VIZ GRAPHIC NOVEL

Descendants of Darkness™

Yami no Matsuei

D1021292

7

Story & Art by **Yoko Matsushita**

Descendants of Darkness
Yami no Matsuei
Vol. 7
Shôjo Edition

Story & Art by
Yoko Matsushita

English Adaptation/Lance Caselman
Translation/David Ury
Touch-Up & Lettering/Gia Cam Luc
Graphics & Cover Design/Courtney Utt
Editor/Pancha Diaz & Nancy Thistlethwaite

Managing Editor/Annette Roman
Director of Production/Noboru Watanabe
Vice President of Publishing/Alvin Lu
Sr. Director of Acquisitions/Rika Inouye
VP of Sales & Marketing/Liza Coppola
Publisher/Hyoe Narita

Printed in the U.S.A.

Published by VIZ Media, LLC
P.O. Box 77064
San Francisco, CA 94107

Shôjo Edition
10 9 8 7 6 5 4 3 2 1
First printing, August 2005

For advertising rates or media kit, e-mail advertising@viz.com

Table of Contents

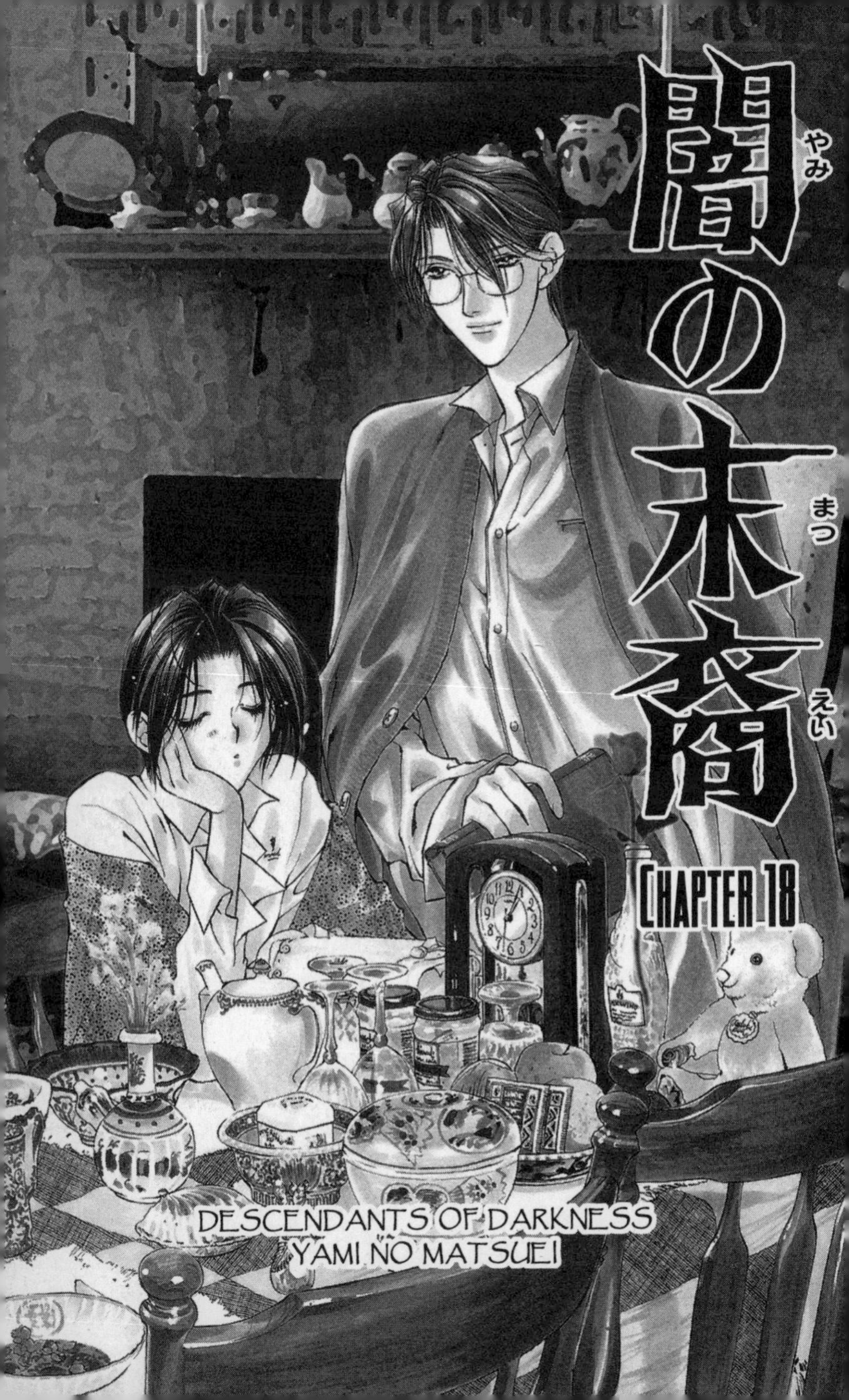

闇の末裔
やみ
まつ
えい
CHAPTER 18
DESCENDANTS OF DARKNESS
YAMI NO MATSUEI

GIVE ME A CHILD.

YOUR CHILD.

IF YOU WON'T LOVE ME, THEN...

...LET ME BEAR YOUR CHILD.

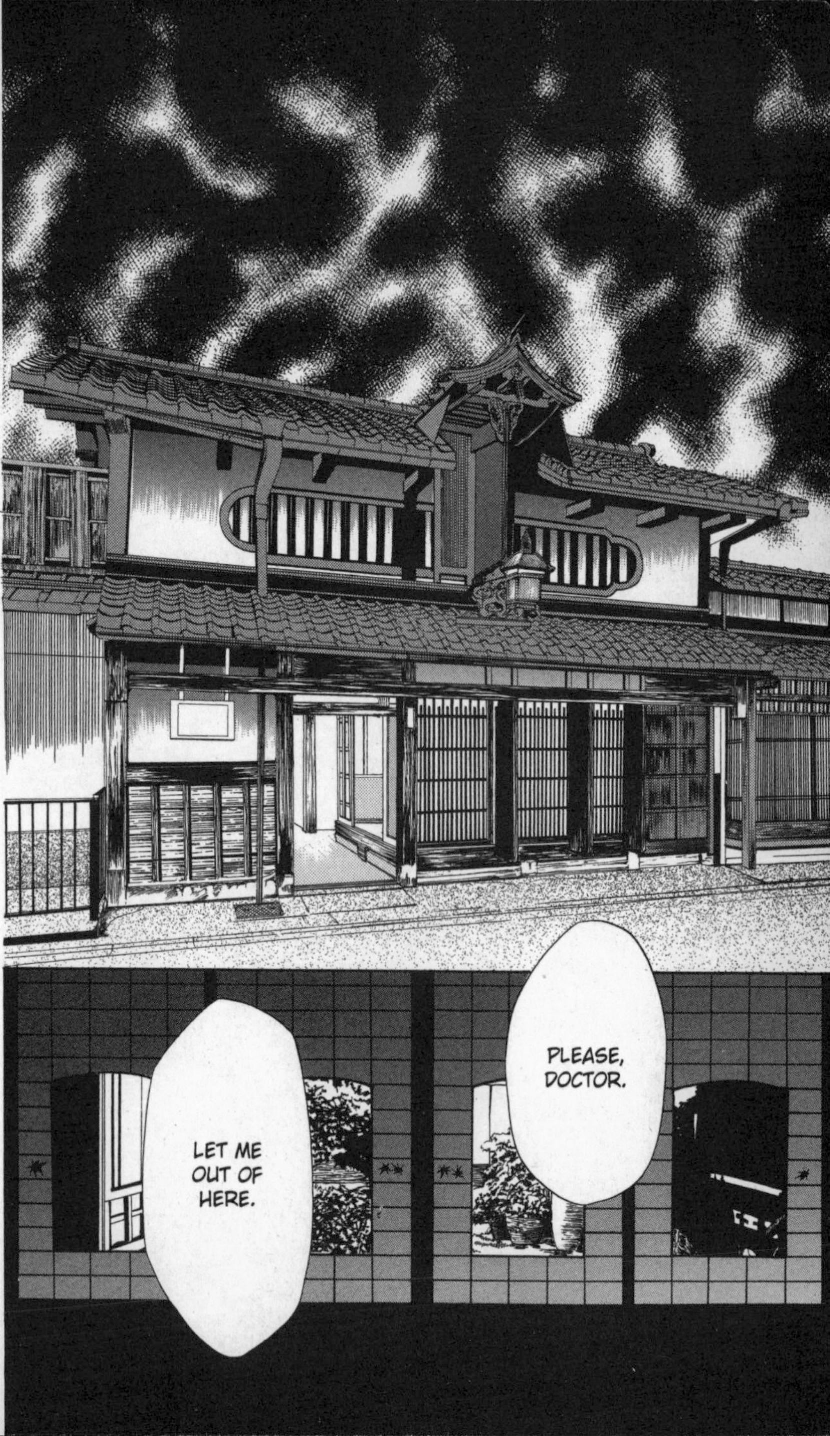
PLEASE, DOCTOR.
LET ME OUT OF HERE.

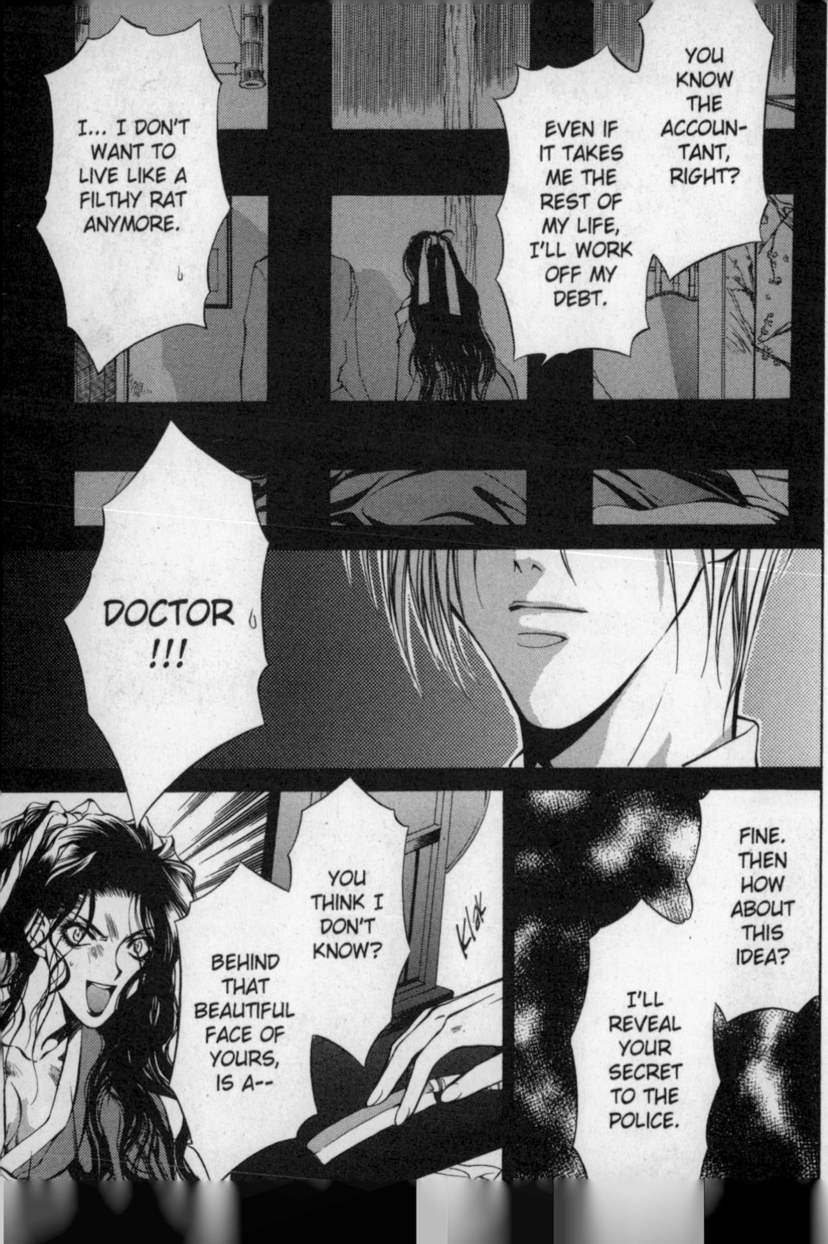
YOU KNOW THE ACCOUNTANT, RIGHT?
EVEN IF IT TAKES ME THE REST OF MY LIFE, I'LL WORK OFF MY DEBT.
I... I DON'T WANT TO LIVE LIKE A FILTHY RAT ANYMORE.
DOCTOR !!!
FINE. THEN HOW ABOUT THIS IDEA?
I'LL REVEAL YOUR SECRET TO THE POLICE.
YOU THINK I DON'T KNOW?
BEHIND THAT BEAUTIFUL FACE OF YOURS, IS A--
Klak

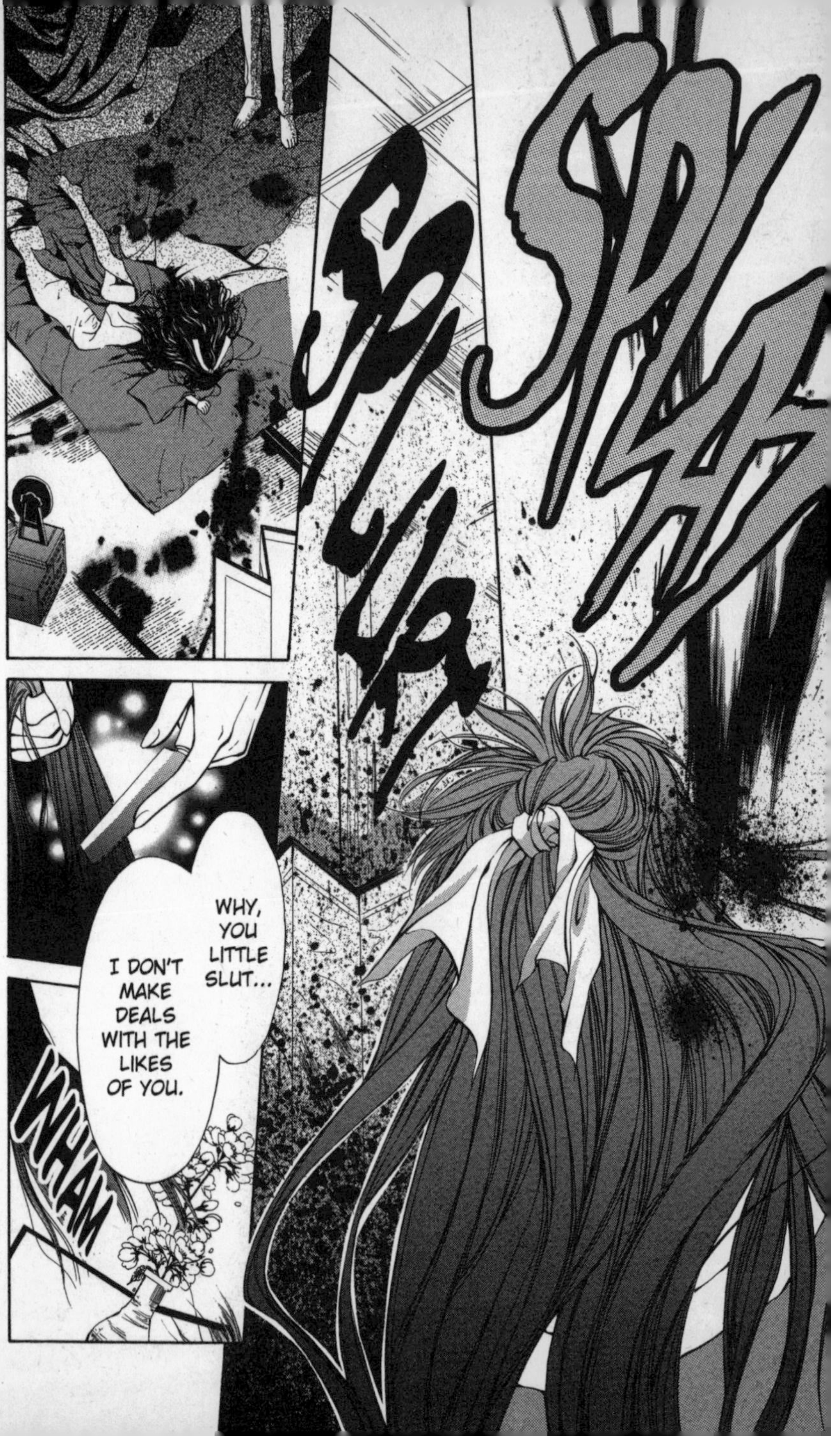
WHY, YOU LITTLE SLUT...
I DON'T MAKE DEALS WITH THE LIKES OF YOU.
WHAM

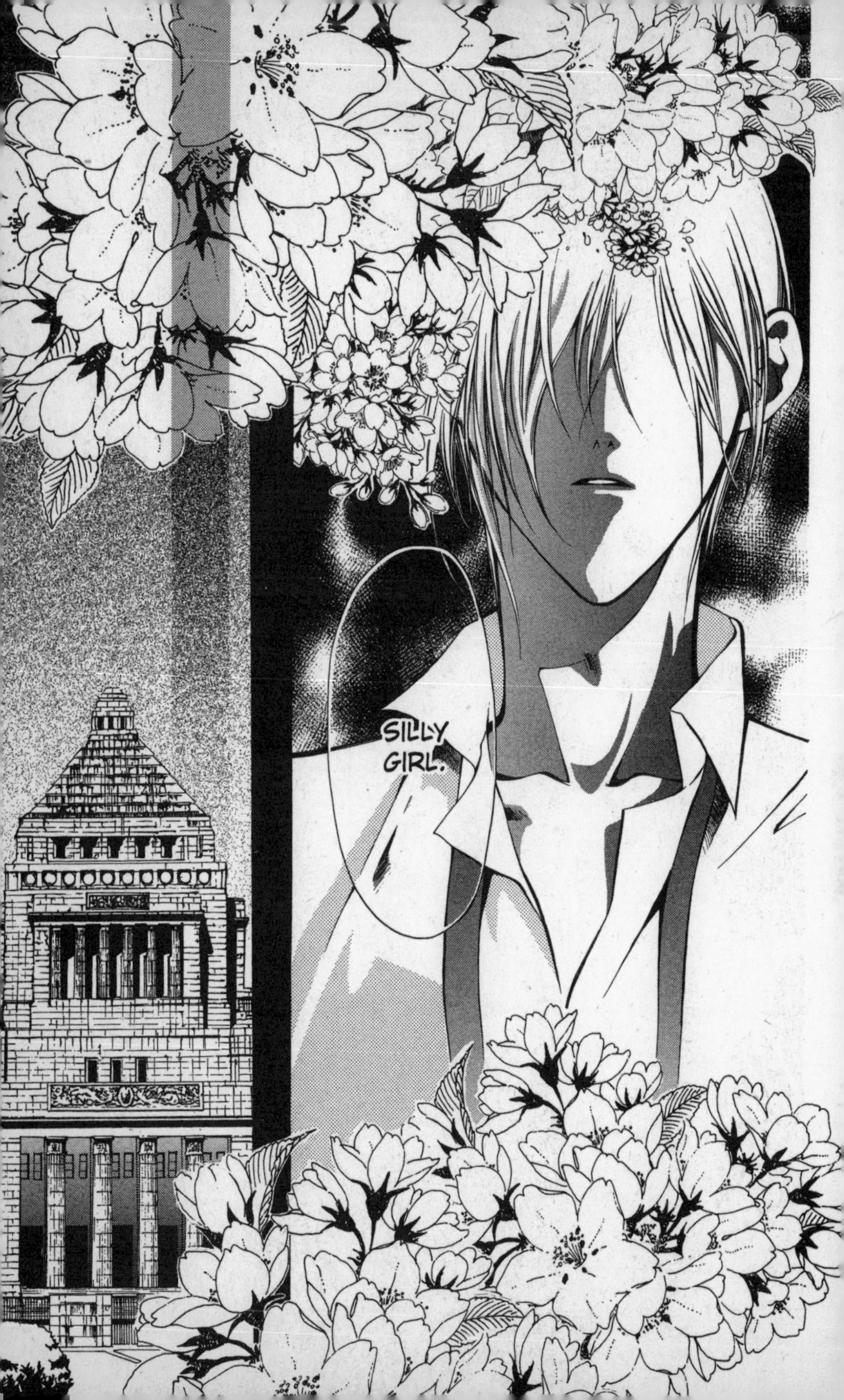
SILLY GIRL.

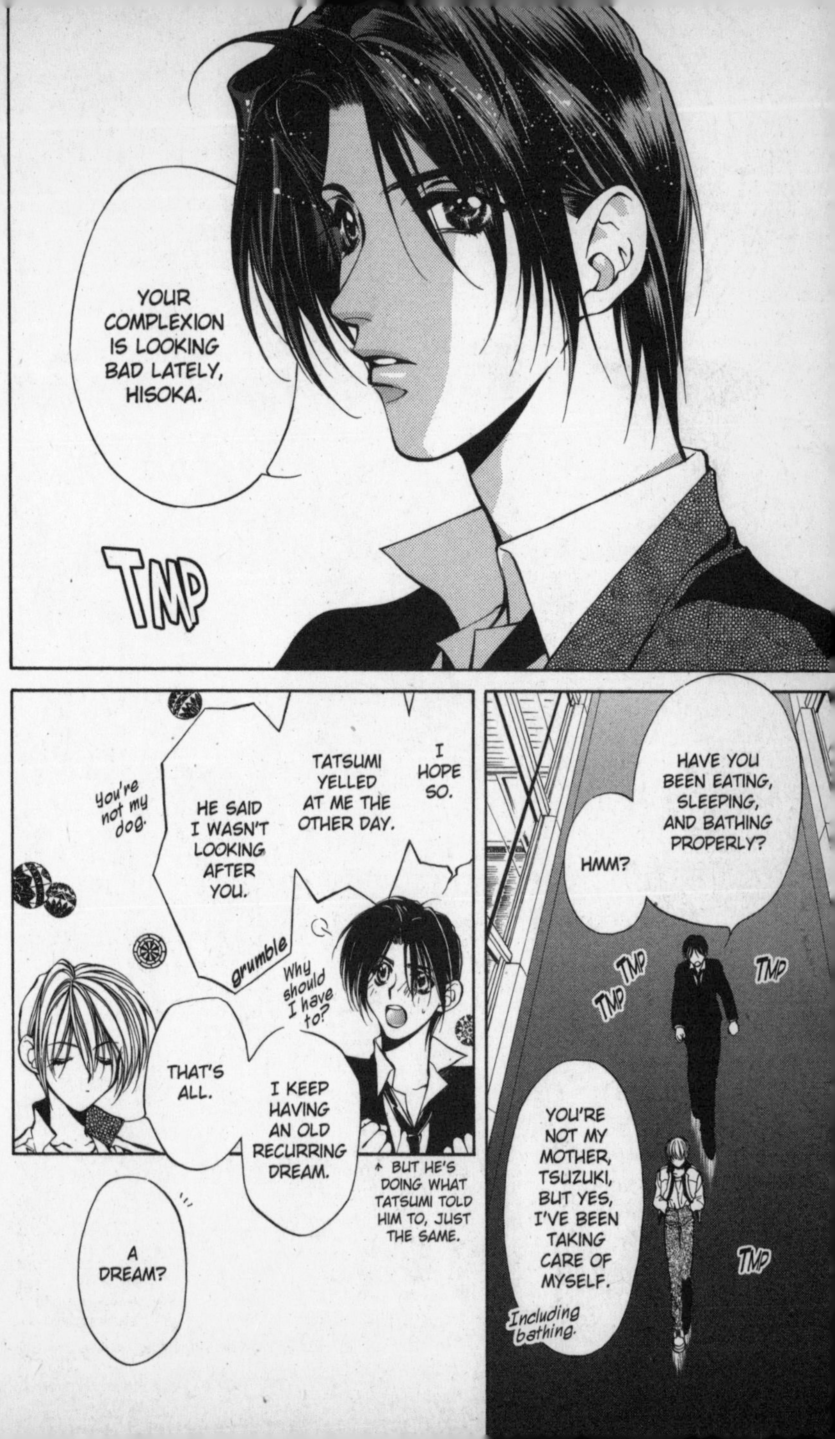
YOUR COMPLEXION IS LOOKING BAD LATELY, HISOKA.
TMP
HAVE YOU BEEN EATING, SLEEPING, AND BATHING PROPERLY?
HMM?
TMP
TMP
TMP
YOU'RE NOT MY MOTHER, TSUZUKI, BUT YES, I'VE BEEN TAKING CARE OF MYSELF.
Including bathing.
TMP
I HOPE SO.
TATSUMI YELLED AT ME THE OTHER DAY.
HE SAID I WASN'T LOOKING AFTER YOU.
you're not my dog.
grumble
Why should I have to?
I KEEP HAVING AN OLD RECURRING DREAM.
THAT'S ALL.
BUT HE'S DOING WHAT TATSUMI TOLD HIM TO, JUST THE SAME.
A DREAM?

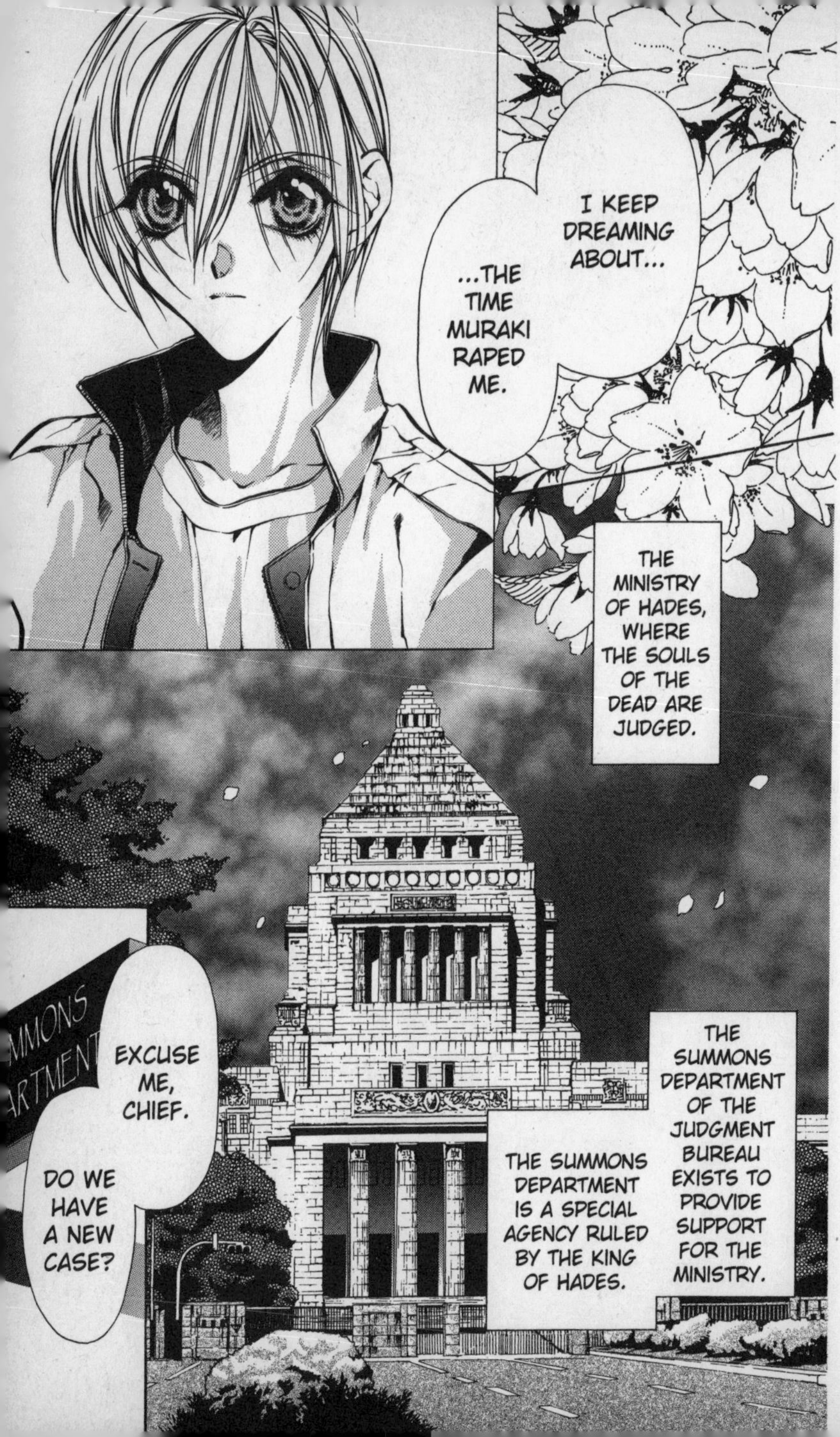
I KEEP DREAMING ABOUT...
...THE TIME MURAKI RAPED ME.
THE MINISTRY OF HADES, WHERE THE SOULS OF THE DEAD ARE JUDGED.
THE SUMMONS DEPARTMENT OF THE JUDGMENT BUREAU EXISTS TO PROVIDE SUPPORT FOR THE MINISTRY.
THE SUMMONS DEPARTMENT IS A SPECIAL AGENCY RULED BY THE KING OF HADES.
MMONS ARTMENT
EXCUSE ME, CHIEF.
DO WE HAVE A NEW CASE?

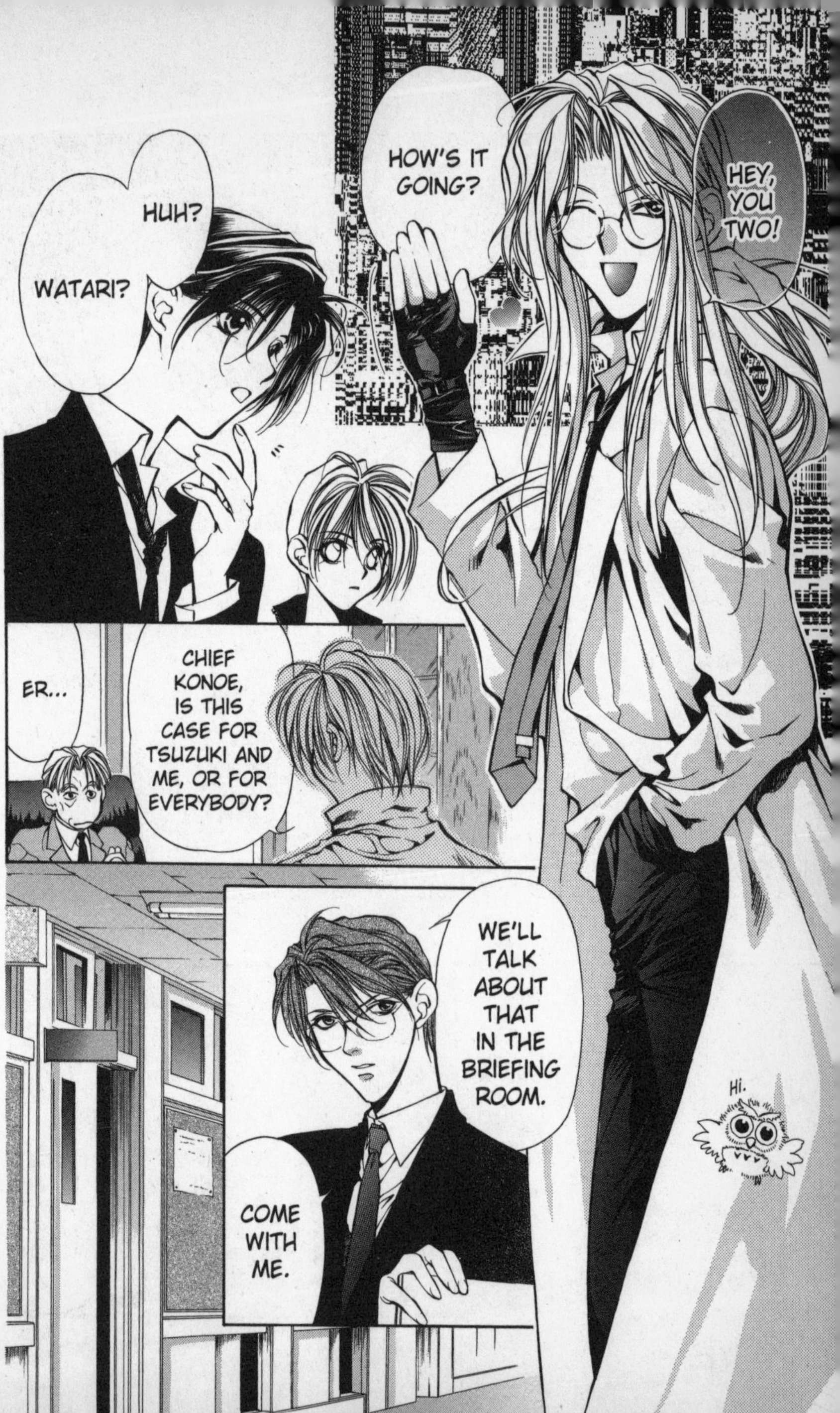
HEY, YOU TWO!
HOW'S IT GOING?
HUH?
WATARI?
CHIEF KONOE, IS THIS CASE FOR TSUZUKI AND ME, OR FOR EVERYBODY?
ER...
WE'LL TALK ABOUT THAT IN THE BRIEFING ROOM.
COME WITH ME.
Hi.

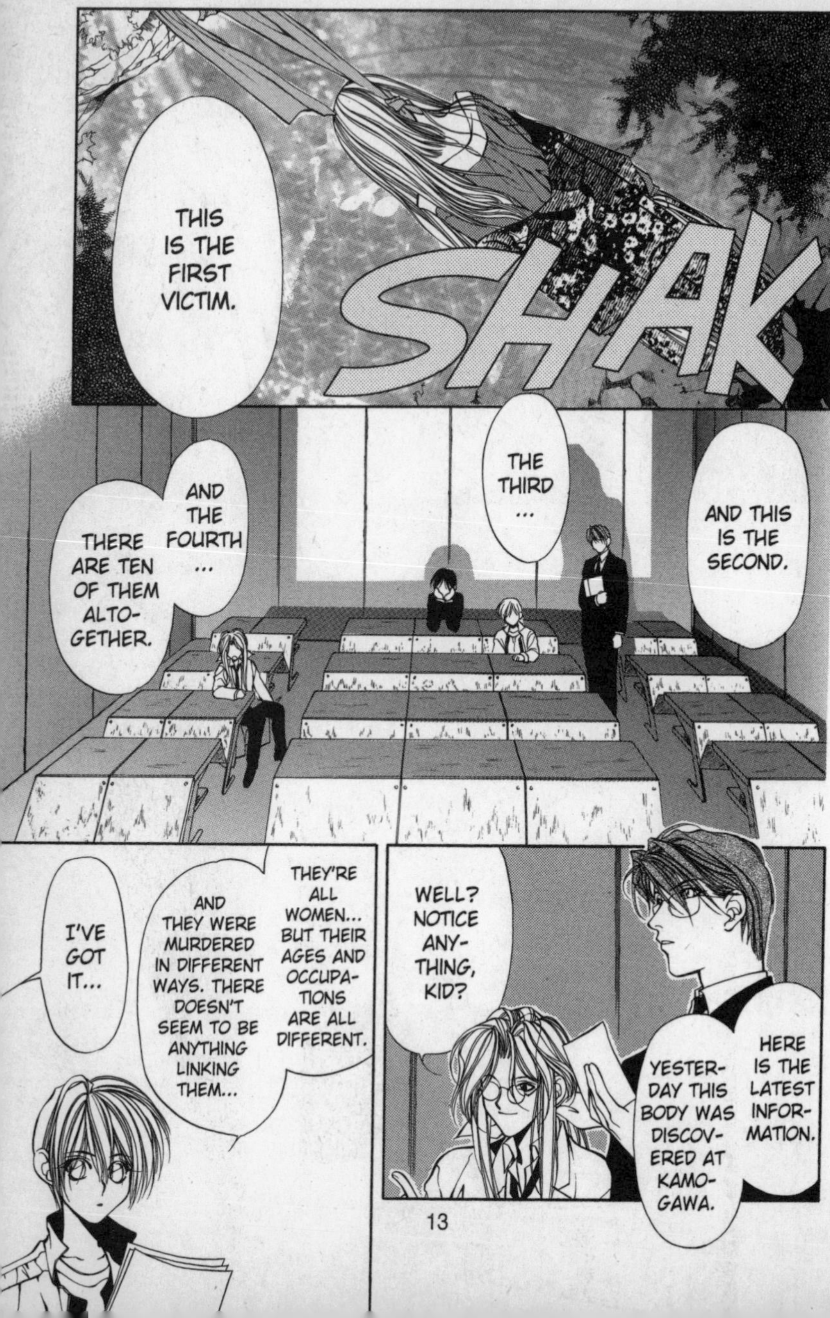
THIS IS THE FIRST VICTIM.
SHAK
AND THIS IS THE SECOND.
THE THIRD ...
AND THE FOURTH ...
THERE ARE TEN OF THEM ALTOGETHER.
HERE IS THE LATEST INFORMATION.
YESTERDAY THIS BODY WAS DISCOVERED AT KAMOGAWA.
WELL? NOTICE ANYTHING, KID?
THEY'RE ALL WOMEN... BUT THEIR AGES AND OCCUPATIONS ARE ALL DIFFERENT.
AND THEY WERE MURDERED IN DIFFERENT WAYS. THERE DOESN'T SEEM TO BE ANYTHING LINKING THEM...
I'VE GOT IT...

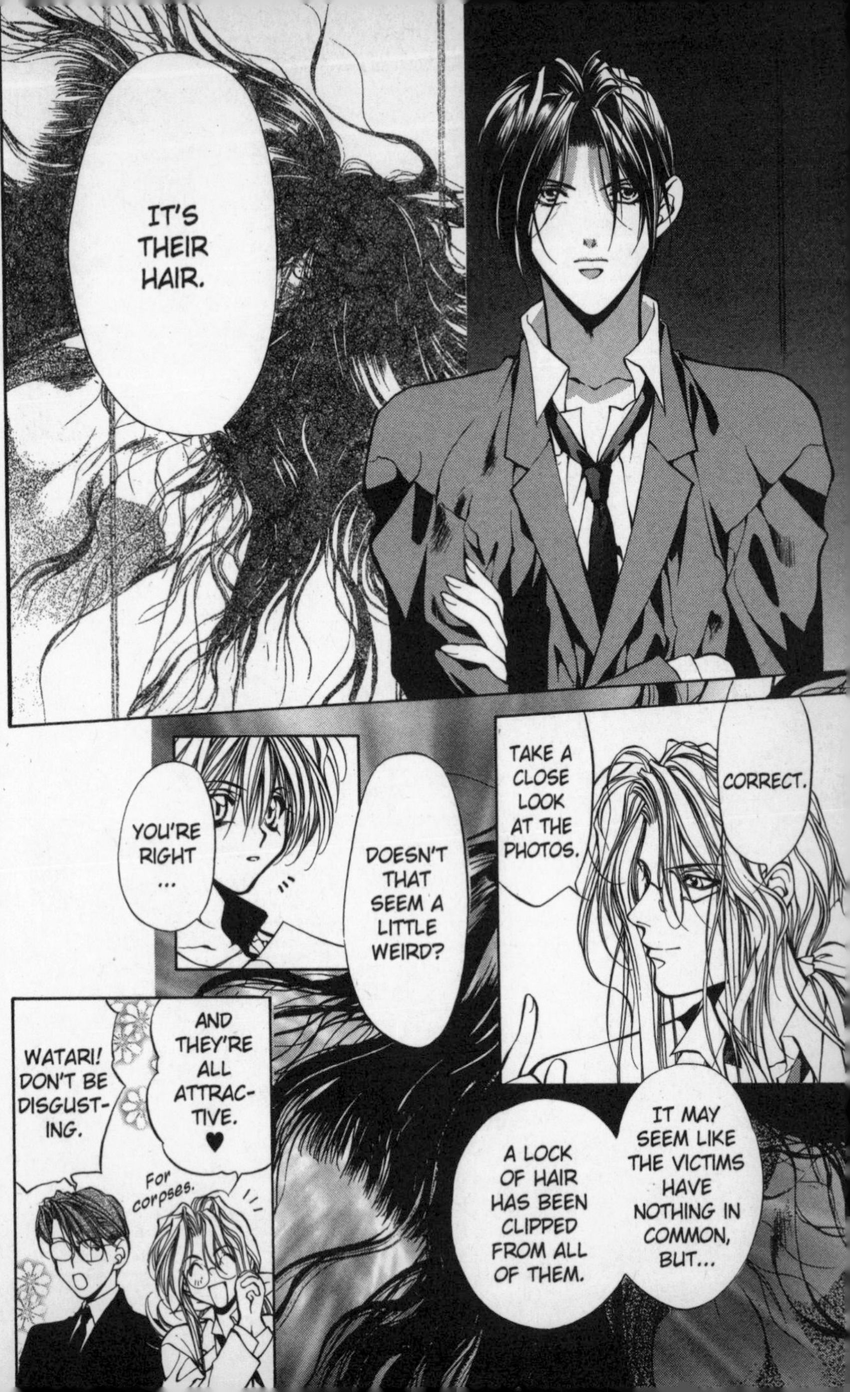
IT'S THEIR HAIR.
CORRECT.
TAKE A CLOSE LOOK AT THE PHOTOS.
DOESN'T THAT SEEM A LITTLE WEIRD?
YOU'RE RIGHT ...
IT MAY SEEM LIKE THE VICTIMS HAVE NOTHING IN COMMON, BUT...
A LOCK OF HAIR HAS BEEN CLIPPED FROM ALL OF THEM.
AND THEY'RE ALL ATTRACTIVE. ♥
WATARI! DON'T BE DISGUSTING.
For corpses.

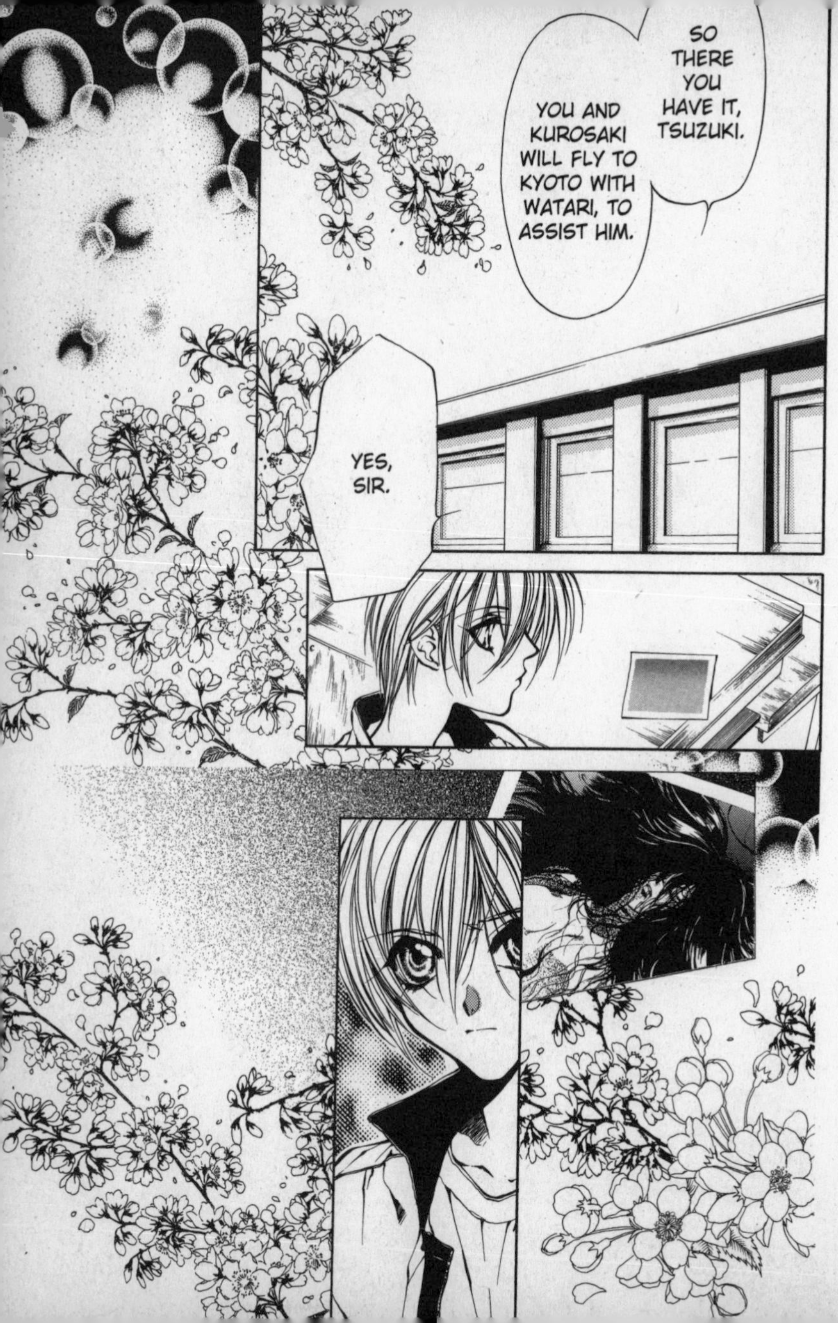
SO THERE YOU HAVE IT, TSUZUKI.
YOU AND KUROSAKI WILL FLY TO KYOTO WITH WATARI, TO ASSIST HIM.
YES, SIR.

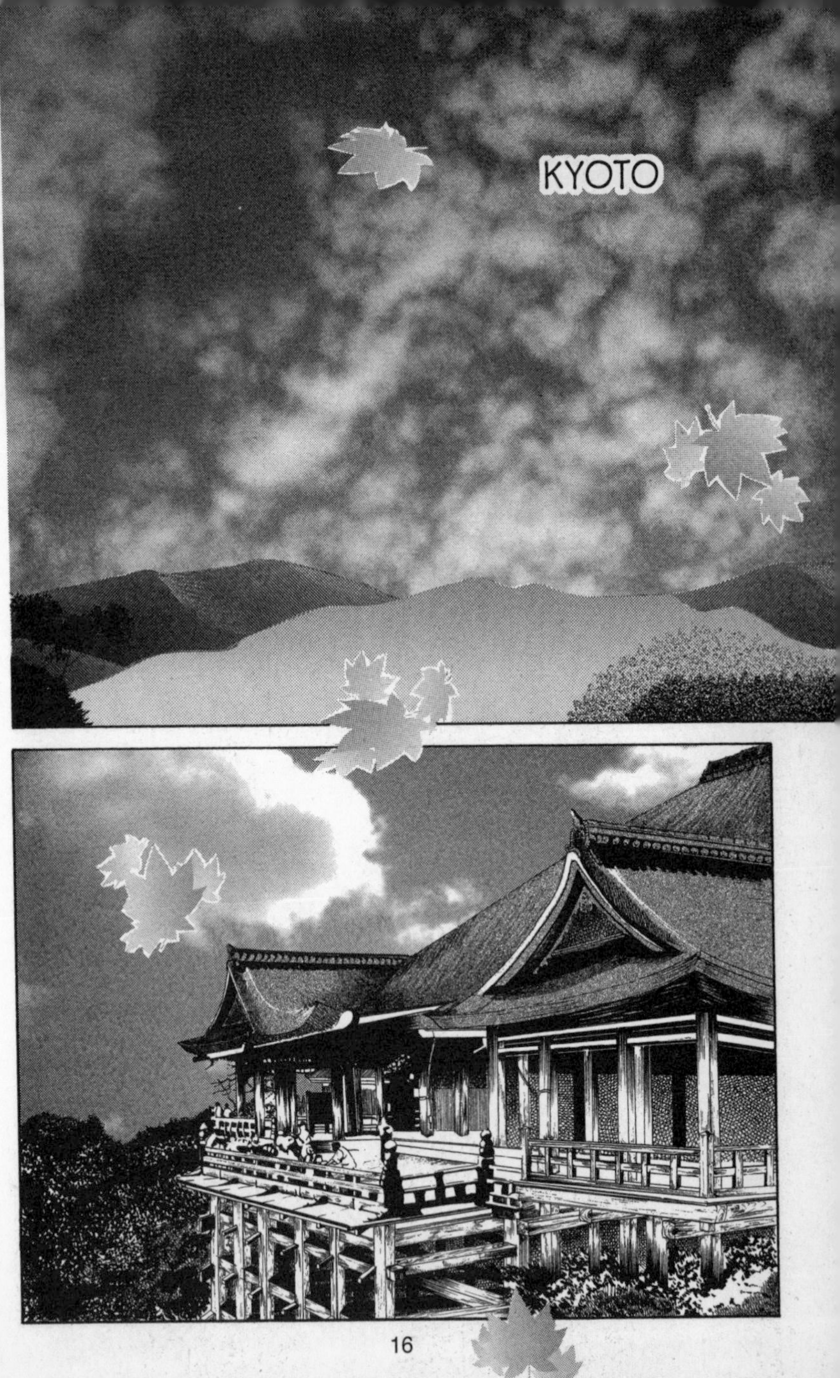
KYOTO

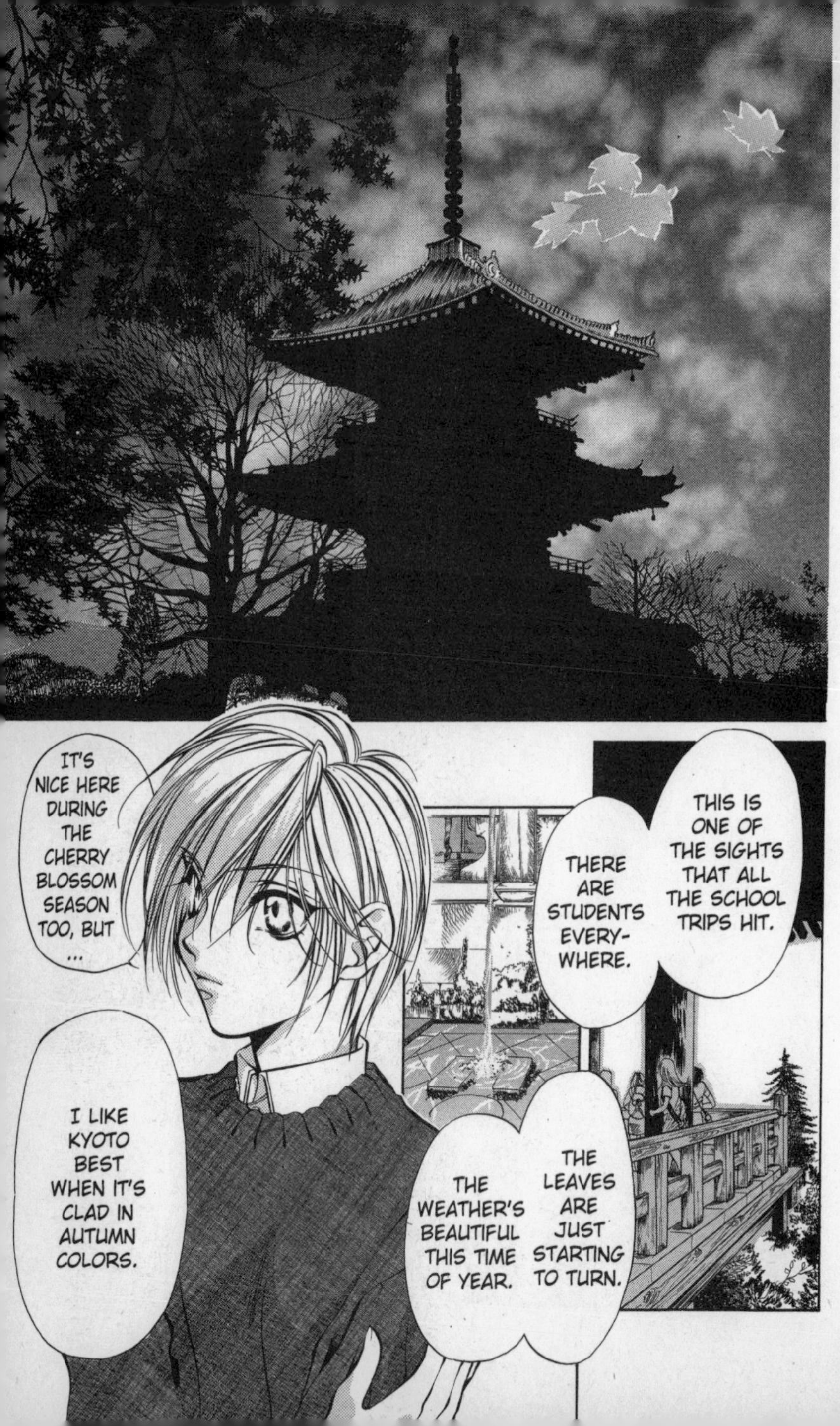
THIS IS ONE OF THE SIGHTS THAT ALL THE SCHOOL TRIPS HIT.
THERE ARE STUDENTS EVERY-WHERE.
IT'S NICE HERE DURING THE CHERRY BLOSSOM SEASON TOO, BUT ...
THE LEAVES ARE JUST STARTING TO TURN. THE WEATHER'S BEAUTIFUL THIS TIME OF YEAR.
I LIKE KYOTO BEST WHEN IT'S CLAD IN AUTUMN COLORS.

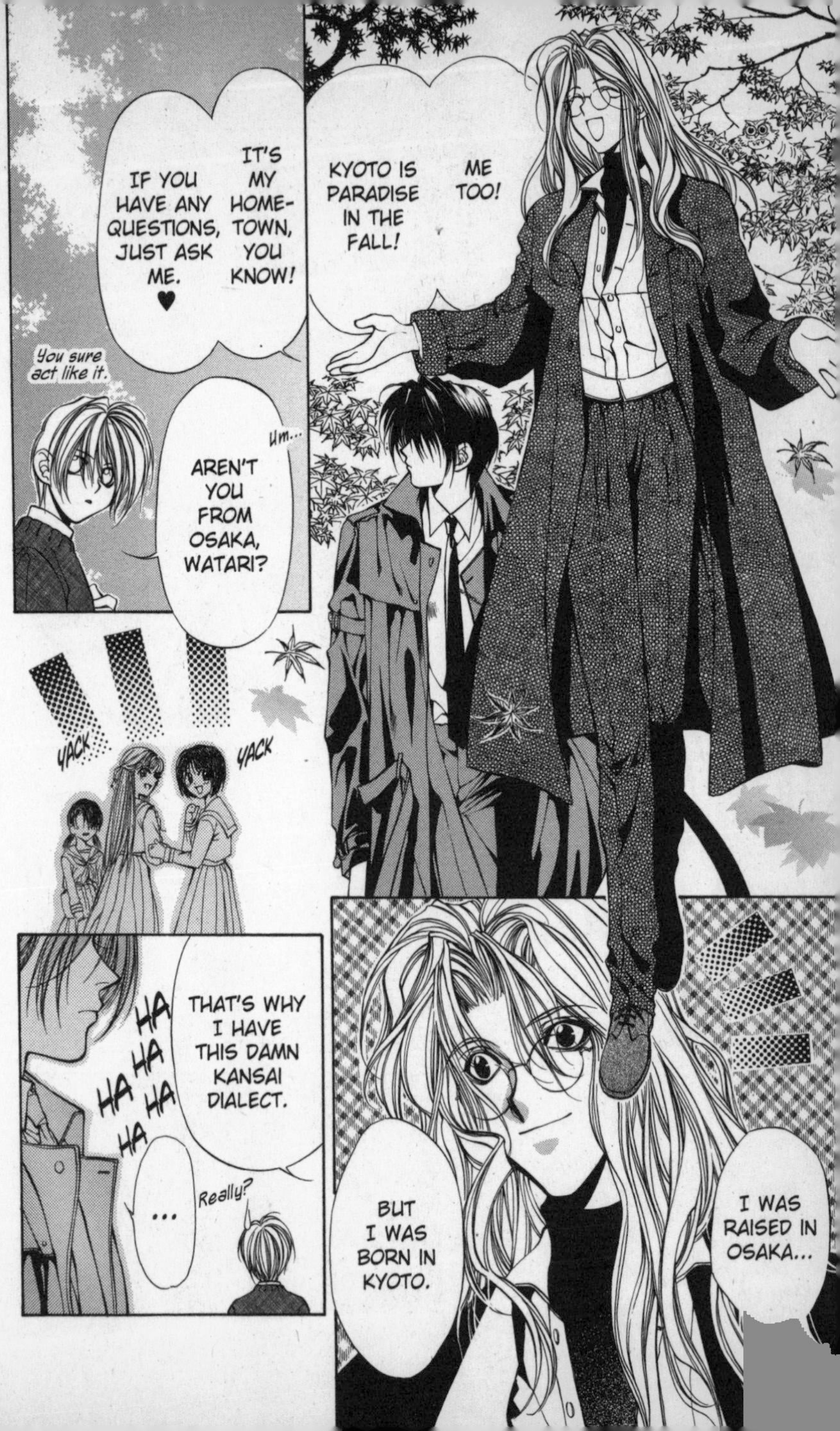
ME TOO!
KYOTO IS PARADISE IN THE FALL!
IT'S MY HOMETOWN, YOU KNOW!
IF YOU HAVE ANY QUESTIONS, JUST ASK ME. ♥
You sure act like it.
Um...
AREN'T YOU FROM OSAKA, WATARI?
YACK
YACK
I WAS RAISED IN OSAKA...
BUT I WAS BORN IN KYOTO.
THAT'S WHY I HAVE THIS DAMN KANSAI DIALECT.
HA HA HA HA HA HA
...
Really?

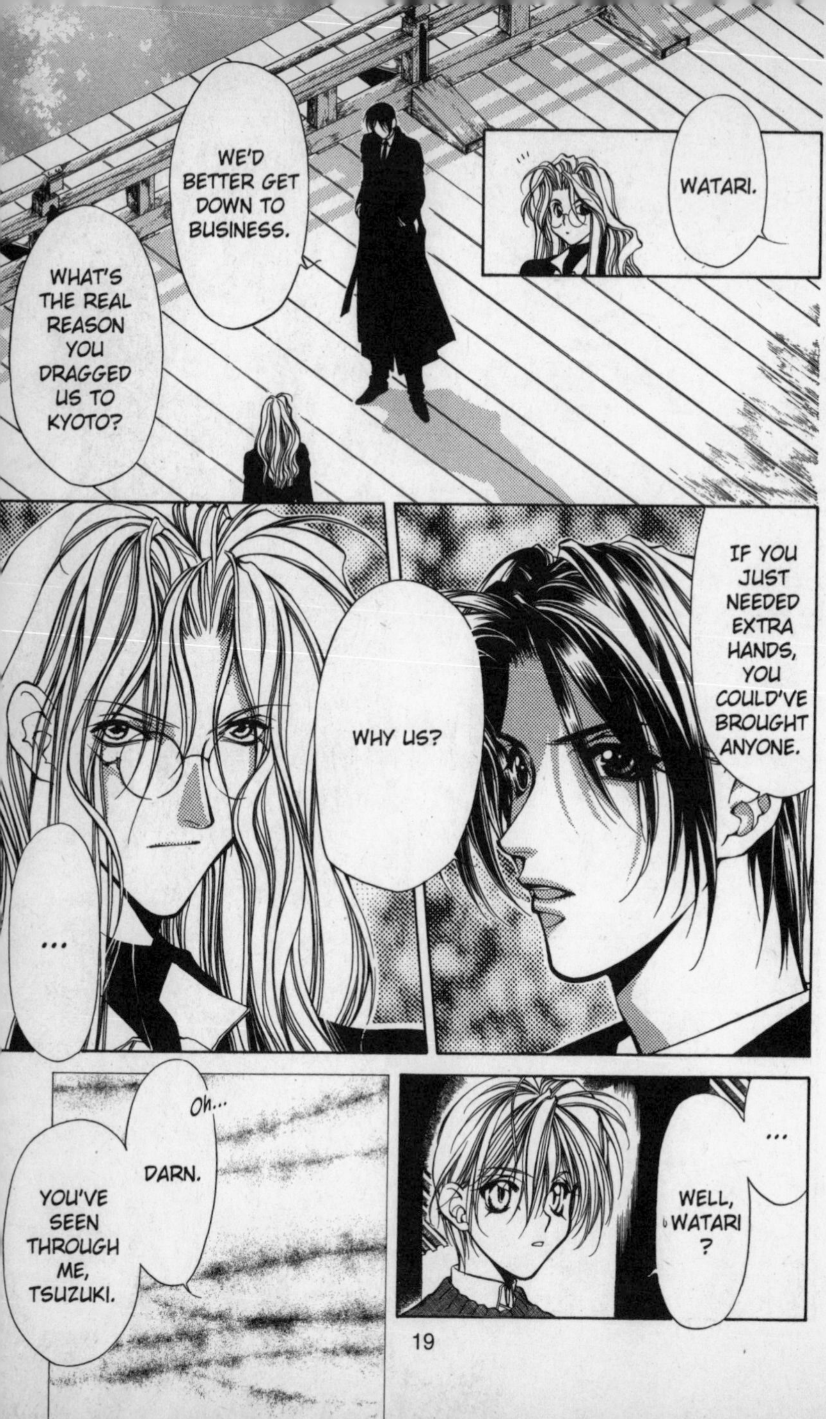
WATARI.
WE'D BETTER GET DOWN TO BUSINESS.
WHAT'S THE REAL REASON YOU DRAGGED US TO KYOTO?
IF YOU JUST NEEDED EXTRA HANDS, YOU COULD'VE BROUGHT ANYONE.
WHY US?
...
...
WELL, WATARI?
Oh...
DARN.
YOU'VE SEEN THROUGH ME, TSUZUKI.

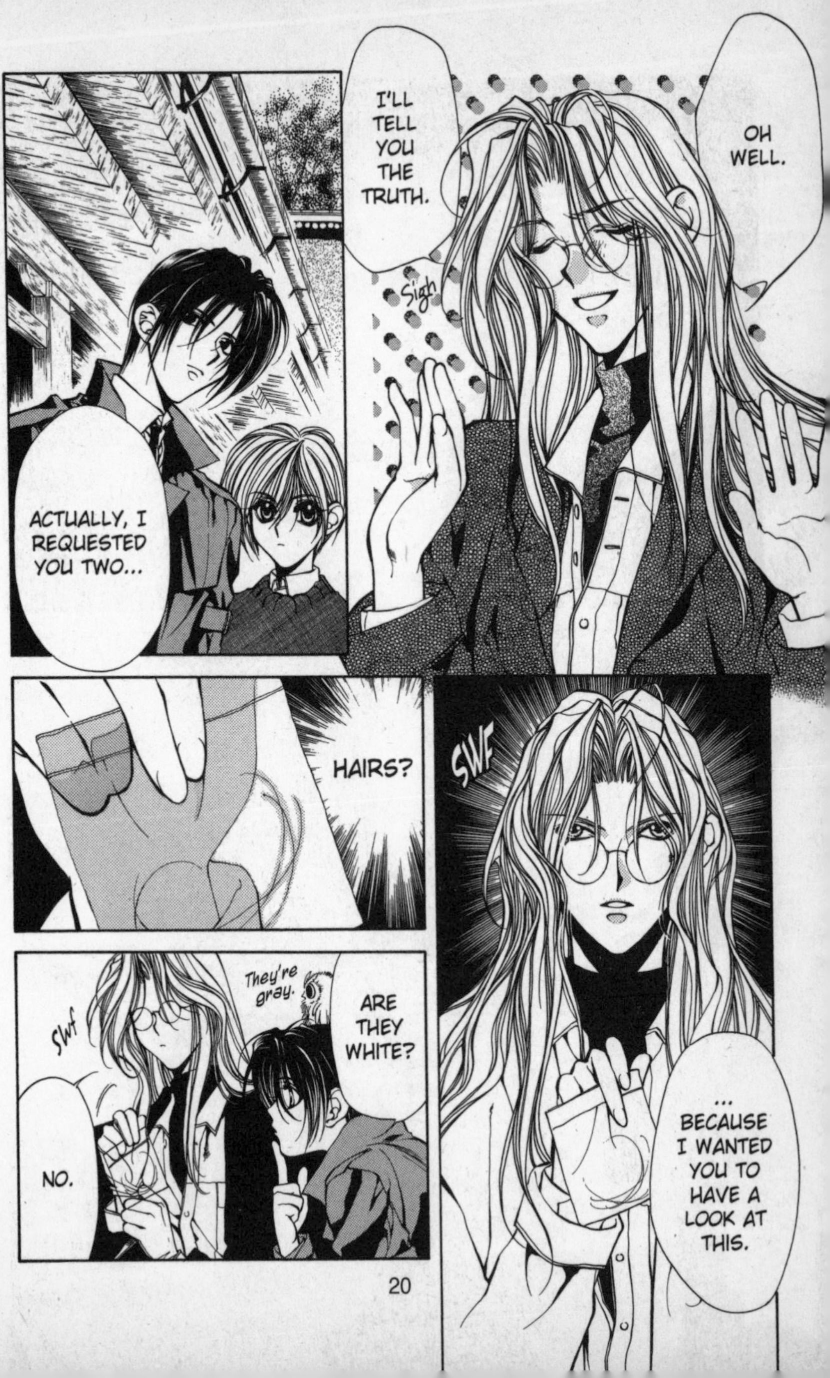
OH WELL.
Sigh
I'LL TELL YOU THE TRUTH.
ACTUALLY, I REQUESTED YOU TWO...
SWF
...BECAUSE I WANTED YOU TO HAVE A LOOK AT THIS.
HAIRS?
ARE THEY WHITE?
They're gray.
Swf
NO.

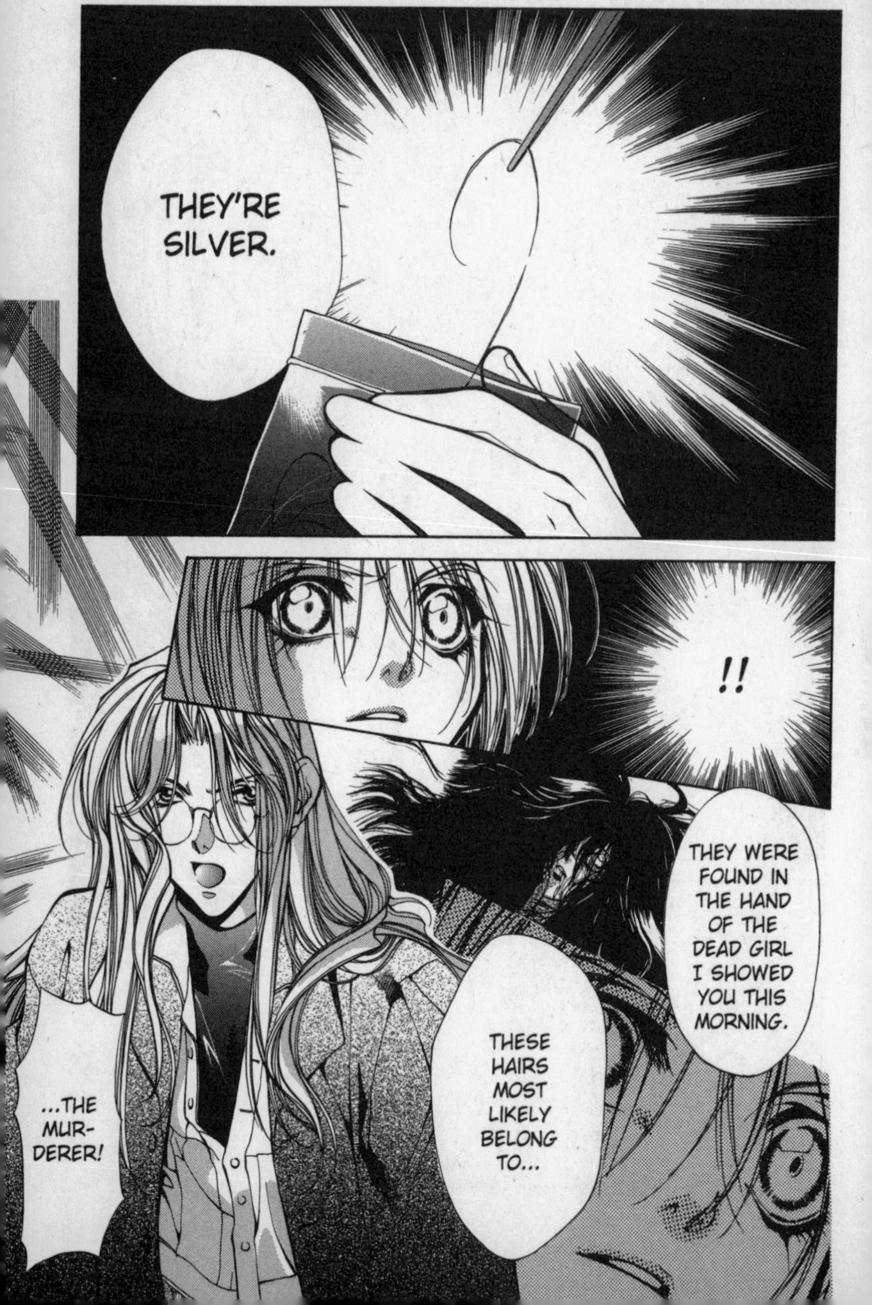
THEY'RE SILVER.
!!
THEY WERE FOUND IN THE HAND OF THE DEAD GIRL I SHOWED YOU THIS MORNING.
THESE HAIRS MOST LIKELY BELONG TO...
...THE MUR-DERER!

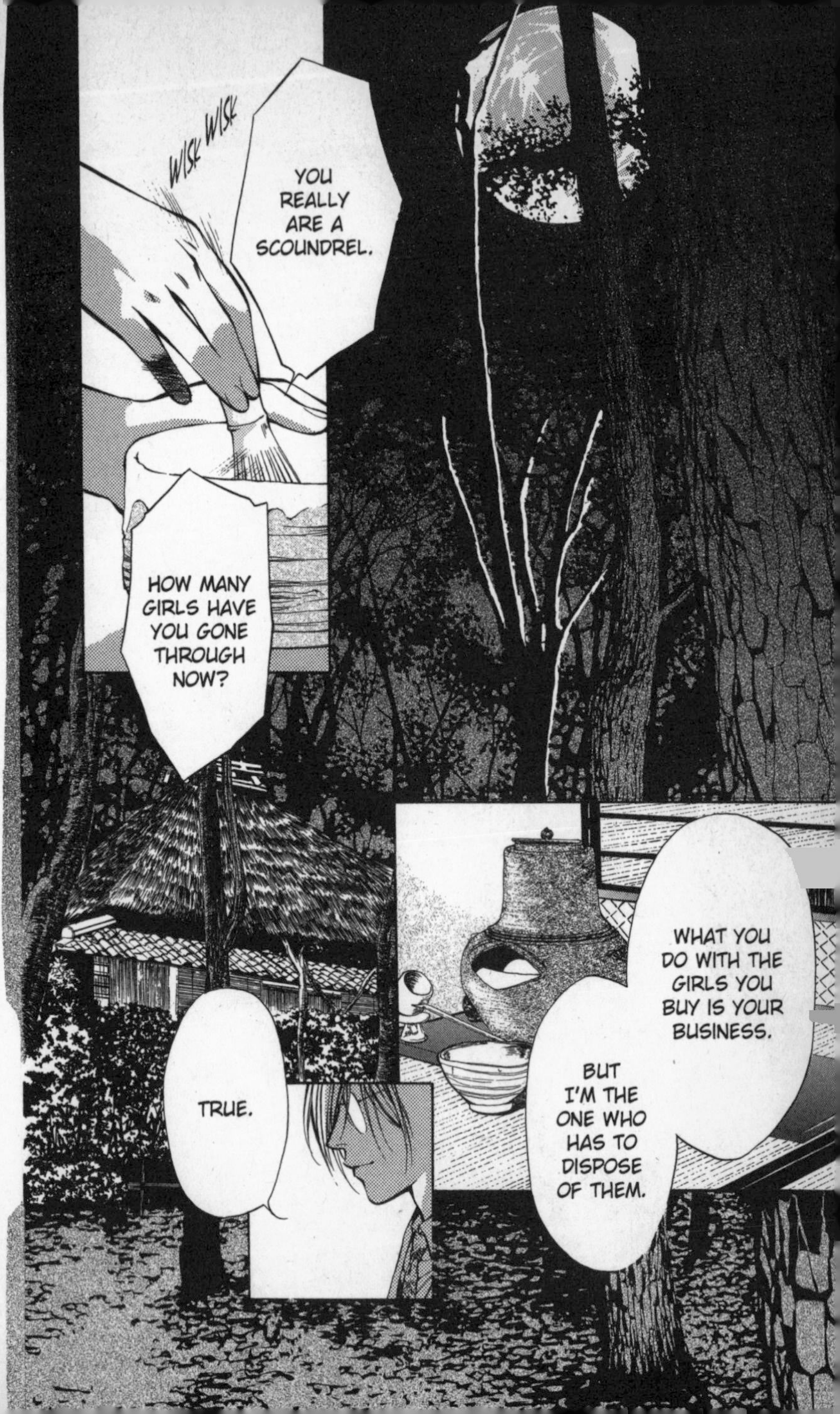
WISK WISK
YOU REALLY ARE A SCOUNDREL.
HOW MANY GIRLS HAVE YOU GONE THROUGH NOW?
WHAT YOU DO WITH THE GIRLS YOU BUY IS YOUR BUSINESS.
BUT I'M THE ONE WHO HAS TO DISPOSE OF THEM.
TRUE.

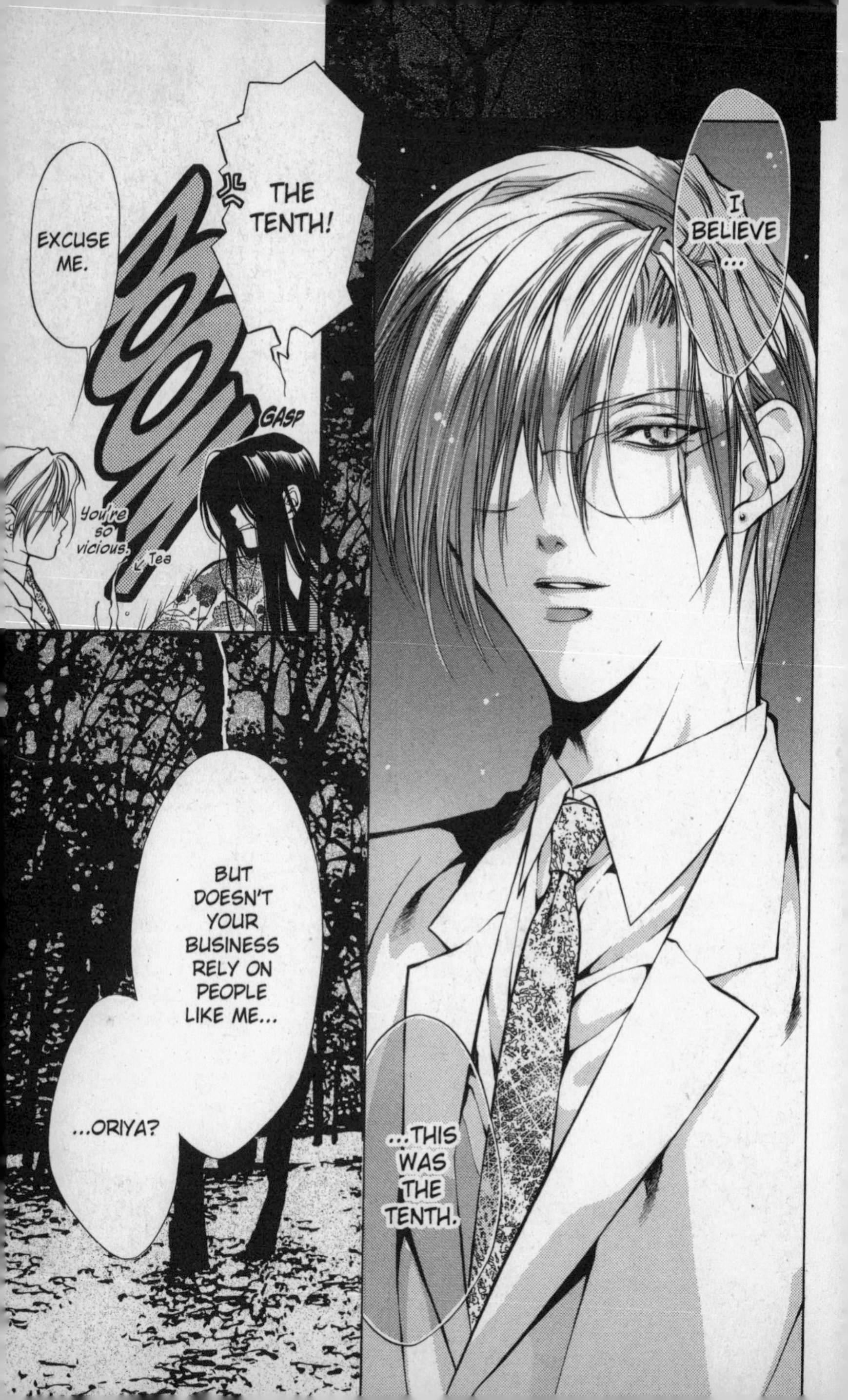
I BELIEVE...
...THIS WAS THE TENTH.
THE TENTH!
EXCUSE ME.
GASP
You're so vicious.
Tea
BUT DOESN'T YOUR BUSINESS RELY ON PEOPLE LIKE ME...
...ORIYA?

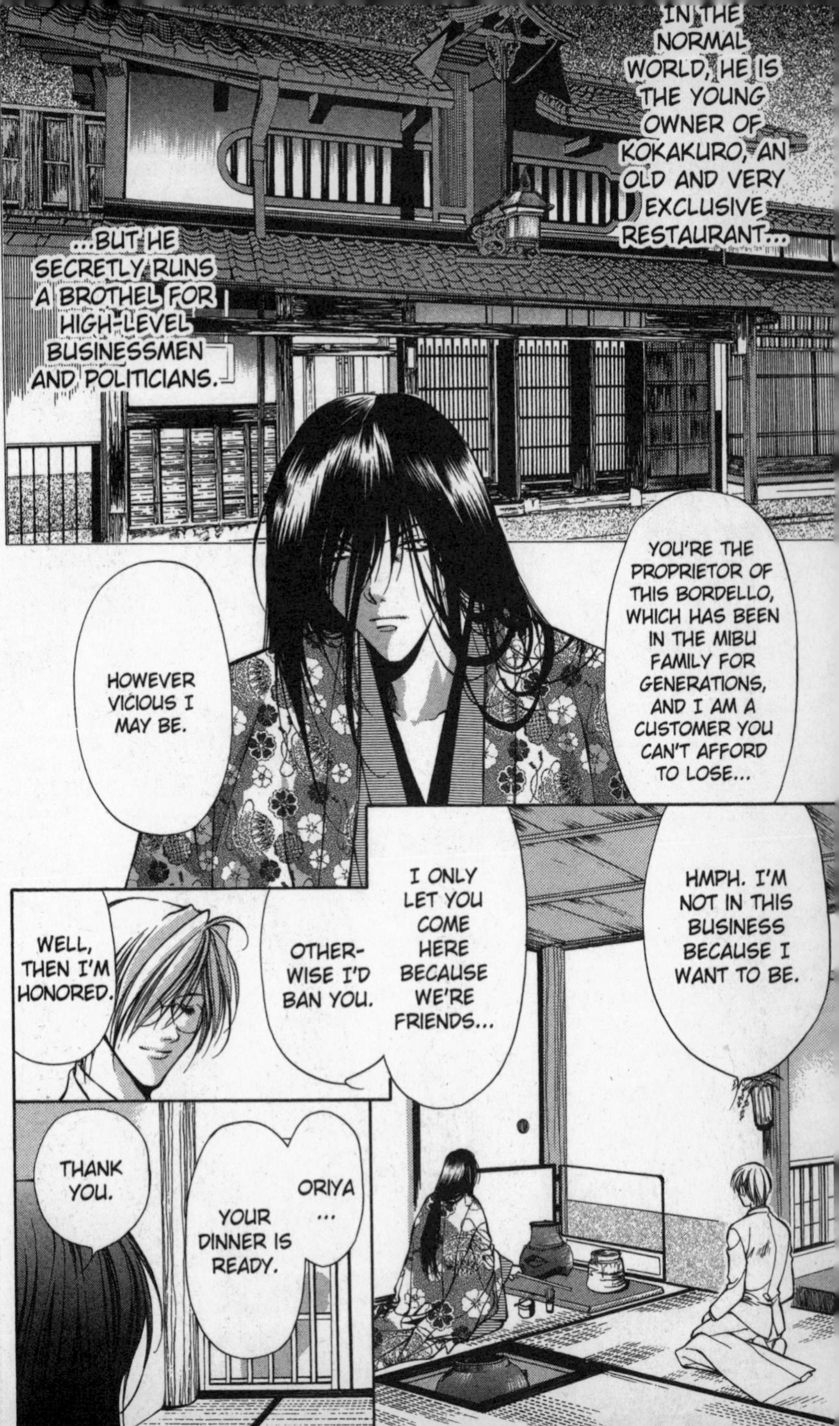
IN THE NORMAL WORLD, HE IS THE YOUNG OWNER OF KOKAKURO, AN OLD AND VERY EXCLUSIVE RESTAURANT...
...BUT HE SECRETLY RUNS A BROTHEL FOR HIGH-LEVEL BUSINESSMEN AND POLITICIANS.
YOU'RE THE PROPRIETOR OF THIS BORDELLO, WHICH HAS BEEN IN THE MIBU FAMILY FOR GENERATIONS, AND I AM A CUSTOMER YOU CAN'T AFFORD TO LOSE...
HOWEVER VICIOUS I MAY BE.
HMPH. I'M NOT IN THIS BUSINESS BECAUSE I WANT TO BE.
I ONLY LET YOU COME HERE BECAUSE WE'RE FRIENDS...
OTHER-WISE I'D BAN YOU.
WELL, THEN I'M HONORED.
ORIYA...
YOUR DINNER IS READY.
THANK YOU.

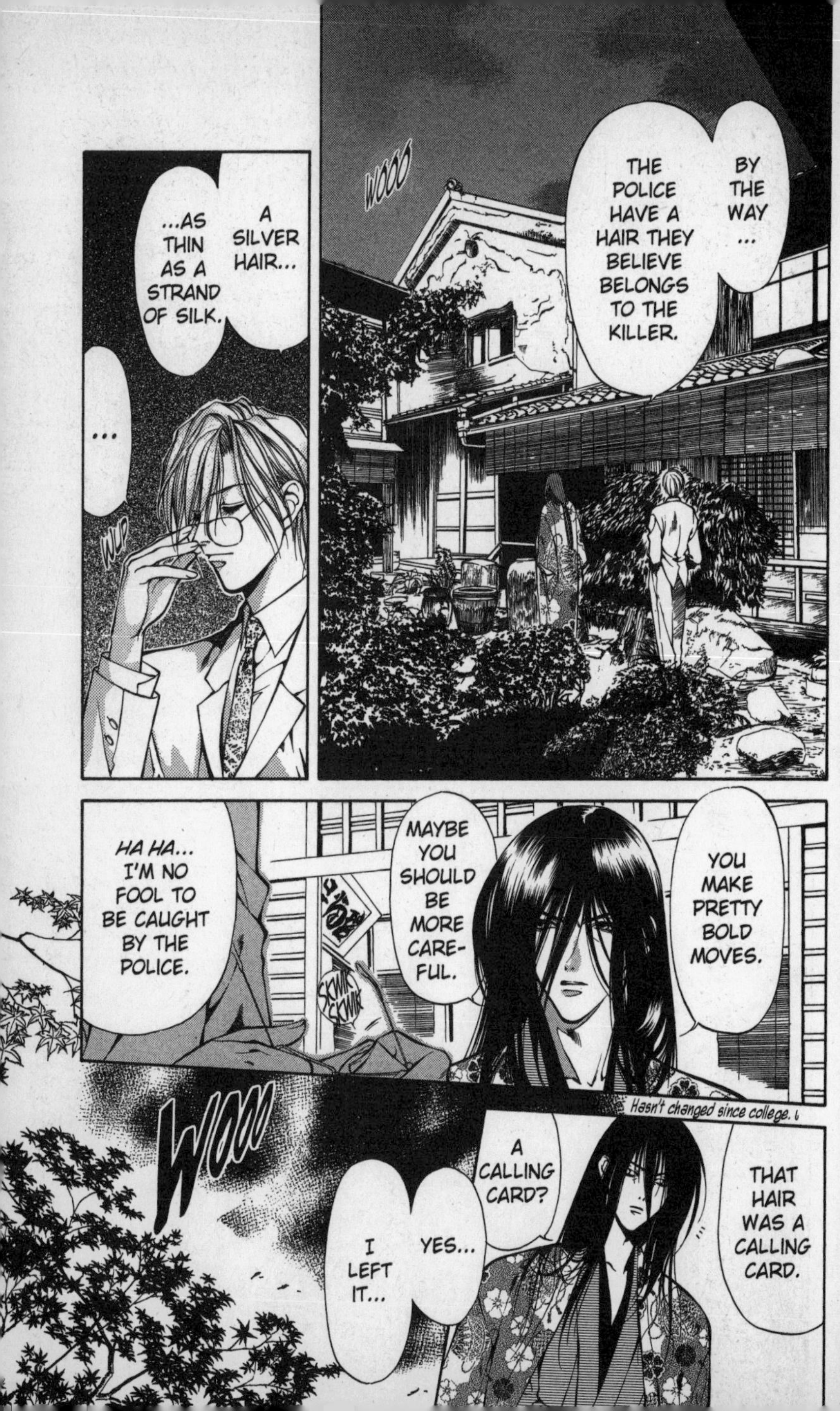
WOOO
BY THE WAY ...
THE POLICE HAVE A HAIR THEY BELIEVE BELONGS TO THE KILLER.
A SILVER HAIR...
...AS THIN AS A STRAND OF SILK.
...
YOU MAKE PRETTY BOLD MOVES.
MAYBE YOU SHOULD BE MORE CARE-FUL.
SKWIK SKWIK
HA HA... I'M NO FOOL TO BE CAUGHT BY THE POLICE.
Hasn't changed since college.
THAT HAIR WAS A CALLING CARD.
A CALLING CARD?
YES...
I LEFT IT...

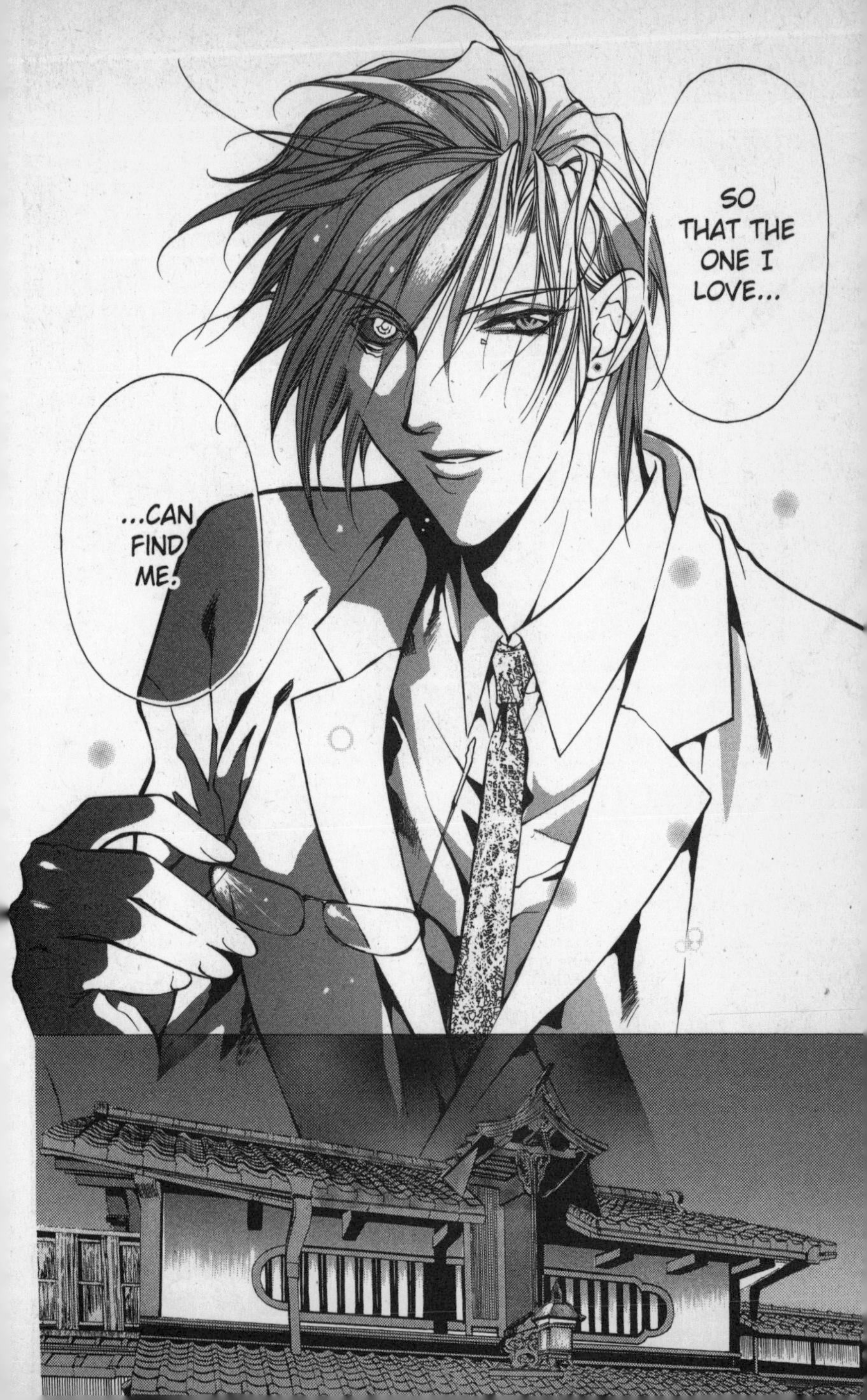
SO THAT THE ONE I LOVE...
...CAN FIND ME.

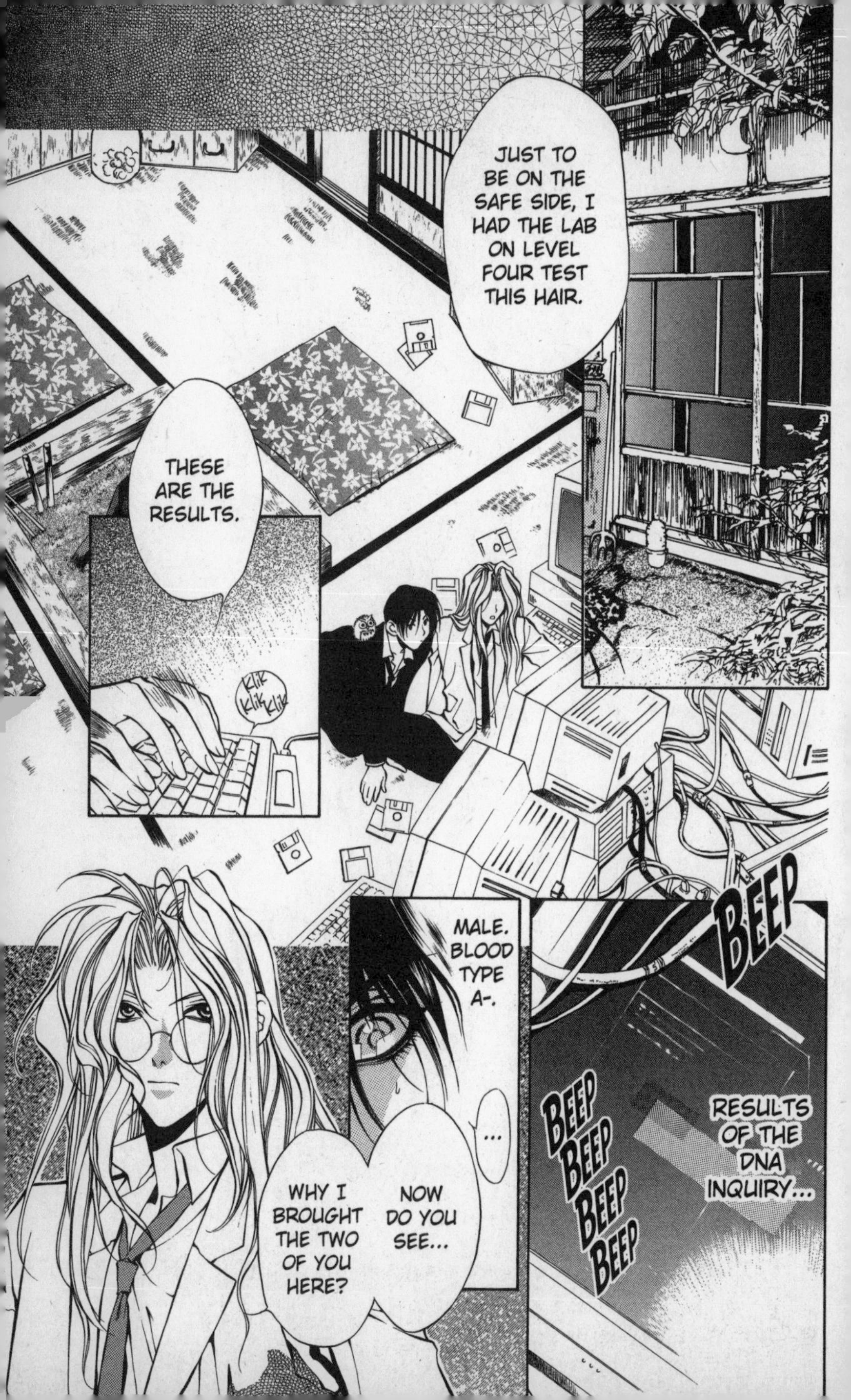
JUST TO BE ON THE SAFE SIDE, I HAD THE LAB ON LEVEL FOUR TEST THIS HAIR.
THESE ARE THE RESULTS.
Klik Klik Klik
BEEP
BEEP BEEP BEEP BEEP
RESULTS OF THE DNA INQUIRY...
MALE. BLOOD TYPE A-.
...
NOW DO YOU SEE...
WHY I BROUGHT THE TWO OF YOU HERE?

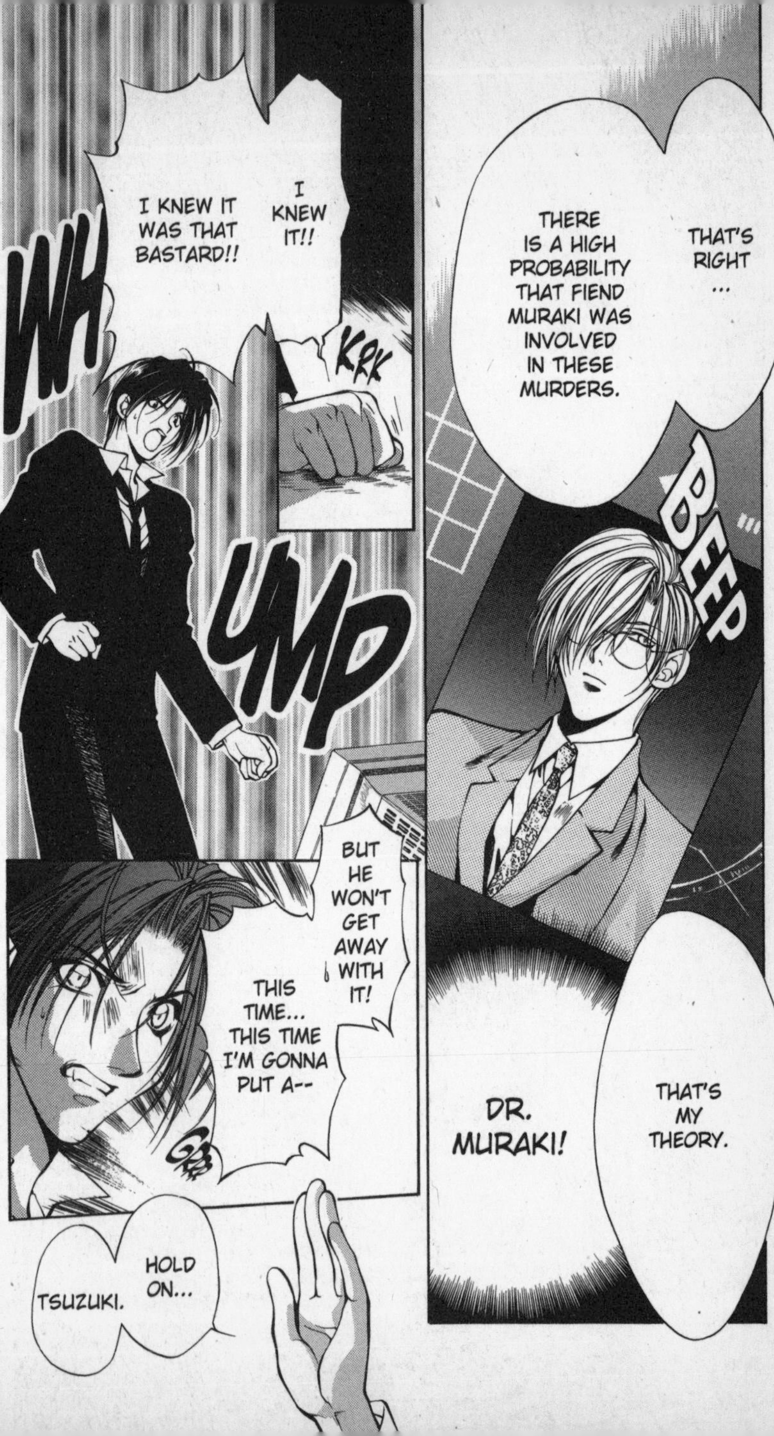
THAT'S RIGHT ...
THERE IS A HIGH PROBABILITY THAT FIEND MURAKI WAS INVOLVED IN THESE MURDERS.
BEEP
THAT'S MY THEORY.
DR. MURAKI!
I KNEW IT!!
I KNEW IT WAS THAT BASTARD!!
KRK
WH
UMP
BUT HE WON'T GET AWAY WITH IT!
THIS TIME... THIS TIME I'M GONNA PUT A--
HOLD ON...
TSUZUKI.

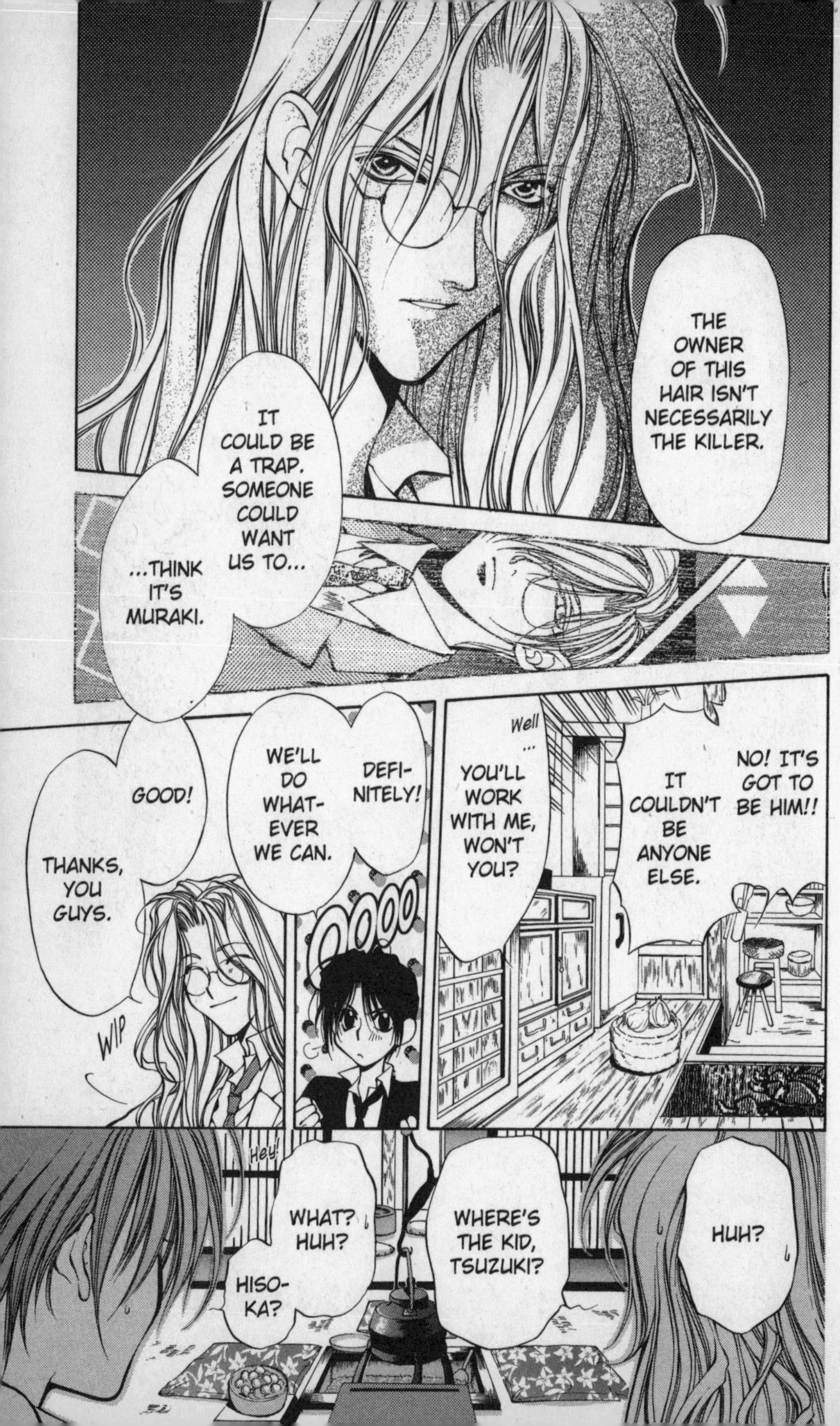
THE OWNER OF THIS HAIR ISN'T NECESSARILY THE KILLER.
IT COULD BE A TRAP. SOMEONE COULD WANT US TO...
...THINK IT'S MURAKI.
NO! IT'S GOT TO BE HIM!!
IT COULDN'T BE ANYONE ELSE.
Well ...
YOU'LL WORK WITH ME, WON'T YOU?
DEFI-NITELY!
WE'LL DO WHAT-EVER WE CAN.
GOOD!
THANKS, YOU GUYS.
WIP
HUH?
WHERE'S THE KID, TSUZUKI?
Hey!
WHAT? HUH?
HISO-KA?

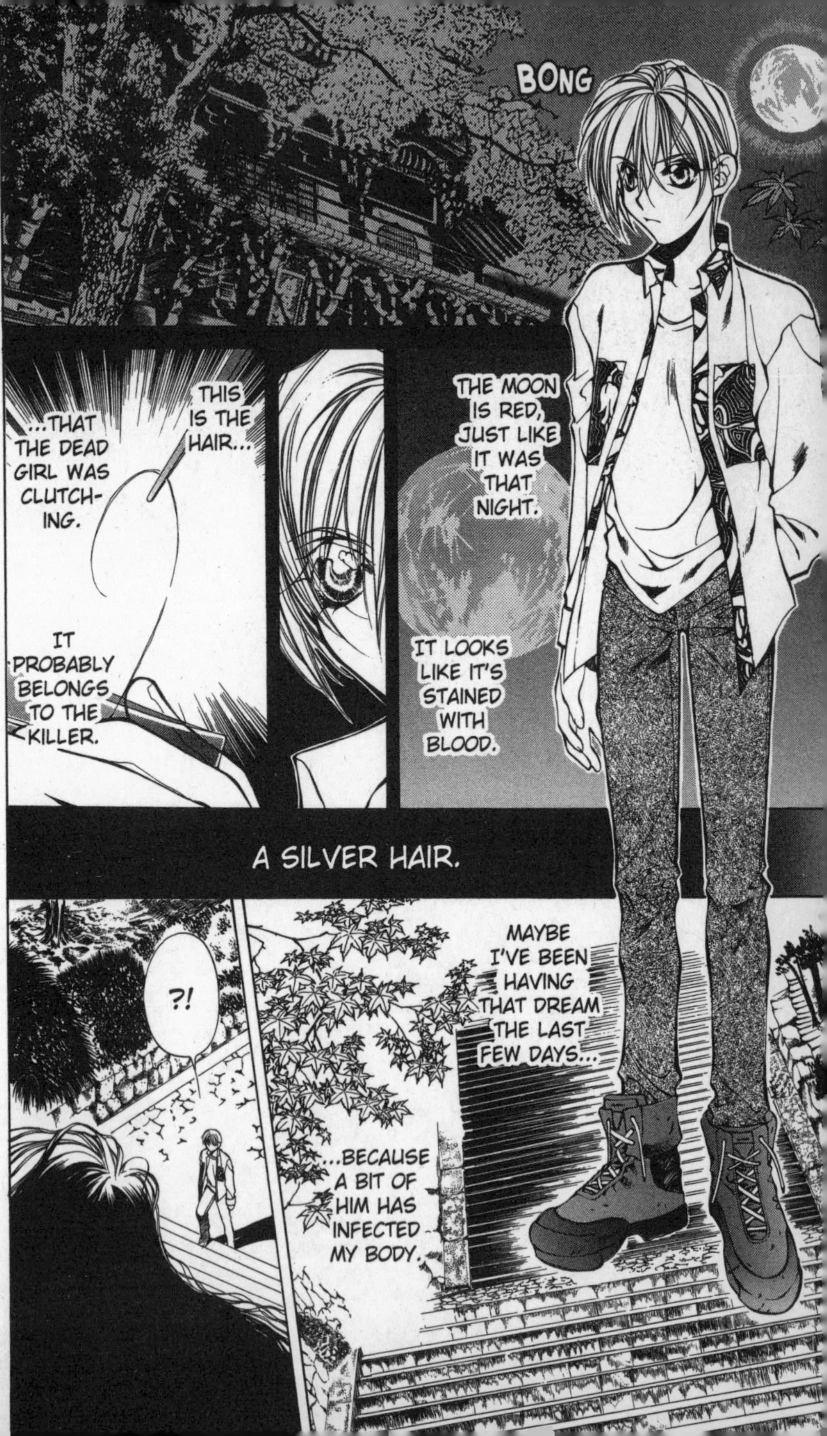
BONG
THE MOON IS RED, JUST LIKE IT WAS THAT NIGHT.
IT LOOKS LIKE IT'S STAINED WITH BLOOD.
THIS IS THE HAIR...
...THAT THE DEAD GIRL WAS CLUTCHING.
IT PROBABLY BELONGS TO THE KILLER.
A SILVER HAIR.
MAYBE I'VE BEEN HAVING THAT DREAM THE LAST FEW DAYS...
...BECAUSE A BIT OF HIM HAS INFECTED MY BODY.
?!

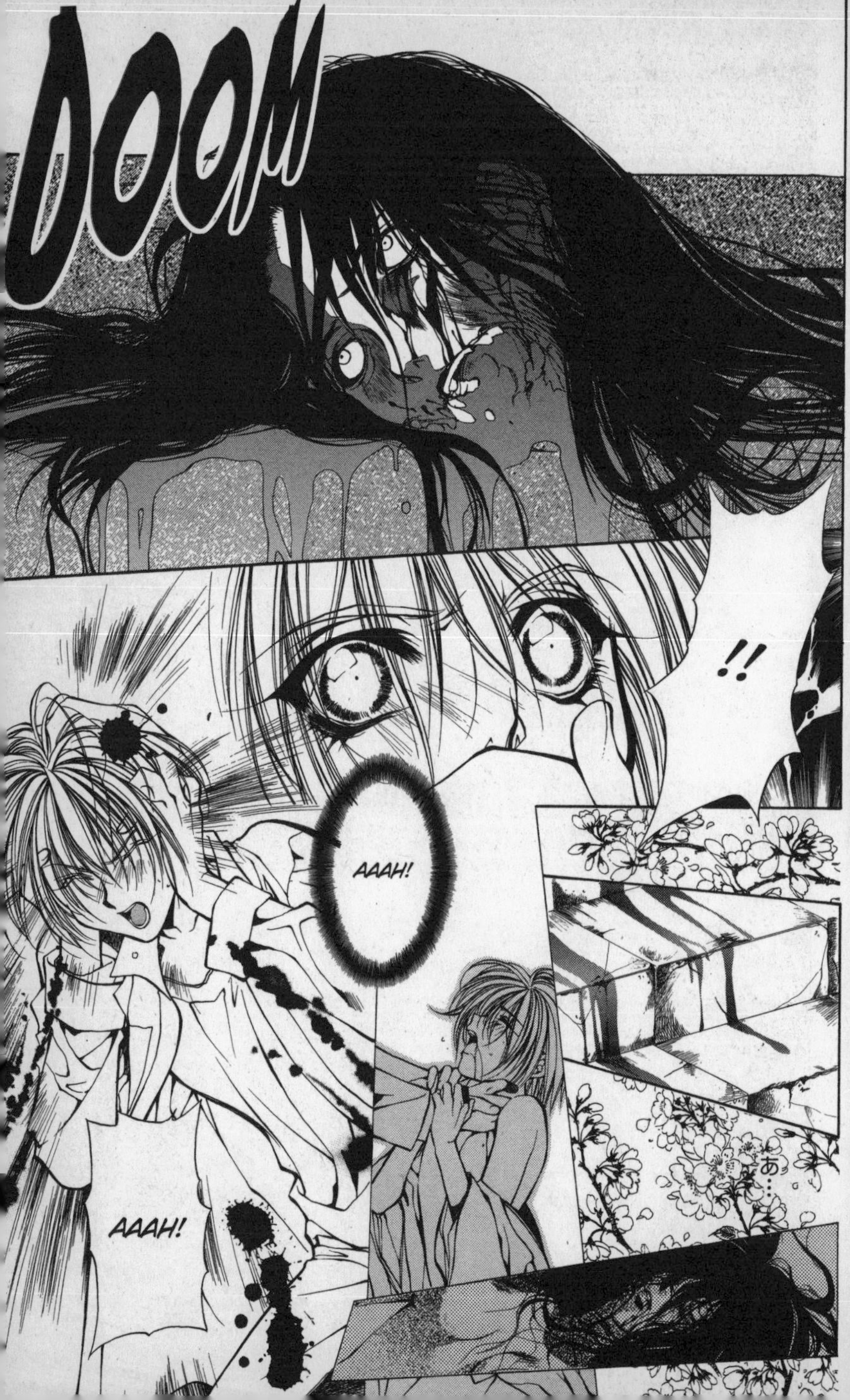
DOOM
!!
AAAH!
あ…
AAAH!

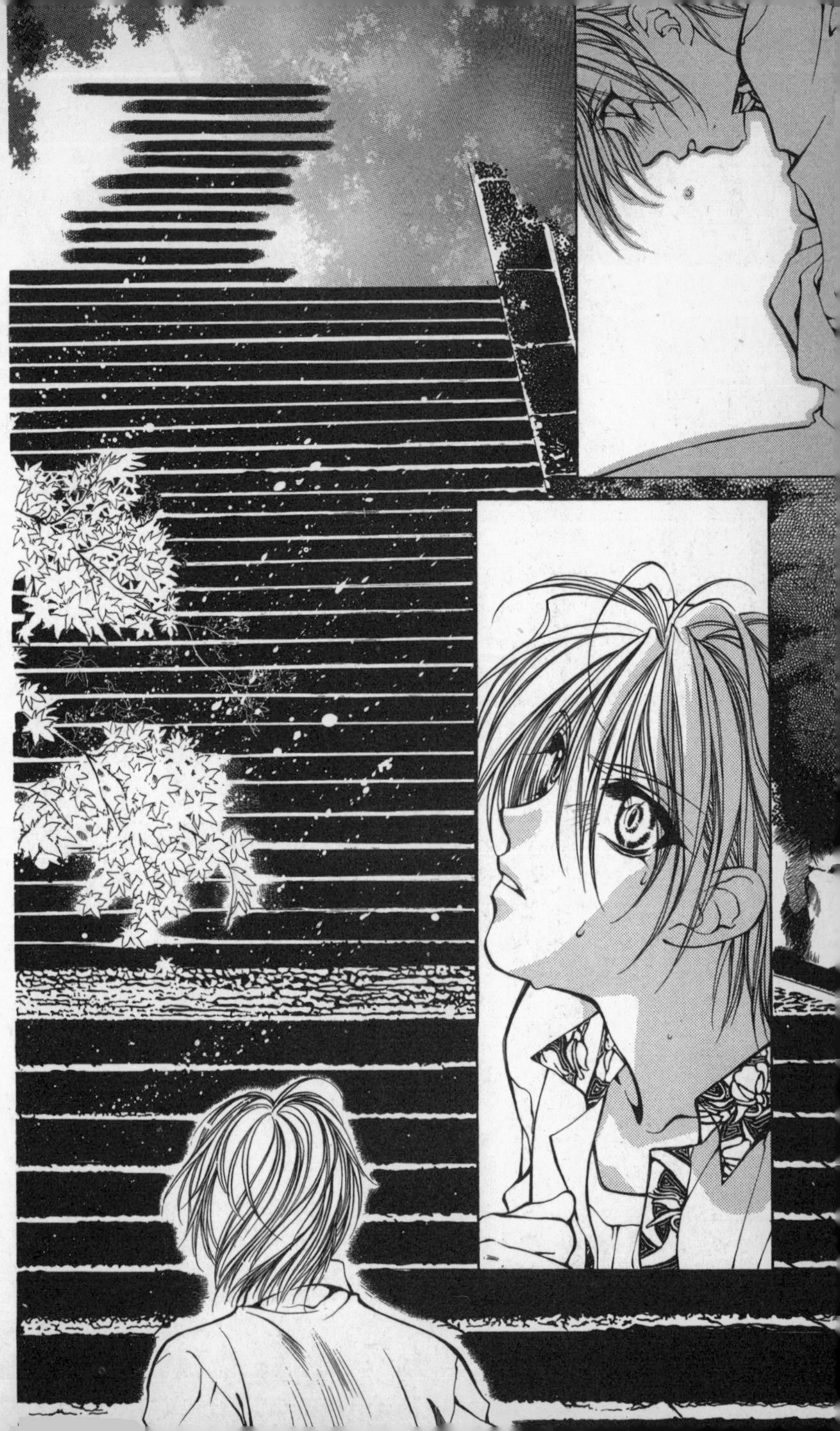

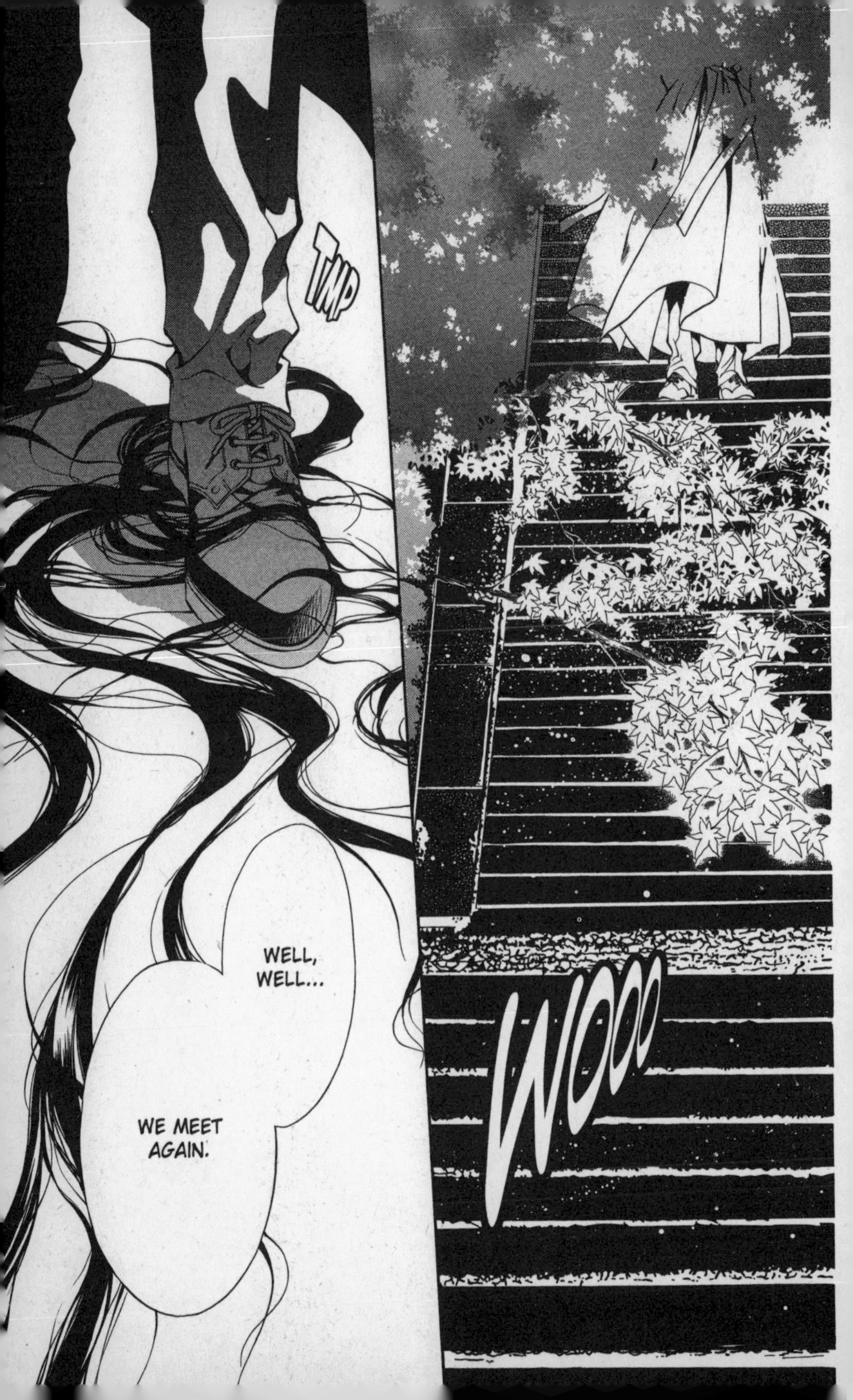
WOOO
TMP
WELL, WELL...
WE MEET AGAIN.

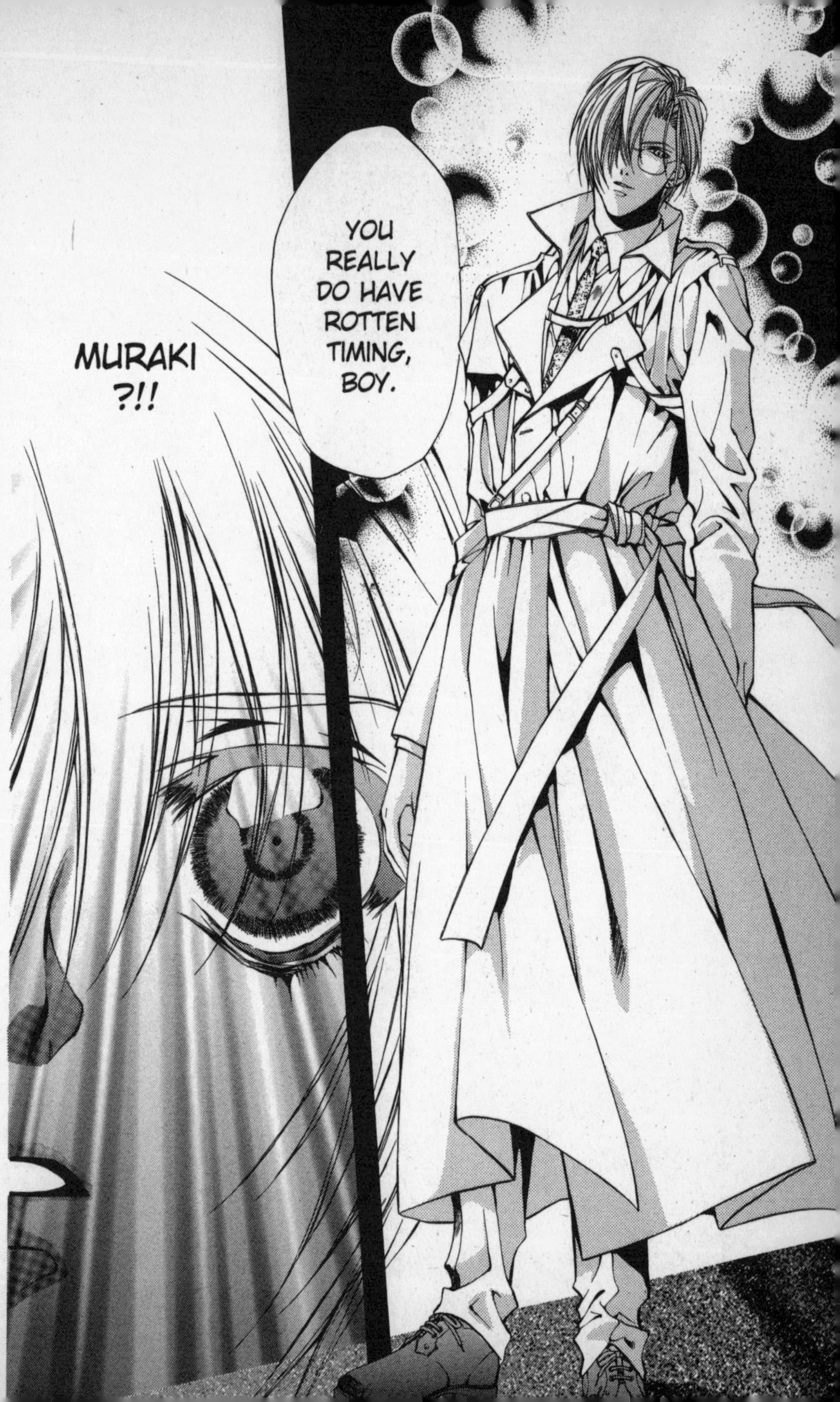
YOU REALLY DO HAVE ROTTEN TIMING, BOY.
MURAKI ?!!

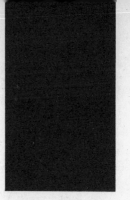

CHAPTER 19

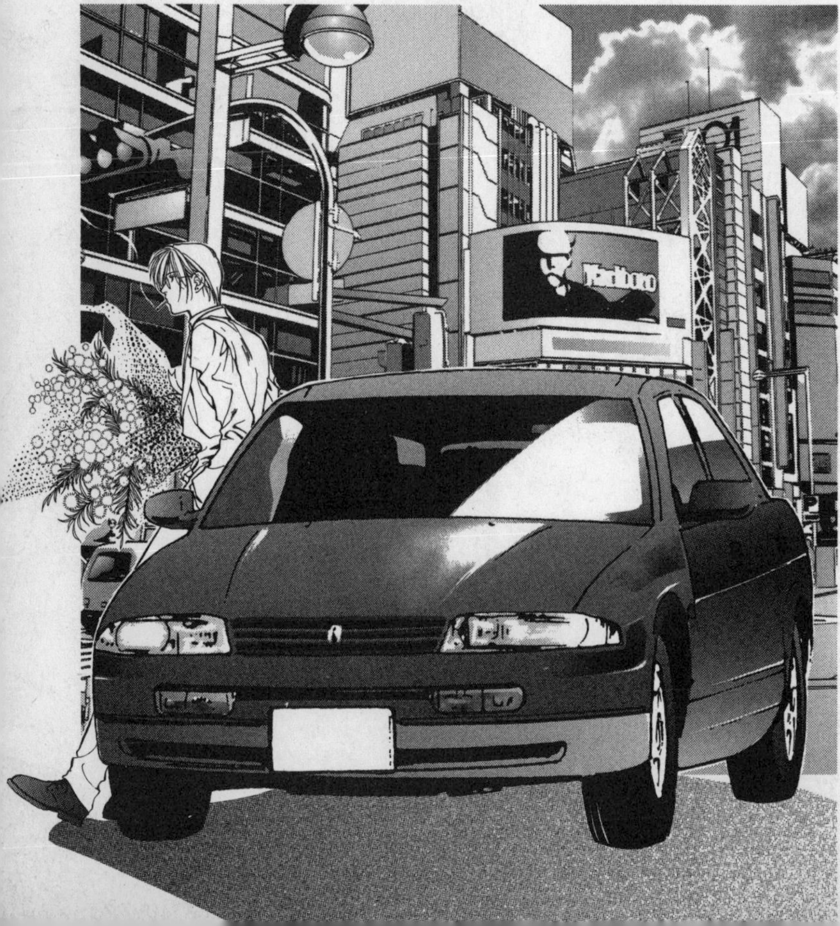

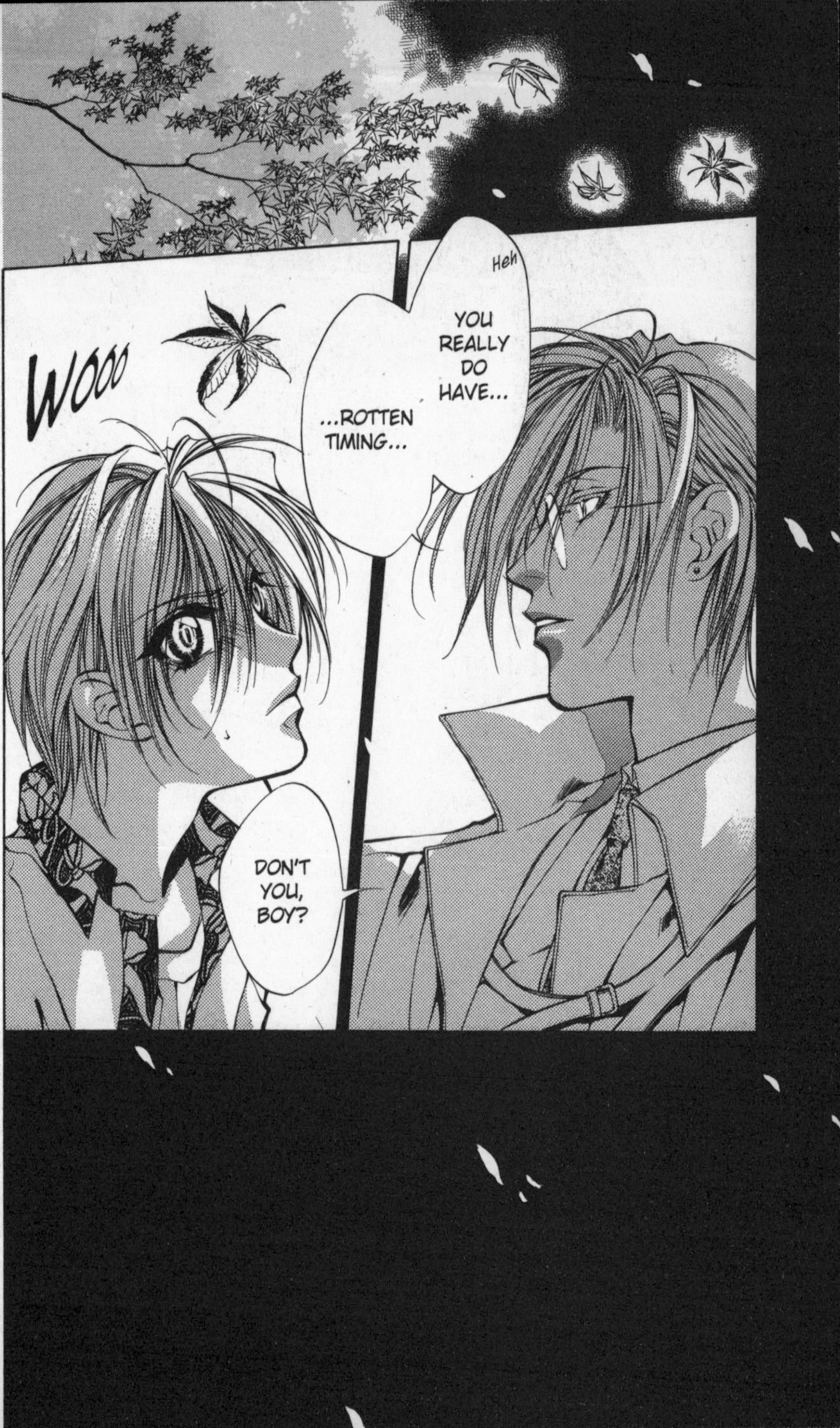
Heh
YOU REALLY DO HAVE...
...ROTTEN TIMING...
WOOO
DON'T YOU, BOY?

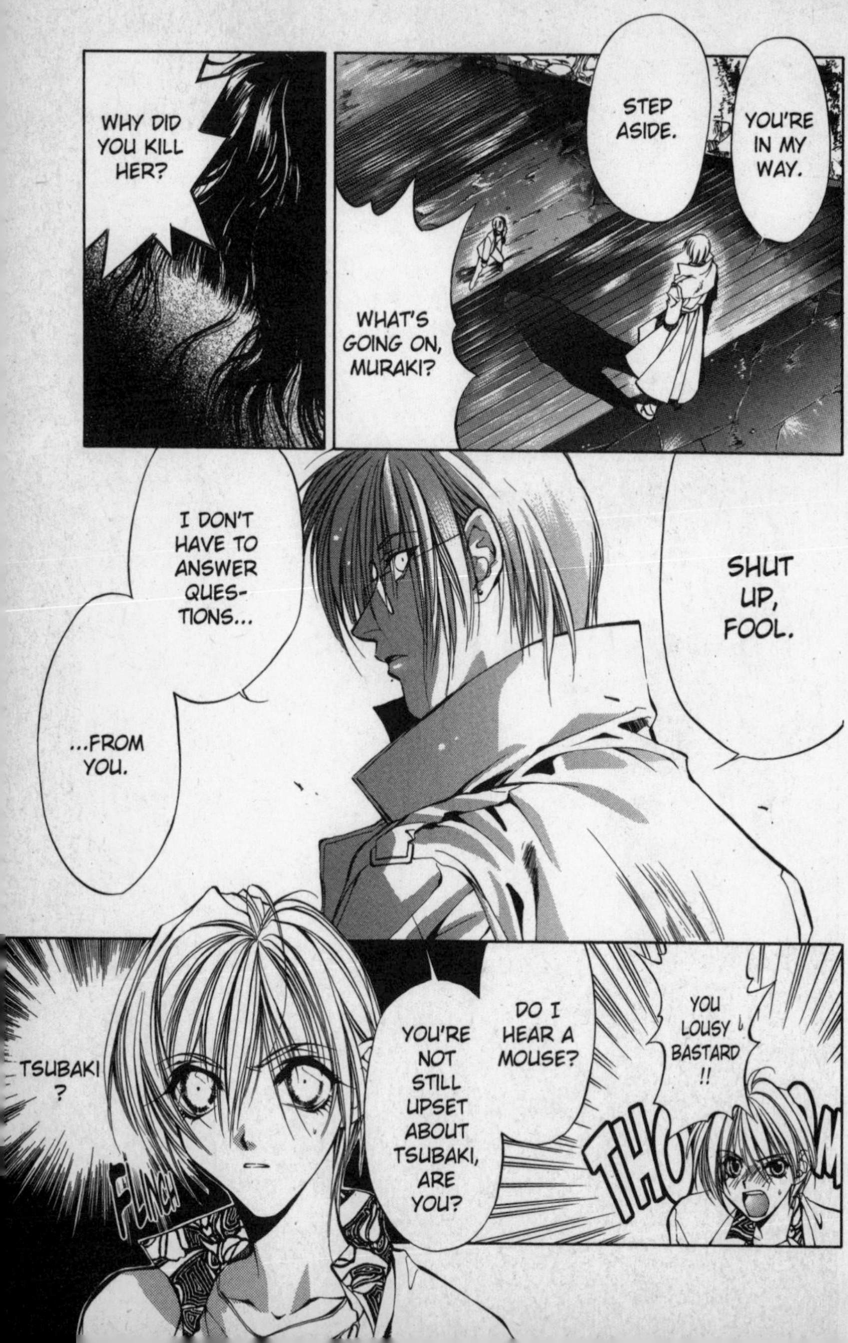
YOU'RE IN MY WAY.
STEP ASIDE.
WHAT'S GOING ON, MURAKI?
WHY DID YOU KILL HER?
SHUT UP, FOOL.
I DON'T HAVE TO ANSWER QUES-TIONS...
...FROM YOU.
YOU LOUSY BASTARD!!
DO I HEAR A MOUSE?
YOU'RE NOT STILL UPSET ABOUT TSUBAKI, ARE YOU?
TSUBAKI?
FLINCH

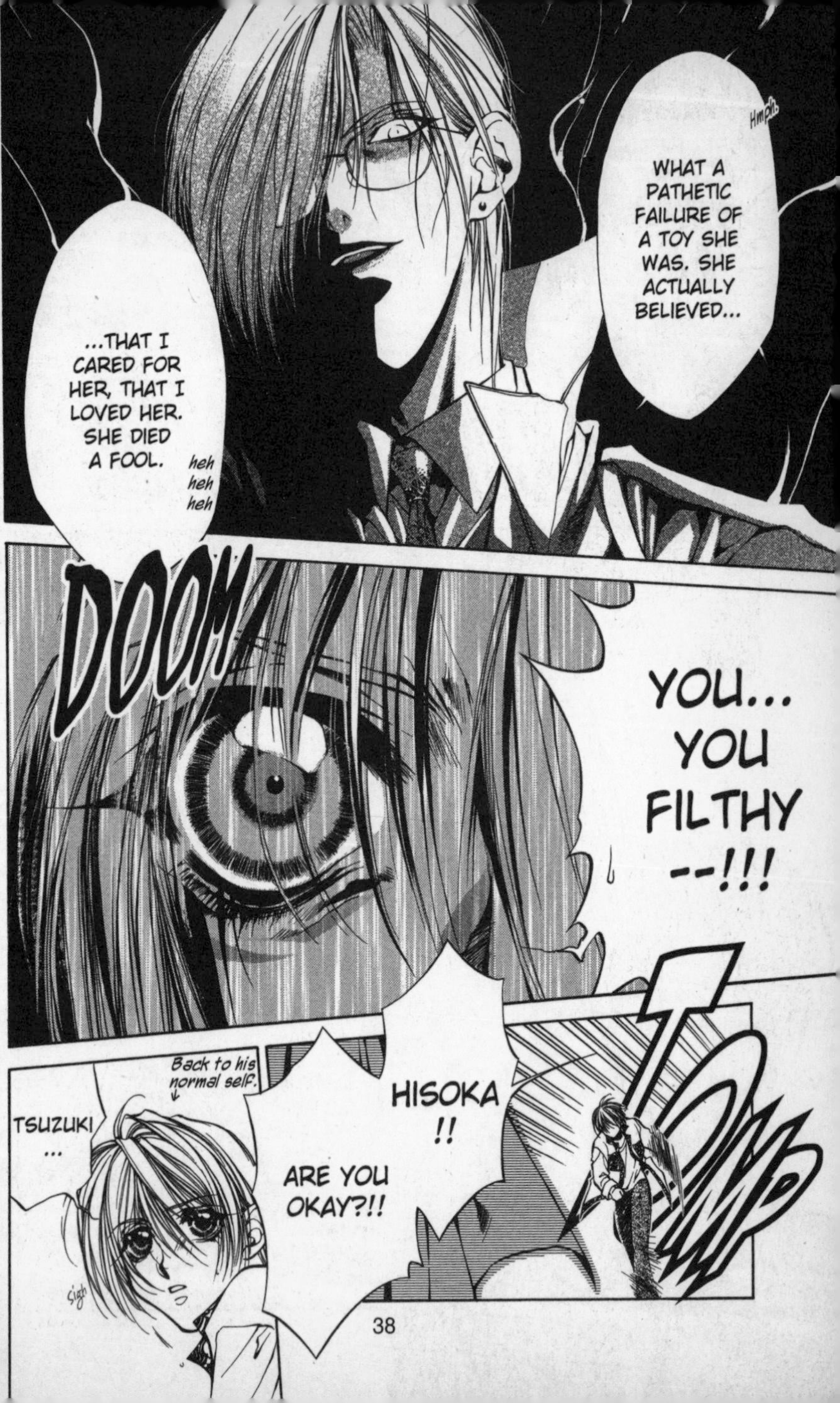
Hmph.
WHAT A PATHETIC FAILURE OF A TOY SHE WAS. SHE ACTUALLY BELIEVED...
...THAT I CARED FOR HER, THAT I LOVED HER. SHE DIED A FOOL.
heh heh heh
YOU... YOU FILTHY --!!!
DOOM
TOMP
HISOKA !!
ARE YOU OKAY?!!
Back to his normal self.
TSUZUKI ...
sigh

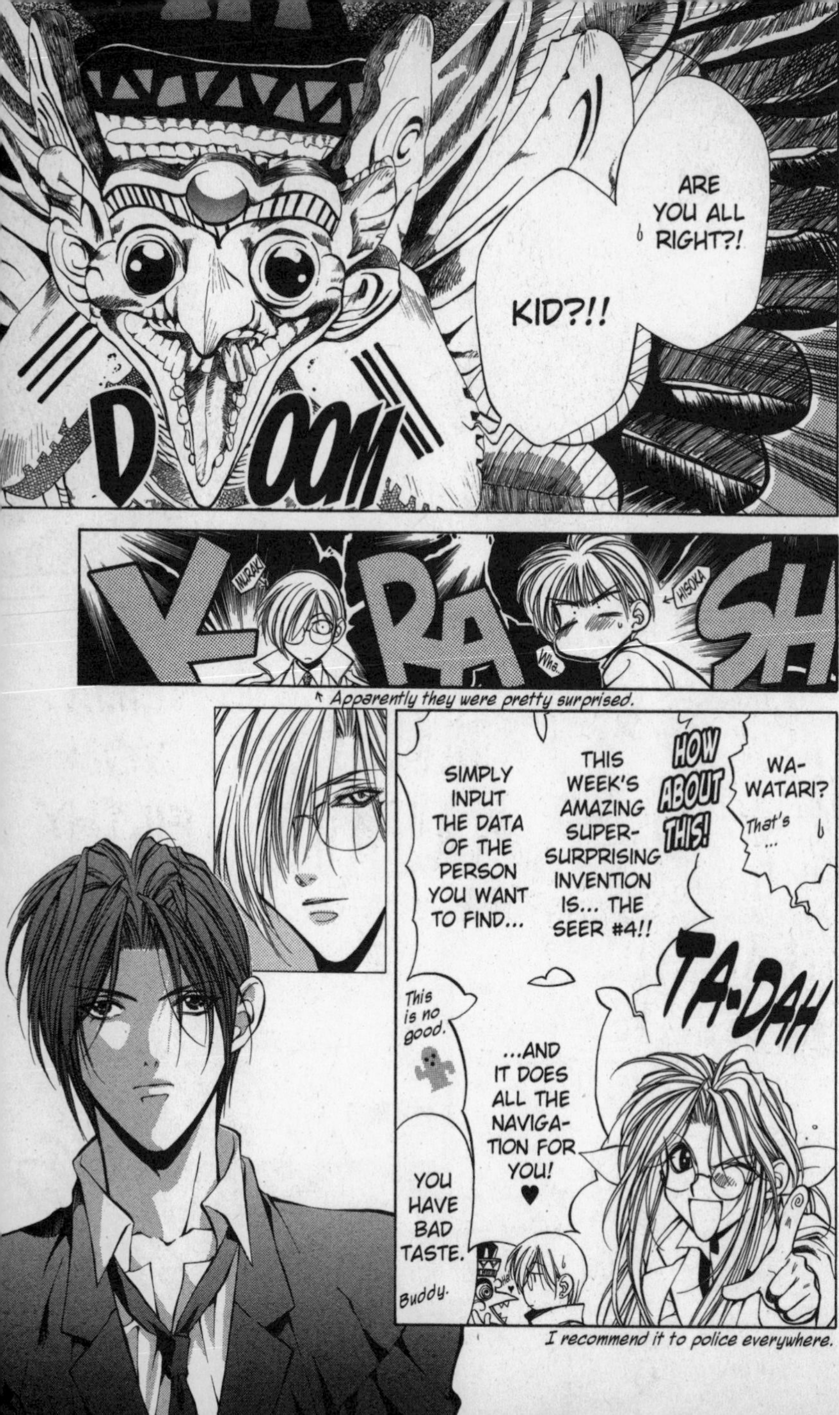

ARE YOU ALL RIGHT?!
KID?!!
DOOM
K-RA-SH
HISOKA
Wha...
MURAKI
Apparently they were pretty surprised.
WA-WATARI?
That's ...
HOW ABOUT THIS!
THIS WEEK'S AMAZING SUPER-SURPRISING INVENTION IS... THE SEER #4!!
SIMPLY INPUT THE DATA OF THE PERSON YOU WANT TO FIND...
TA-DAH
...AND IT DOES ALL THE NAVIGA-TION FOR YOU! ♥
This is no good.
YOU HAVE BAD TASTE.
Buddy.
I recommend it to police everywhere.

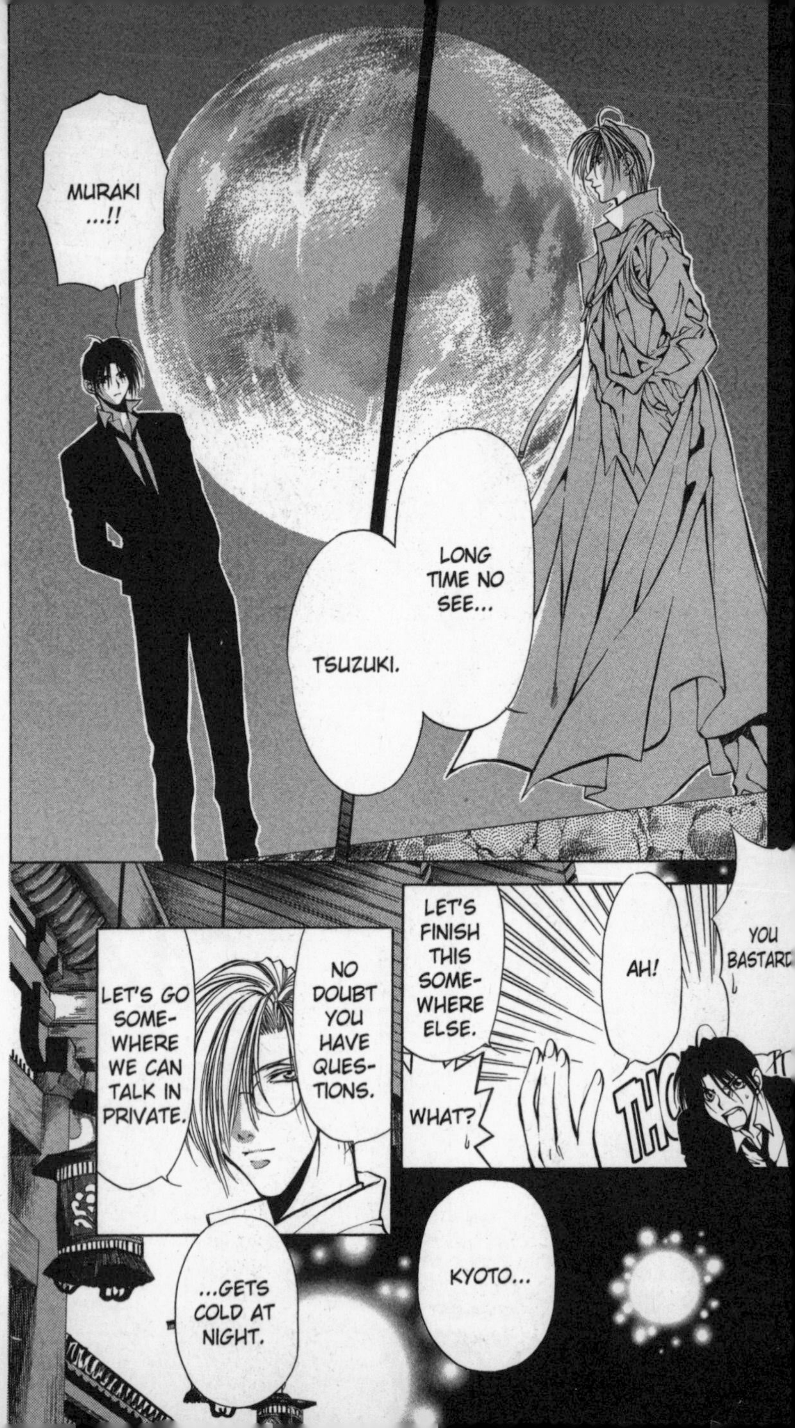
MURAKI ...!!
LONG TIME NO SEE...
TSUZUKI.
YOU BASTARD
AH!
LET'S FINISH THIS SOME-WHERE ELSE.
WHAT?
NO DOUBT YOU HAVE QUES-TIONS.
LET'S GO SOME-WHERE WE CAN TALK IN PRIVATE.
KYOTO...
...GETS COLD AT NIGHT.

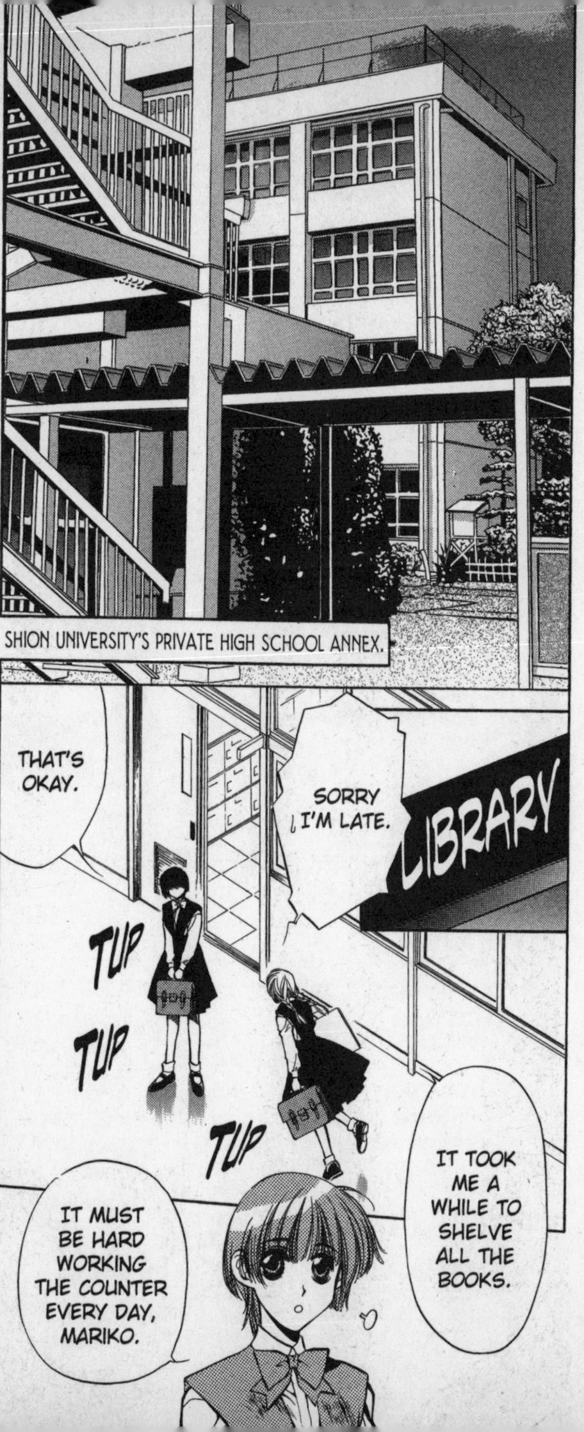
SHION UNIVERSITY'S PRIVATE HIGH SCHOOL ANNEX.
LIBRARY
SORRY I'M LATE.
THAT'S OKAY.
TUP
TUP
TUP
IT TOOK ME A WHILE TO SHELVE ALL THE BOOKS.
IT MUST BE HARD WORKING THE COUNTER EVERY DAY, MARIKO.

Lately I've felt... ...a little bit flashy.

Hello, Matsushita here. It's already volume seven of Descendents of Darkness. I wonder how many volumes there will be in this series--even I don't know. This is my first long-running series so, I want it to go on for as long as possible. (Hee!) Thank you, everyone!

The Kyoto story here is the longest one so far. It's 10 chapters! It continues in the next volume. I actually wanted to make it even longer, but my editor said the readers would get bored if it was too long.

Knows from experience.

So I ended it after only 10 chapters, but since it was originally only supposed to go for eight chapters, I should feel lucky--I got to draw two extra chapters. But then... (sigh)

↑ I'm still a little disappointed.

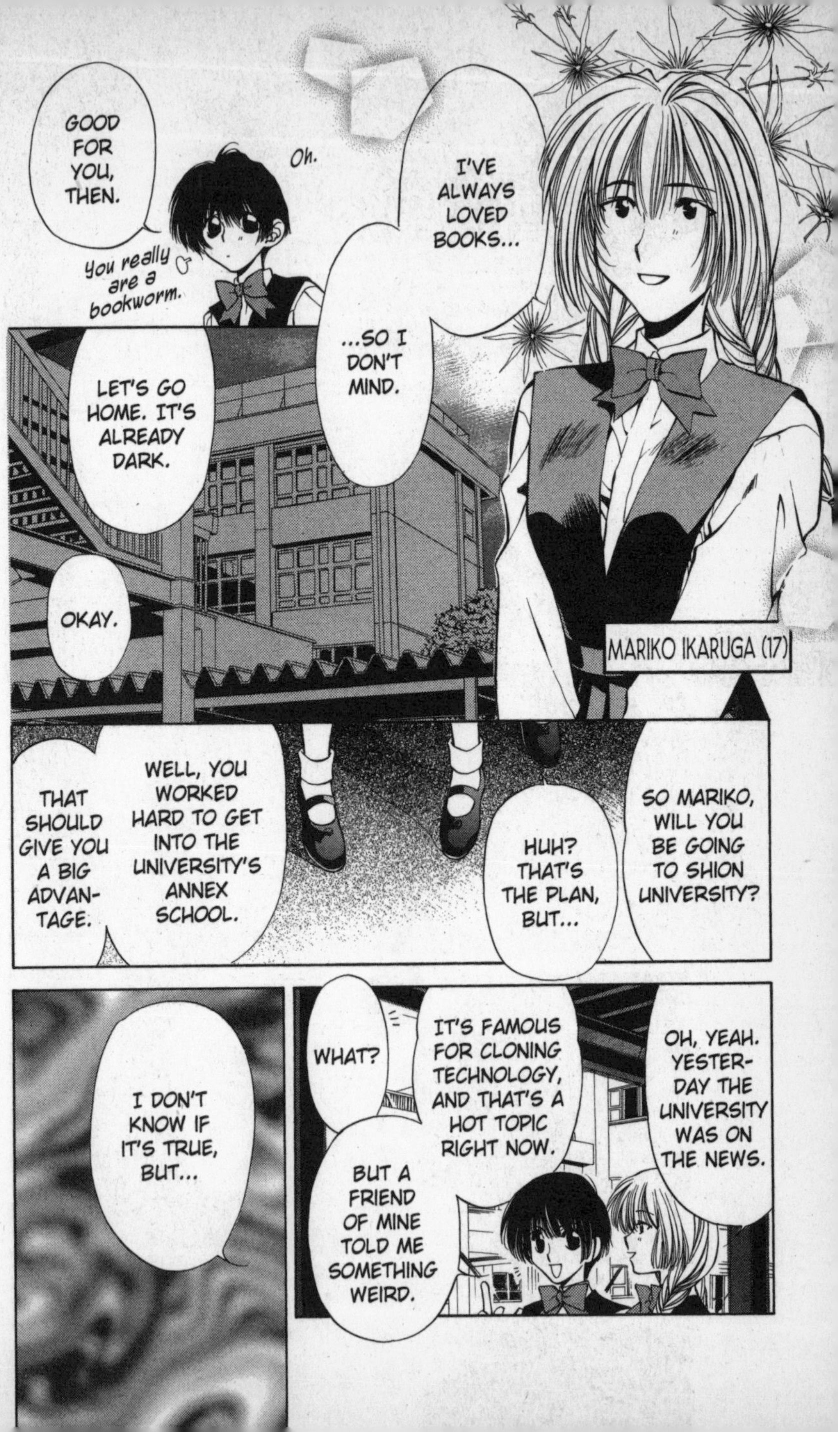
I'VE ALWAYS LOVED BOOKS...
...SO I DON'T MIND.
MARIKO IKARUGA (17)
Oh.
GOOD FOR YOU, THEN.
You really are a bookworm.
LET'S GO HOME. IT'S ALREADY DARK.
OKAY.
SO MARIKO, WILL YOU BE GOING TO SHION UNIVERSITY?
HUH? THAT'S THE PLAN, BUT...
WELL, YOU WORKED HARD TO GET INTO THE UNIVERSITY'S ANNEX SCHOOL.
THAT SHOULD GIVE YOU A BIG ADVANTAGE.
OH, YEAH. YESTERDAY THE UNIVERSITY WAS ON THE NEWS.
IT'S FAMOUS FOR CLONING TECHNOLOGY, AND THAT'S A HOT TOPIC RIGHT NOW.
WHAT?
BUT A FRIEND OF MINE TOLD ME SOMETHING WEIRD.
I DON'T KNOW IF IT'S TRUE, BUT...

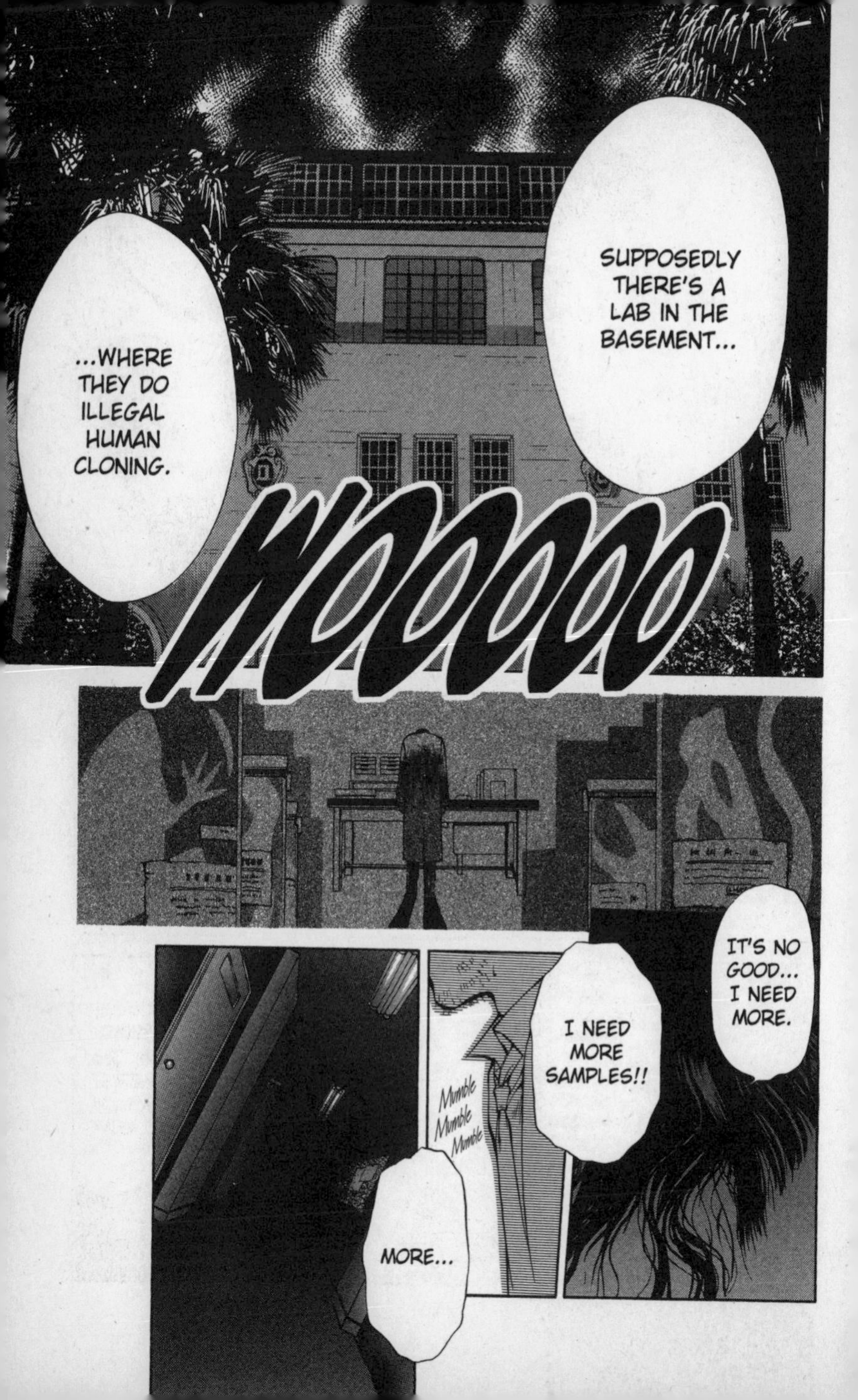
SUPPOSEDLY THERE'S A LAB IN THE BASEMENT...
...WHERE THEY DO ILLEGAL HUMAN CLONING.
IT'S NO GOOD... I NEED MORE.
I NEED MORE SAMPLES!!
Mumble Mumble Mumble
MORE...

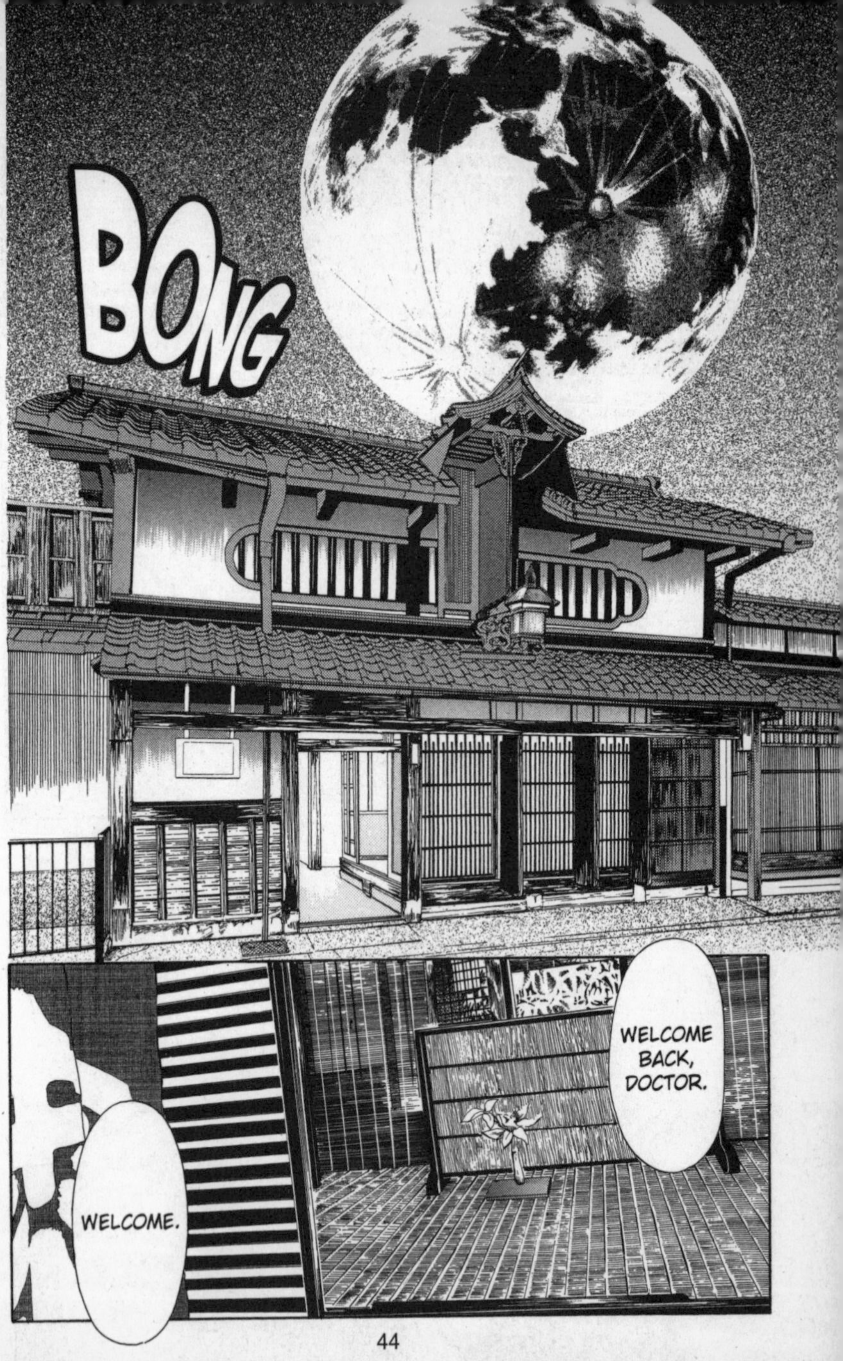
BONG
WELCOME BACK, DOCTOR.
WELCOME.

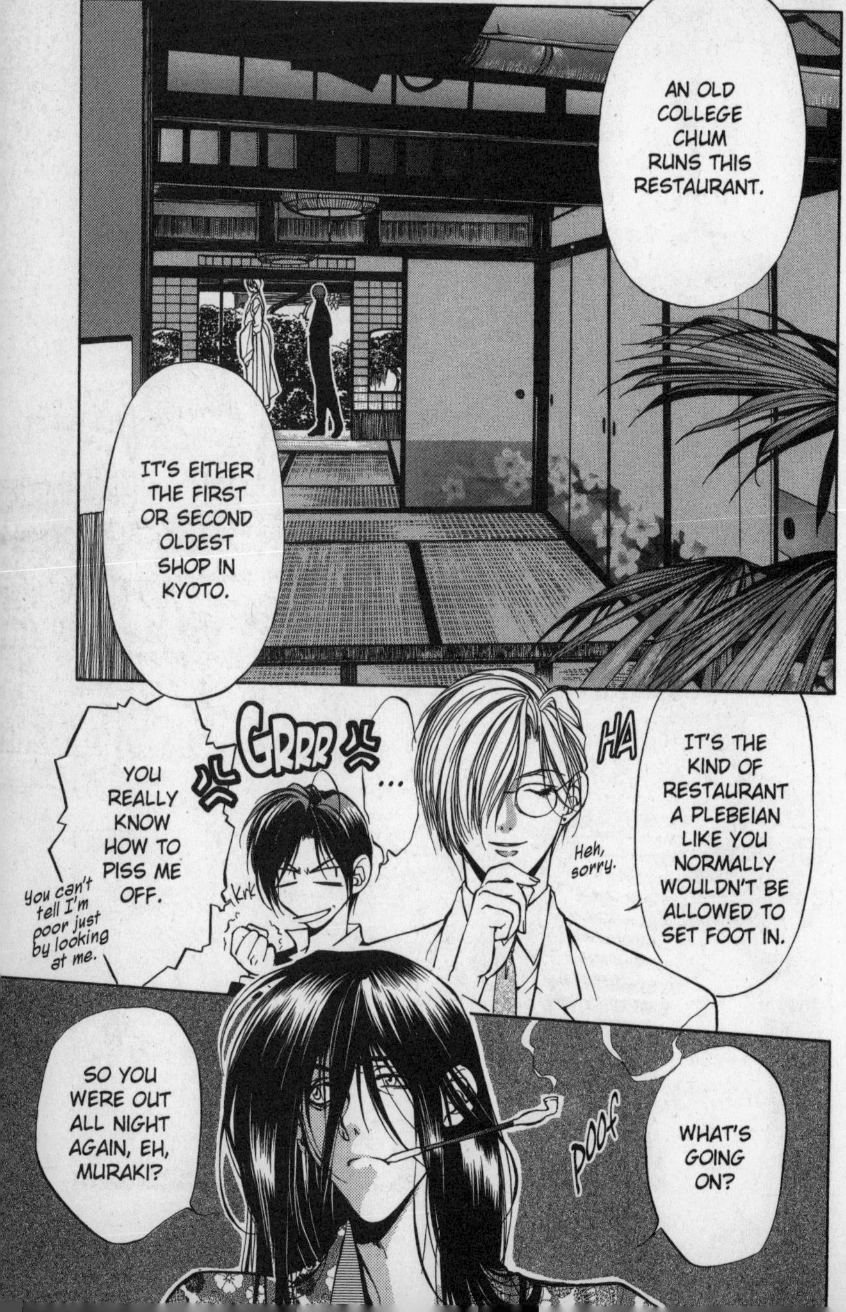
AN OLD COLLEGE CHUM RUNS THIS RESTAURANT.
IT'S EITHER THE FIRST OR SECOND OLDEST SHOP IN KYOTO.
HA
IT'S THE KIND OF RESTAURANT A PLEBEIAN LIKE YOU NORMALLY WOULDN'T BE ALLOWED TO SET FOOT IN.
Heh, sorry.
...
GRRR
YOU REALLY KNOW HOW TO PISS ME OFF.
Krk
You can't tell I'm poor just by looking at me.
WHAT'S GOING ON?
POOF
SO YOU WERE OUT ALL NIGHT AGAIN, EH, MURAKI?

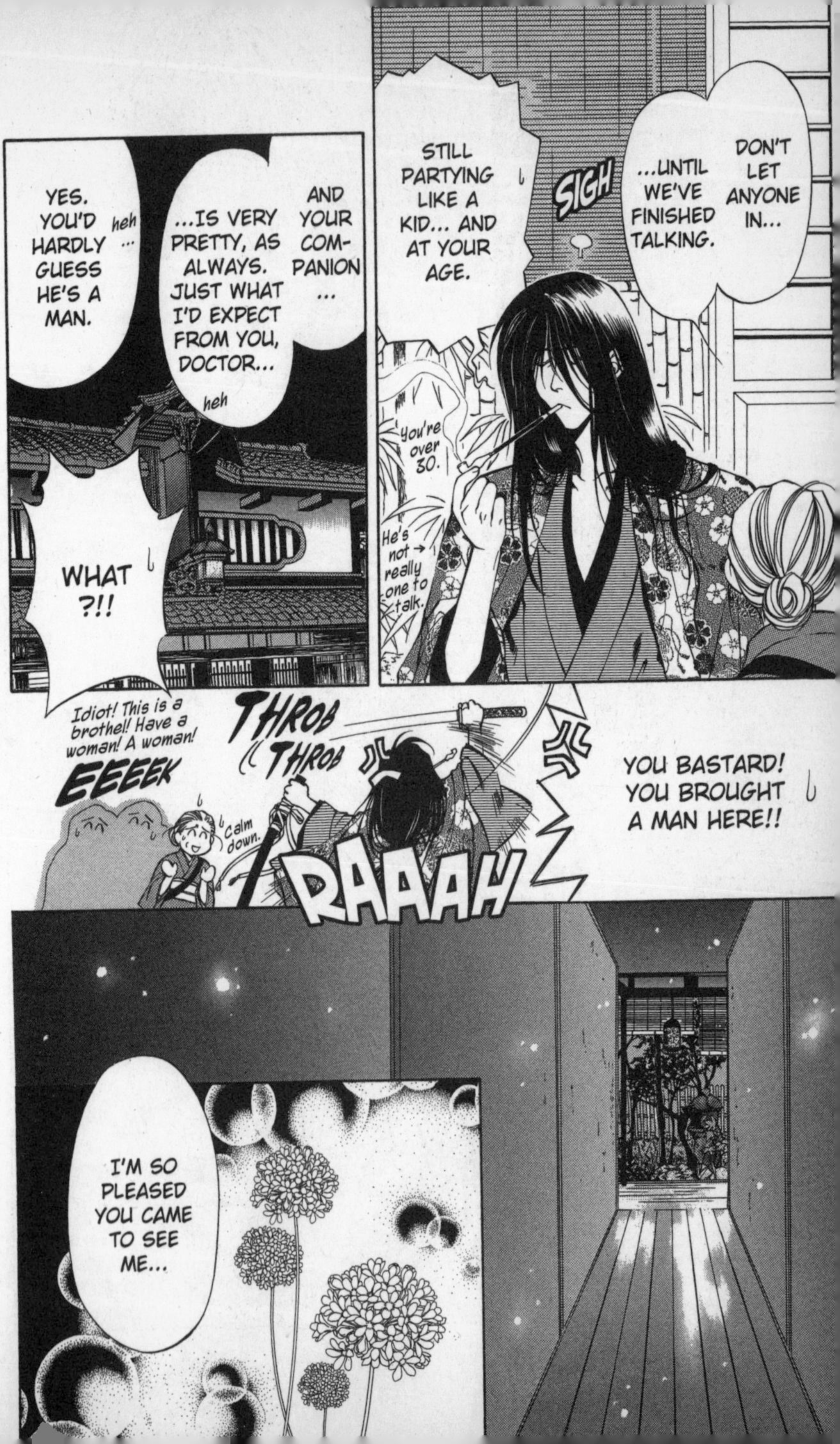
DON'T LET ANYONE IN...
...UNTIL WE'VE FINISHED TALKING.
SIGH
STILL PARTYING LIKE A KID... AND AT YOUR AGE.
You're over 30.
He's not really one to talk.
AND YOUR COMPANION...
...IS VERY PRETTY, AS ALWAYS. JUST WHAT I'D EXPECT FROM YOU, DOCTOR...
heh
heh...
YES. YOU'D HARDLY GUESS HE'S A MAN.
WHAT?!!
YOU BASTARD! YOU BROUGHT A MAN HERE!!
RAAAH
THROB THROB
Calm down.
Idiot! This is a brothel! Have a woman! A woman!
EEEEK
I'M SO PLEASED YOU CAME TO SEE ME...

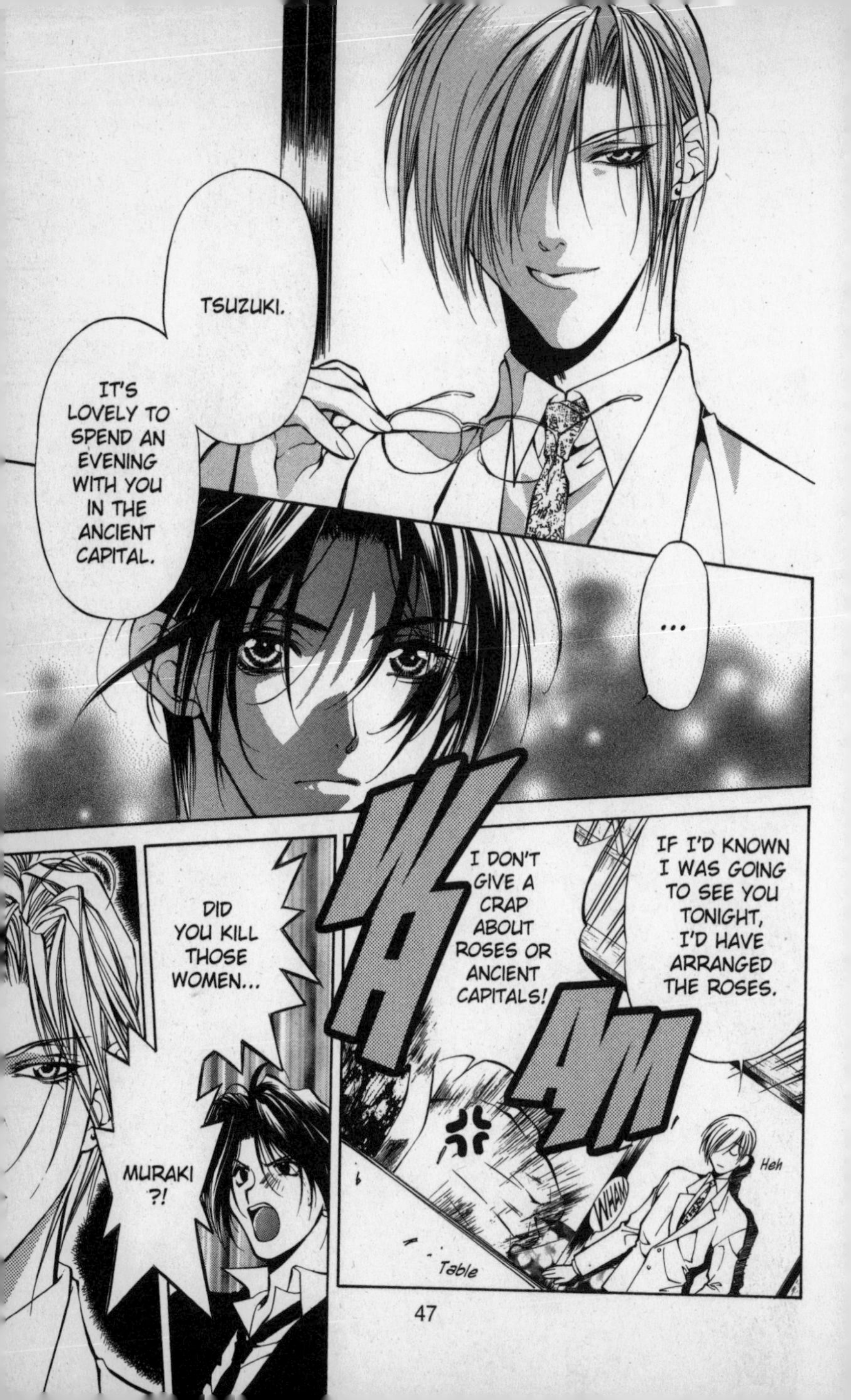
TSUZUKI.
IT'S LOVELY TO SPEND AN EVENING WITH YOU IN THE ANCIENT CAPITAL.
...
IF I'D KNOWN I WAS GOING TO SEE YOU TONIGHT, I'D HAVE ARRANGED THE ROSES.
I DON'T GIVE A CRAP ABOUT ROSES OR ANCIENT CAPITALS!
WHAM
Heh
WHAM
Table
DID YOU KILL THOSE WOMEN...
MURAKI ?!

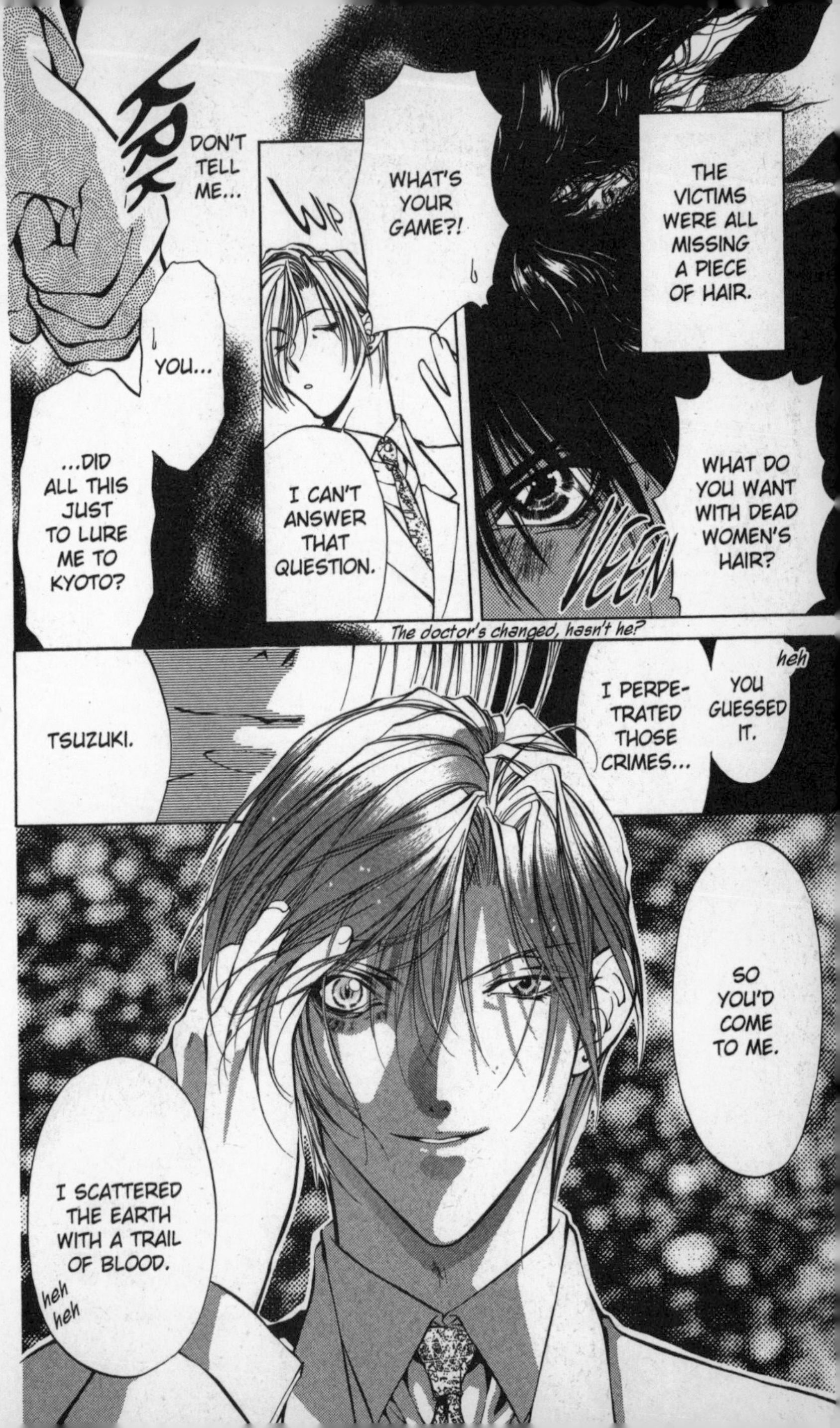
THE VICTIMS WERE ALL MISSING A PIECE OF HAIR.
WHAT DO YOU WANT WITH DEAD WOMEN'S HAIR?
VEEN
WHAT'S YOUR GAME?!
WIP
I CAN'T ANSWER THAT QUESTION.
KRRK
DON'T TELL ME...
YOU...
...DID ALL THIS JUST TO LURE ME TO KYOTO?
The doctor's changed, hasn't he?
heh
YOU GUESSED IT.
I PERPE-TRATED THOSE CRIMES...
TSUZUKI.
SO YOU'D COME TO ME.
I SCATTERED THE EARTH WITH A TRAIL OF BLOOD.
heh heh

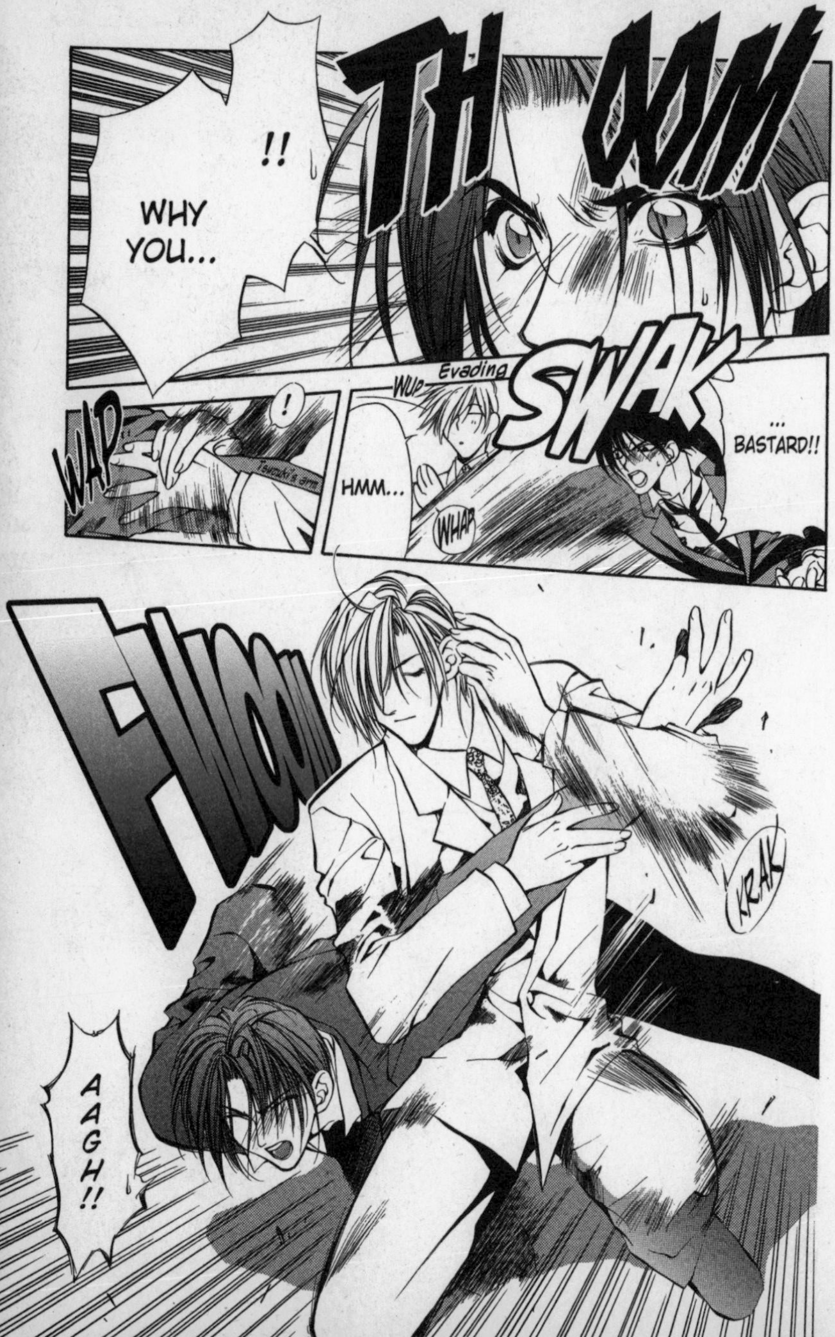
THOOM
!!
WHY YOU...
SWAK
... BASTARD!!
Evading
WUP
HMM...
WHAP
!
WAP
Tsuzuki's arm
KRAK
FWOOM
AAGH!!

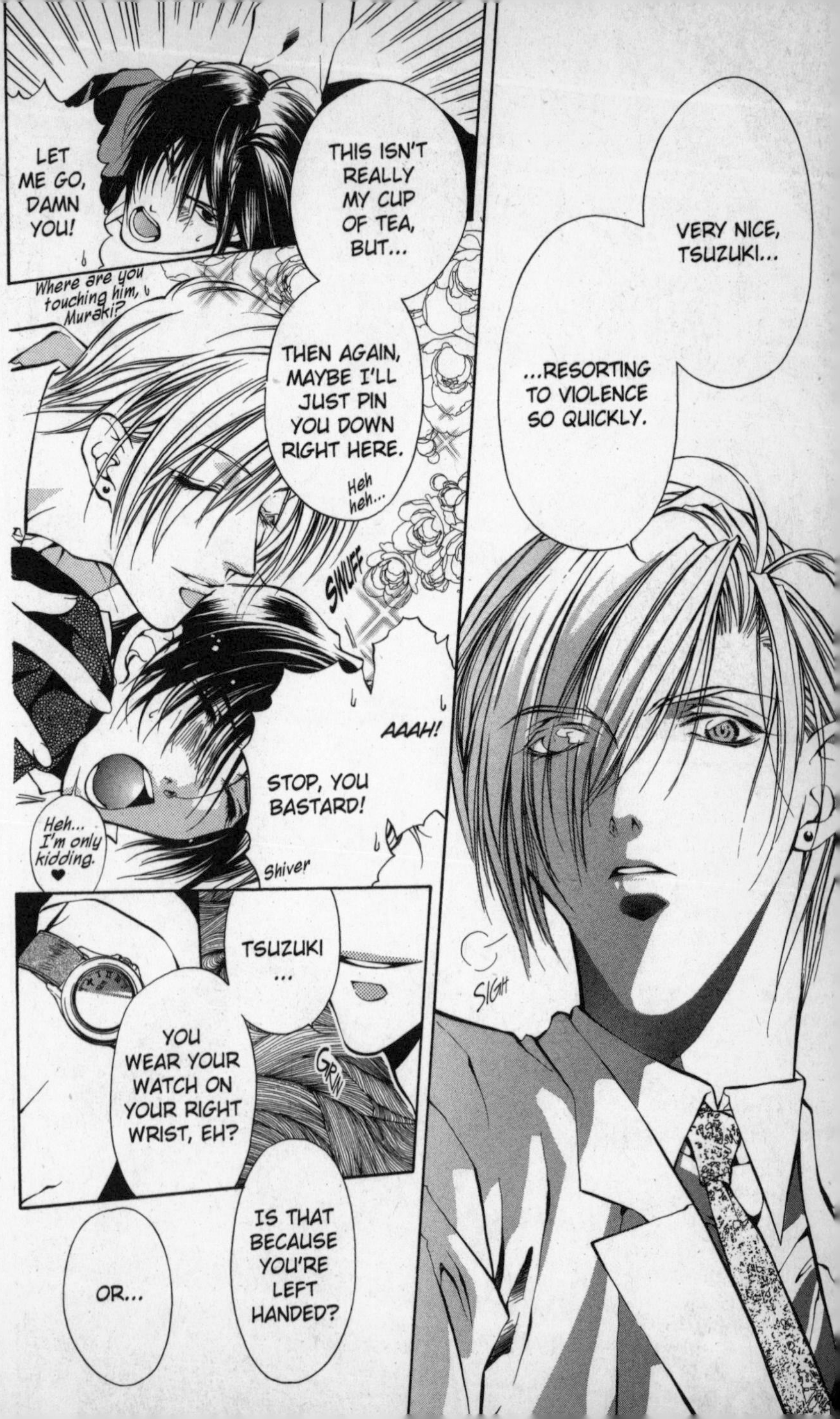
VERY NICE, TSUZUKI...
...RESORTING TO VIOLENCE SO QUICKLY.
SIGH
THIS ISN'T REALLY MY CUP OF TEA, BUT...
LET ME GO, DAMN YOU!
Where are you touching him, Muraki?
THEN AGAIN, MAYBE I'LL JUST PIN YOU DOWN RIGHT HERE.
Heh heh...
SNIFF
AAAH!
STOP, YOU BASTARD!
Shiver
Heh... I'm only kidding. ♥
TSUZUKI...
YOU WEAR YOUR WATCH ON YOUR RIGHT WRIST, EH?
GRIN
IS THAT BECAUSE YOU'RE LEFT HANDED?
OR...

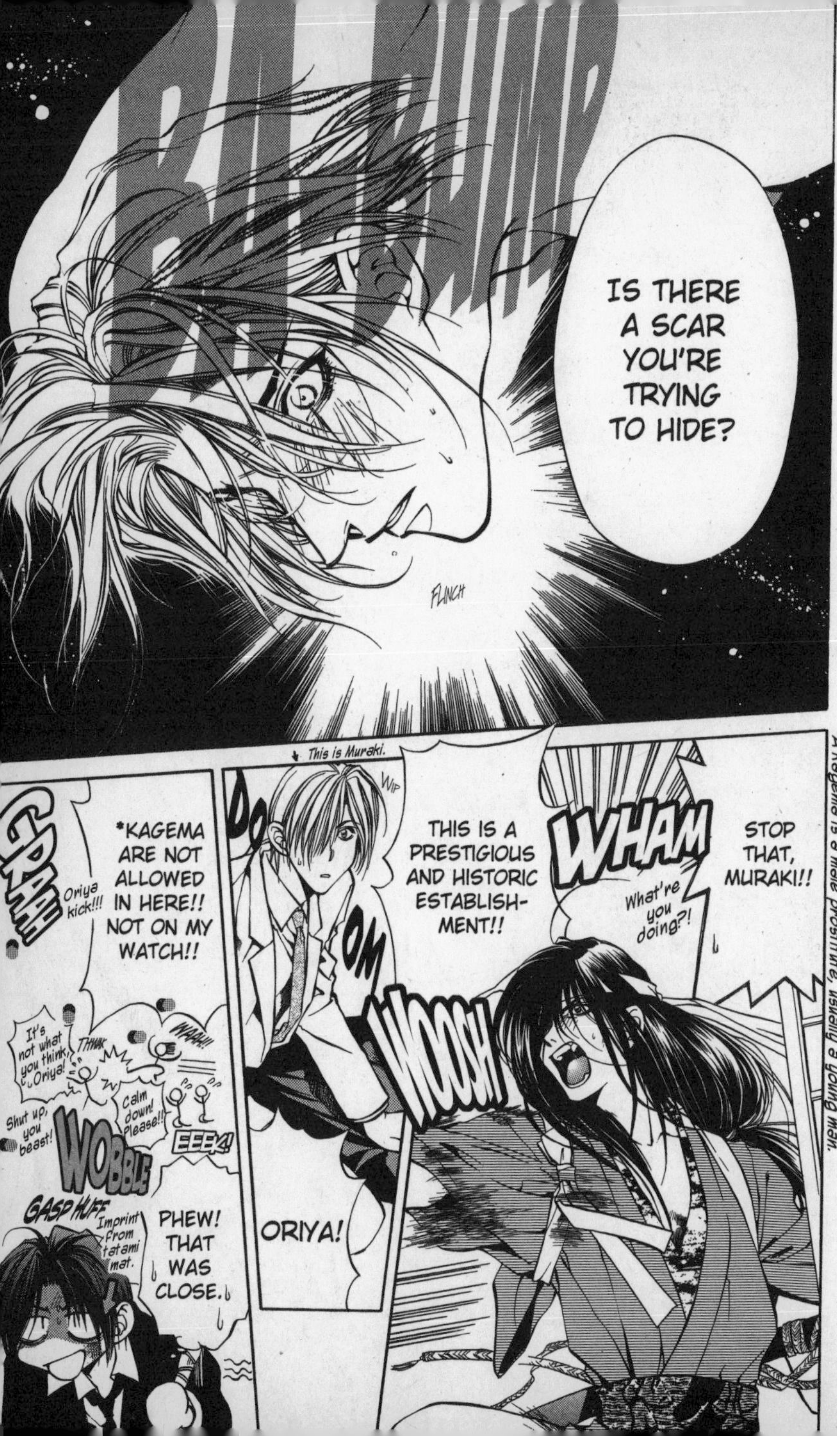
BA-BUMP
IS THERE A SCAR YOU'RE TRYING TO HIDE?
FLINCH
STOP THAT, MURAKI!!
WHAM
What're you doing?!
THIS IS A PRESTIGIOUS AND HISTORIC ESTABLISH-MENT!!
This is Muraki.
WIP
DOOM
WOOSH
ORIYA!
*KAGEMA ARE NOT ALLOWED IN HERE!! NOT ON MY WATCH!!
GRAAH!
Oriya kick!!!
It's not what you think, Oriya!
THWAK
WAAH!!
Calm down! Please!!
EEEK!
Shut up, you beast!
WOBBLE
GASP HUFF
Imprint from tatami mat.
PHEW! THAT WAS CLOSE.

*A kagema is a male prostitute, usually a young man.

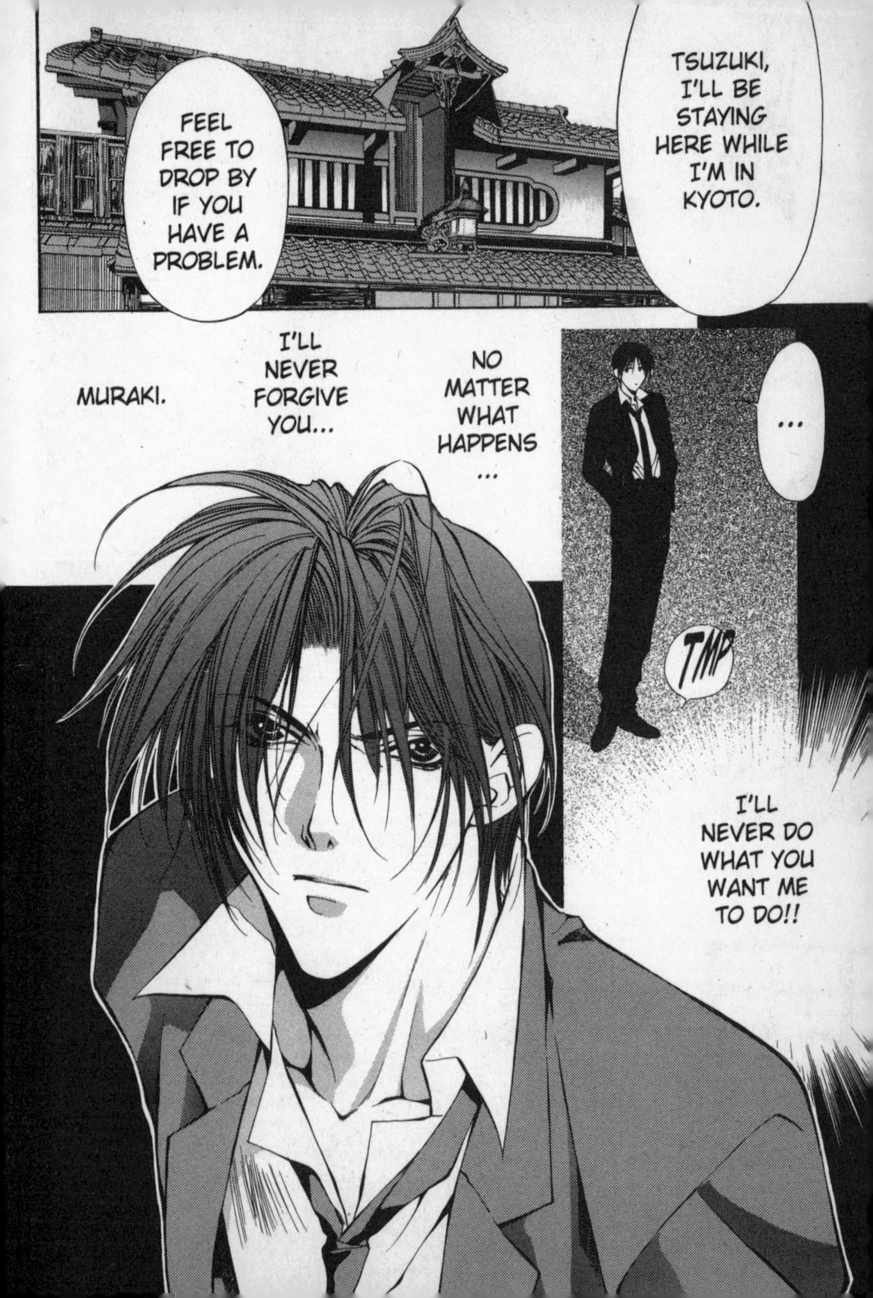
TSUZUKI, I'LL BE STAYING HERE WHILE I'M IN KYOTO.
FEEL FREE TO DROP BY IF YOU HAVE A PROBLEM.
...
TMP
NO MATTER WHAT HAPPENS...
I'LL NEVER FORGIVE YOU...
MURAKI.
I'LL NEVER DO WHAT YOU WANT ME TO DO!!

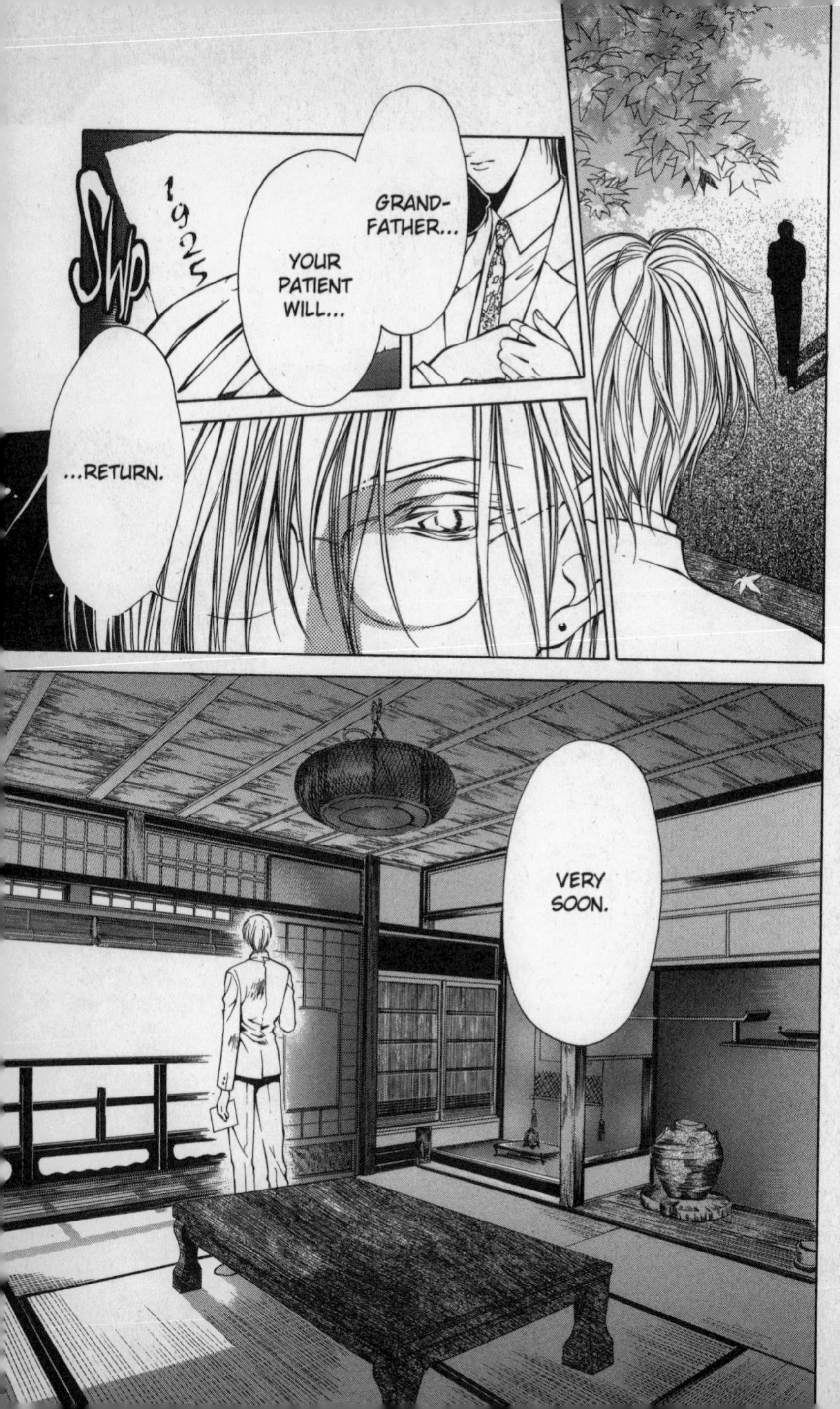
GRAND-FATHER... YOUR PATIENT WILL...
1925
SWP
...RETURN.
VERY SOON.

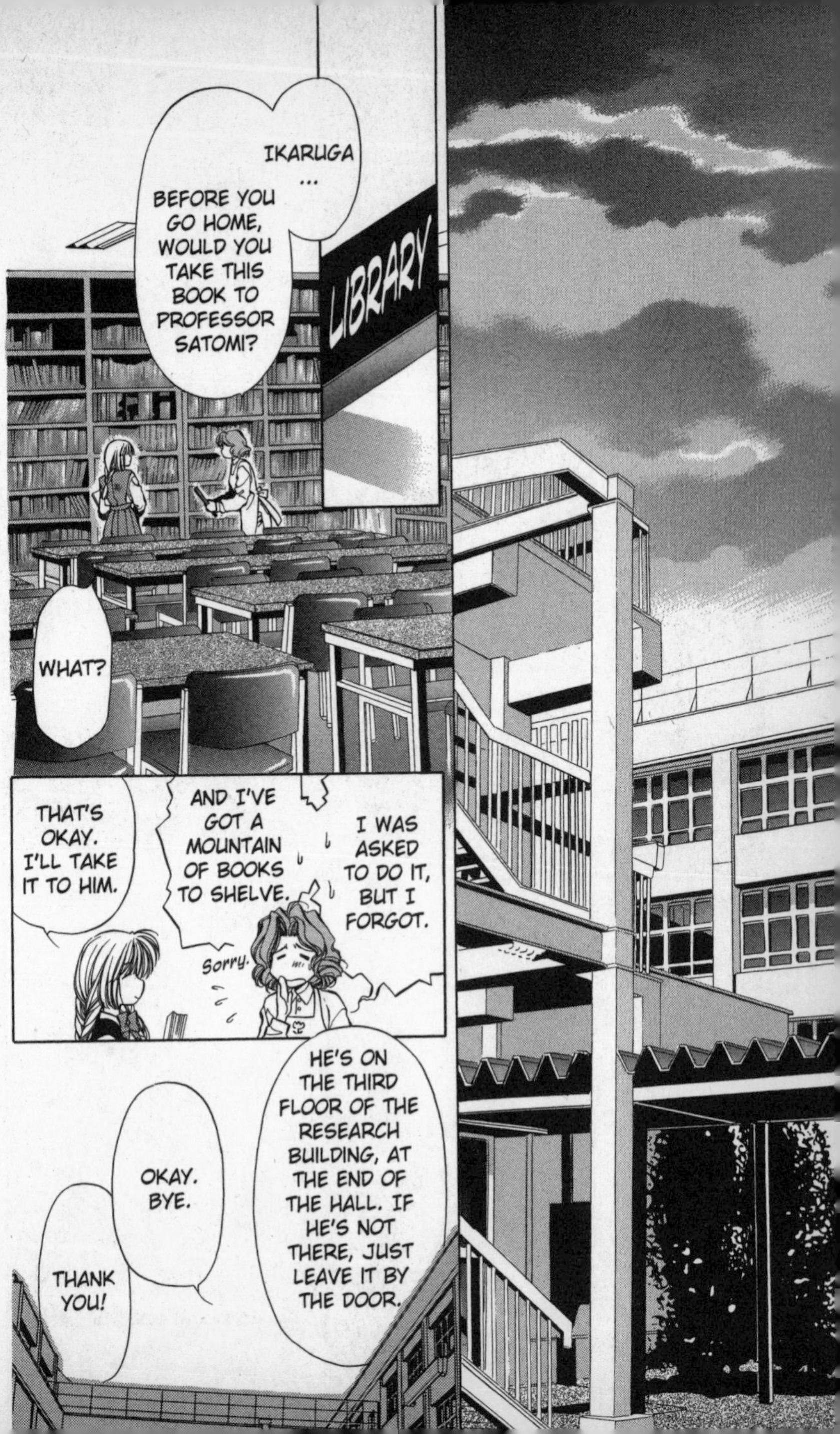
IKARUGA ... BEFORE YOU GO HOME, WOULD YOU TAKE THIS BOOK TO PROFESSOR SATOMI?
LIBRARY
WHAT?
I WAS ASKED TO DO IT, BUT I FORGOT.
AND I'VE GOT A MOUNTAIN OF BOOKS TO SHELVE.
Sorry.
THAT'S OKAY. I'LL TAKE IT TO HIM.
HE'S ON THE THIRD FLOOR OF THE RESEARCH BUILDING, AT THE END OF THE HALL. IF HE'S NOT THERE, JUST LEAVE IT BY THE DOOR.
OKAY. BYE.
THANK YOU!

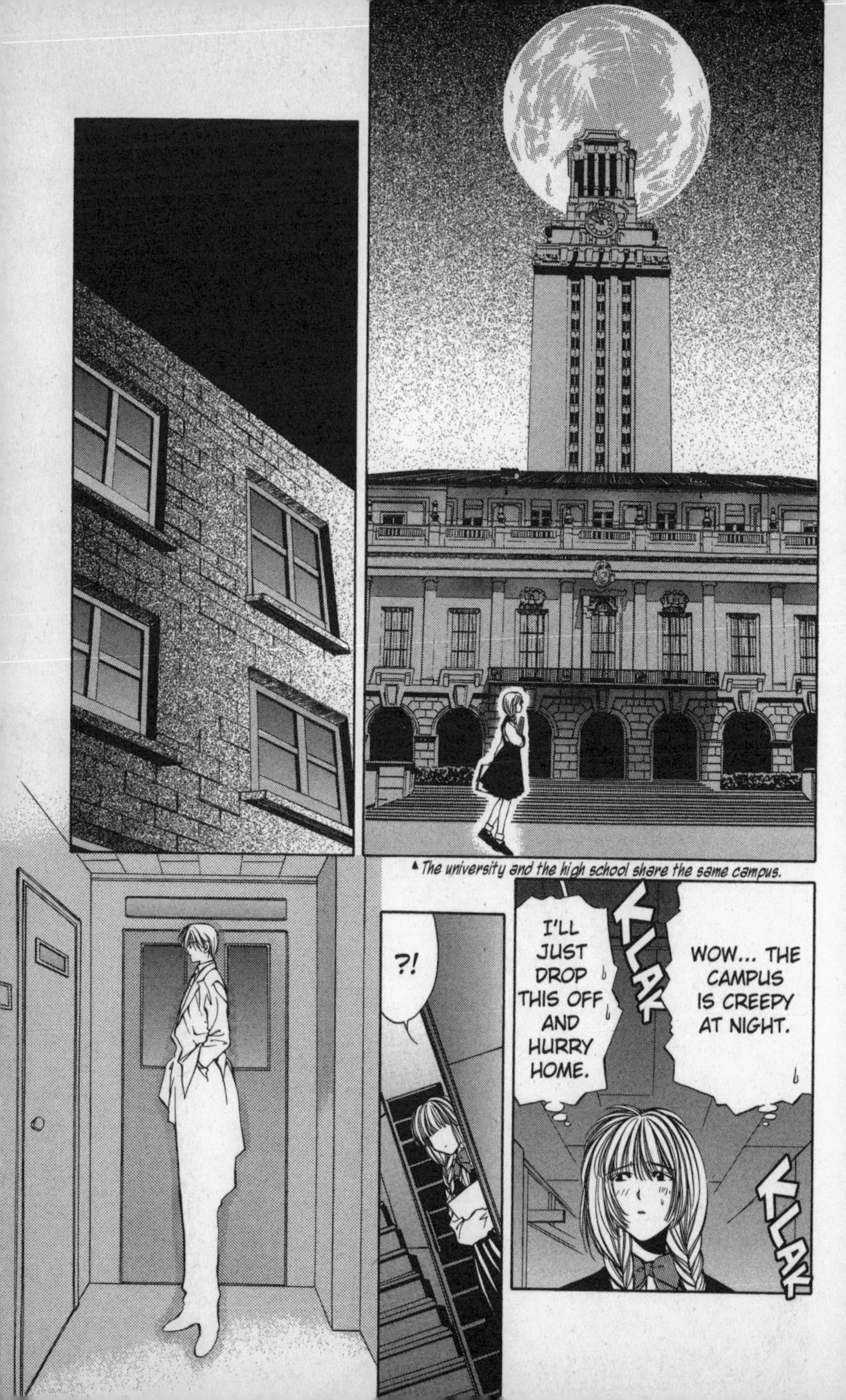
▲The university and the high school share the same campus.
WOW... THE CAMPUS IS CREEPY AT NIGHT.
KLAK
I'LL JUST DROP THIS OFF AND HURRY HOME.
KLAK
?!

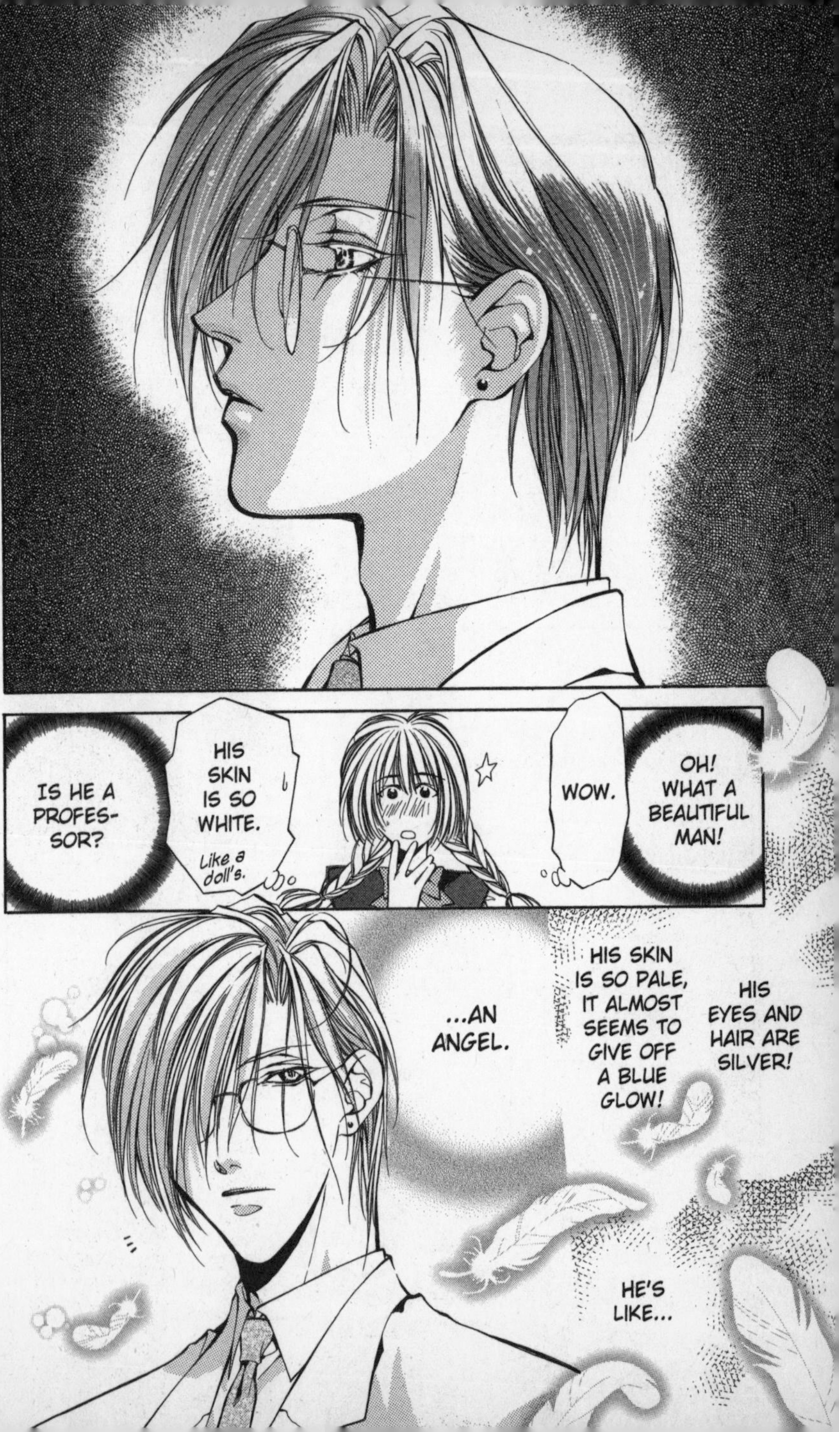
OH! WHAT A BEAUTIFUL MAN!
WOW.
HIS SKIN IS SO WHITE.
Like a doll's.
IS HE A PROFES-SOR?
HIS EYES AND HAIR ARE SILVER!
HIS SKIN IS SO PALE, IT ALMOST SEEMS TO GIVE OFF A BLUE GLOW!
HE'S LIKE...
...AN ANGEL.

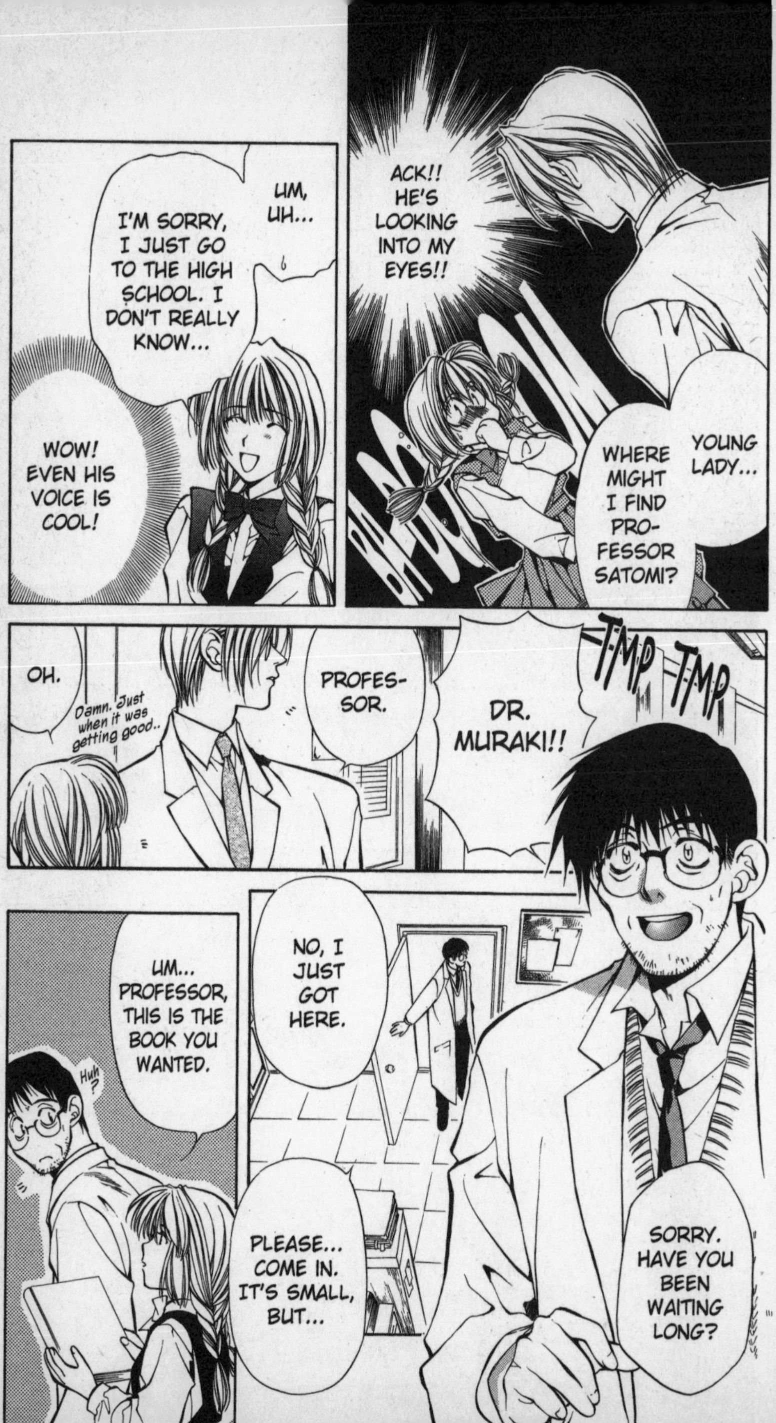
ACK!! HE'S LOOKING INTO MY EYES!!
YOUNG LADY...
WHERE MIGHT I FIND PRO-FESSOR SATOMI?
UM, UH...
I'M SORRY, I JUST GO TO THE HIGH SCHOOL. I DON'T REALLY KNOW...
WOW! EVEN HIS VOICE IS COOL!
TMP TMP
DR. MURAKI!!
PROFES-SOR.
OH.
Damn. Just when it was getting good..
SORRY. HAVE YOU BEEN WAITING LONG?
NO, I JUST GOT HERE.
PLEASE... COME IN. IT'S SMALL, BUT...
UM... PROFESSOR, THIS IS THE BOOK YOU WANTED.
Huh?

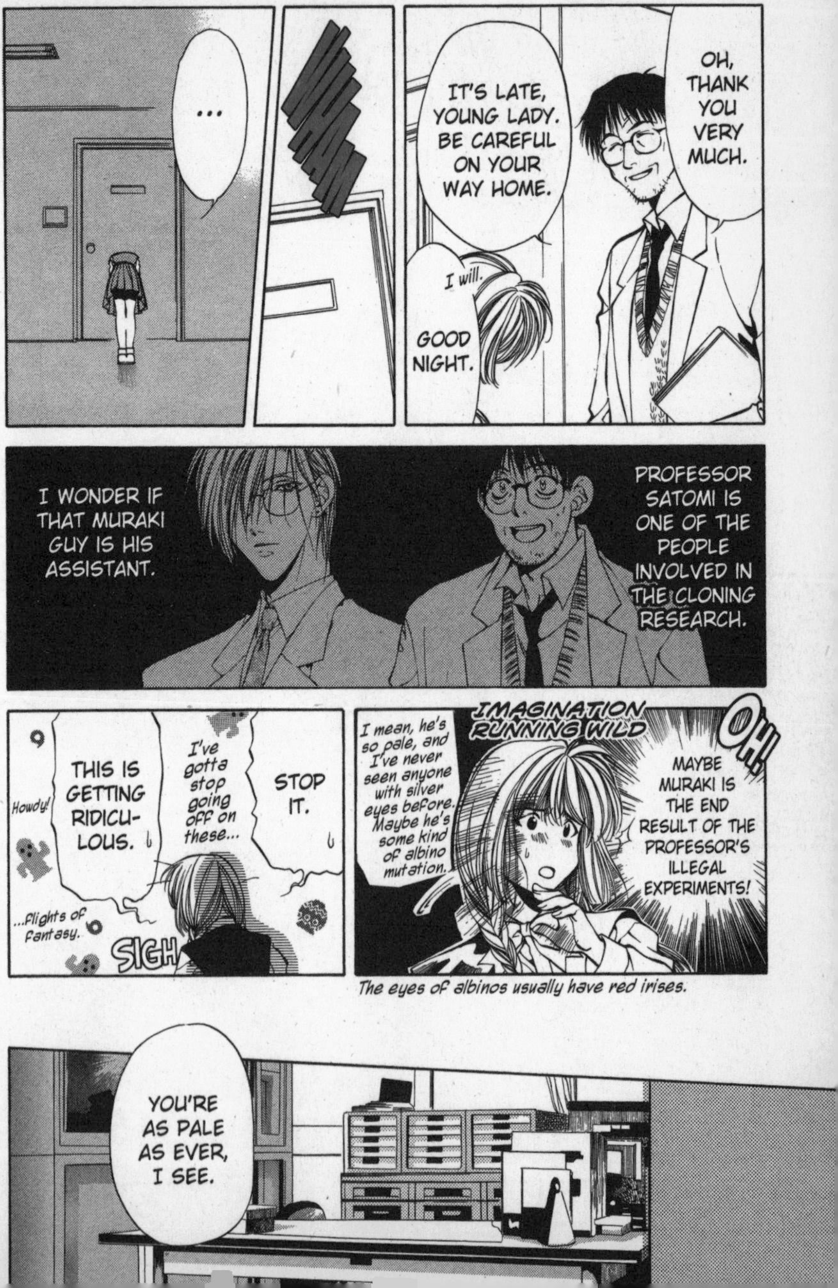
OH, THANK YOU VERY MUCH.
IT'S LATE, YOUNG LADY. BE CAREFUL ON YOUR WAY HOME.
I will.
GOOD NIGHT.
...
PROFESSOR SATOMI IS ONE OF THE PEOPLE INVOLVED IN THE CLONING RESEARCH.
I WONDER IF THAT MURAKI GUY IS HIS ASSISTANT.
OH!
IMAGINATION RUNNING WILD
MAYBE MURAKI IS THE END RESULT OF THE PROFESSOR'S ILLEGAL EXPERIMENTS!
I mean, he's so pale, and I've never seen anyone with silver eyes before. Maybe he's some kind of albino mutation.
STOP IT.
I've gotta stop going off on these...
THIS IS GETTING RIDICU-LOUS.
Howdy!
...flights of fantasy.
SIGH
The eyes of albinos usually have red irises.
YOU'RE AS PALE AS EVER, I SEE.

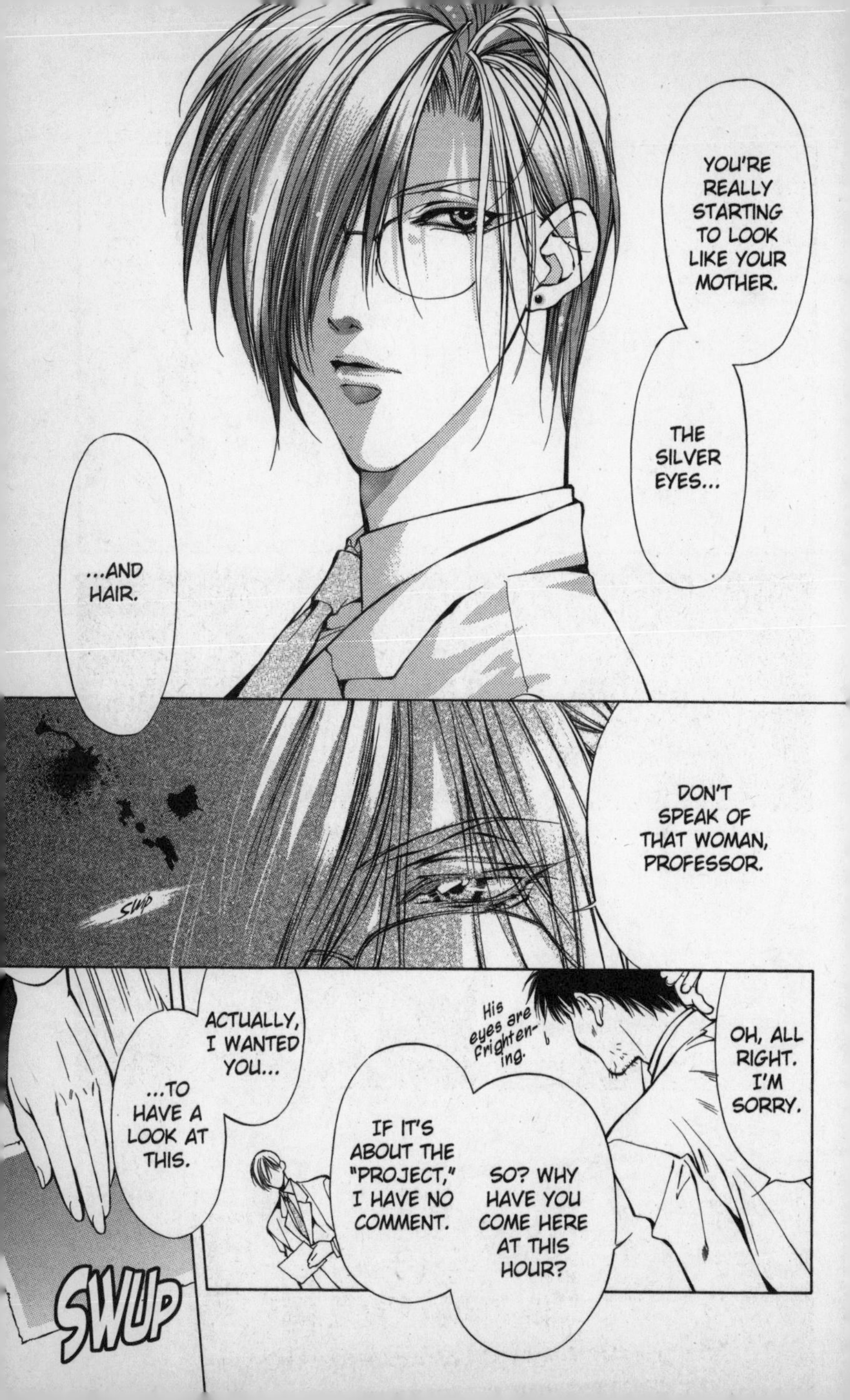
YOU'RE REALLY STARTING TO LOOK LIKE YOUR MOTHER.
THE SILVER EYES...
...AND HAIR.
DON'T SPEAK OF THAT WOMAN, PROFESSOR.
SWUP
OH, ALL RIGHT. I'M SORRY.
His eyes are frightening.
SO? WHY HAVE YOU COME HERE AT THIS HOUR?
IF IT'S ABOUT THE "PROJECT," I HAVE NO COMMENT.
ACTUALLY, I WANTED YOU...
...TO HAVE A LOOK AT THIS.
SWUP

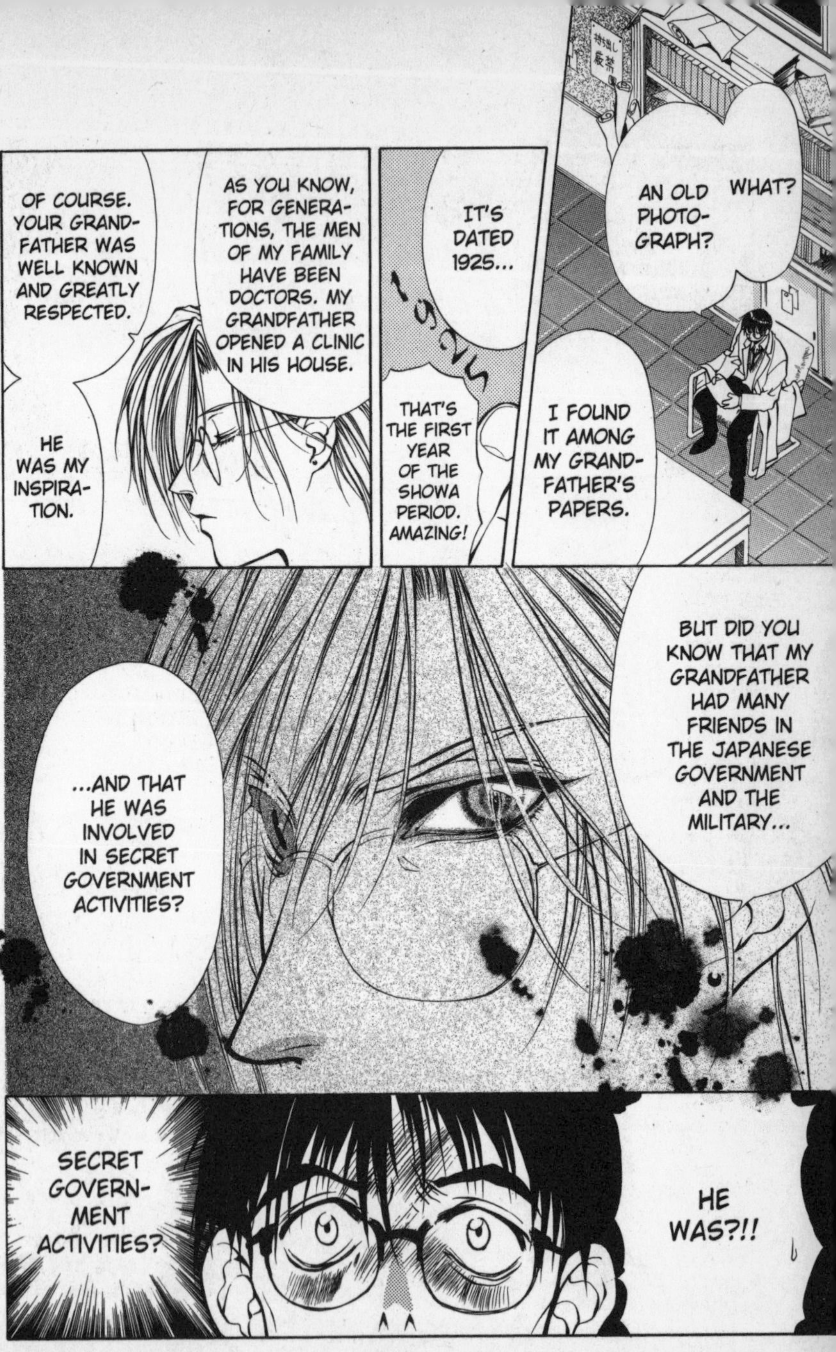
WHAT?
AN OLD PHOTOGRAPH?
I FOUND IT AMONG MY GRANDFATHER'S PAPERS.
IT'S DATED 1925...
THAT'S THE FIRST YEAR OF THE SHOWA PERIOD. AMAZING!
AS YOU KNOW, FOR GENERATIONS, THE MEN OF MY FAMILY HAVE BEEN DOCTORS. MY GRANDFATHER OPENED A CLINIC IN HIS HOUSE.
OF COURSE. YOUR GRANDFATHER WAS WELL KNOWN AND GREATLY RESPECTED.
HE WAS MY INSPIRATION.
BUT DID YOU KNOW THAT MY GRANDFATHER HAD MANY FRIENDS IN THE JAPANESE GOVERNMENT AND THE MILITARY...
...AND THAT HE WAS INVOLVED IN SECRET GOVERNMENT ACTIVITIES?
HE WAS?!!
SECRET GOVERNMENT ACTIVITIES?

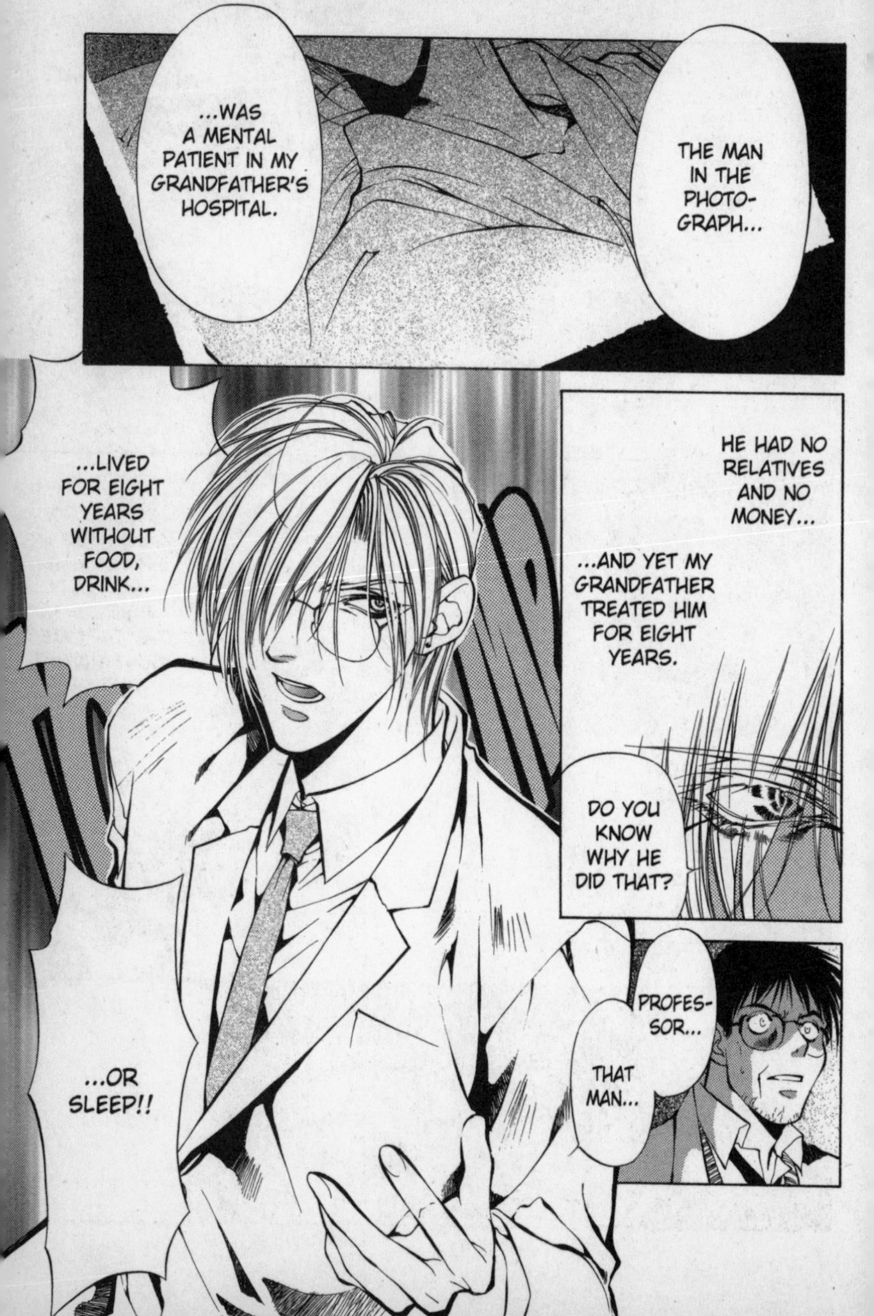
THE MAN IN THE PHOTOGRAPH...
...WAS A MENTAL PATIENT IN MY GRANDFATHER'S HOSPITAL.
HE HAD NO RELATIVES AND NO MONEY...
...AND YET MY GRANDFATHER TREATED HIM FOR EIGHT YEARS.
DO YOU KNOW WHY HE DID THAT?
...LIVED FOR EIGHT YEARS WITHOUT FOOD, DRINK...
...OR SLEEP!!
PROFESSOR...
THAT MAN...

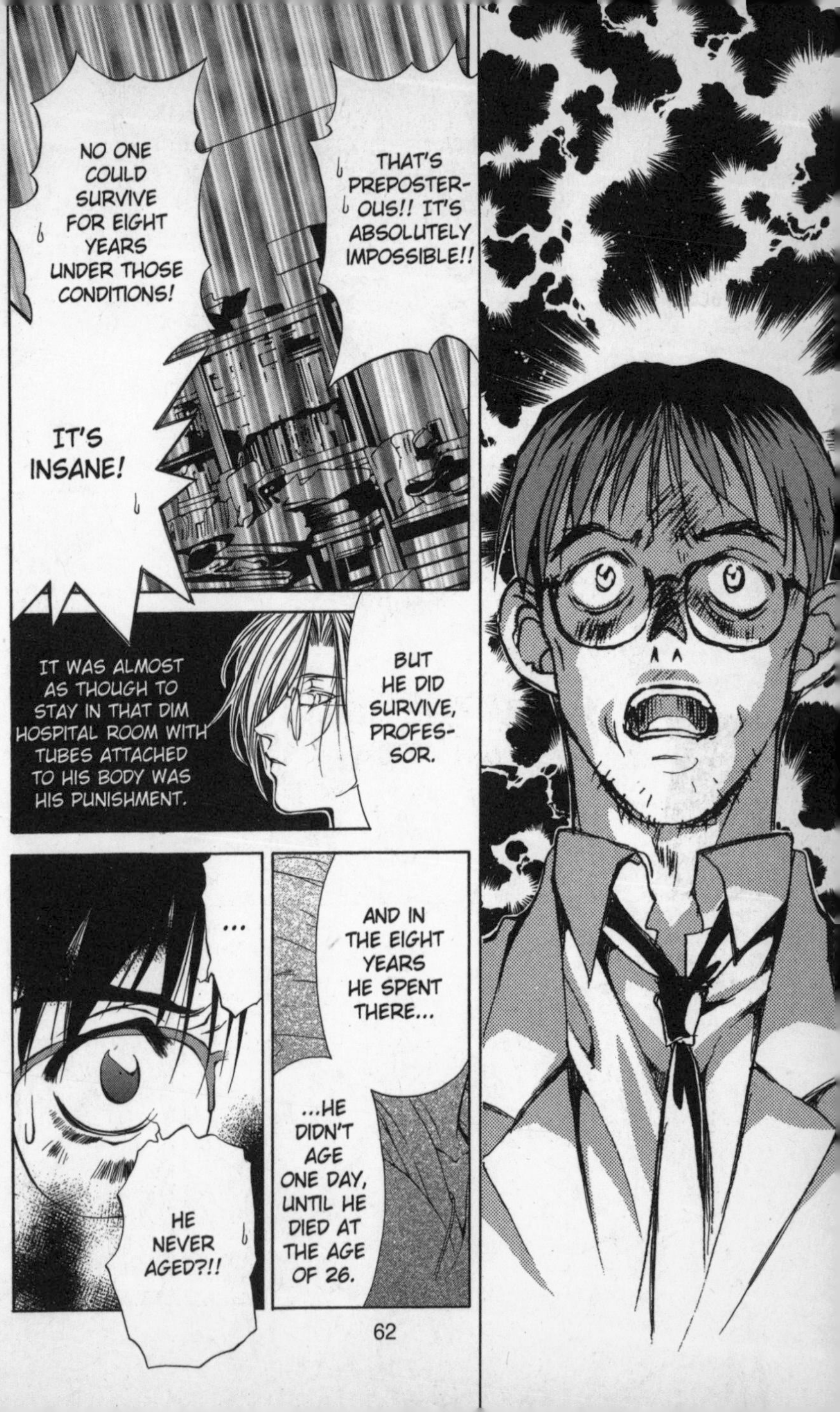

THAT'S PREPOSTER-OUS!! IT'S ABSOLUTELY IMPOSSIBLE!!
NO ONE COULD SURVIVE FOR EIGHT YEARS UNDER THOSE CONDITIONS!
IT'S INSANE!
BUT HE DID SURVIVE, PROFES-SOR.
IT WAS ALMOST AS THOUGH TO STAY IN THAT DIM HOSPITAL ROOM WITH TUBES ATTACHED TO HIS BODY WAS HIS PUNISHMENT.
AND IN THE EIGHT YEARS HE SPENT THERE...
...HE DIDN'T AGE ONE DAY, UNTIL HE DIED AT THE AGE OF 26.
...
HE NEVER AGED?!!

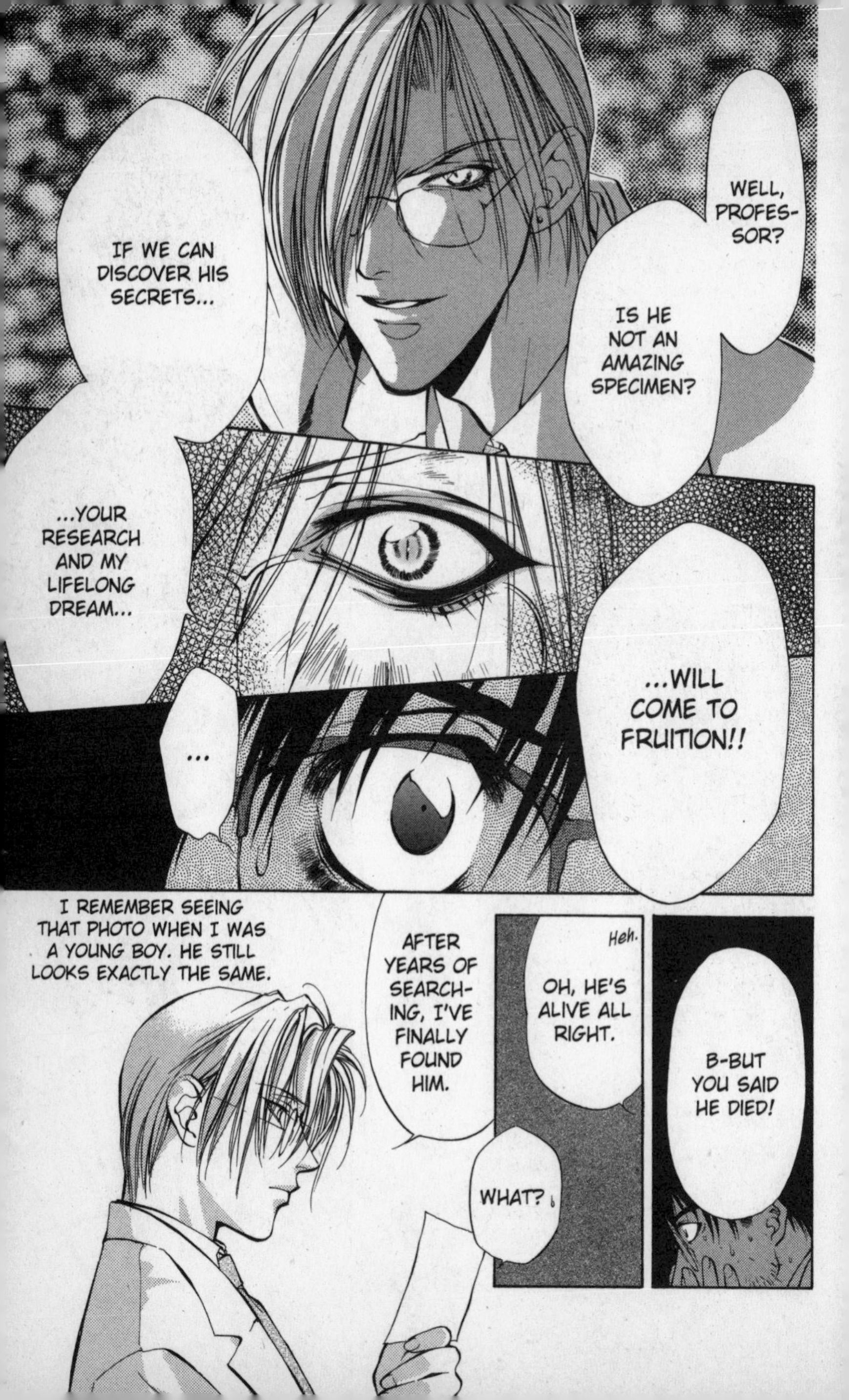
WELL, PROFES-SOR?
IS HE NOT AN AMAZING SPECIMEN?
IF WE CAN DISCOVER HIS SECRETS...
...YOUR RESEARCH AND MY LIFELONG DREAM...
...WILL COME TO FRUITION!!
...
B-BUT YOU SAID HE DIED!
Heh.
OH, HE'S ALIVE ALL RIGHT.
WHAT?
AFTER YEARS OF SEARCH-ING, I'VE FINALLY FOUND HIM.
I REMEMBER SEEING THAT PHOTO WHEN I WAS A YOUNG BOY. HE STILL LOOKS EXACTLY THE SAME.

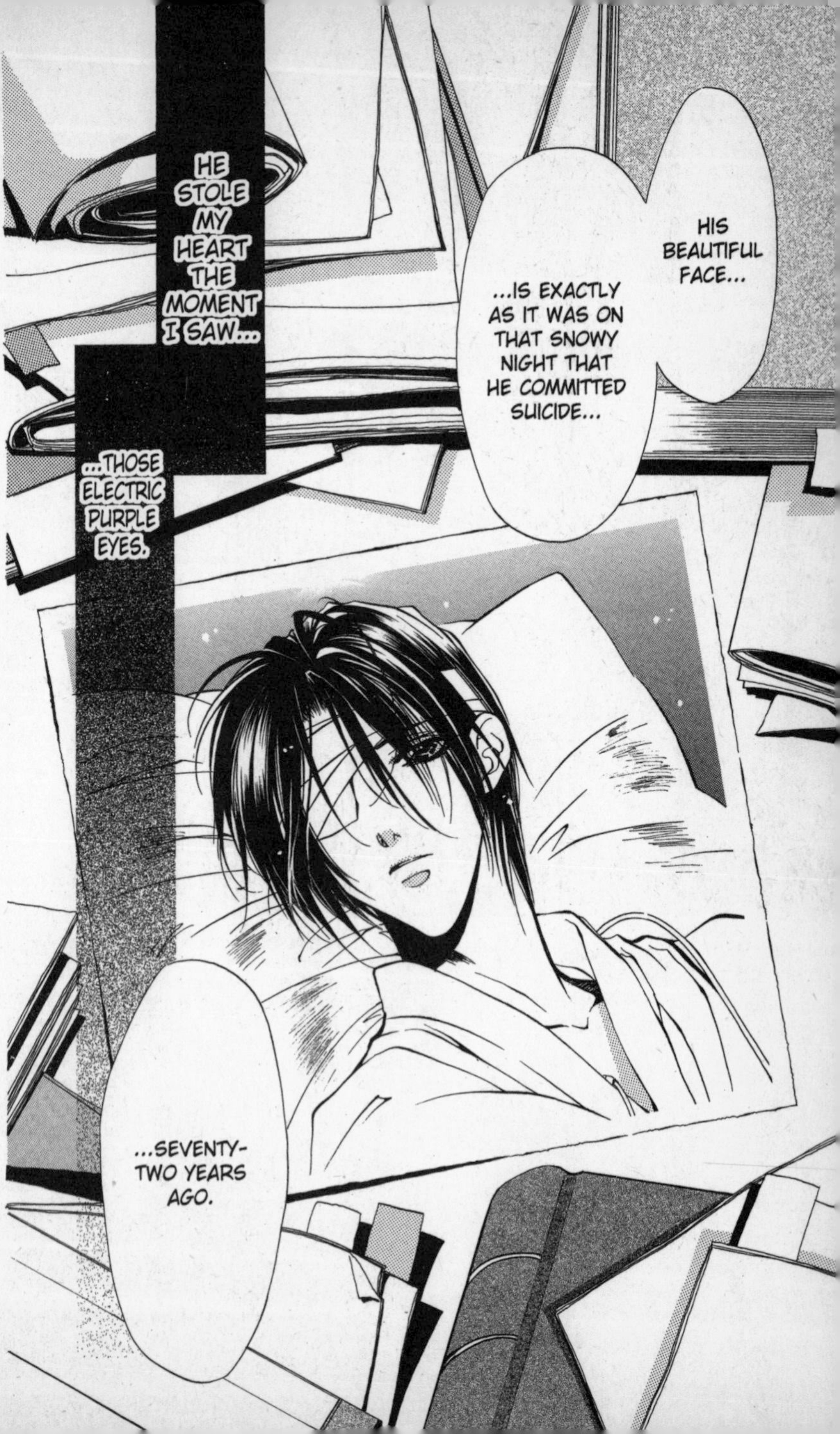
HIS BEAUTIFUL FACE...
...IS EXACTLY AS IT WAS ON THAT SNOWY NIGHT THAT HE COMMITTED SUICIDE...
HE STOLE MY HEART THE MOMENT I SAW...
...THOSE ELECTRIC PURPLE EYES.
...SEVENTY-TWO YEARS AGO.

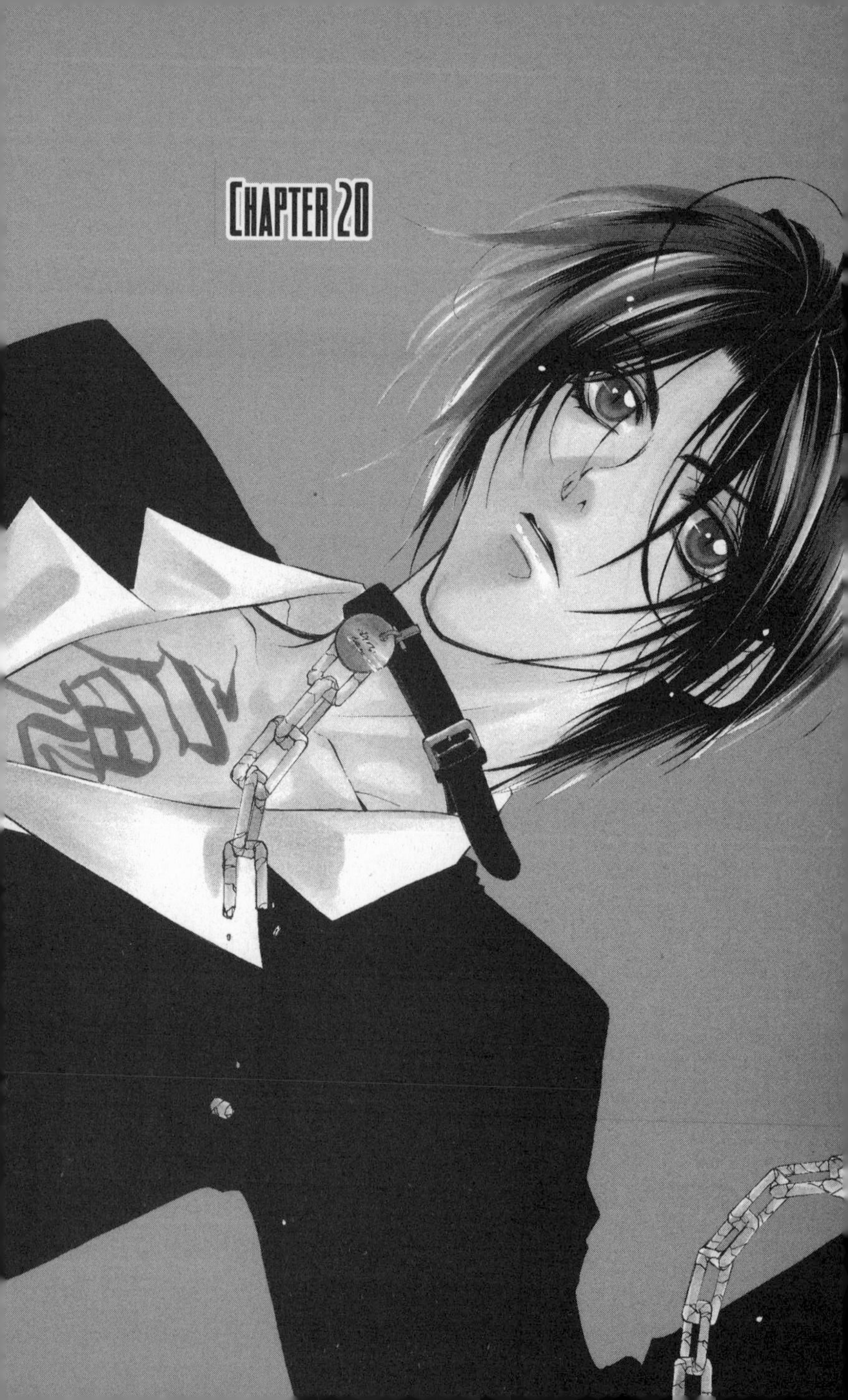
CHAPTER 20

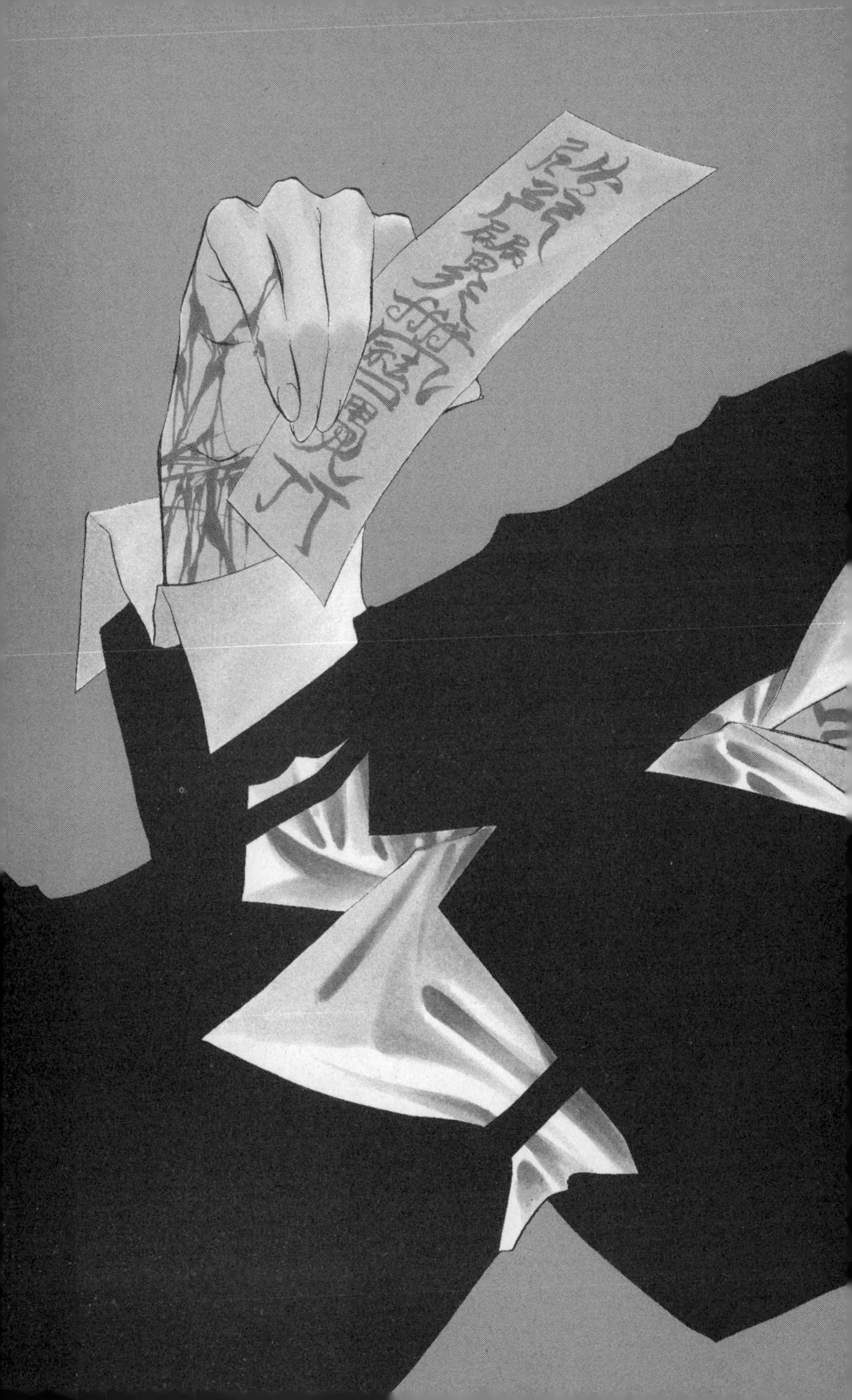

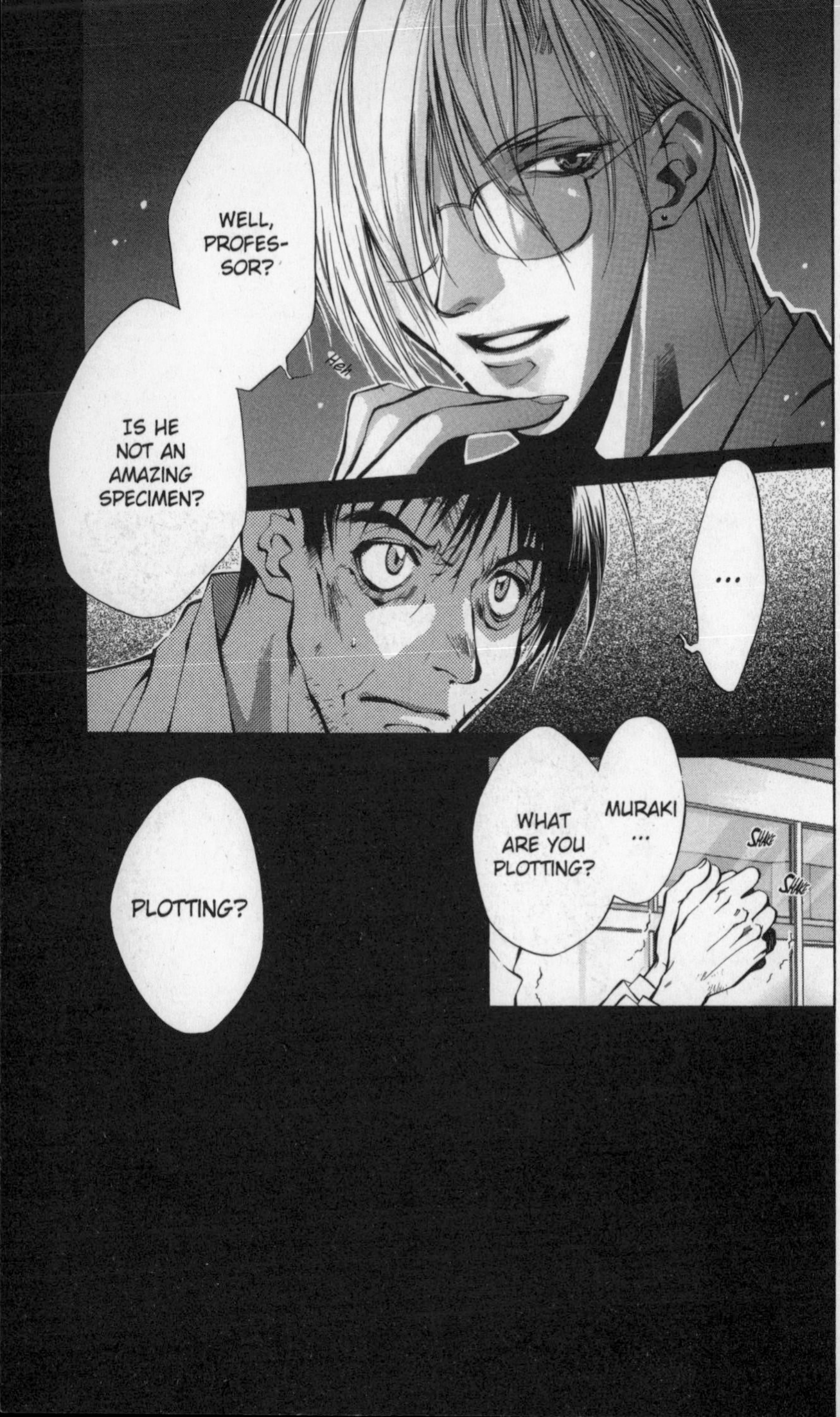
WELL, PROFES- SOR?
Heh
IS HE NOT AN AMAZING SPECIMEN?
...
MURAKI ...
WHAT ARE YOU PLOTTING?
SHAKE
SHAKE
PLOTTING?

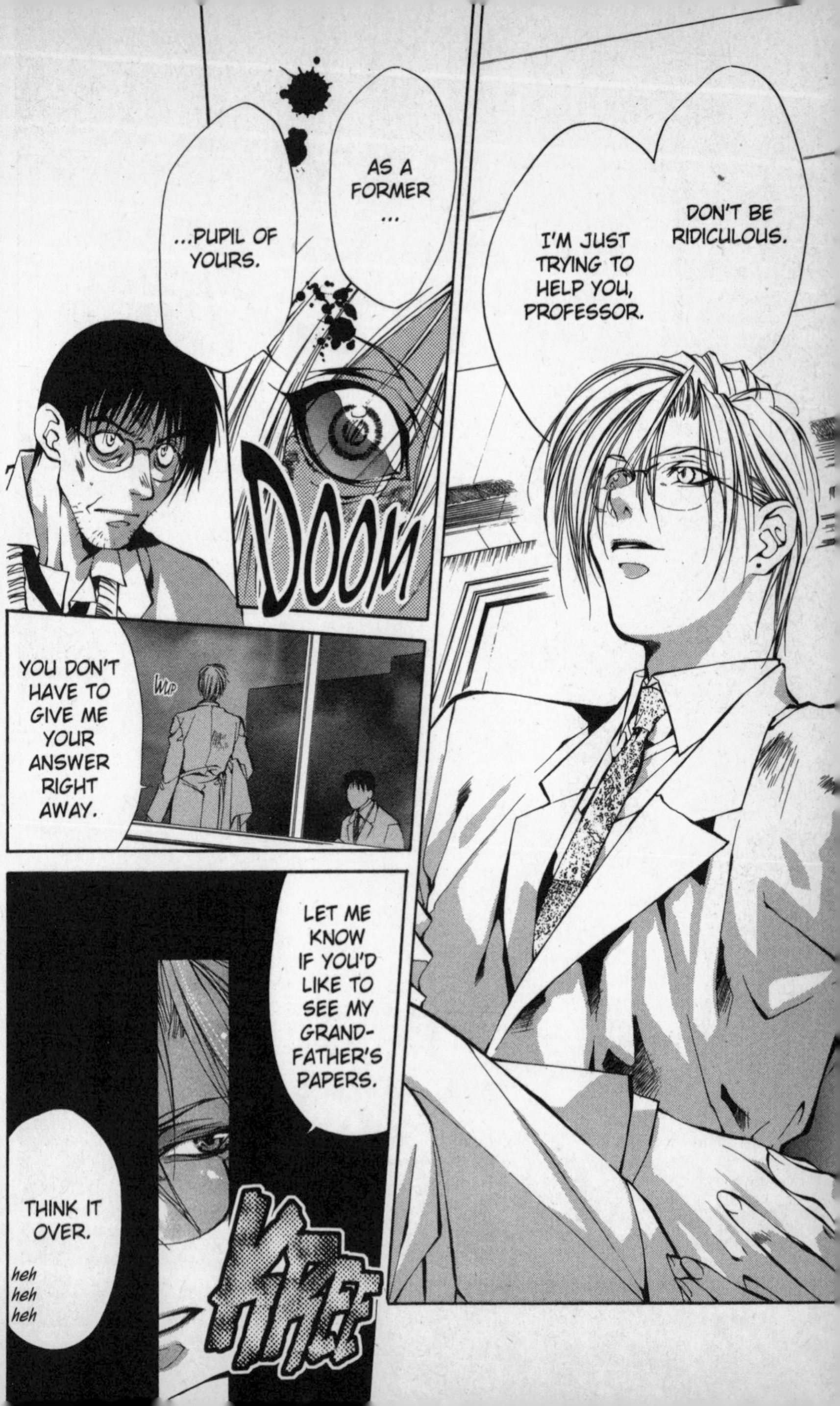
DON'T BE RIDICULOUS.
I'M JUST TRYING TO HELP YOU, PROFESSOR.
AS A FORMER ...
...PUPIL OF YOURS.
DOOM
YOU DON'T HAVE TO GIVE ME YOUR ANSWER RIGHT AWAY.
WUP
LET ME KNOW IF YOU'D LIKE TO SEE MY GRAND-FATHER'S PAPERS.
THINK IT OVER.
heh heh heh

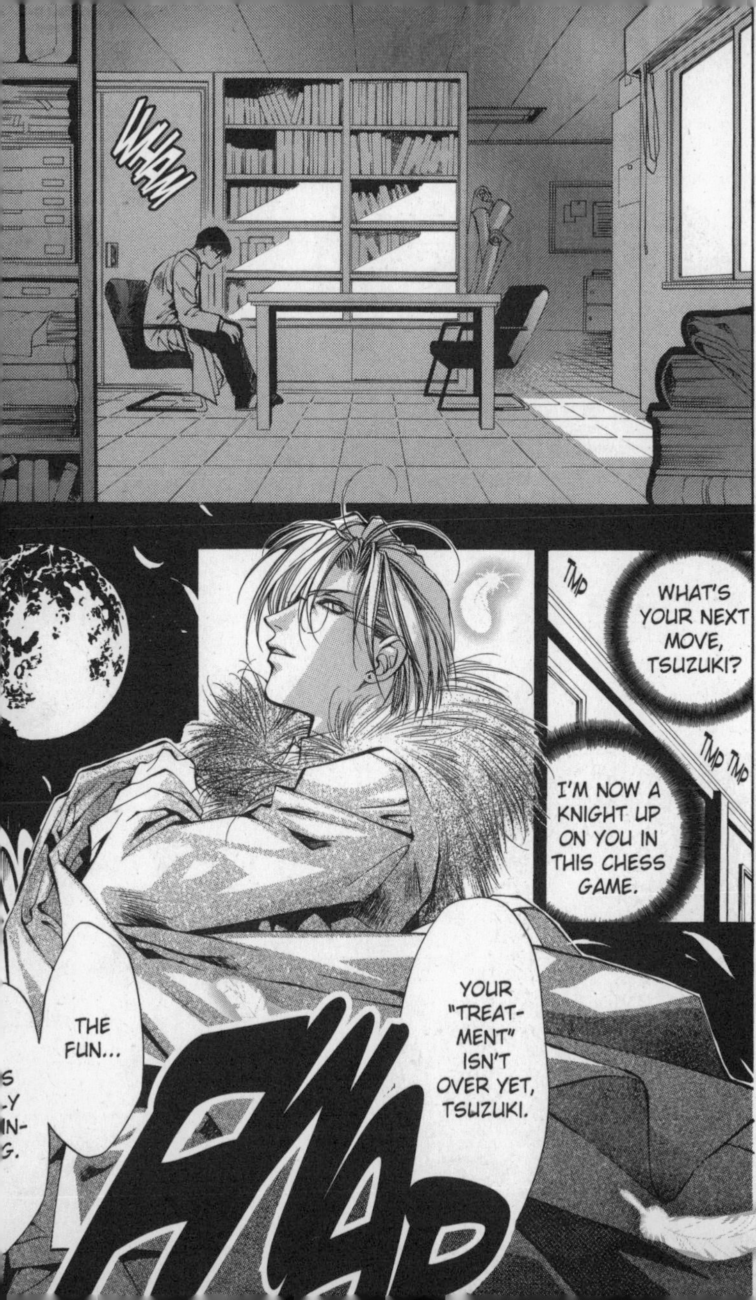
WHAM
TMP
WHAT'S YOUR NEXT MOVE, TSUZUKI?
TMP TMP
I'M NOW A KNIGHT UP ON YOU IN THIS CHESS GAME.
YOUR "TREAT-MENT" ISN'T OVER YET, TSUZUKI.
THE FUN...

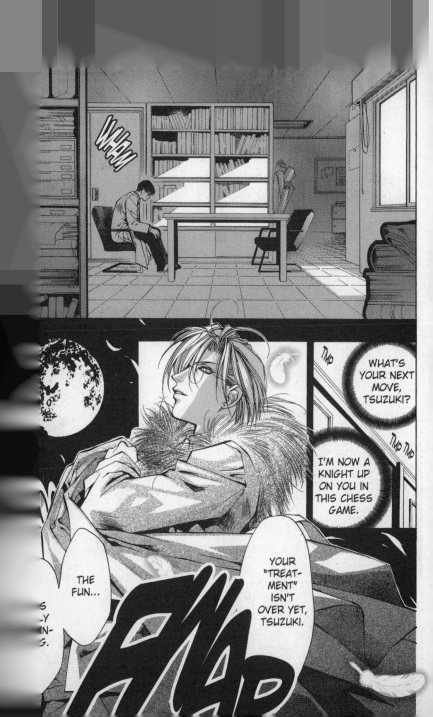

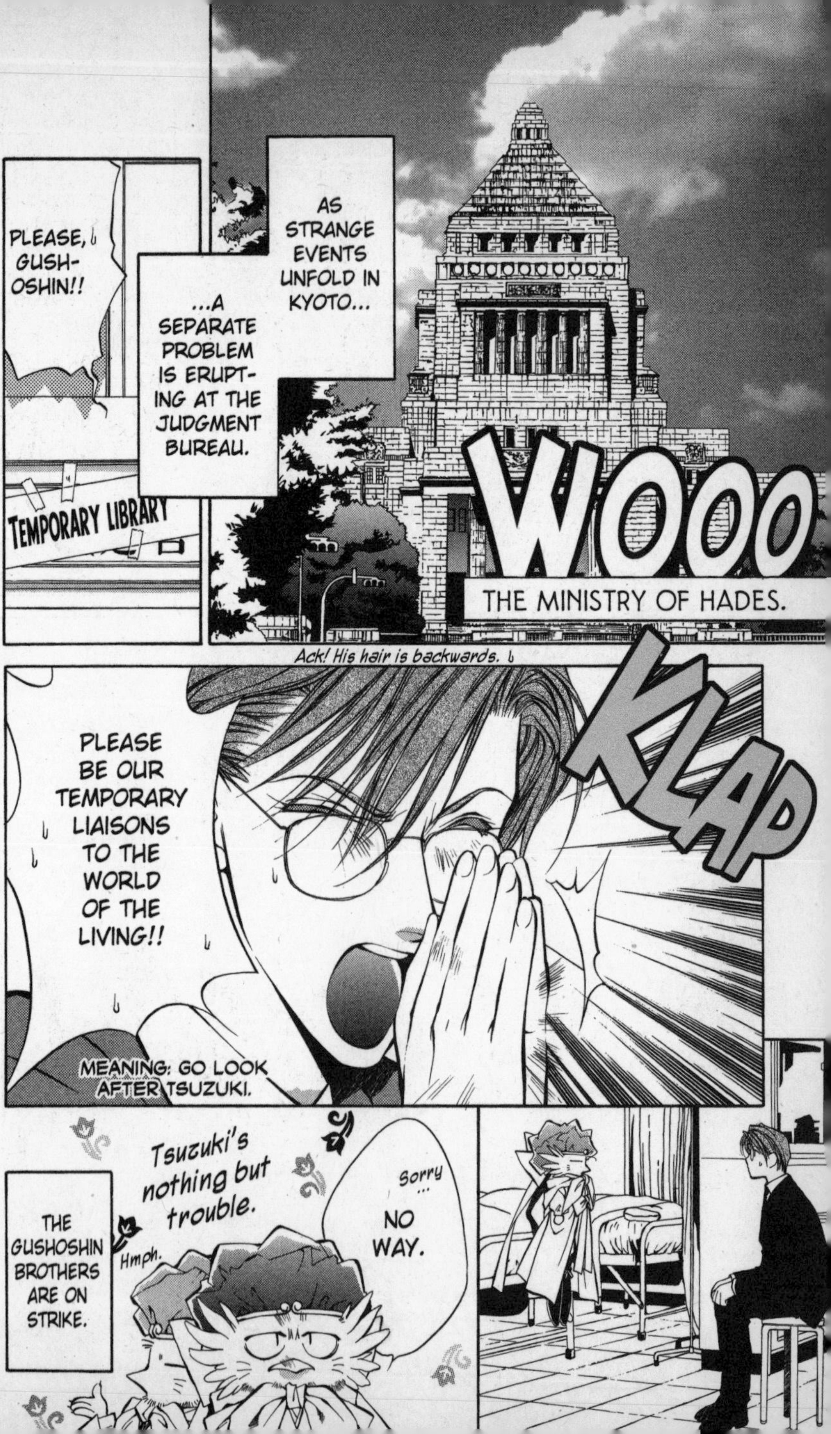
AS STRANGE EVENTS UNFOLD IN KYOTO...
...A SEPARATE PROBLEM IS ERUPTING AT THE JUDGMENT BUREAU.
WOOO
THE MINISTRY OF HADES.
PLEASE, GUSH-OSHIN!!
TEMPORARY LIBRARY
Ack! His hair is backwards.
KLAP
PLEASE BE OUR TEMPORARY LIAISONS TO THE WORLD OF THE LIVING!!
MEANING: GO LOOK AFTER TSUZUKI.
Sorry ...
NO WAY.
Tsuzuki's nothing but trouble.
Hmph.
THE GUSHOSHIN BROTHERS ARE ON STRIKE.

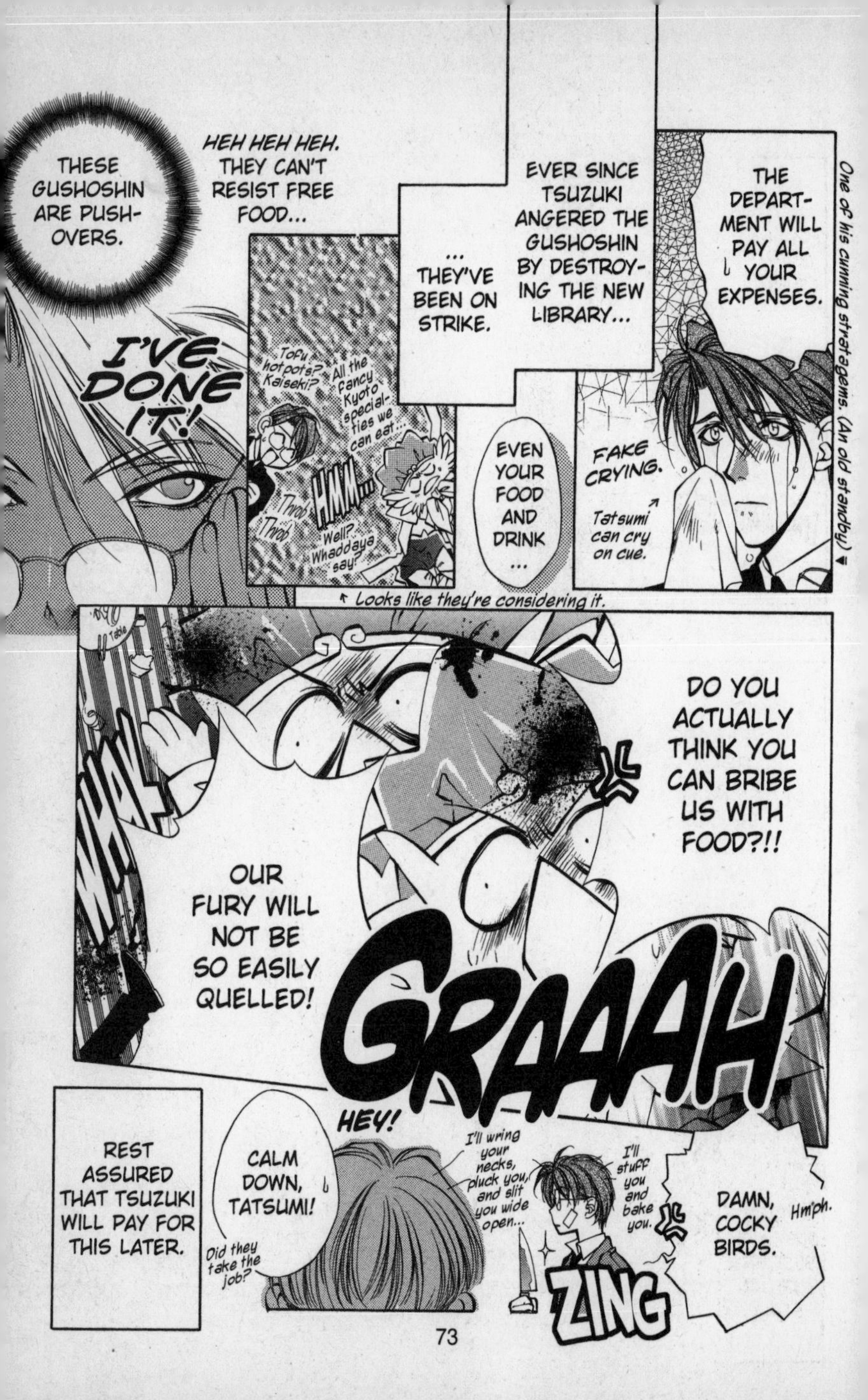
THE DEPART-MENT WILL PAY ALL YOUR EXPENSES.
One of his cunning stratagems. (An old standby)
FAKE CRYING.
Tatsumi can cry on cue.
EVER SINCE TSUZUKI ANGERED THE GUSHOSHIN BY DESTROY-ING THE NEW LIBRARY...
... THEY'VE BEEN ON STRIKE.
EVEN YOUR FOOD AND DRINK ...
All the fancy Kyoto special-ties we can eat...
Tofu hotpots? Kaiseki?
HMM...
Throb Throb
Well? Whaddaya say?
Looks like they're considering it.
HEH HEH HEH. THEY CAN'T RESIST FREE FOOD...
THESE GUSHOSHIN ARE PUSH-OVERS.
I'VE DONE IT!
DO YOU ACTUALLY THINK YOU CAN BRIBE US WITH FOOD?!!
OUR FURY WILL NOT BE SO EASILY QUELLED!
GRAAAH
Table
DAMN, COCKY BIRDS.
Hmph.
I'll stuff you and bake you.
I'll wring your necks, pluck you, and slit you wide open...
ZING
HEY!
CALM DOWN, TATSUMI!
Did they take the job?
REST ASSURED THAT TSUZUKI WILL PAY FOR THIS LATER.

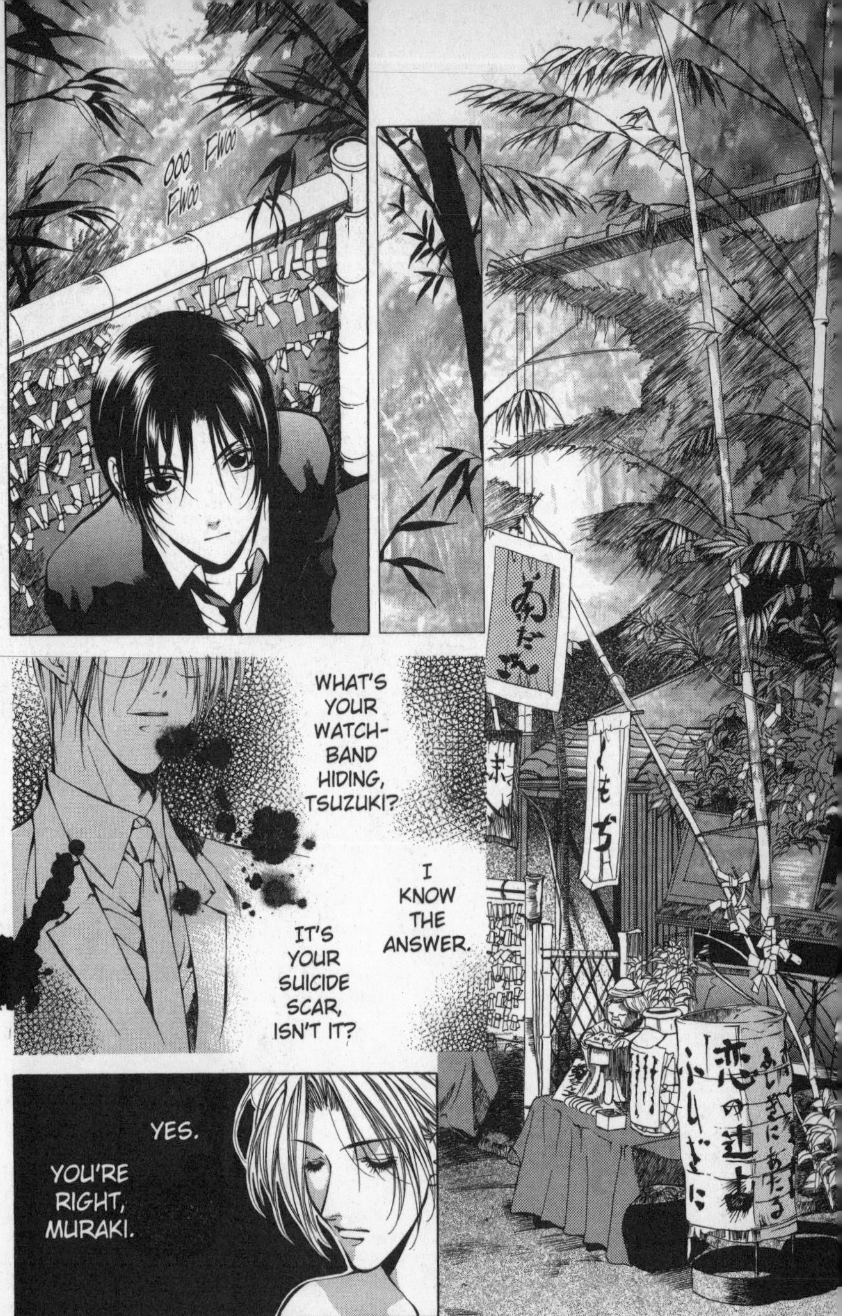
OOO FWOO FWOO
WHAT'S YOUR WATCH-BAND HIDING, TSUZUKI?
I KNOW THE ANSWER.
IT'S YOUR SUICIDE SCAR, ISN'T IT?
YES.
YOU'RE RIGHT, MURAKI.

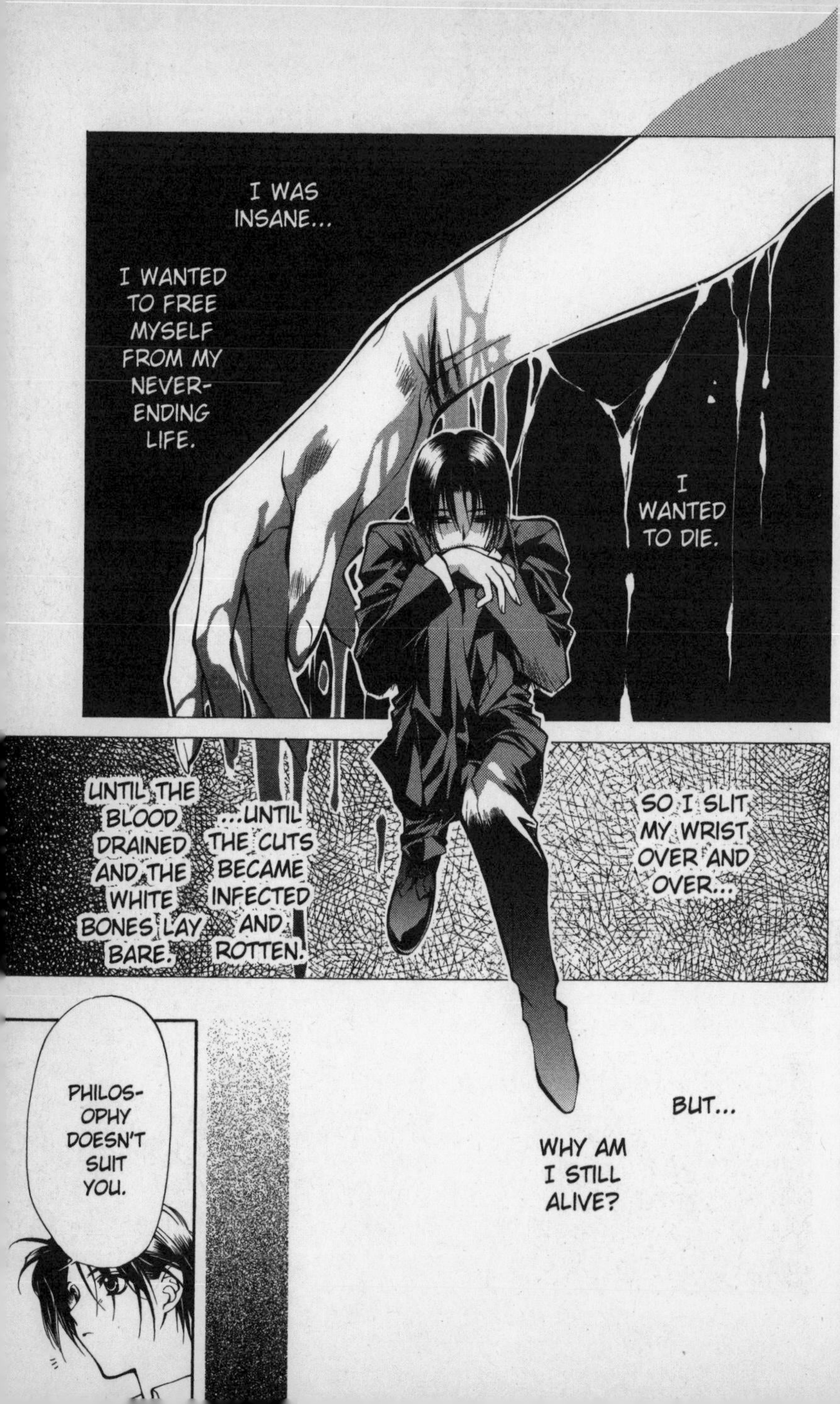
I WAS INSANE...
I WANTED TO FREE MYSELF FROM MY NEVER-ENDING LIFE.
I WANTED TO DIE.
SO I SLIT MY WRIST OVER AND OVER...
...UNTIL THE CUTS BECAME INFECTED AND ROTTEN.
UNTIL THE BLOOD DRAINED AND THE WHITE BONES LAY BARE.
BUT...
WHY AM I STILL ALIVE?
PHILOSOPHY DOESN'T SUIT YOU.

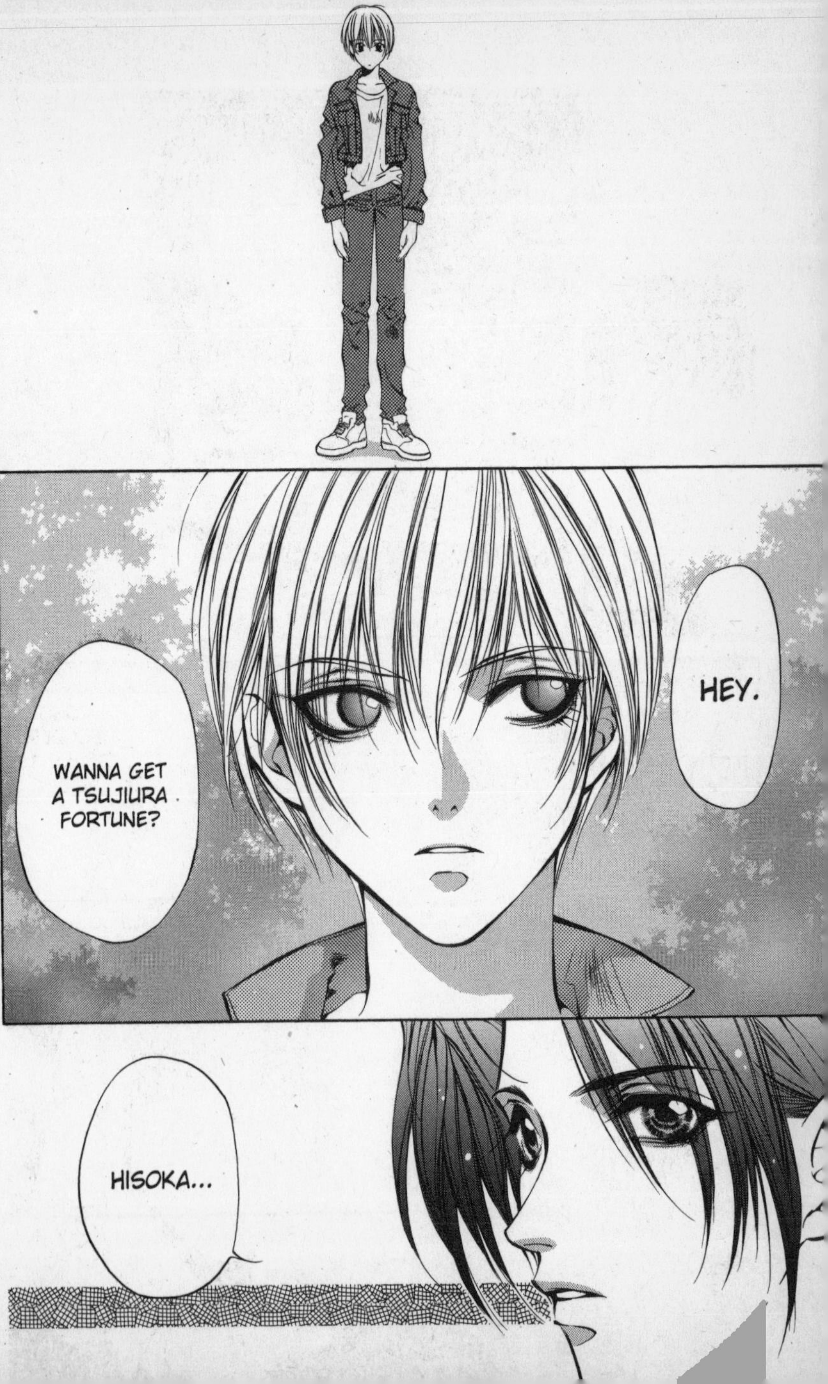
HEY.
WANNA GET A TSUJIURA FORTUNE?
HISOKA...

TSUJIURA WAS ORIGINALLY A KIND OF FORTUNETELLING IN WHICH ONE STOOD AT A CROSS-ROADS AND BASED THE FORTUNE UPON THE WORDS OF THE FIRST PERSON WHO PASSED BY.

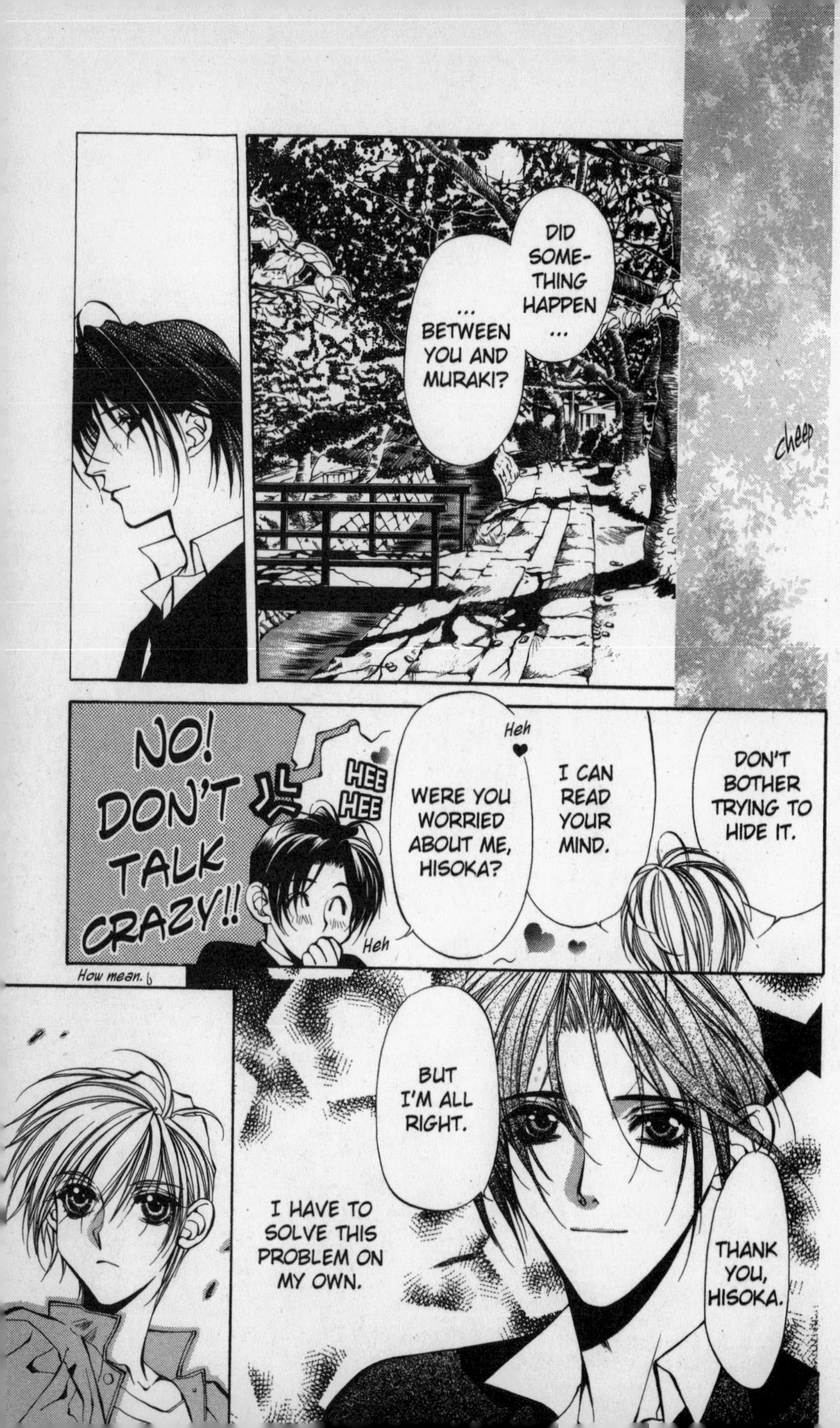
cheep
DID SOME-THING HAPPEN ...
... BETWEEN YOU AND MURAKI?
DON'T BOTHER TRYING TO HIDE IT.
I CAN READ YOUR MIND.
Heh
WERE YOU WORRIED ABOUT ME, HISOKA?
HEE HEE
Heh
NO! DON'T TALK CRAZY!!
How mean.
THANK YOU, HISOKA.
BUT I'M ALL RIGHT.
I HAVE TO SOLVE THIS PROBLEM ON MY OWN.

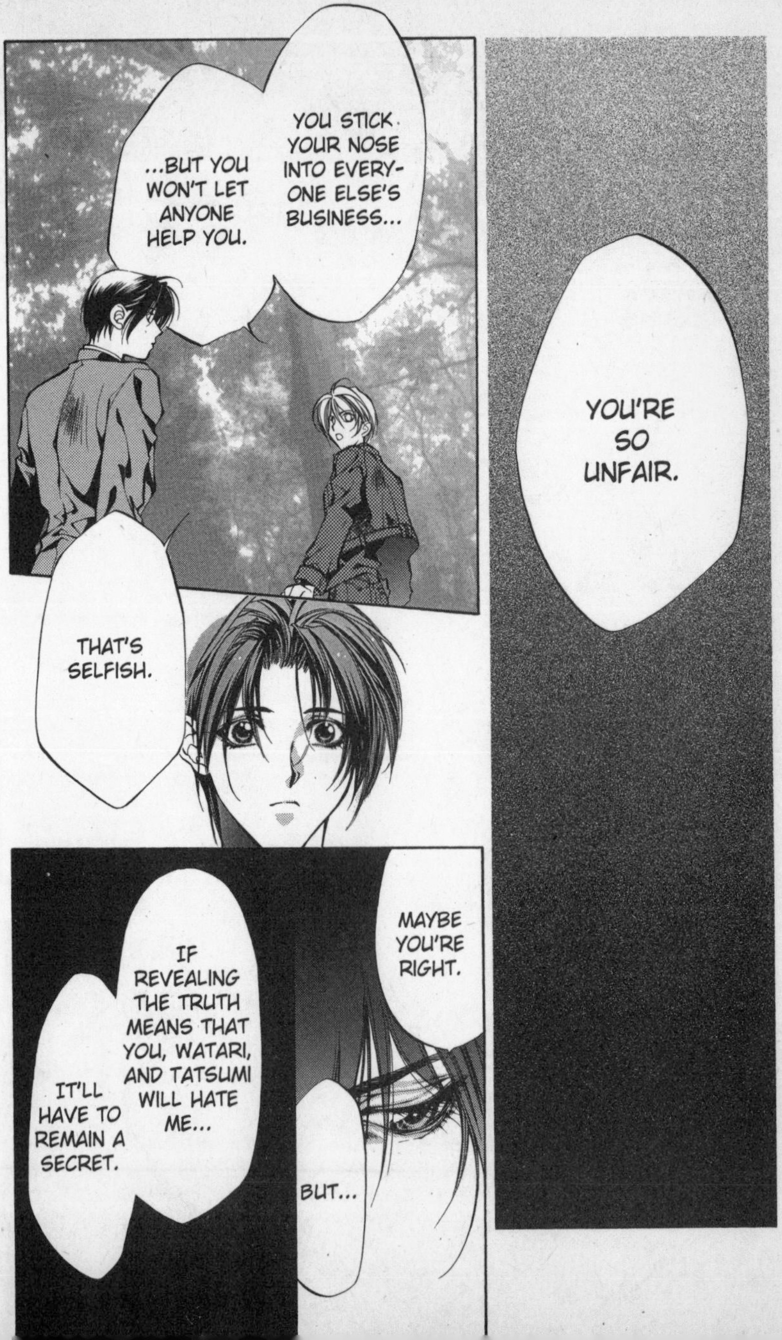

YOU'RE SO UNFAIR.
YOU STICK YOUR NOSE INTO EVERY-ONE ELSE'S BUSINESS...
...BUT YOU WON'T LET ANYONE HELP YOU.
THAT'S SELFISH.
MAYBE YOU'RE RIGHT.
IF REVEALING THE TRUTH MEANS THAT YOU, WATARI, AND TATSUMI WILL HATE ME...
BUT...
IT'LL HAVE TO REMAIN A SECRET.

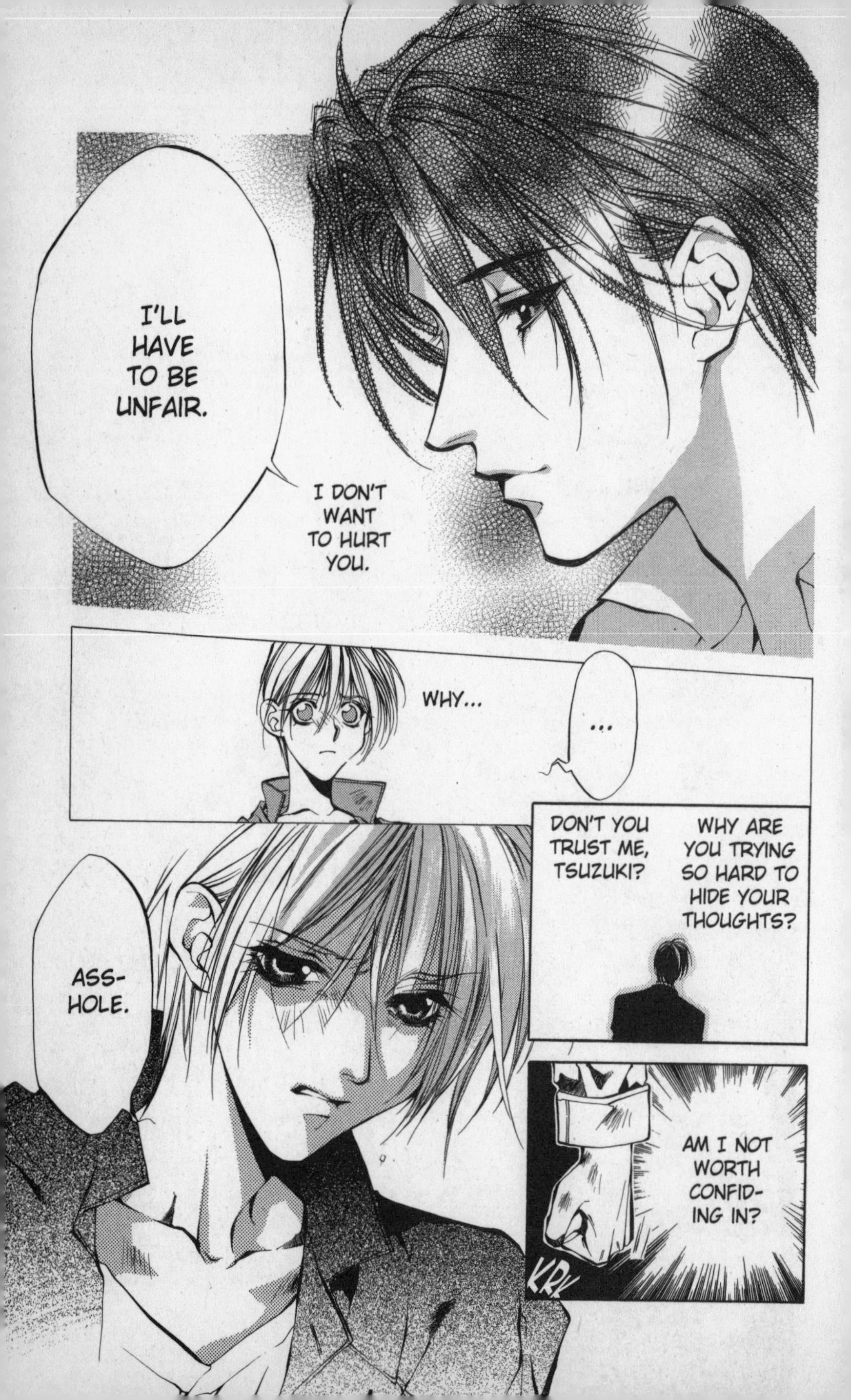

I'LL HAVE TO BE UNFAIR.
I DON'T WANT TO HURT YOU.
...
WHY...
WHY ARE YOU TRYING SO HARD TO HIDE YOUR THOUGHTS?
DON'T YOU TRUST ME, TSUZUKI?
AM I NOT WORTH CONFID-ING IN?
KRK
ASS-HOLE.

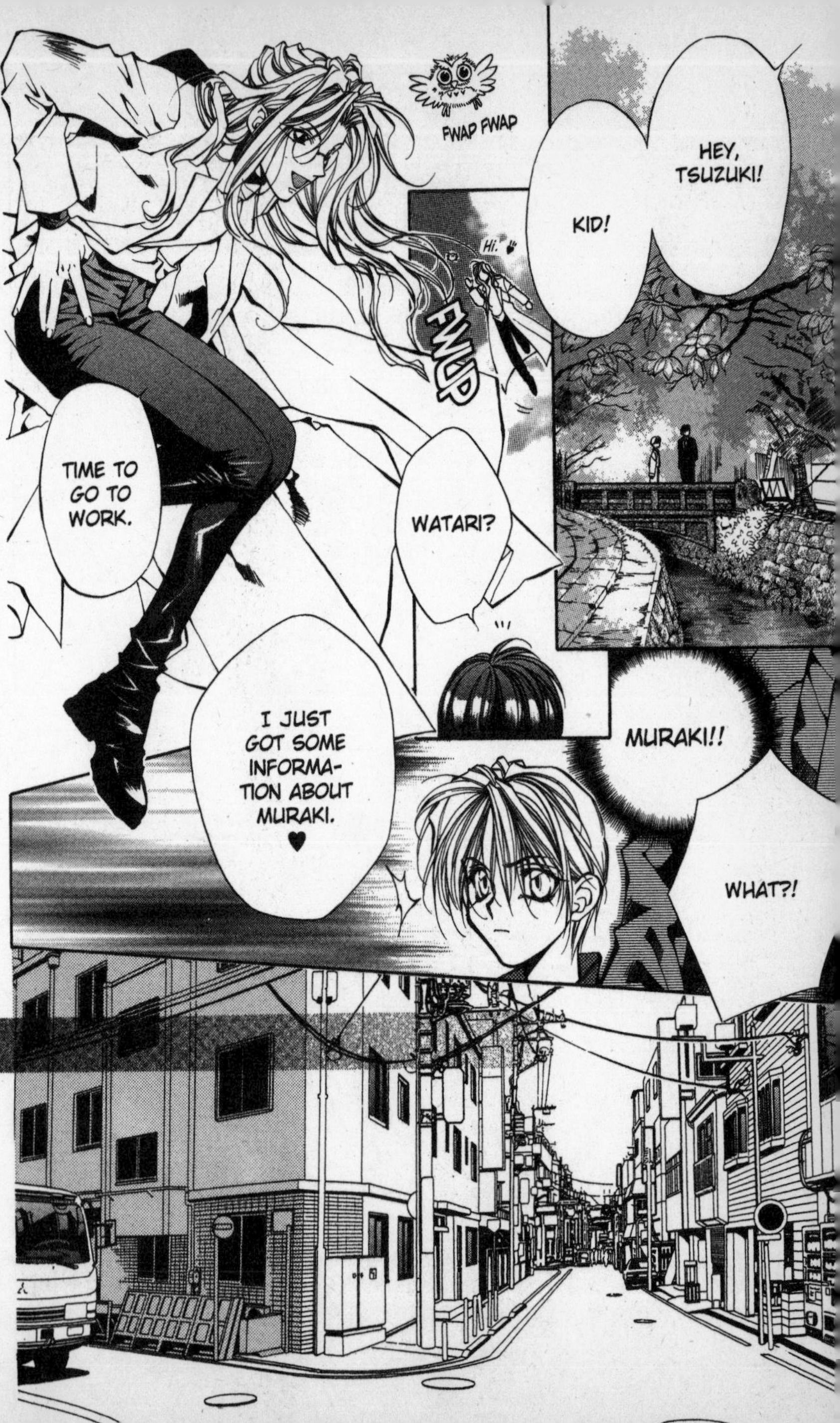
HEY, TSUZUKI!
KID!
FWAP FWAP
Hi. ♥
FWUP
WATARI?
TIME TO GO TO WORK.
I JUST GOT SOME INFORMATION ABOUT MURAKI. ♥
MURAKI!!
WHAT?!

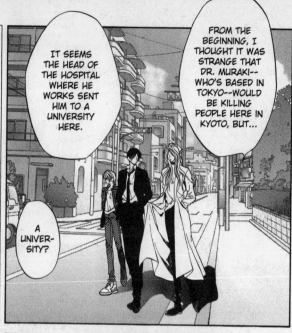

FROM THE BEGINNING, I THOUGHT IT WAS STRANGE THAT DR. MURAKI--WHO'S BASED IN TOKYO--WOULD BE KILLING PEOPLE HERE IN KYOTO, BUT...
IT SEEMS THE HEAD OF THE HOSPITAL WHERE HE WORKS SENT HIM TO A UNIVERSITY HERE.
A UNIVERSITY?
I DON'T KNOW EXACTLY WHAT IT'S ALL ABOUT, BUT...
...HE'S AT THE UNIVERSITY HOSPITAL'S DEPARTMENT OF SURGERY.
WHAT UNIVERSITY?
Hmm...
I THINK THE KID ALREADY KNOWS, BUT...
FWIP
IT'S RIGHT THERE.

So anyway, I went to Kyoto, where this story takes place, to take pictures and do research. I was practically on a military schedule. And it was September and it was really hot! I didn't have much time, so I rented a taxi for the day. Thank you very much, Mr. Cabdriver! I'm sorry for making you take me all over town.

My primary objective was to take pictures, but since I'd come all the way from Kyushu, I decided to meet up with all of the fans I'd met online. We had tea at a famous teahouse called Tsujisato, and then had a wild karaoke party. We talked, drank, and ate while the restaurant kept playing a remix of Lupan. It was very nice of the fans to do that for me. It was the type of research trip where I ended up thinking, "Wait, what am I supposed to be doing here?" (Ha!) Sorry for taking over the whole third floor, Tsujisato. I was the one who ordered coffee. (Ha) How embarrassing.

↑ Who would order coffee at a teahouse?

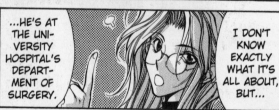

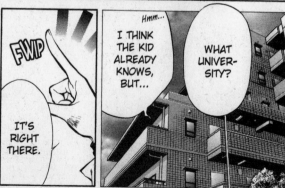

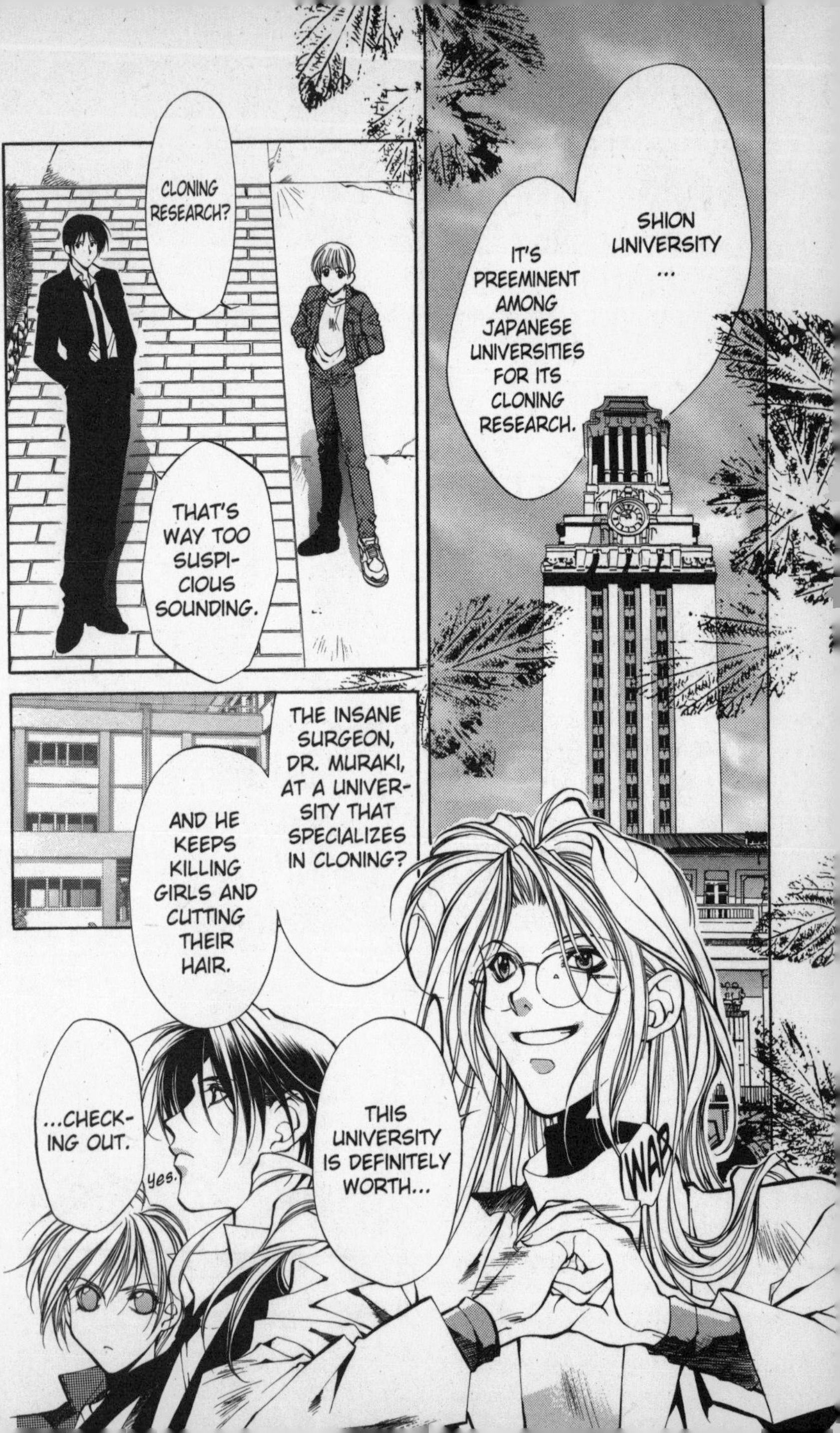
SHION UNIVERSITY ...
IT'S PREEMINENT AMONG JAPANESE UNIVERSITIES FOR ITS CLONING RESEARCH.
CLONING RESEARCH?
THAT'S WAY TOO SUSPI-CIOUS SOUNDING.
THE INSANE SURGEON, DR. MURAKI, AT A UNIVER-SITY THAT SPECIALIZES IN CLONING?
AND HE KEEPS KILLING GIRLS AND CUTTING THEIR HAIR.
THIS UNIVERSITY IS DEFINITELY WORTH...
WAP
yes.
...CHECK-ING OUT.

AND NOW IT'S TIME FOR...

PROFESSOR WATARI OF THE JUDGMENT BUREAU'S EASY Course on Cloning

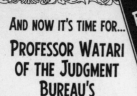

A CLONE IS BASICALLY A COPY.
FIRST, YOU HAVE TO GET A SAMPLE OF AN ORGANISM'S DNA.
AND THEN YOU MAKE A GENETIC COPY OF IT.
LOOKS FAKE.
WATARI, ↗ THE FAKE PROFESSOR.
EXCUSE ME, PROFES-SOR.
Tsuzuki, the bad student. (failed entrance exam 3 times)
Hisoka, the excellent student. (passed exam on first try)
HOW DO YOU MAKE A CLONE USING DNA?
WHUP
I'm sleepy.
When were they students?
WELL ...
DNA HAS TWO FUNCTIONS-- REPLICATION AND REPRO-DUCTION.
CHROMOSOME (A GROUP OF GENES)
RIBOSOMES
MITOCHONDRIA
NUCLEUS
CELL MEMBRANE
ILLUSTRATION OF A CELL
THE REASON CHILDREN RESEMBLE THEIR PARENTS IS THAT THEY SHARE THEIR DNA.

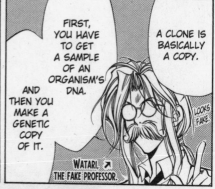

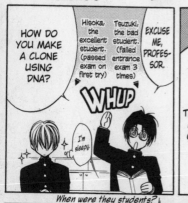

THIS IS HOW CLONES ARE MADE!!
IN CLONING, GENETIC MATERIAL IS TAKEN FROM A PERSON, A PLANT, OR AN ANIMAL AND INSERTED INTO THE NUCLEUS OF A HOST CELL WHOSE DNA HAS BEEN REMOVED OR DESTROYED.
HOST CELL
a
NUTRIENTS
a′
a′
a′
a′
HOW DNA CLONING WORKS
THE DNA REPLICATES TO PRODUCE AN EXACT GENETIC COPY OF THE ORIGINAL DONOR ORGANISM.

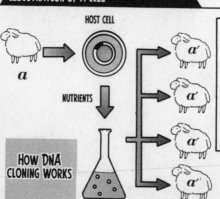

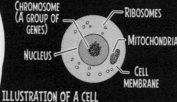

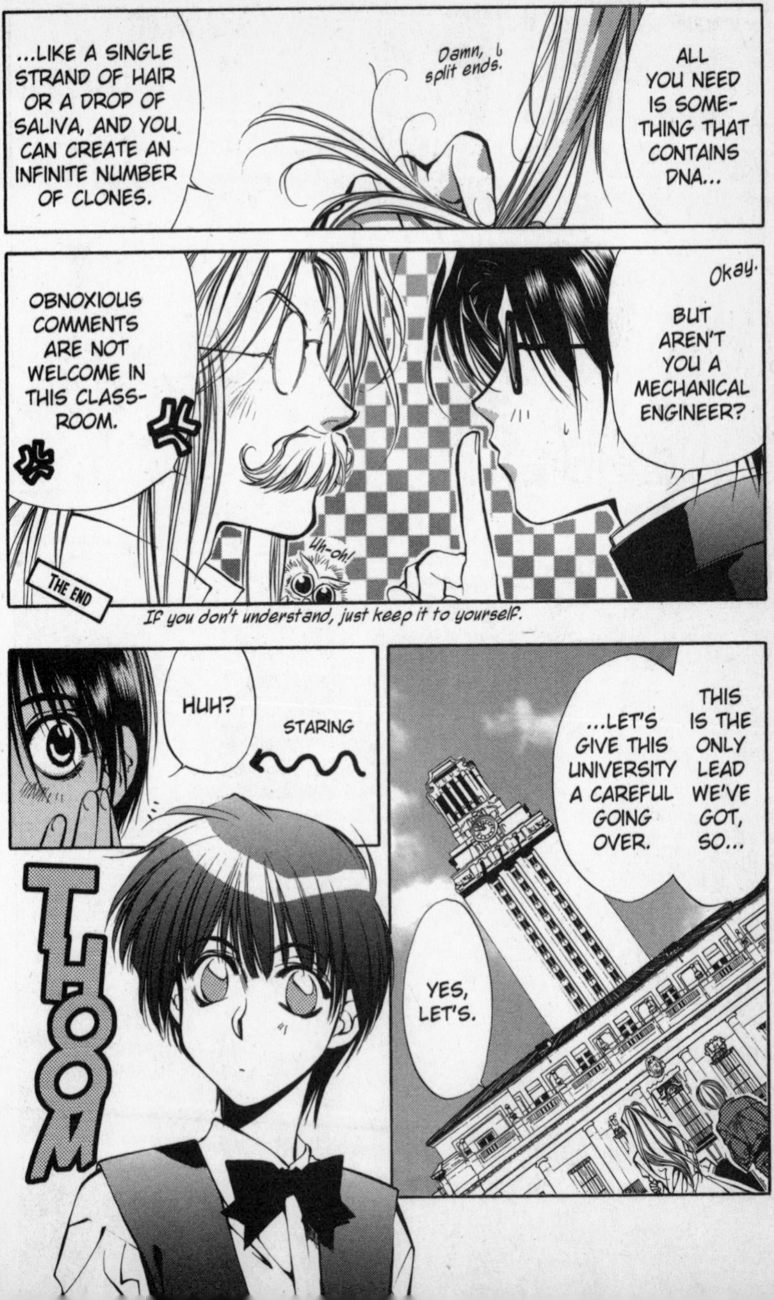
ALL YOU NEED IS SOMETHING THAT CONTAINS DNA...
Damn, split ends.
...LIKE A SINGLE STRAND OF HAIR OR A DROP OF SALIVA, AND YOU CAN CREATE AN INFINITE NUMBER OF CLONES.
Okay.
BUT AREN'T YOU A MECHANICAL ENGINEER?
OBNOXIOUS COMMENTS ARE NOT WELCOME IN THIS CLASSROOM.
Uh-oh!
THE END
If you don't understand, just keep it to yourself.
THIS IS THE ONLY LEAD WE'VE GOT, SO...
...LET'S GIVE THIS UNIVERSITY A CAREFUL GOING OVER.
YES, LET'S.
HUH?
STARING
THOOM

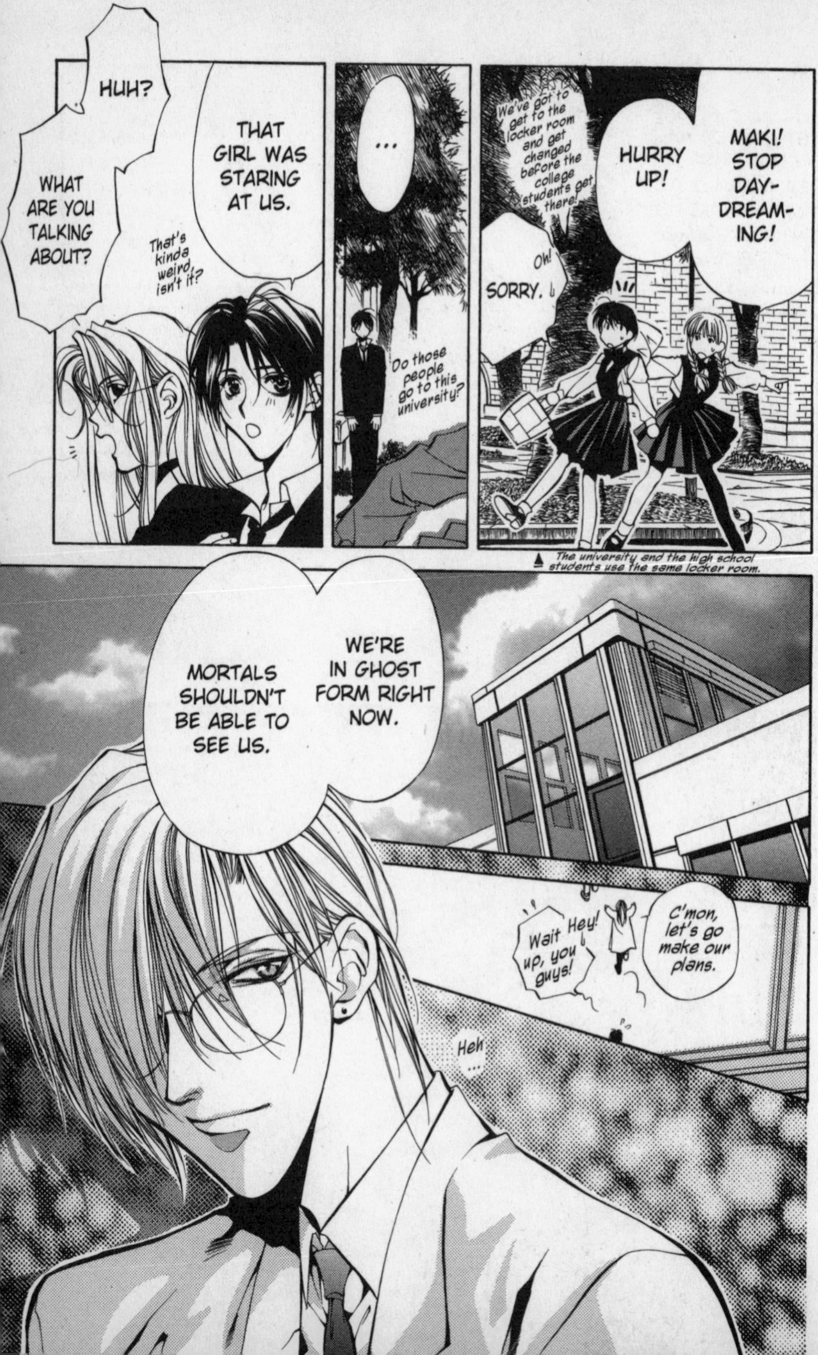
MAKI! STOP DAY-DREAMING!
HURRY UP!
We've got to get to the locker room and get changed before the college students get there!
Oh!
SORRY.
The university and the high school students use the same locker room.
...
Do those people go to this university?
THAT GIRL WAS STARING AT US.
That's kinda weird, isn't it?
HUH?
WHAT ARE YOU TALKING ABOUT?
WE'RE IN GHOST FORM RIGHT NOW.
MORTALS SHOULDN'T BE ABLE TO SEE US.
C'mon, let's go make our plans.
Hey!
Wait up, you guys!
Heh...

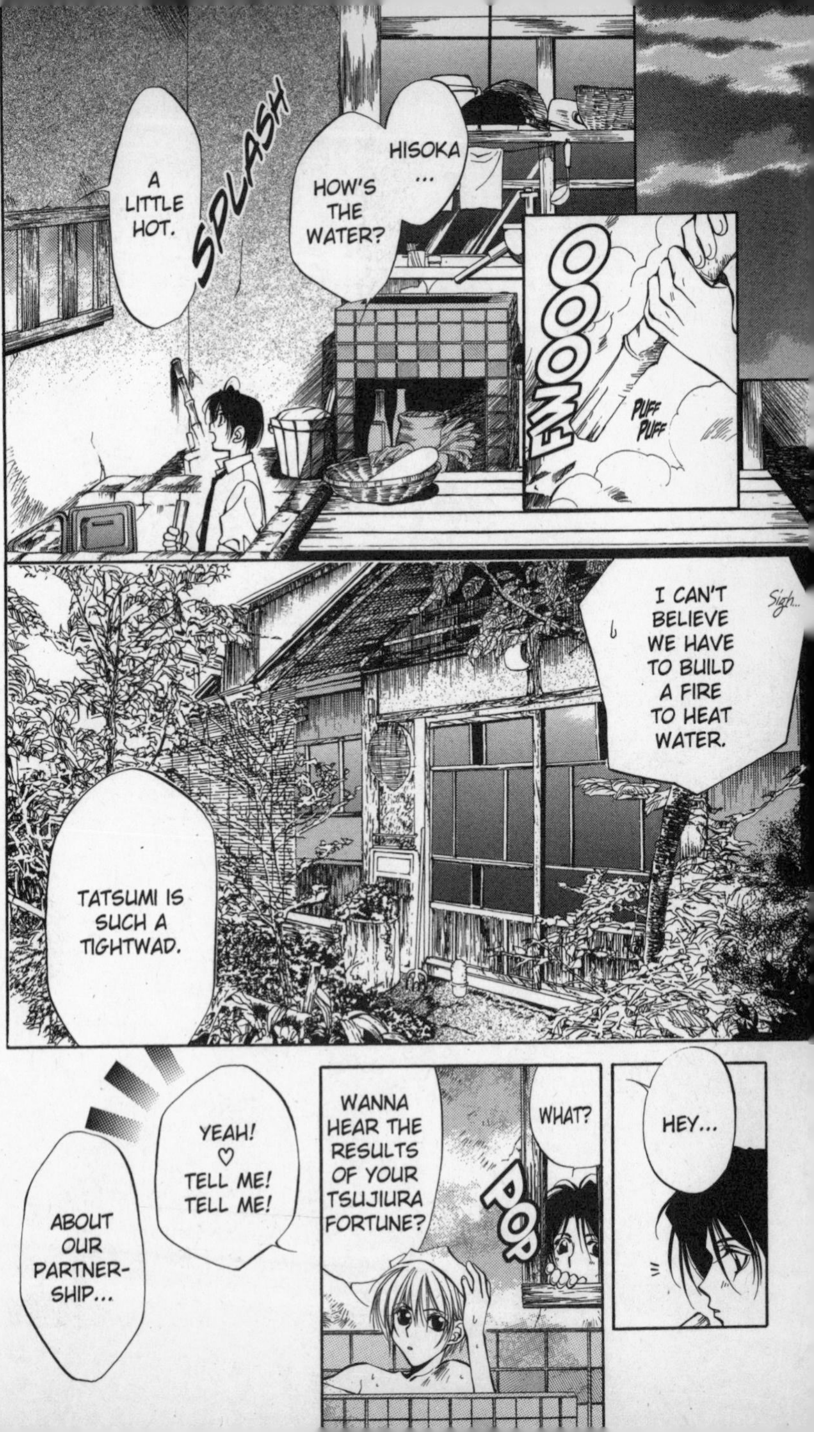
HISOKA...
HOW'S THE WATER?
SPLASH
A LITTLE HOT.
FWOOOOM
PUFF PUFF
Sigh...
I CAN'T BELIEVE WE HAVE TO BUILD A FIRE TO HEAT WATER.
TATSUMI IS SUCH A TIGHTWAD.
HEY...
WHAT?
POP
WANNA HEAR THE RESULTS OF YOUR TSUJIURA FORTUNE?
YEAH! ♡ TELL ME! TELL ME!
ABOUT OUR PARTNER-SHIP...

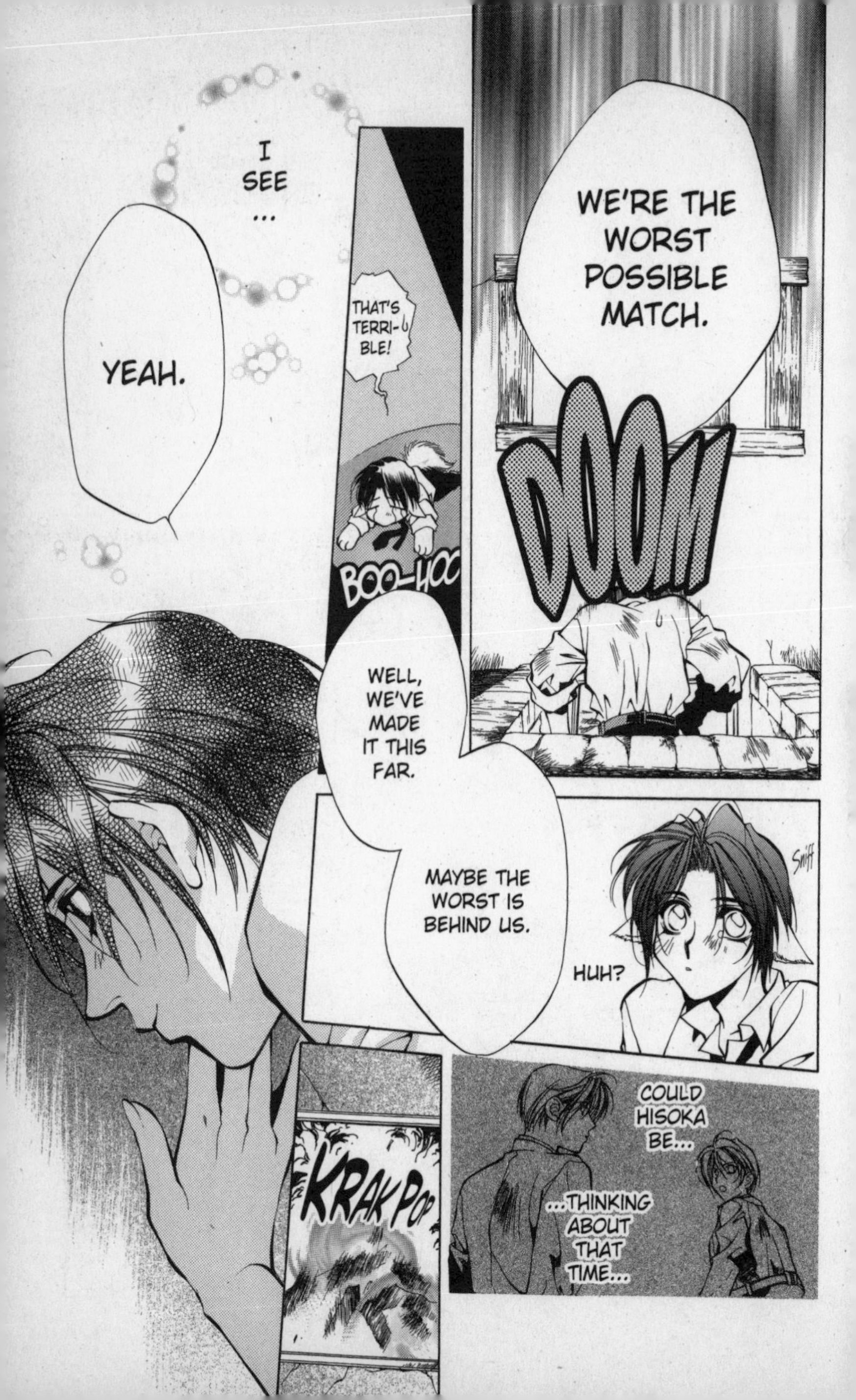
WE'RE THE WORST POSSIBLE MATCH.
DOOM
THAT'S TERRI-BLE!
BOO-HOO
I SEE ...
YEAH.
WELL, WE'VE MADE IT THIS FAR.
MAYBE THE WORST IS BEHIND US.
Sniff
HUH?
COULD HISOKA BE...
...THINKING ABOUT THAT TIME...
KRAK POP

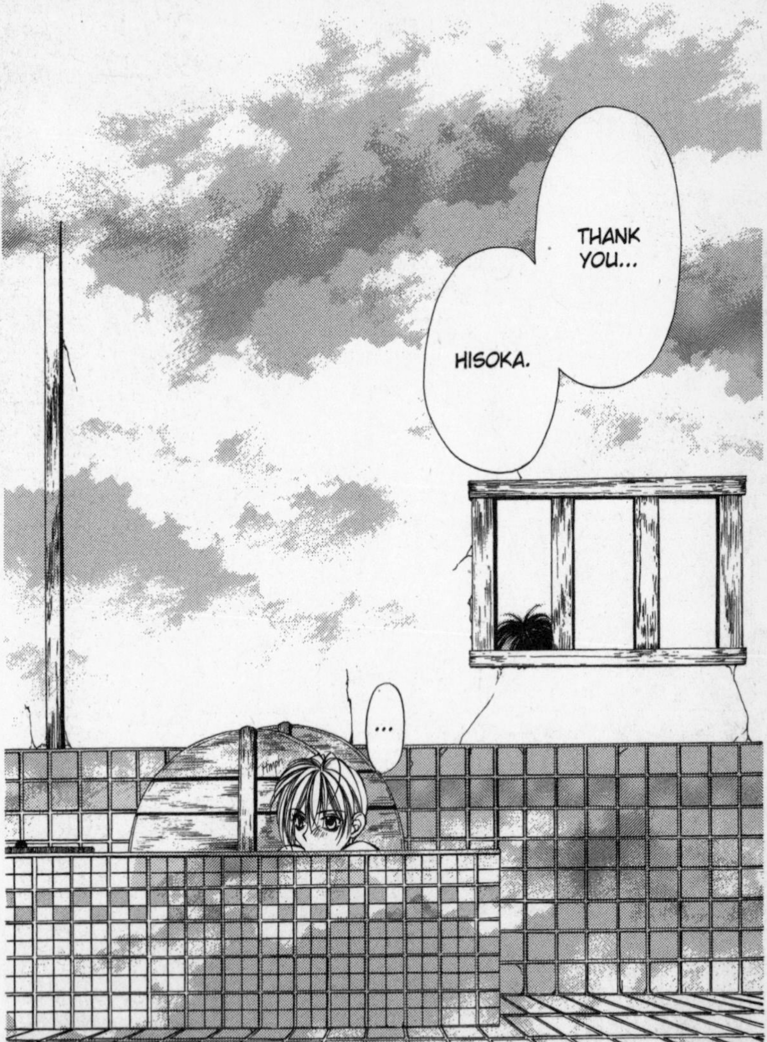
THANK YOU...
HISOKA.
...
Hmph

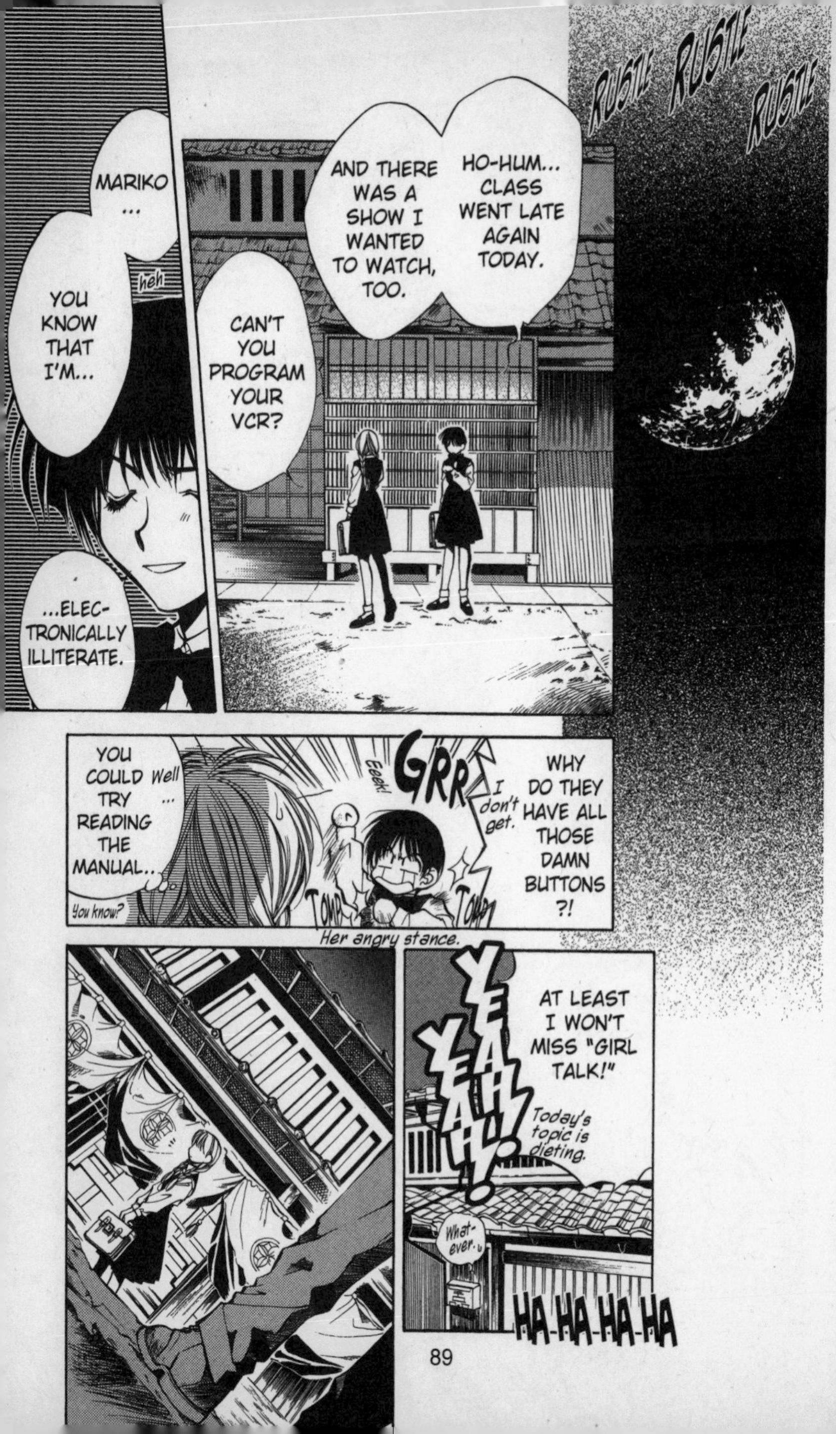
RUSTLE RUSTLE RUSTLE
HO-HUM... CLASS WENT LATE AGAIN TODAY.
AND THERE WAS A SHOW I WANTED TO WATCH, TOO.
CAN'T YOU PROGRAM YOUR VCR?
MARIKO...
heh
YOU KNOW THAT I'M...
...ELECTRONICALLY ILLITERATE.
WHY DO THEY HAVE ALL THOSE DAMN BUTTONS?!
I don't get.
GRR
TOMP TOMP
Eeek!
YOU COULD TRY READING THE MANUAL...
Well...
You know?
Her angry stance.
AT LEAST I WON'T MISS "GIRL TALK!"
Today's topic is dieting.
YEAH YEAH!
Whatever.
HA-HA-HA-HA

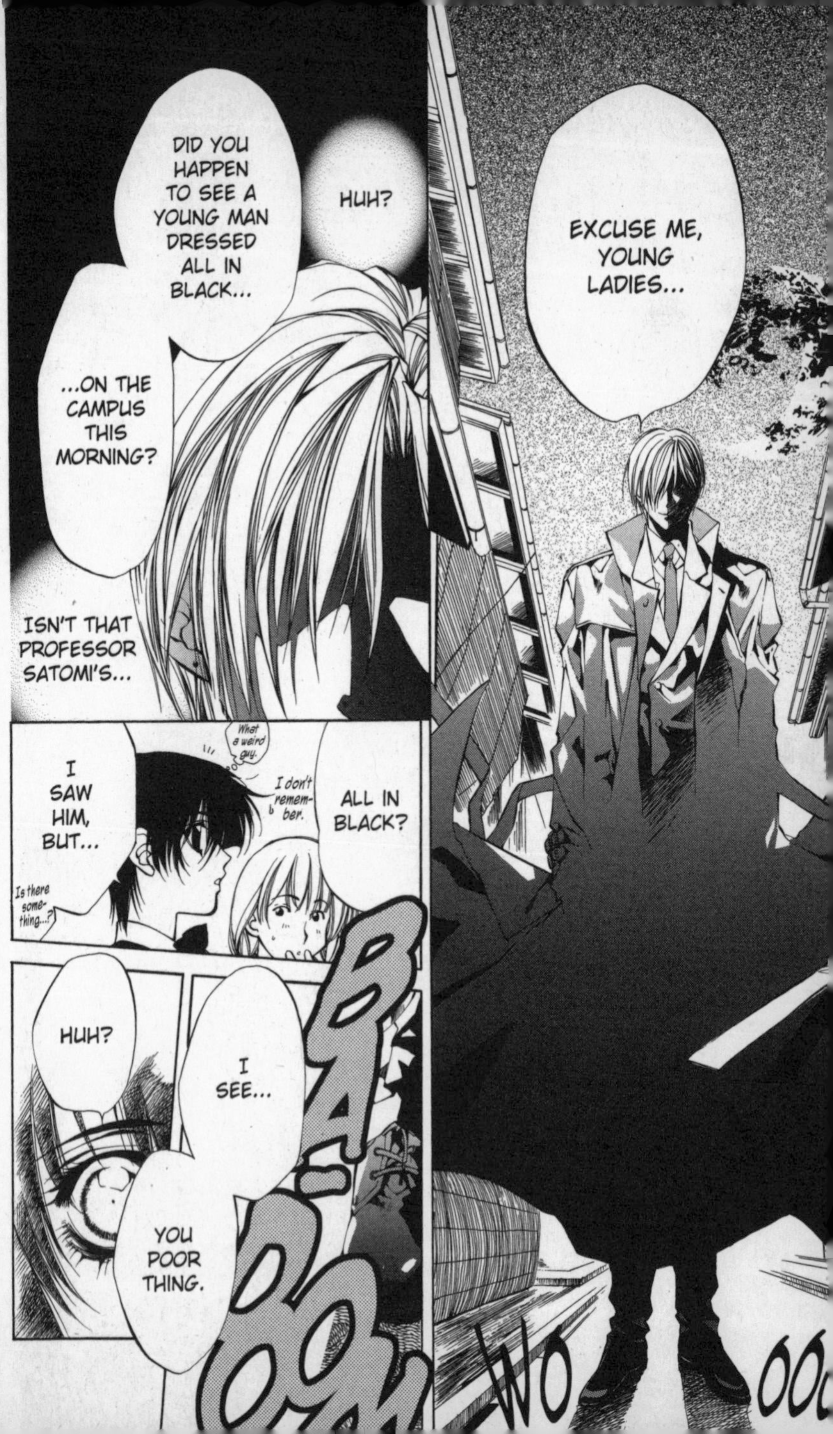
EXCUSE ME, YOUNG LADIES...
DID YOU HAPPEN TO SEE A YOUNG MAN DRESSED ALL IN BLACK...
HUH?
...ON THE CAMPUS THIS MORNING?
ISN'T THAT PROFESSOR SATOMI'S...
ALL IN BLACK?
I don't remember.
What a weird guy.
I SAW HIM, BUT...
Is there something...?
I SEE...
YOU POOR THING.
HUH?

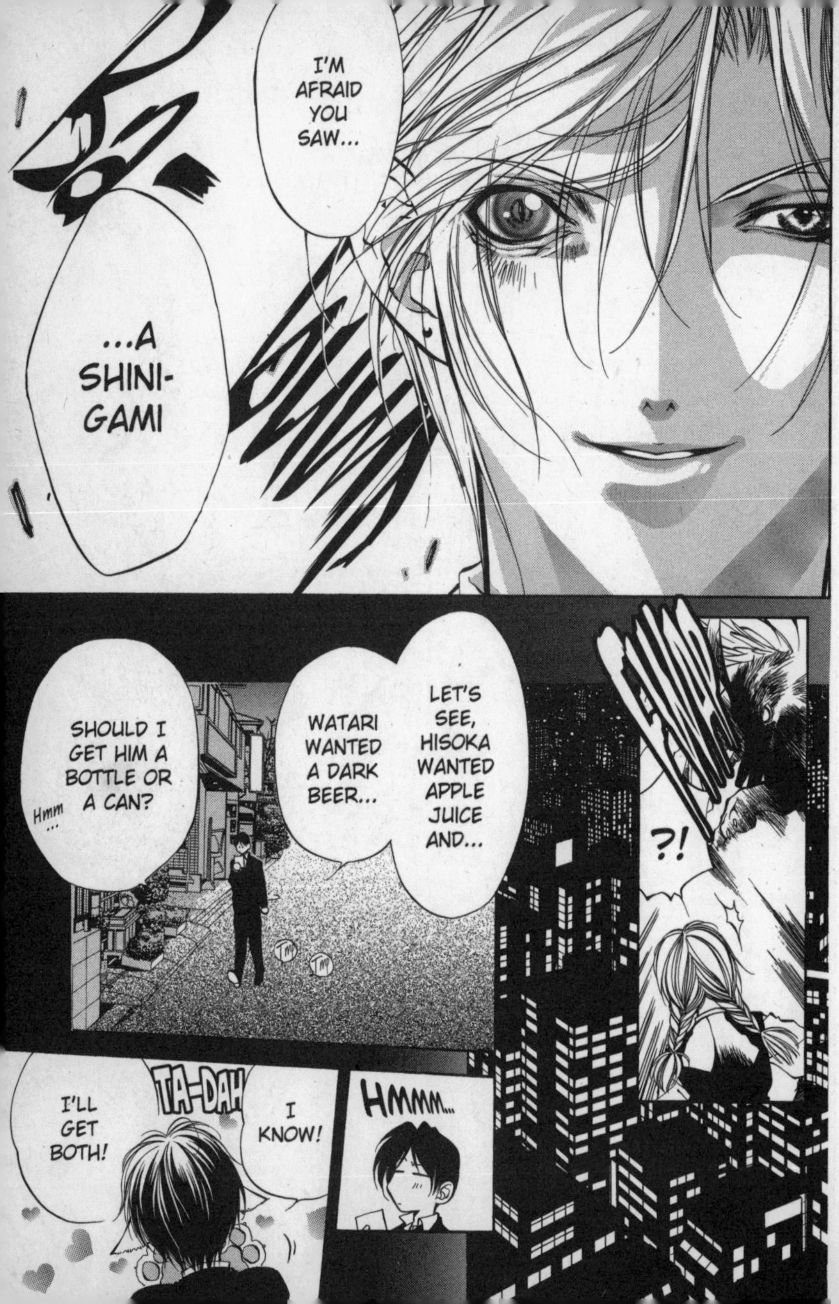
I'M AFRAID YOU SAW...
...A SHINI-GAMI
?!
LET'S SEE, HISOKA WANTED APPLE JUICE AND...
WATARI WANTED A DARK BEER...
SHOULD I GET HIM A BOTTLE OR A CAN?
Hmm ...
HMMM...
I KNOW!
TA-DAH
I'LL GET BOTH!

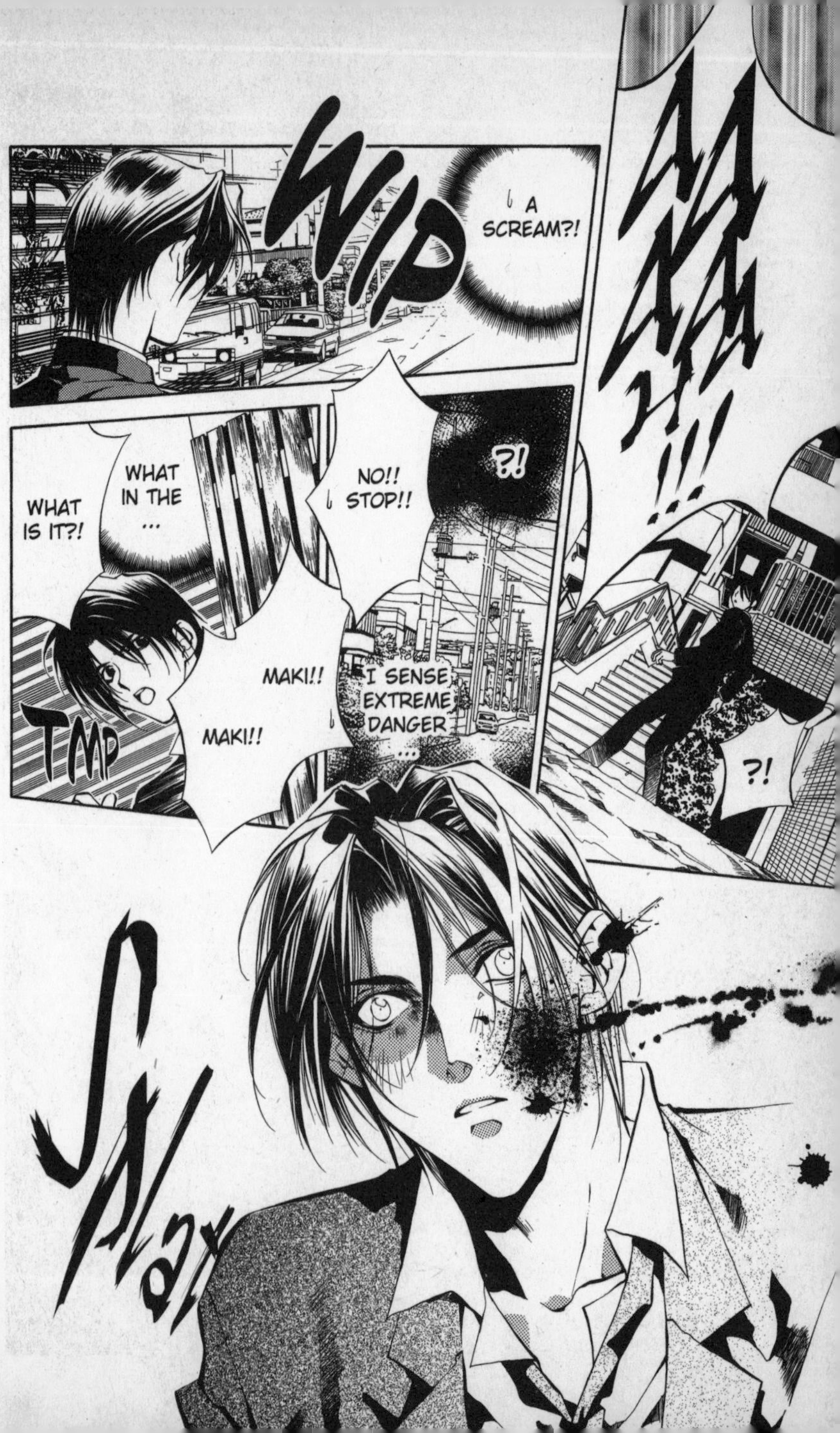

WIP
A SCREAM?!
?!
?!
NO!! STOP!!
WHAT IN THE ...
WHAT IS IT?!
TMP
MAKI!!
MAKI!!
I SENSE EXTREME DANGER ...
Splat

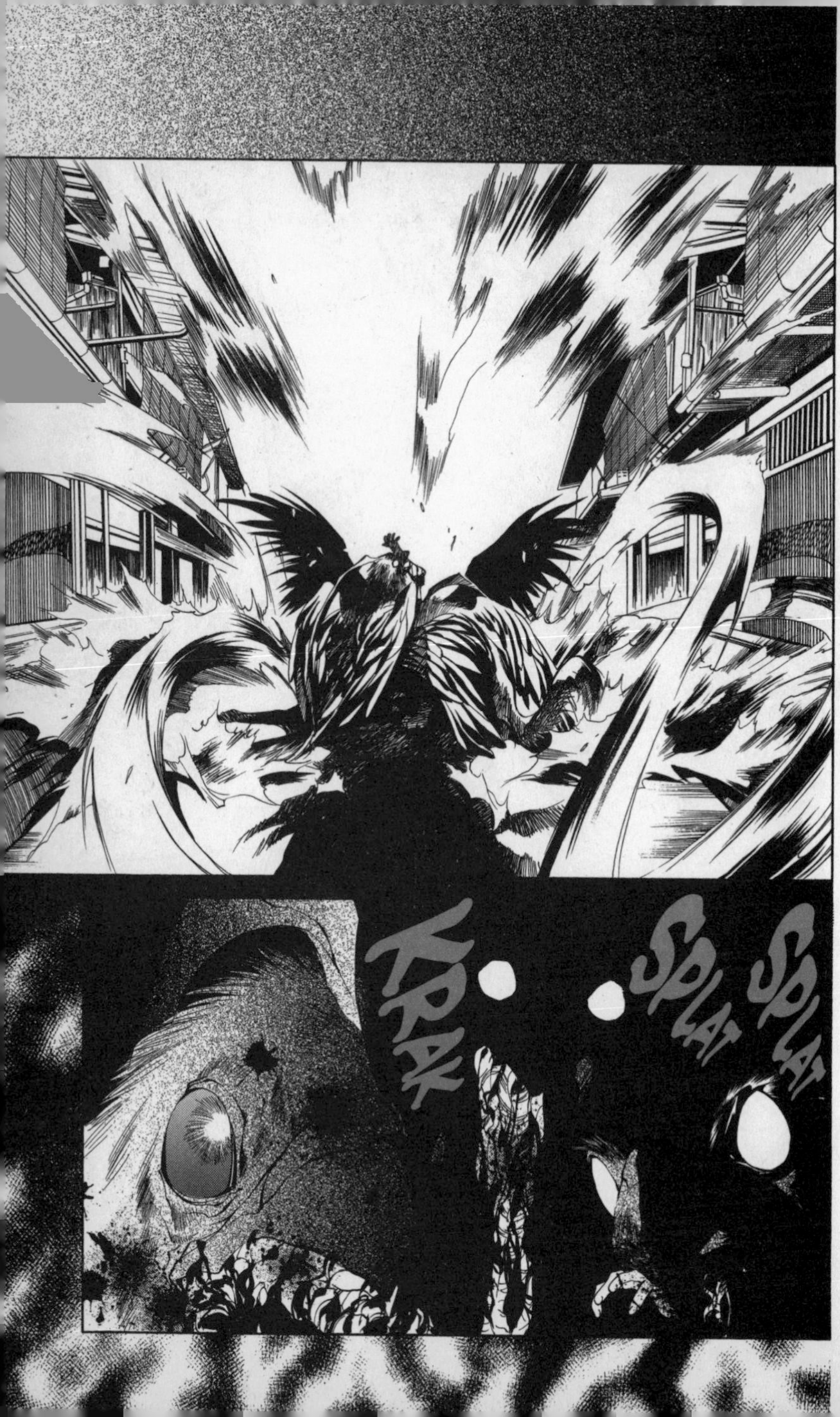
SPLAT
SPLAT
KRAK

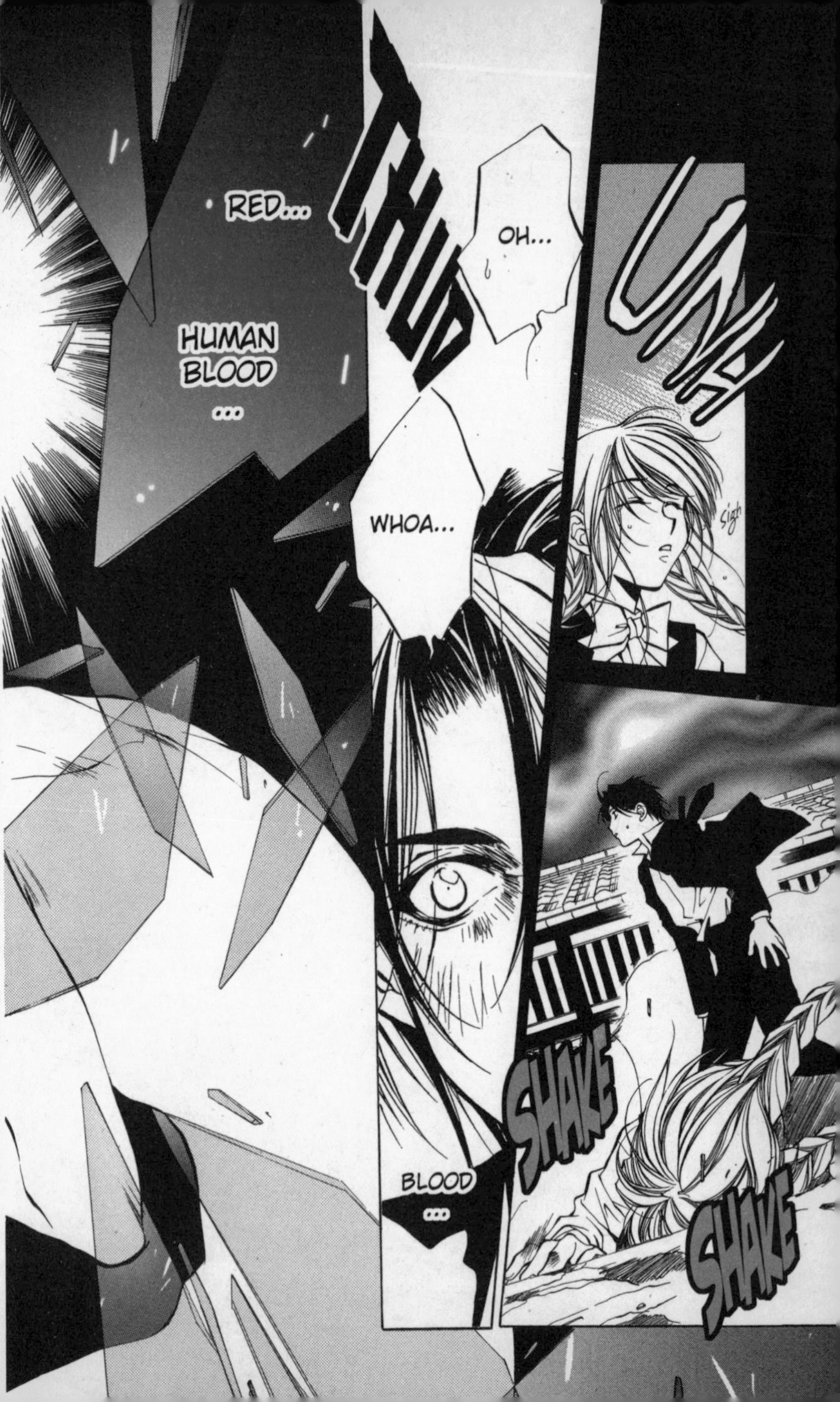
UNYA
Sigh
SHAKE
SHAKE
THUD
OH...
WHOA...
BLOOD
...
RED...
HUMAN
BLOOD
...

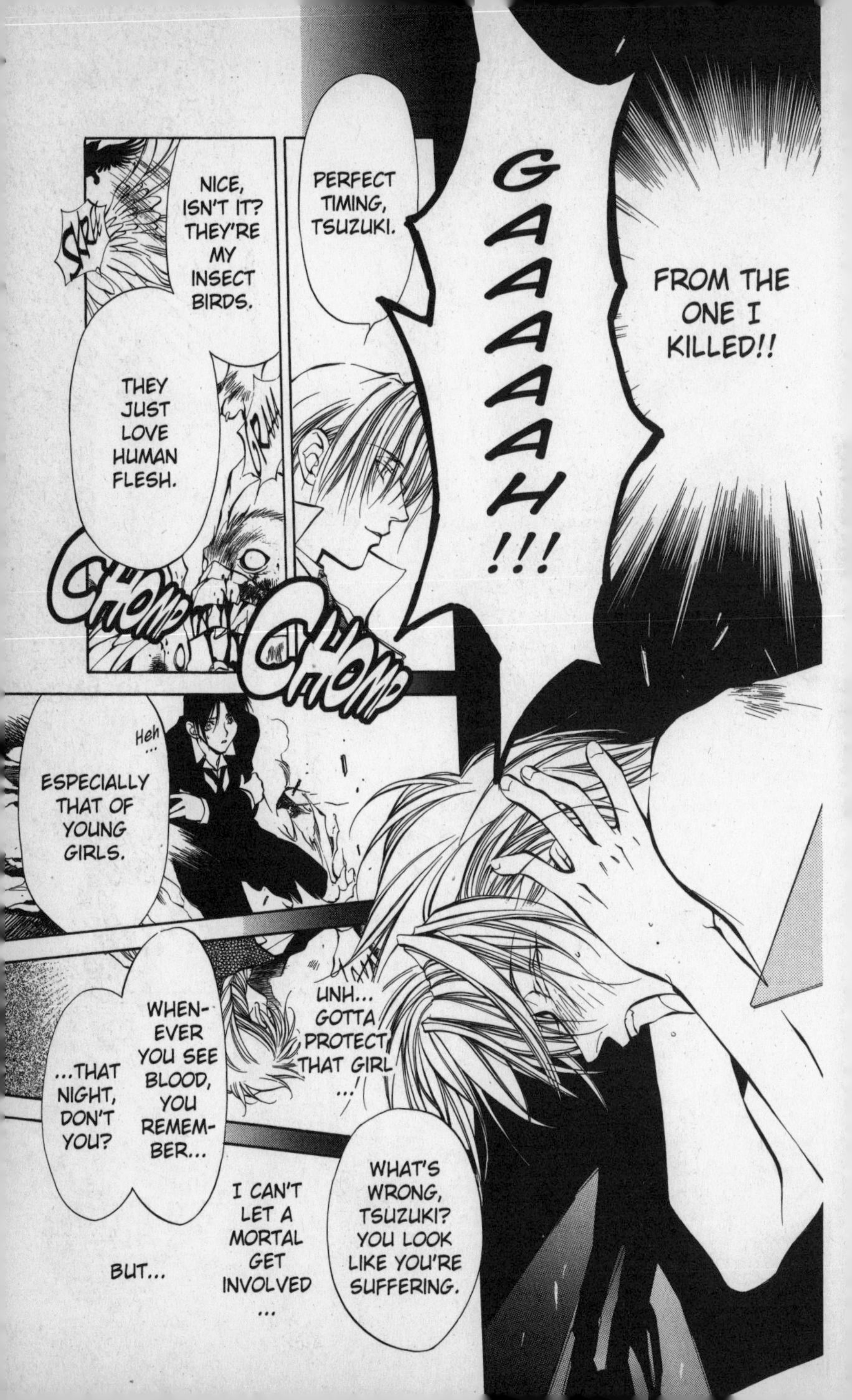
FROM THE ONE I KILLED!!
GAAAAAAH!!!
PERFECT TIMING, TSUZUKI.
NICE, ISN'T IT? THEY'RE MY INSECT BIRDS.
THEY JUST LOVE HUMAN FLESH.
CHOMP
CHOMP
Heh...
ESPECIALLY THAT OF YOUNG GIRLS.
UNH... GOTTA PROTECT THAT GIRL...
WHAT'S WRONG, TSUZUKI? YOU LOOK LIKE YOU'RE SUFFERING.
WHEN-EVER YOU SEE BLOOD, YOU REMEM-BER...
...THAT NIGHT, DON'T YOU?
I CAN'T LET A MORTAL GET INVOLVED...
BUT...

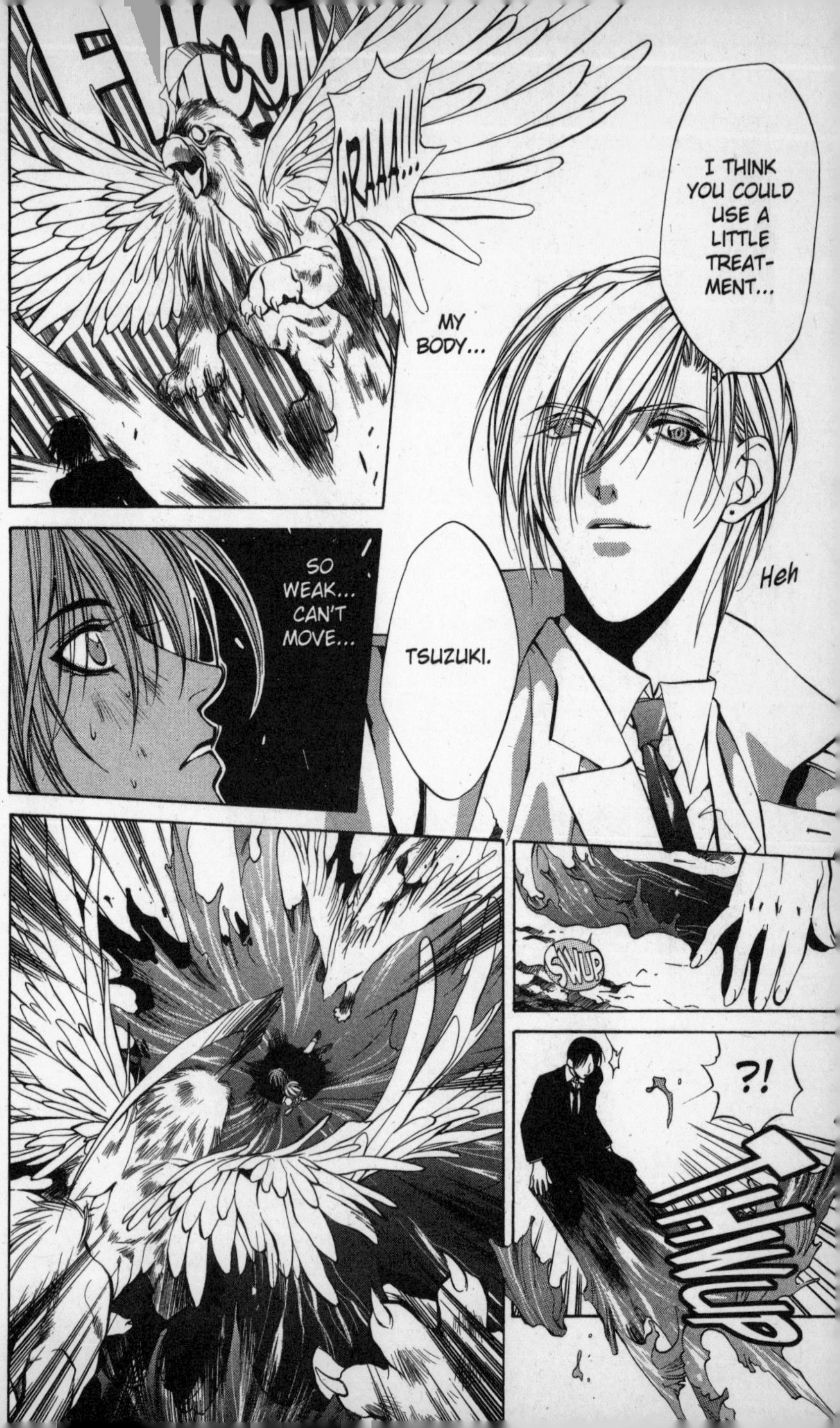
I THINK YOU COULD USE A LITTLE TREATMENT...
Heh
TSUZUKI.
GRAAA!!!...
MY BODY...
SO WEAK... CAN'T MOVE...
SWUP
?!
THWUP

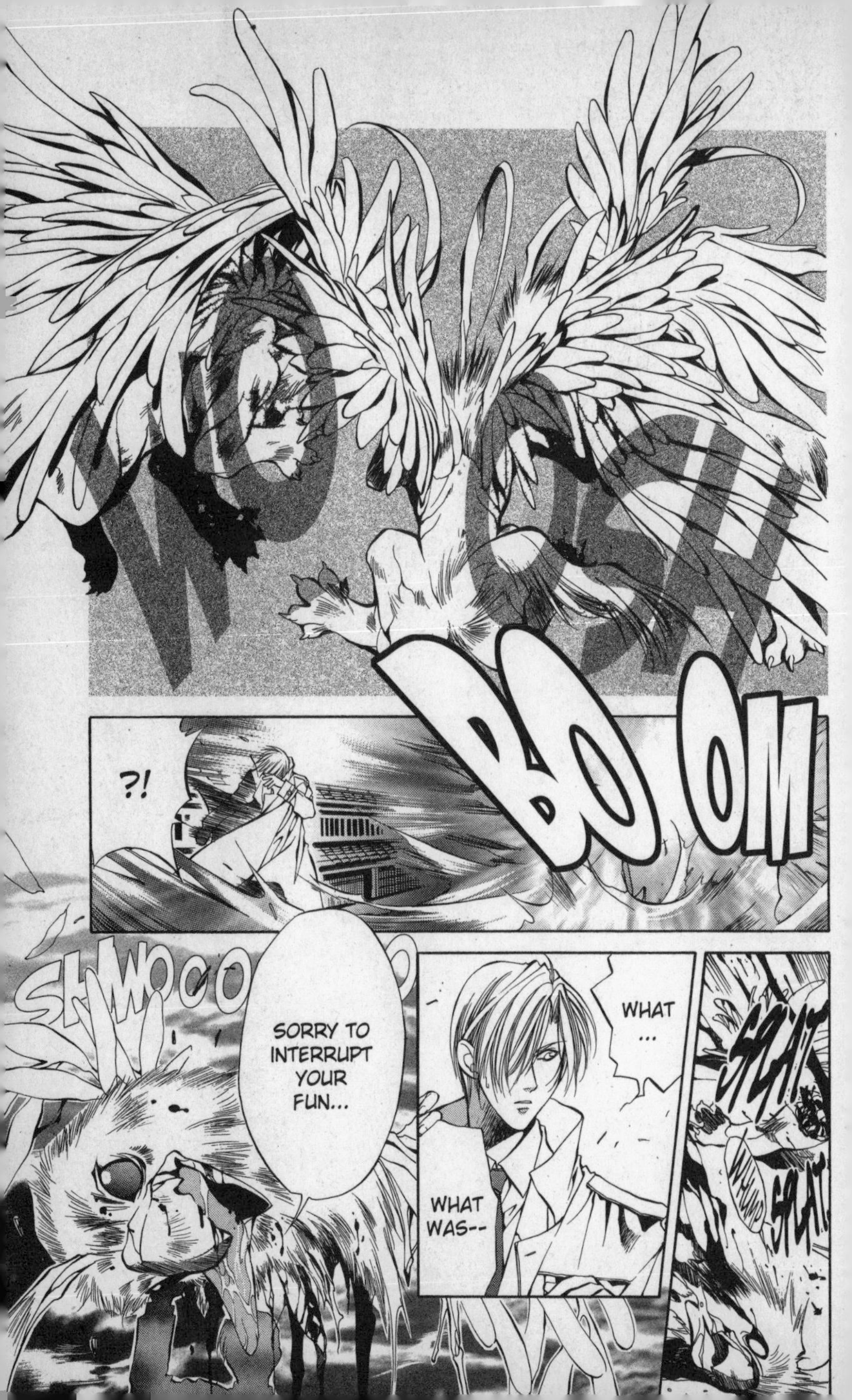
WOOSH
BOOM
?!
SPLAT
WHUMP
SPLAT
WHAT ...
WHAT WAS--
SHWOOO
SORRY TO INTERRUPT YOUR FUN...

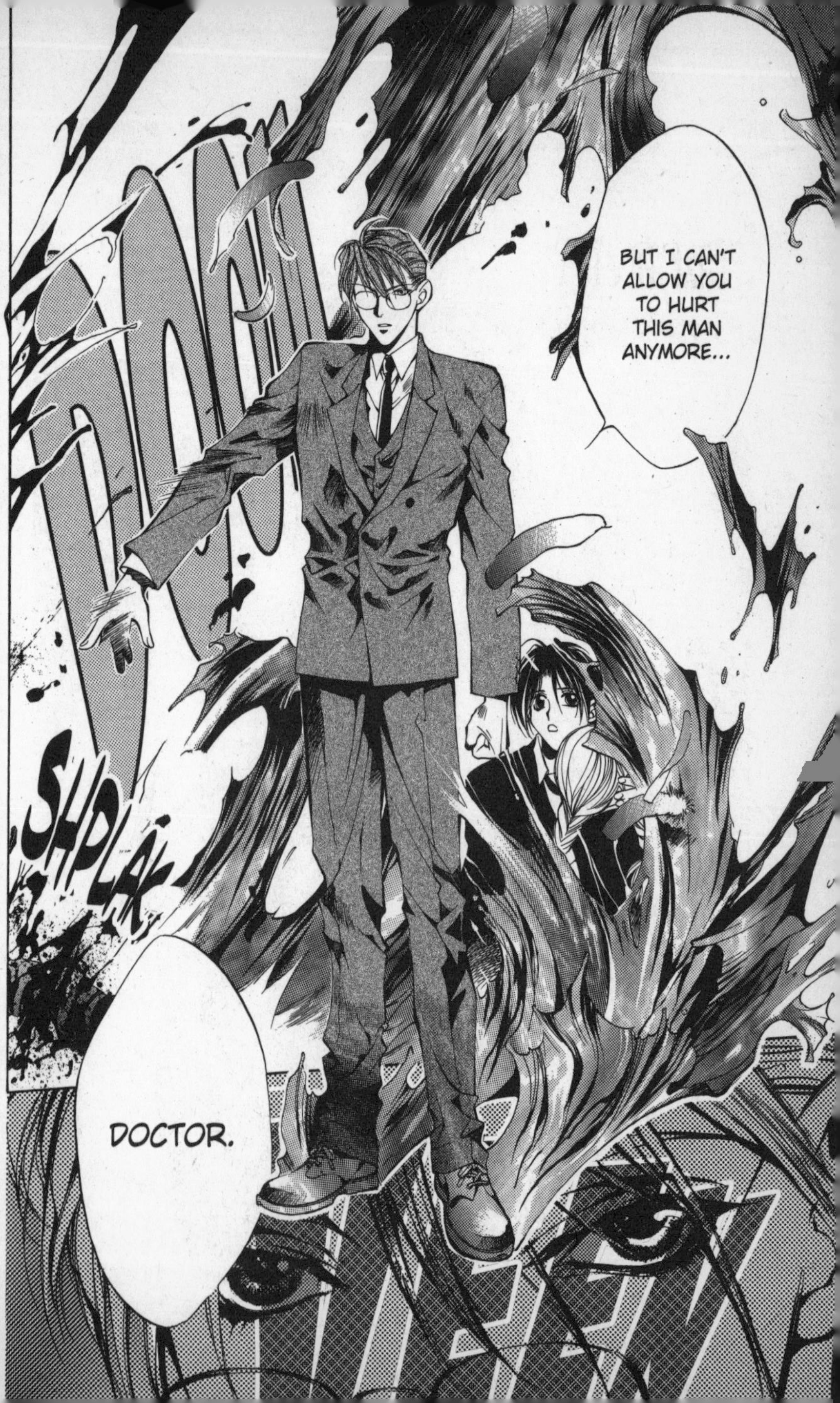
BUT I CAN'T ALLOW YOU TO HURT THIS MAN ANYMORE...
DOOM
SHPLAK
DOCTOR.

CHAPTER 21

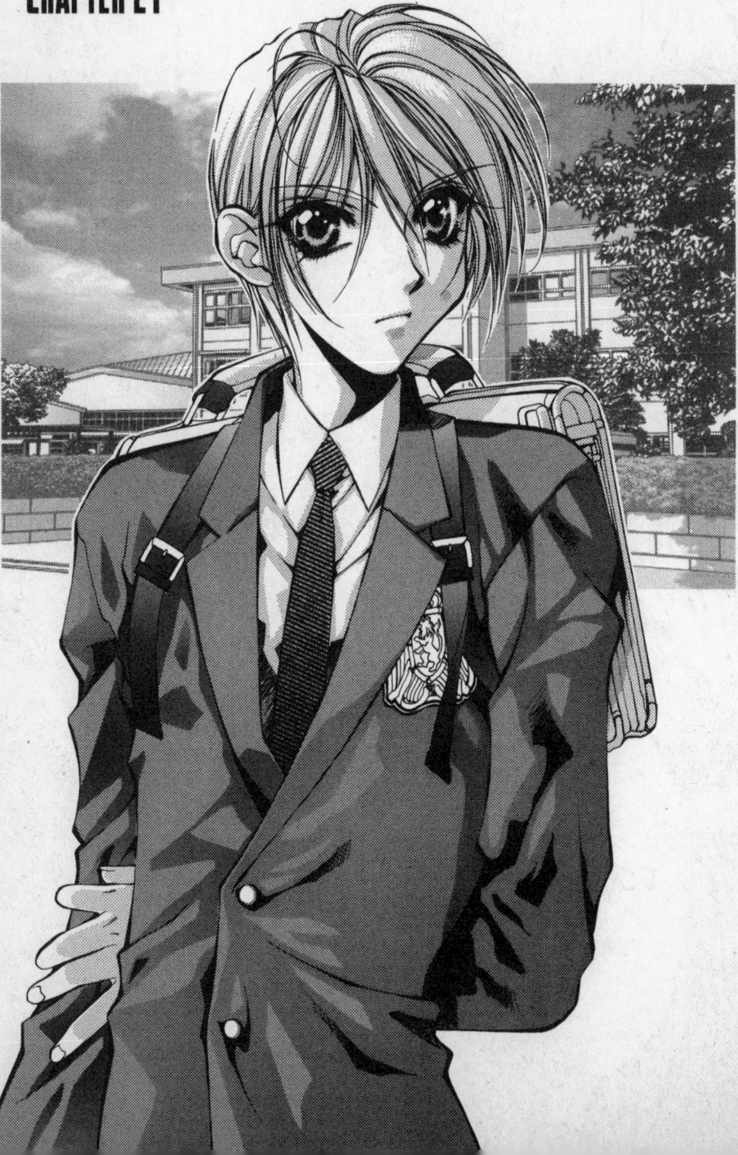

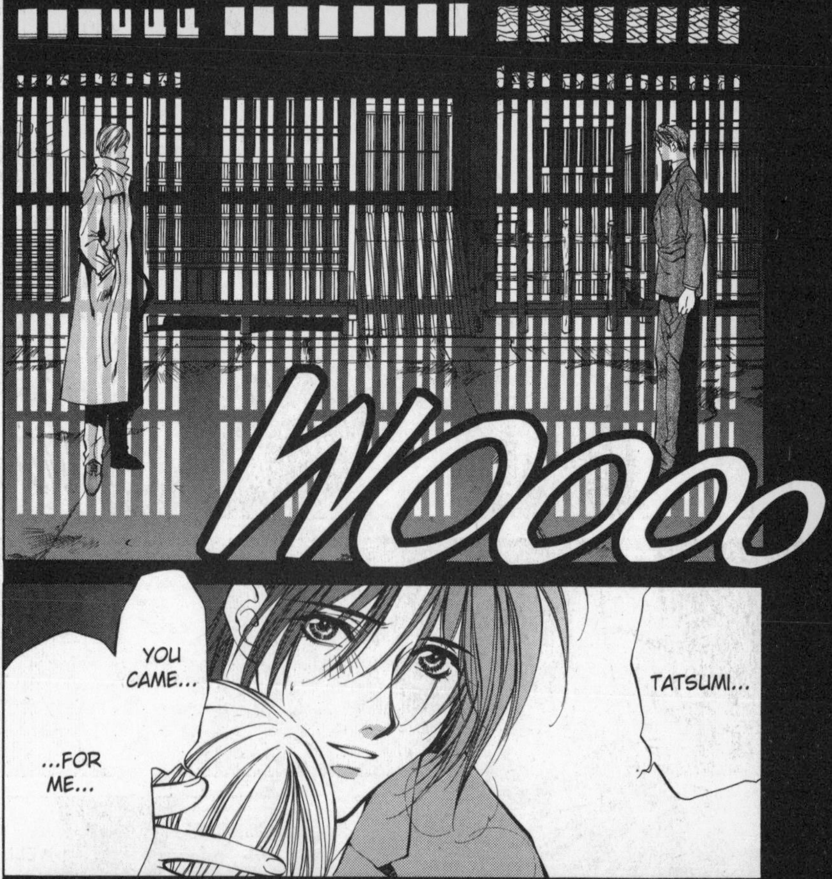
WOOOO
TATSUMI...
YOU CAME...
...FOR ME...

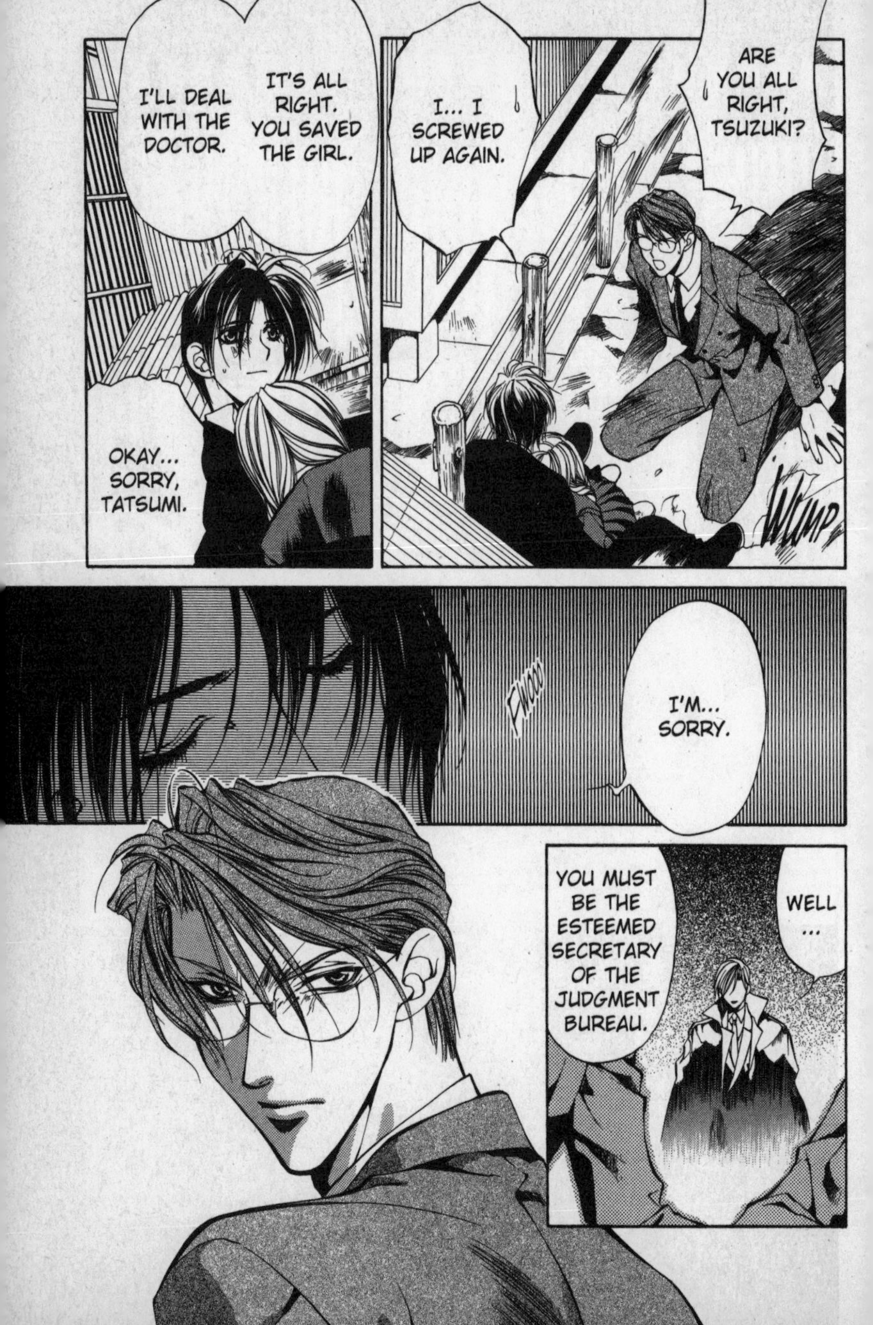
ARE YOU ALL RIGHT, TSUZUKI?
I... I SCREWED UP AGAIN.
WUMP
IT'S ALL RIGHT. YOU SAVED THE GIRL.
I'LL DEAL WITH THE DOCTOR.
OKAY... SORRY, TATSUMI.
I'M... SORRY.
FWOOO
WELL ...
YOU MUST BE THE ESTEEMED SECRETARY OF THE JUDGMENT BUREAU.

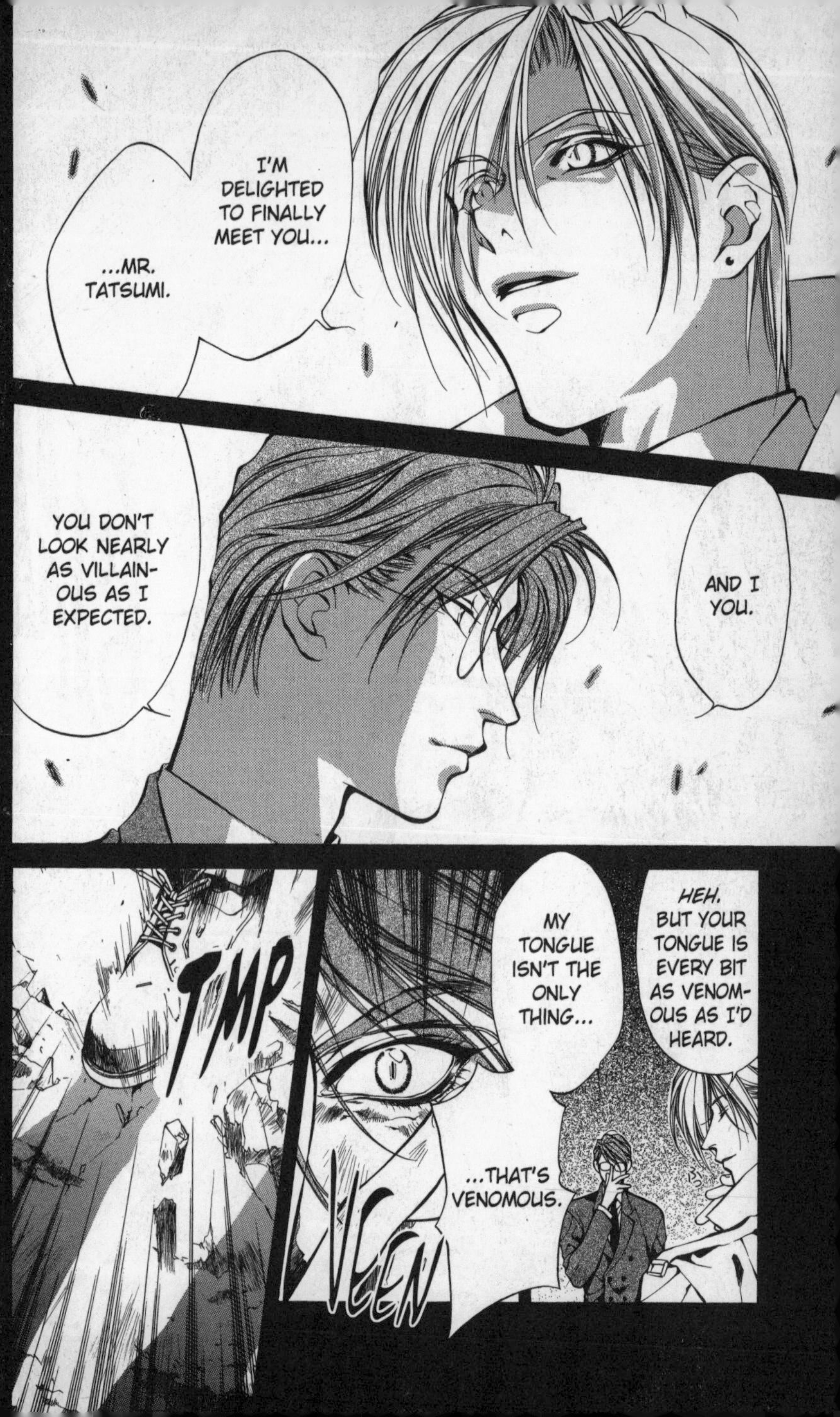
I'M DELIGHTED TO FINALLY MEET YOU...
...MR. TATSUMI.
AND I YOU.
YOU DON'T LOOK NEARLY AS VILLAIN-OUS AS I EXPECTED.
HEH. BUT YOUR TONGUE IS EVERY BIT AS VENOM-OUS AS I'D HEARD.
MY TONGUE ISN'T THE ONLY THING...
...THAT'S VENOMOUS.
TMP
VEEN

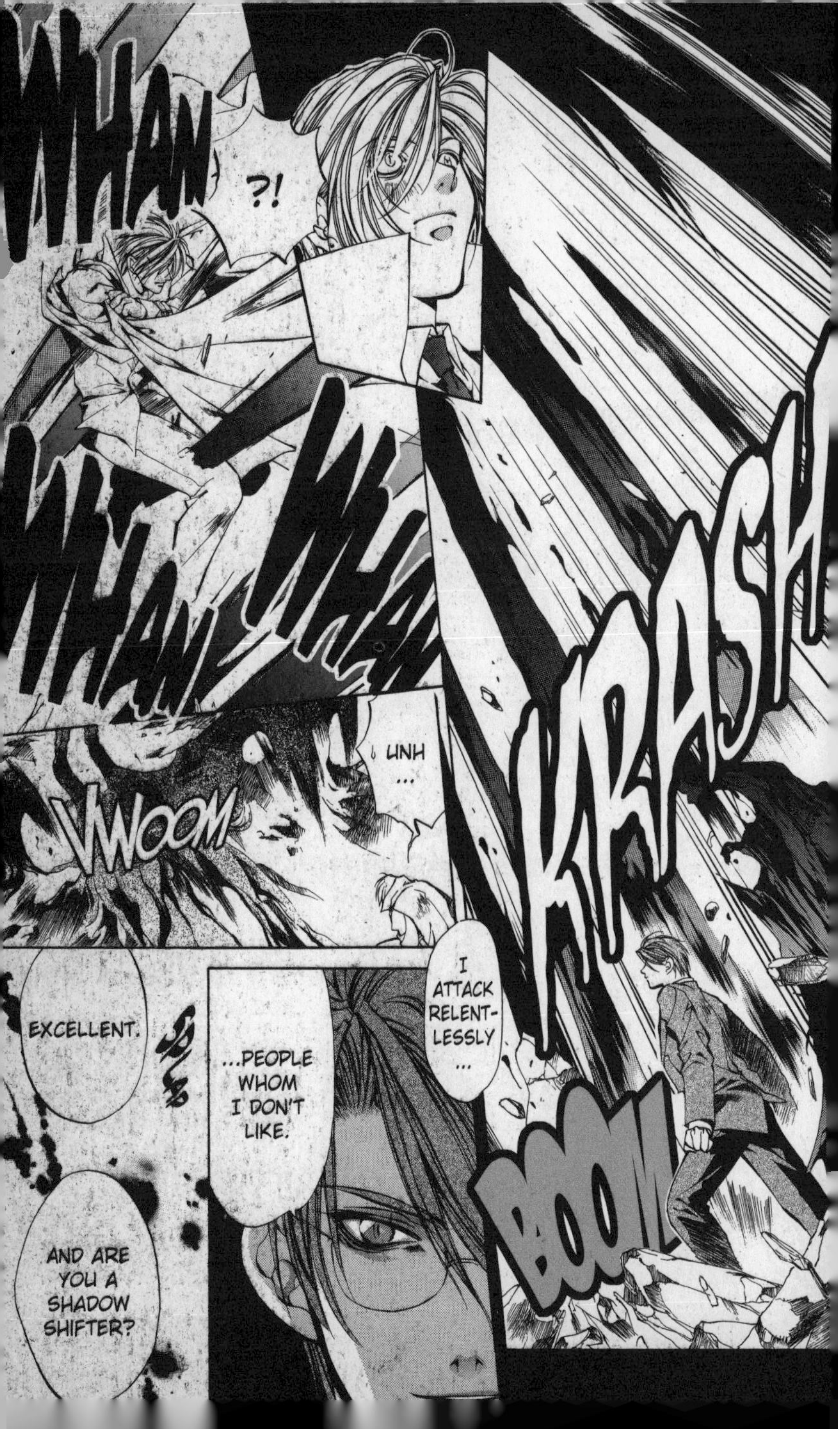
?!
WHAM
WHAM
WHAM
KRASH
UNH ...
VWOOM
I ATTACK RELENT-LESSLY ...
BOOM
...PEOPLE WHOM I DON'T LIKE.
EXCELLENT.
AND ARE YOU A SHADOW SHIFTER?

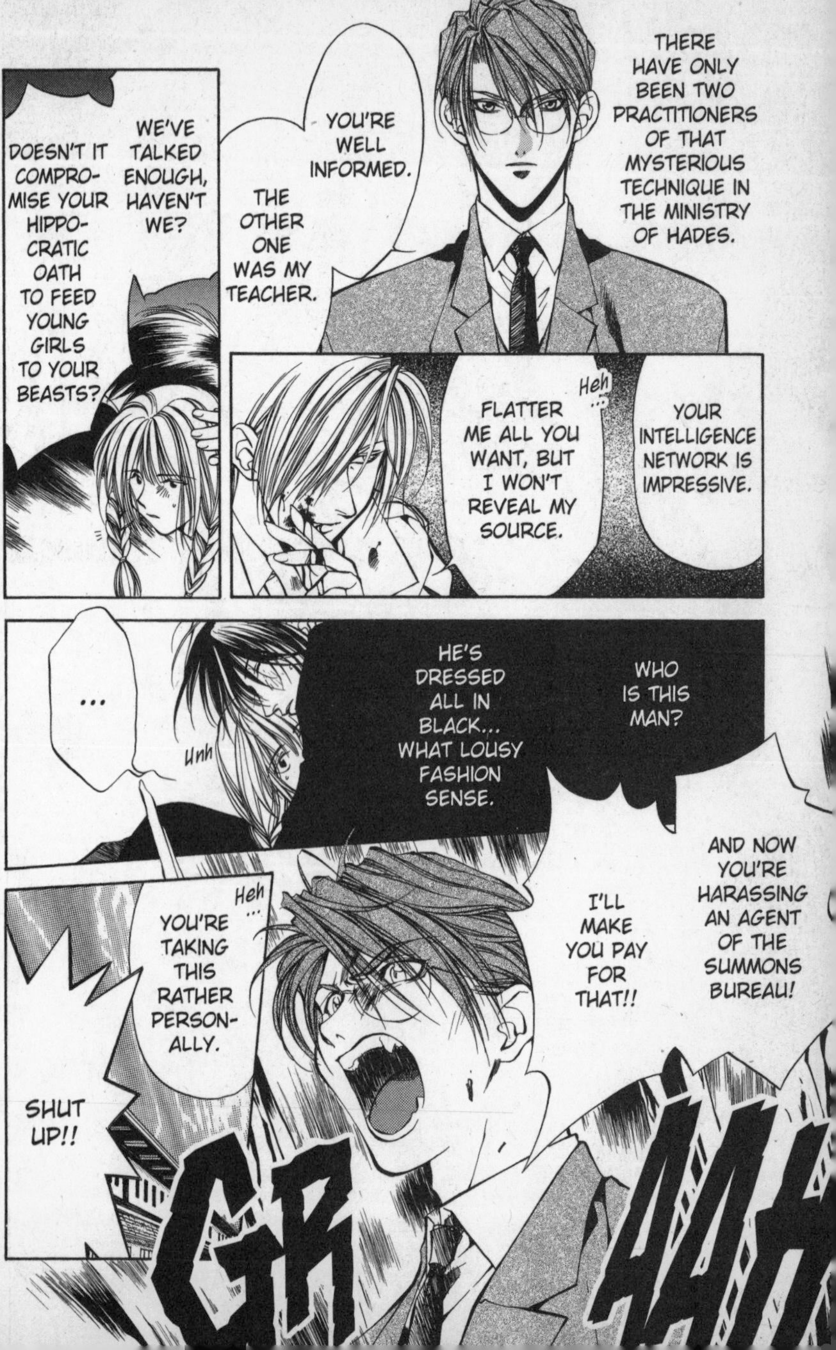
THERE HAVE ONLY BEEN TWO PRACTITIONERS OF THAT MYSTERIOUS TECHNIQUE IN THE MINISTRY OF HADES.
YOU'RE WELL INFORMED.
THE OTHER ONE WAS MY TEACHER.
YOUR INTELLIGENCE NETWORK IS IMPRESSIVE.
Heh...
FLATTER ME ALL YOU WANT, BUT I WON'T REVEAL MY SOURCE.
WE'VE TALKED ENOUGH, HAVEN'T WE?
DOESN'T IT COMPROMISE YOUR HIPPOCRATIC OATH TO FEED YOUNG GIRLS TO YOUR BEASTS?
WHO IS THIS MAN?
HE'S DRESSED ALL IN BLACK... WHAT LOUSY FASHION SENSE.
Unh
...
AND NOW YOU'RE HARASSING AN AGENT OF THE SUMMONS BUREAU!
I'LL MAKE YOU PAY FOR THAT!!
Heh...
YOU'RE TAKING THIS RATHER PERSONALLY.
SHUT UP!!

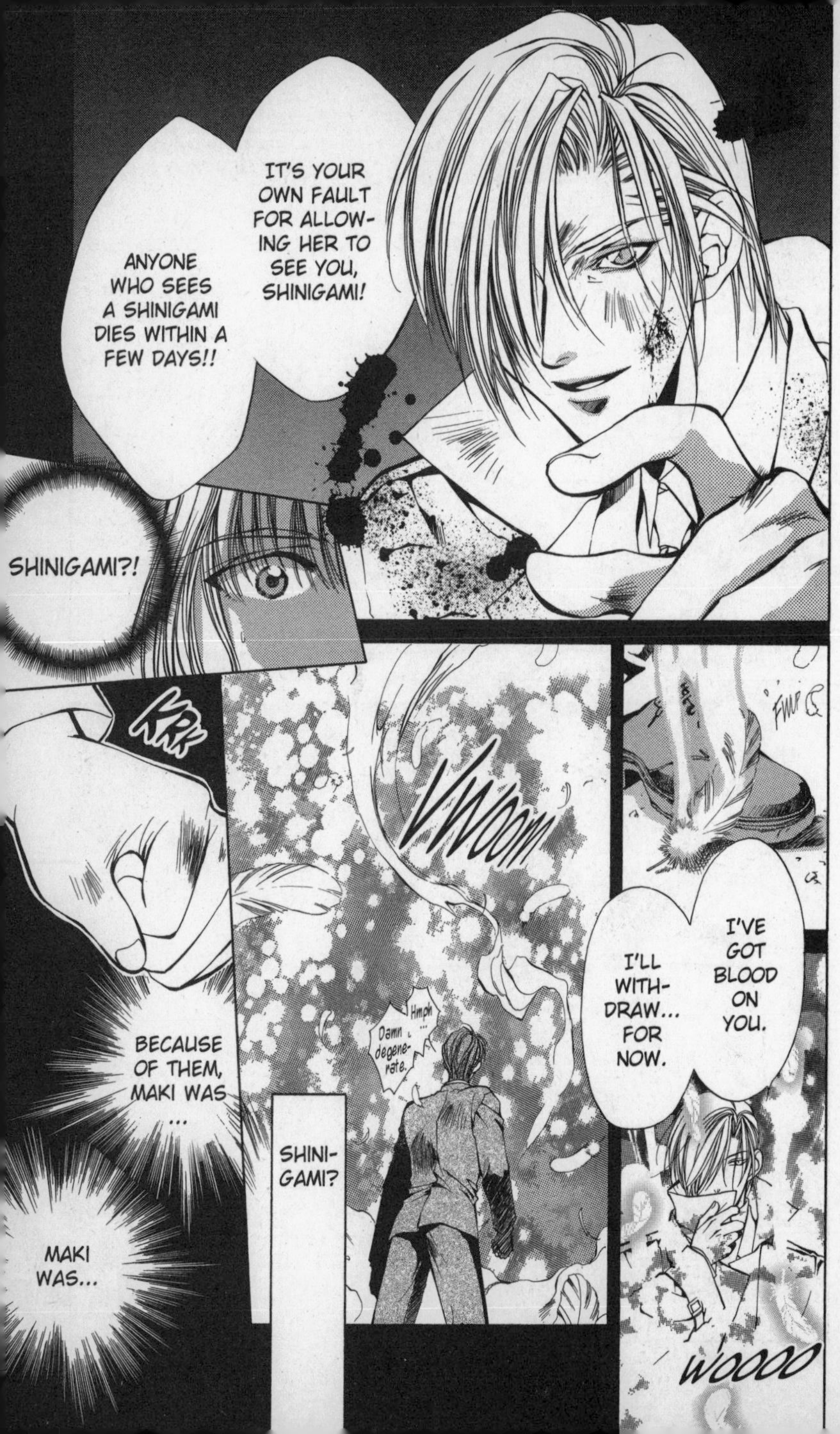
IT'S YOUR OWN FAULT FOR ALLOWING HER TO SEE YOU, SHINIGAMI!
ANYONE WHO SEES A SHINIGAMI DIES WITHIN A FEW DAYS!!
SHINIGAMI?!
FWUP
I'VE GOT BLOOD ON YOU.
I'LL WITHDRAW... FOR NOW.
WOOOO
VWOOM
Hmph...
Damn degenerate.
SHINIGAMI?
KRK
BECAUSE OF THEM, MAKI WAS ...
MAKI WAS...

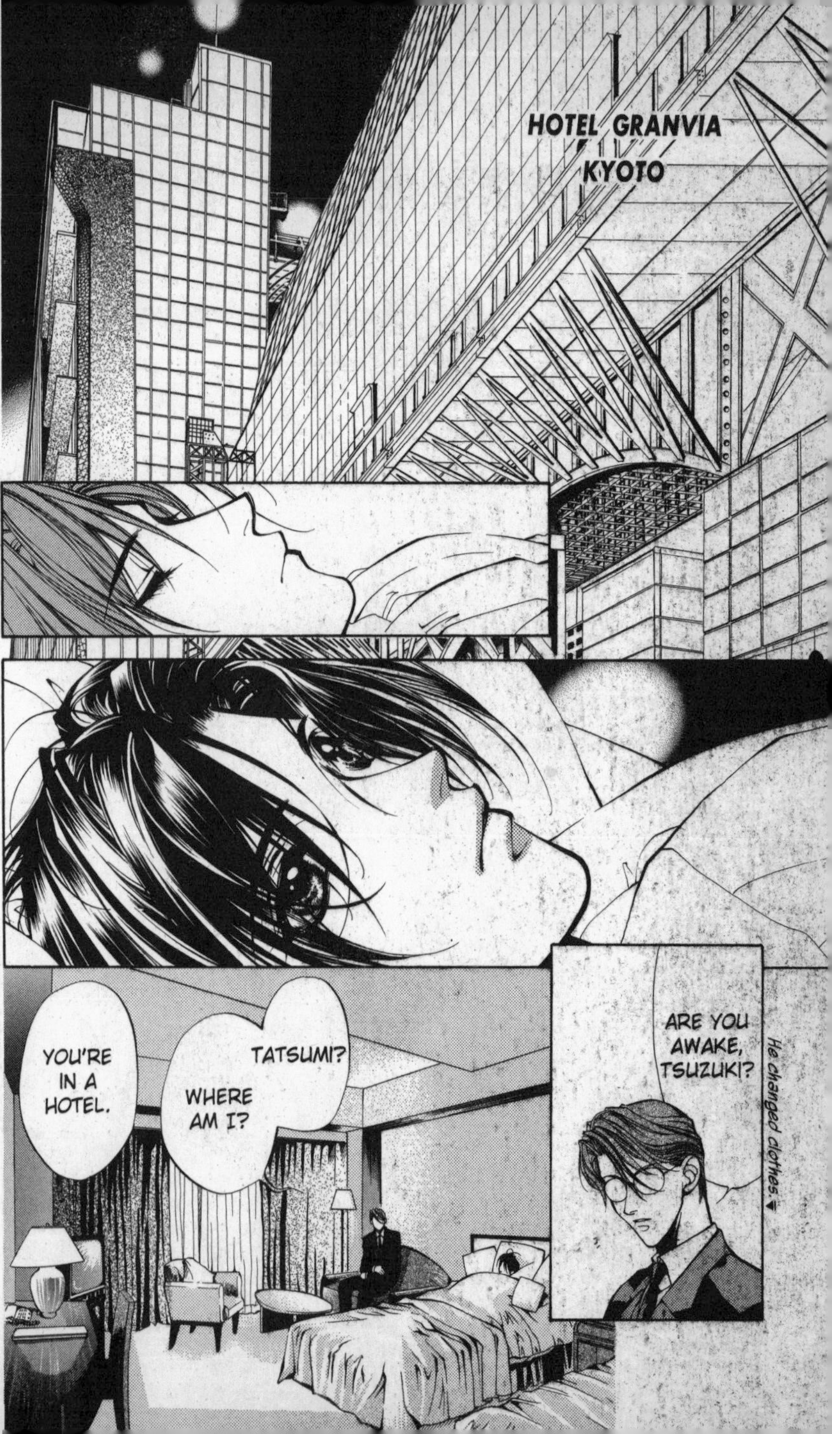
HOTEL GRANVIA KYOTO
ARE YOU AWAKE, TSUZUKI?
He changed clothes.♥
TATSUMI?
WHERE AM I?
YOU'RE IN A HOTEL.

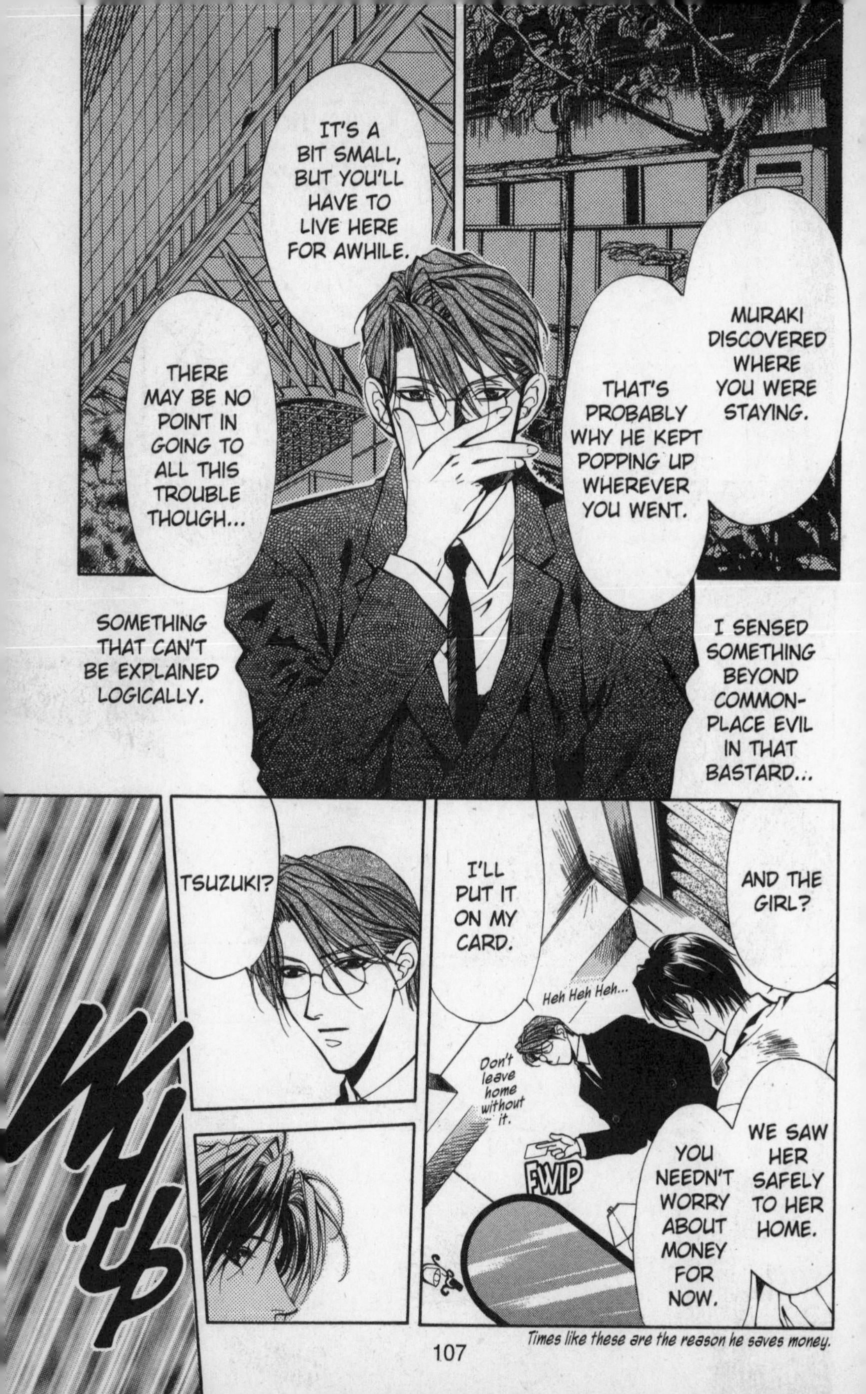
IT'S A BIT SMALL, BUT YOU'LL HAVE TO LIVE HERE FOR AWHILE.
MURAKI DISCOVERED WHERE YOU WERE STAYING.
THAT'S PROBABLY WHY HE KEPT POPPING UP WHEREVER YOU WENT.
THERE MAY BE NO POINT IN GOING TO ALL THIS TROUBLE THOUGH...
I SENSED SOMETHING BEYOND COMMON-PLACE EVIL IN THAT BASTARD...
SOMETHING THAT CAN'T BE EXPLAINED LOGICALLY.
AND THE GIRL?
WE SAW HER SAFELY TO HER HOME.
YOU NEEDN'T WORRY ABOUT MONEY FOR NOW.
I'LL PUT IT ON MY CARD.
Heh Heh Heh...
Don't leave home without it.
FWIP
TSUZUKI?
WHUP

Times like these are the reason he saves money.

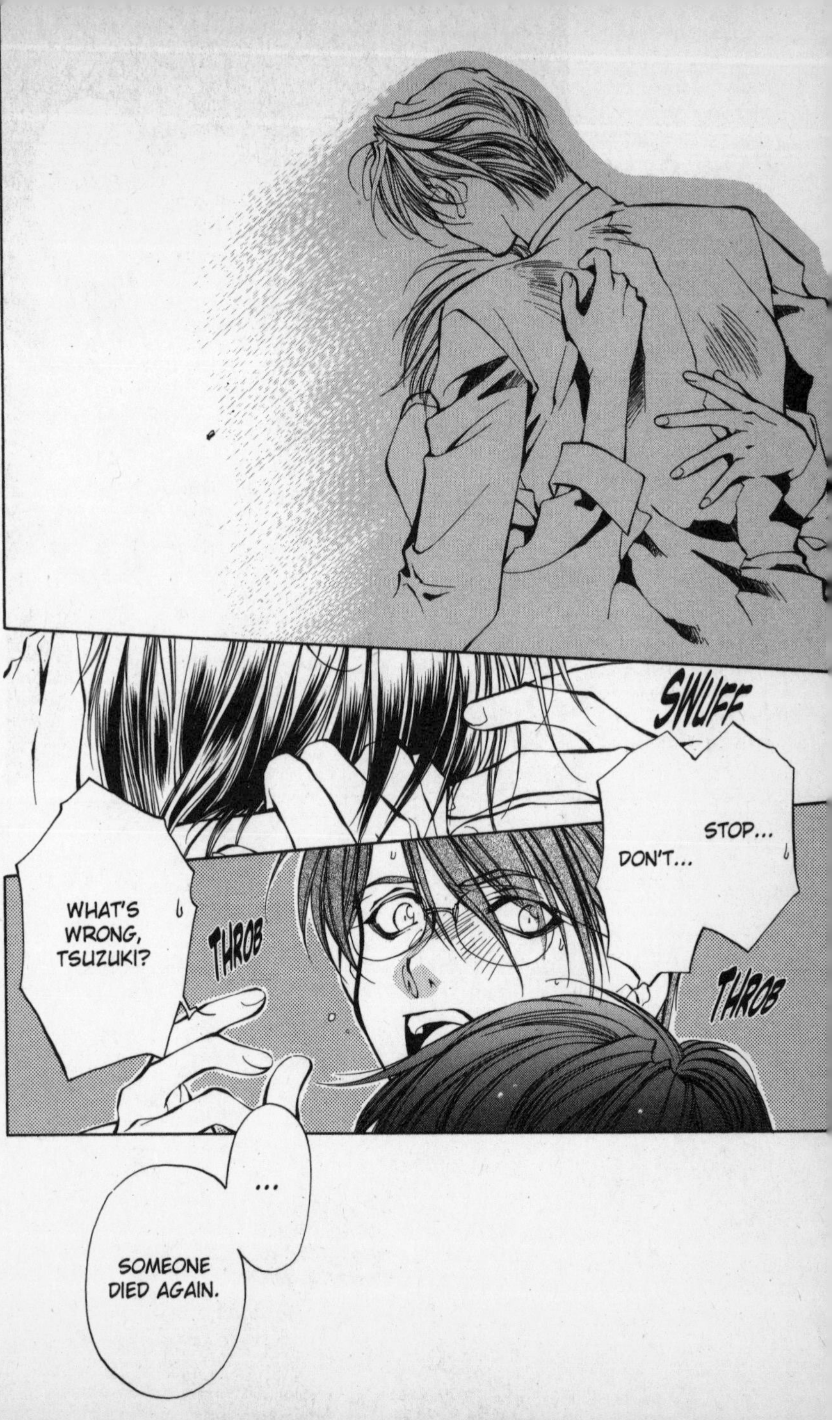
SWUFF
STOP...
DON'T...
THROB
THROB
WHAT'S WRONG, TSUZUKI?
...
SOMEONE DIED AGAIN.

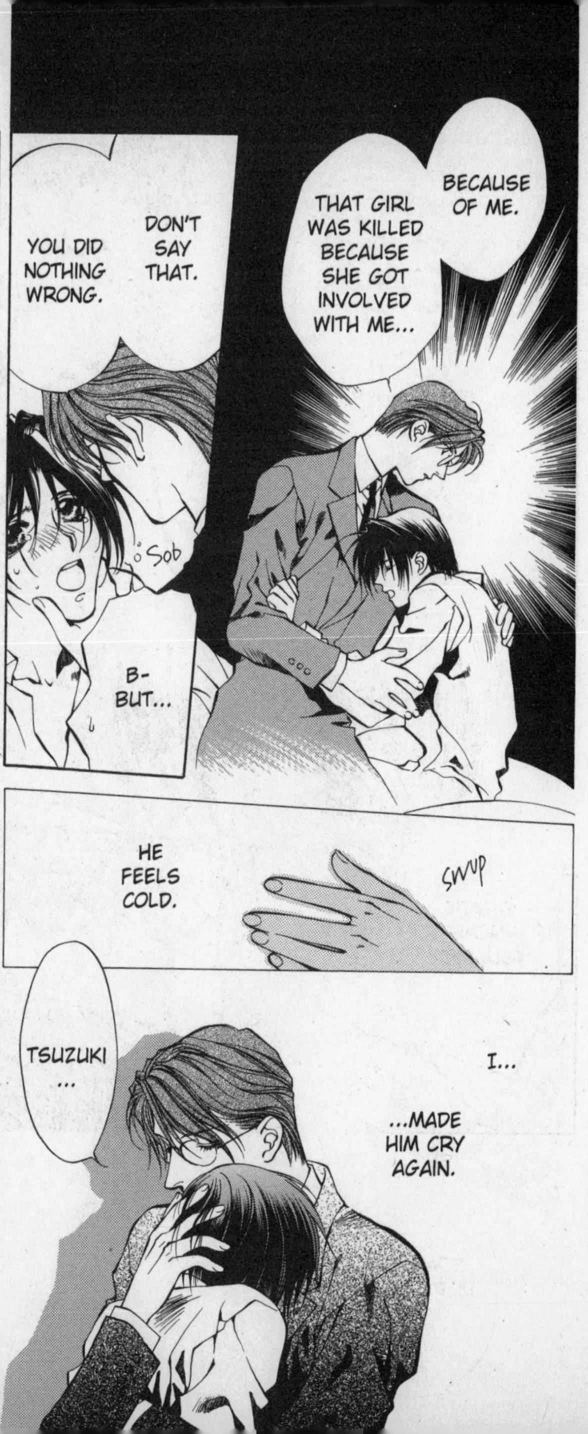
BECAUSE OF ME.
THAT GIRL WAS KILLED BECAUSE SHE GOT INVOLVED WITH ME...
DON'T SAY THAT.
YOU DID NOTHING WRONG.
Sob
B- BUT...
SWUP
HE FEELS COLD.
I...
...MADE HIM CRY AGAIN.
TSUZUKI ...

Green tea is good!

Well, the Tsujiri tea that's mentioned in this book comes from the Tsujiri teashop. At the end of book five I wrote something like, "By the way, at Gion Ujiri they have a tea called "Tatsumi of Kyoto." If you're ever in Kyoto, check it out!" Apparently the president of Tsujiri heard about that (Hee!) and sent me a gift package of teas! Thank you so much, Mr. President. My assistant and I really enjoyed the green tea cookies and tea.

I've been so busy with work I haven't had time to send a "thank you" note. I'm sorry. Next time I'm in Kyoto I'll definitely drop by. So listen everybody, if you go to Kyoto, make sure to go to Tsujiri in Gion and get some Tatsumi of Kyoto tea! (Ha!) But seriously, Tatsumi of Kyoto is really good. I've already used up all of mine, so next time I go I'll have to stock up.

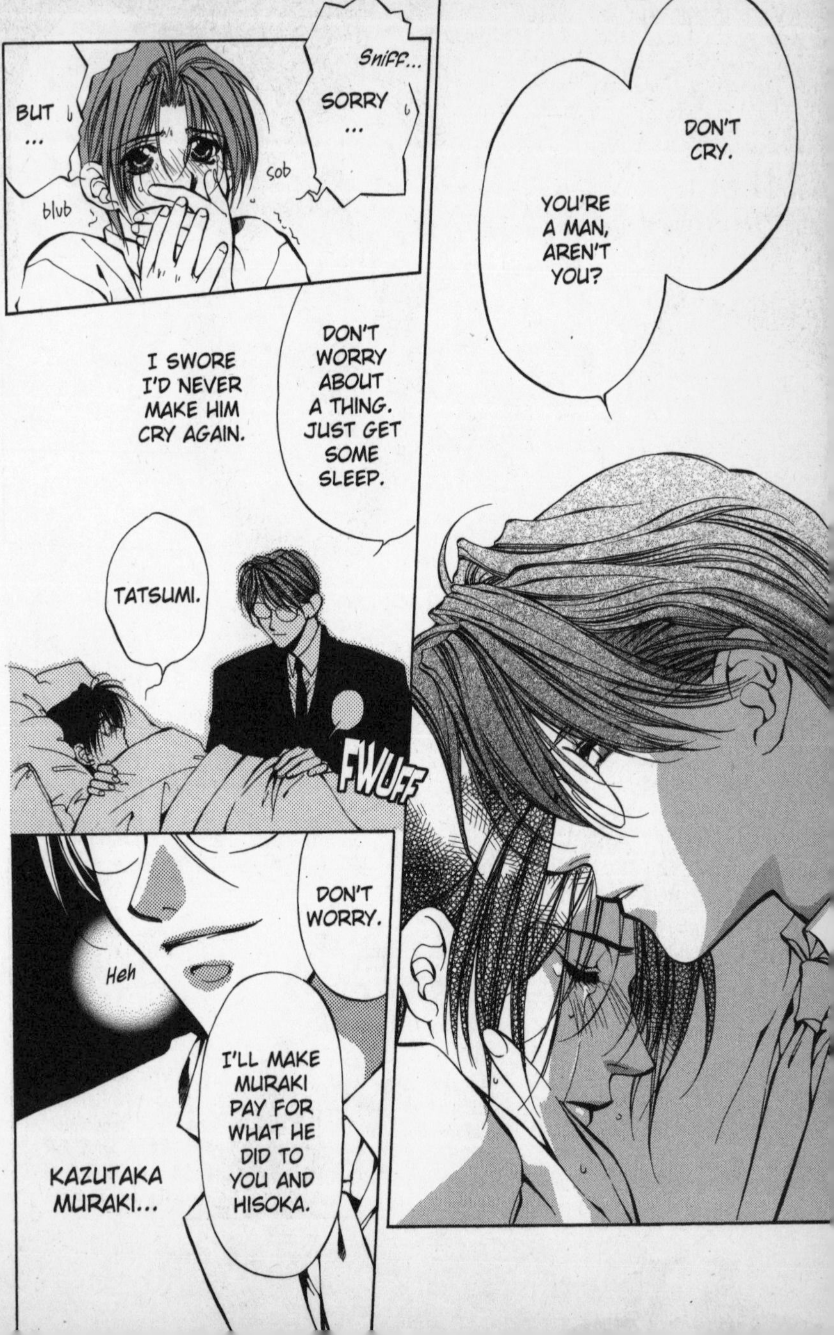
DON'T CRY.
YOU'RE A MAN, AREN'T YOU?
Sniff...
SORRY ...
BUT ...
sob
blub
DON'T WORRY ABOUT A THING. JUST GET SOME SLEEP.
I SWORE I'D NEVER MAKE HIM CRY AGAIN.
TATSUMI.
FWUFF
DON'T WORRY.
I'LL MAKE MURAKI PAY FOR WHAT HE DID TO YOU AND HISOKA.
Heh
KAZUTAKA MURAKI...

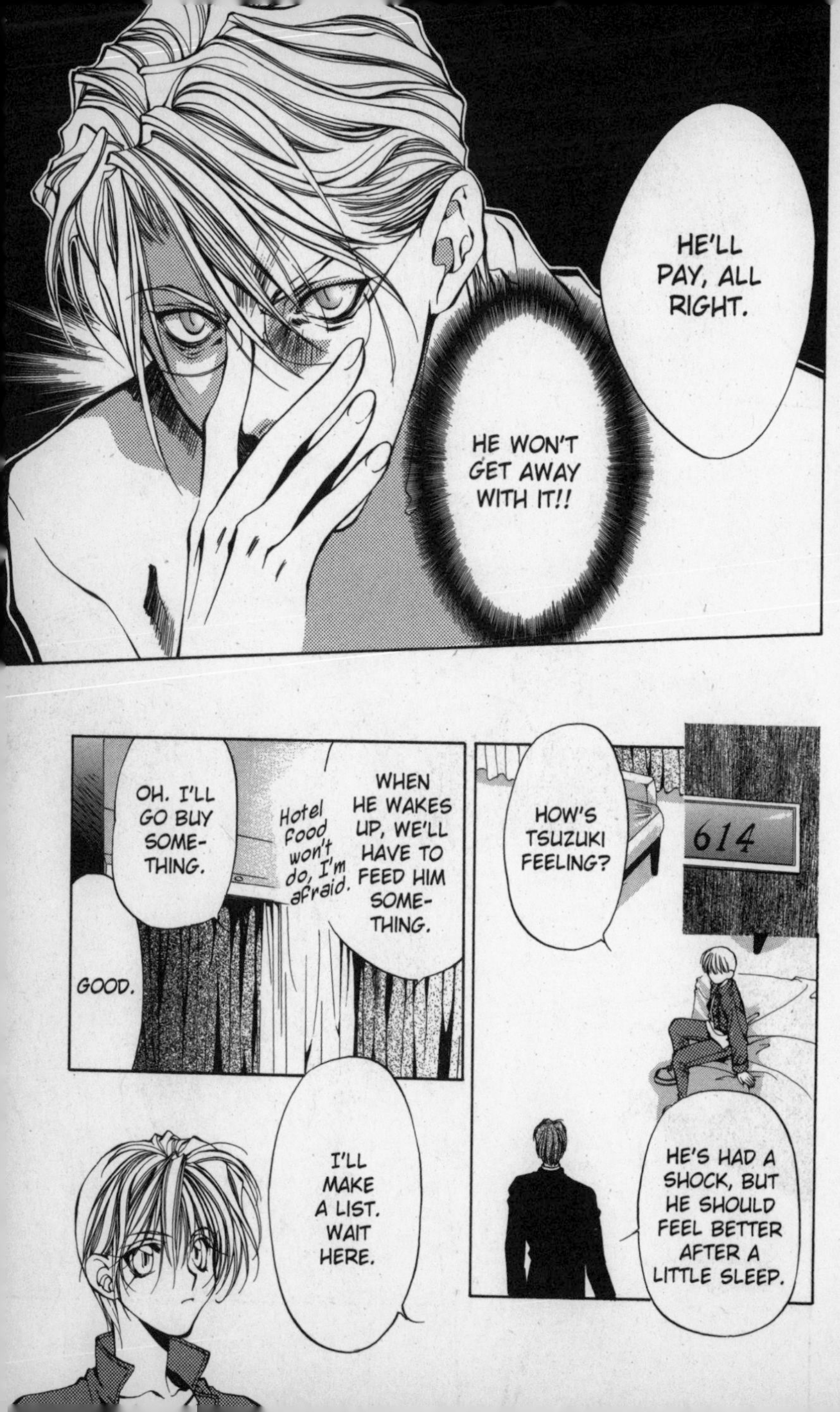
HE'LL PAY, ALL RIGHT.
HE WON'T GET AWAY WITH IT!!
HOW'S TSUZUKI FEELING?
614
HE'S HAD A SHOCK, BUT HE SHOULD FEEL BETTER AFTER A LITTLE SLEEP.
WHEN HE WAKES UP, WE'LL HAVE TO FEED HIM SOMETHING.
Hotel food won't do, I'm afraid.
OH. I'LL GO BUY SOMETHING.
GOOD.
I'LL MAKE A LIST. WAIT HERE.

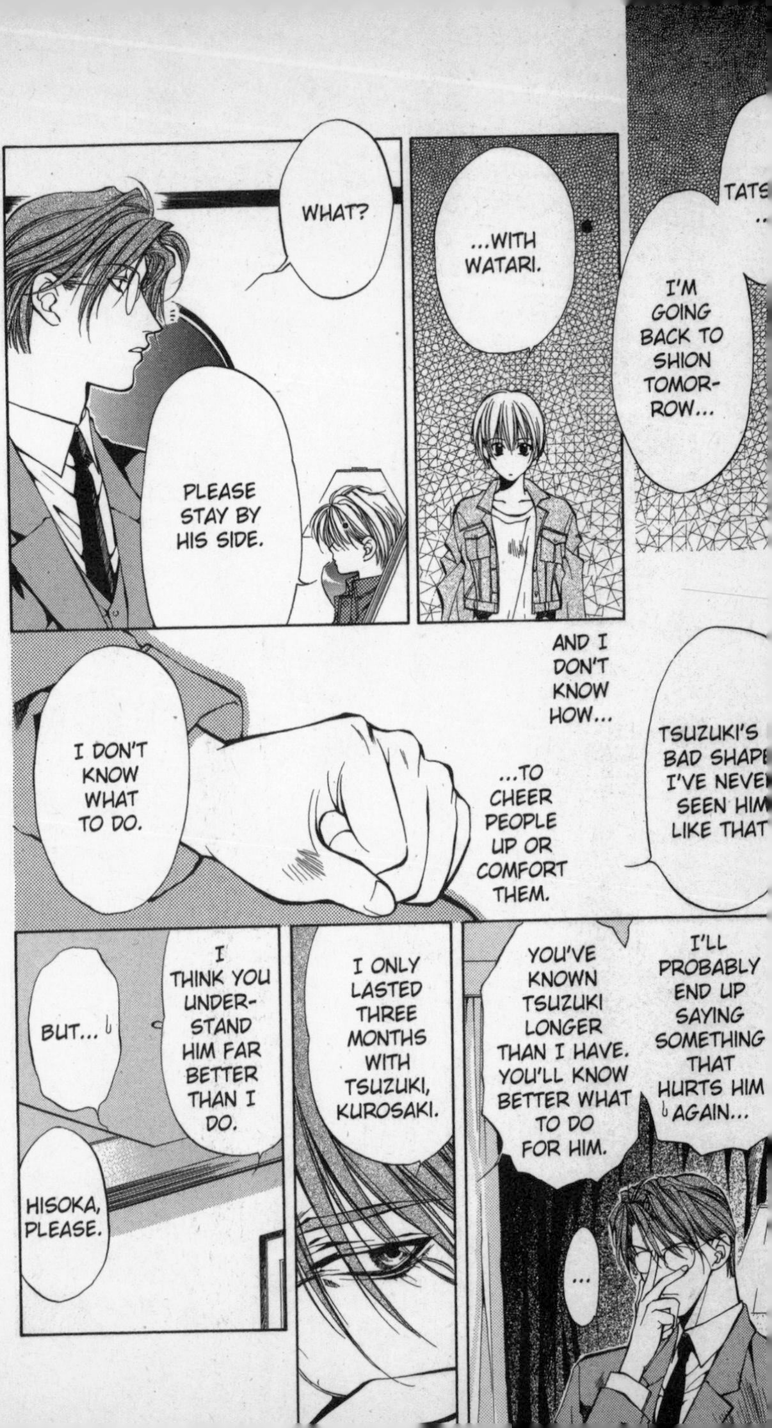
TATS
...
I'M GOING BACK TO SHION TOMORROW...
...WITH WATARI.
WHAT?
PLEASE STAY BY HIS SIDE.
TSUZUKI'S BAD SHAPE I'VE NEVE SEEN HIM LIKE THAT
AND I DON'T KNOW HOW...
...TO CHEER PEOPLE UP OR COMFORT THEM.
I DON'T KNOW WHAT TO DO.
I'LL PROBABLY END UP SAYING SOMETHING THAT HURTS HIM AGAIN...
YOU'VE KNOWN TSUZUKI LONGER THAN I HAVE. YOU'LL KNOW BETTER WHAT TO DO FOR HIM.
...
I ONLY LASTED THREE MONTHS WITH TSUZUKI, KUROSAKI.
I THINK YOU UNDER-STAND HIM FAR BETTER THAN I DO.
BUT...
HISOKA, PLEASE.

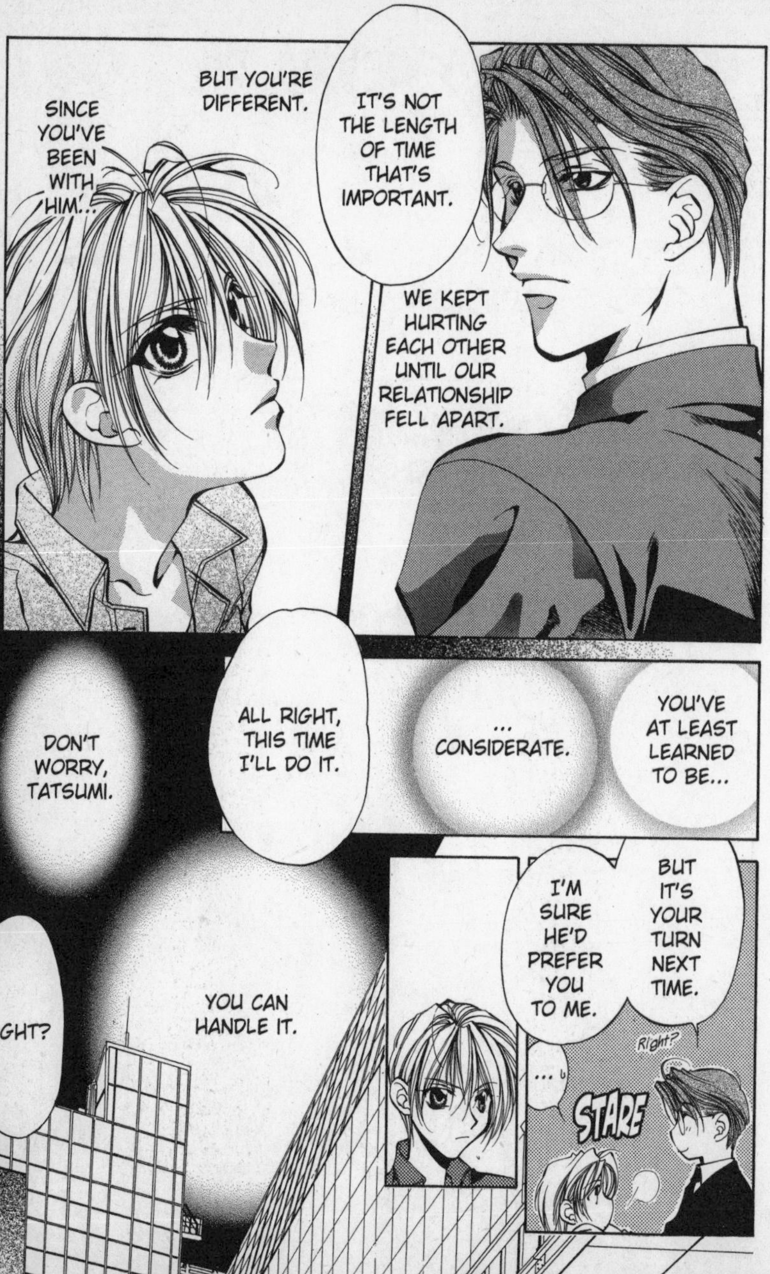
IT'S NOT THE LENGTH OF TIME THAT'S IMPORTANT.
WE KEPT HURTING EACH OTHER UNTIL OUR RELATIONSHIP FELL APART.
BUT YOU'RE DIFFERENT.
SINCE YOU'VE BEEN WITH HIM...
YOU'VE AT LEAST LEARNED TO BE...
... CONSIDERATE.
ALL RIGHT, THIS TIME I'LL DO IT.
DON'T WORRY, TATSUMI.
BUT IT'S YOUR TURN NEXT TIME.
I'M SURE HE'D PREFER YOU TO ME.
Right?
STARE
...
YOU CAN HANDLE IT.
RIGHT?

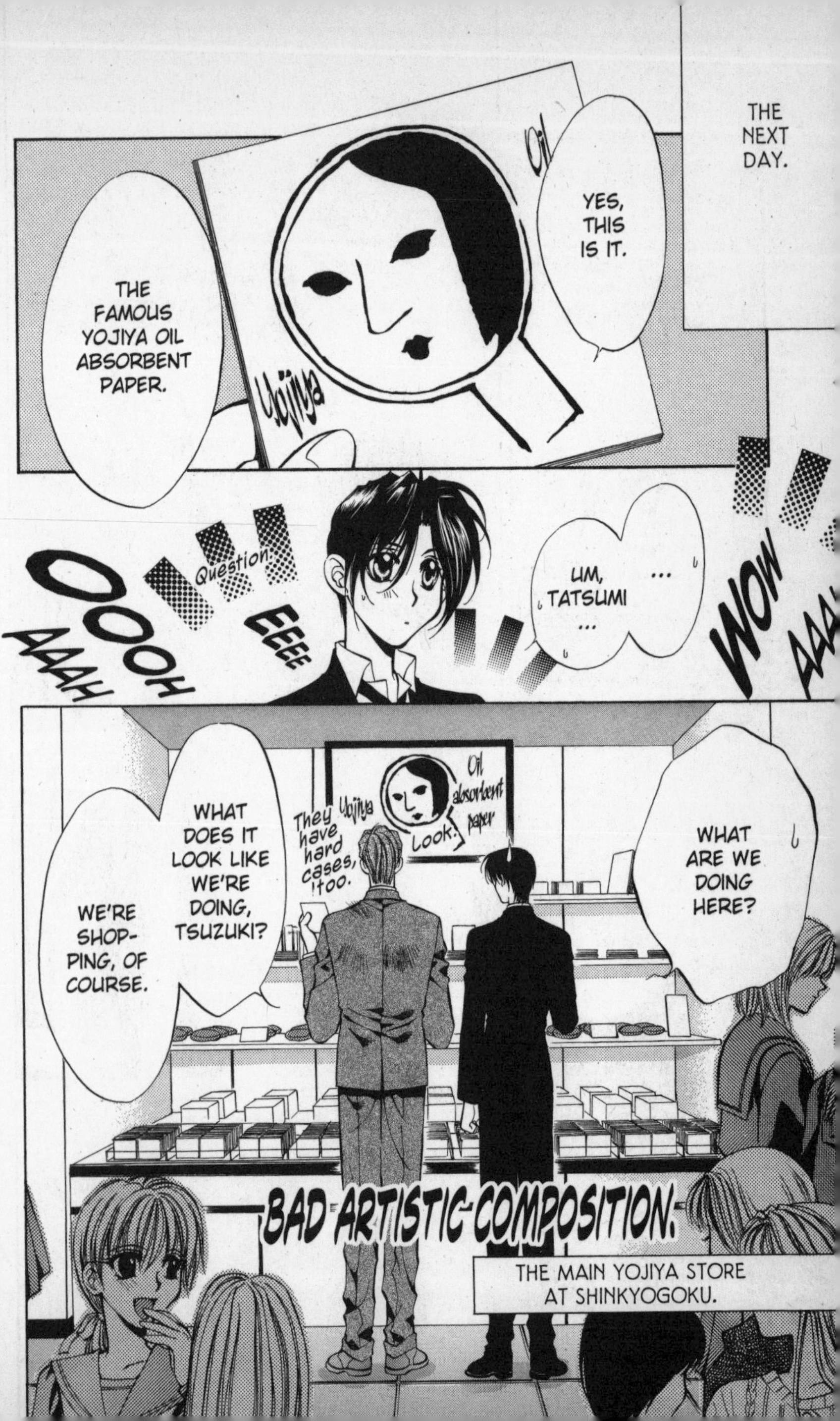
THE NEXT DAY.
Oil
Yojiya
YES, THIS IS IT.
THE FAMOUS YOJIYA OIL ABSORBENT PAPER.
WOW
UM, TATSUMI ...
...
Question.
EEEE
OOOH AAAH
WHAT ARE WE DOING HERE?
Oil absorbent paper
Yojiya
Look.
They have hard cases, too!
WHAT DOES IT LOOK LIKE WE'RE DOING, TSUZUKI?
WE'RE SHOP-PING, OF COURSE.
BAD ARTISTIC COMPOSITION.
THE MAIN YOJIYA STORE AT SHINKYOGOKU.

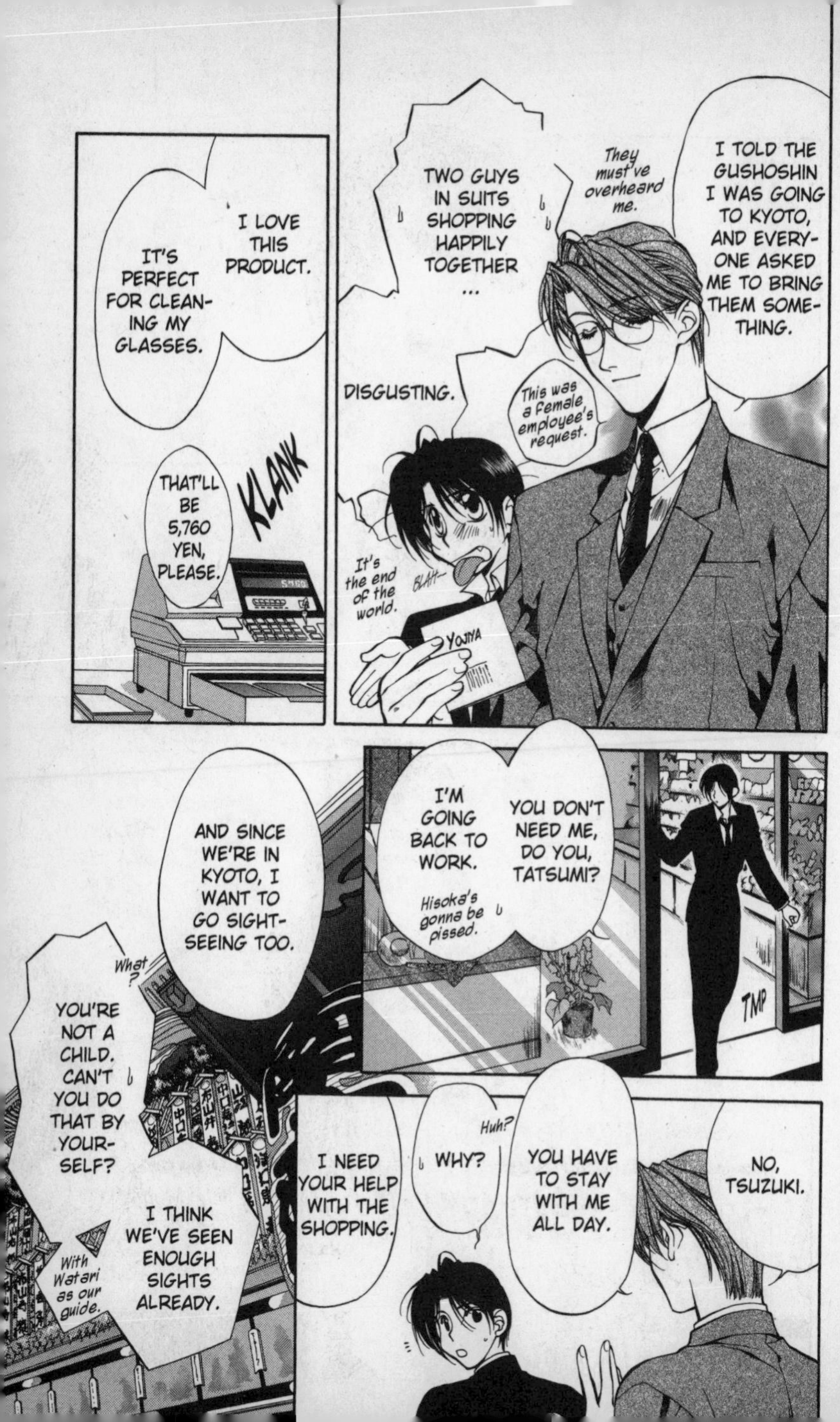
I TOLD THE GUSHOSHIN I WAS GOING TO KYOTO, AND EVERY-ONE ASKED ME TO BRING THEM SOME-THING.
They must've overheard me.
TWO GUYS IN SUITS SHOPPING HAPPILY TOGETHER ...
This was a female employee's request.
DISGUSTING.
BLAH—
It's the end of the world.
YOJIYA
I LOVE THIS PRODUCT.
IT'S PERFECT FOR CLEAN-ING MY GLASSES.
KLANK
THAT'LL BE 5,760 YEN, PLEASE.
YOU DON'T NEED ME, DO YOU, TATSUMI?
I'M GOING BACK TO WORK.
Hisoka's gonna be pissed.
TMP
NO, TSUZUKI.
YOU HAVE TO STAY WITH ME ALL DAY.
Huh?
WHY?
I NEED YOUR HELP WITH THE SHOPPING.
AND SINCE WE'RE IN KYOTO, I WANT TO GO SIGHT-SEEING TOO.
What?
YOU'RE NOT A CHILD. CAN'T YOU DO THAT BY YOUR-SELF?
I THINK WE'VE SEEN ENOUGH SIGHTS ALREADY.
With Watari as our guide.

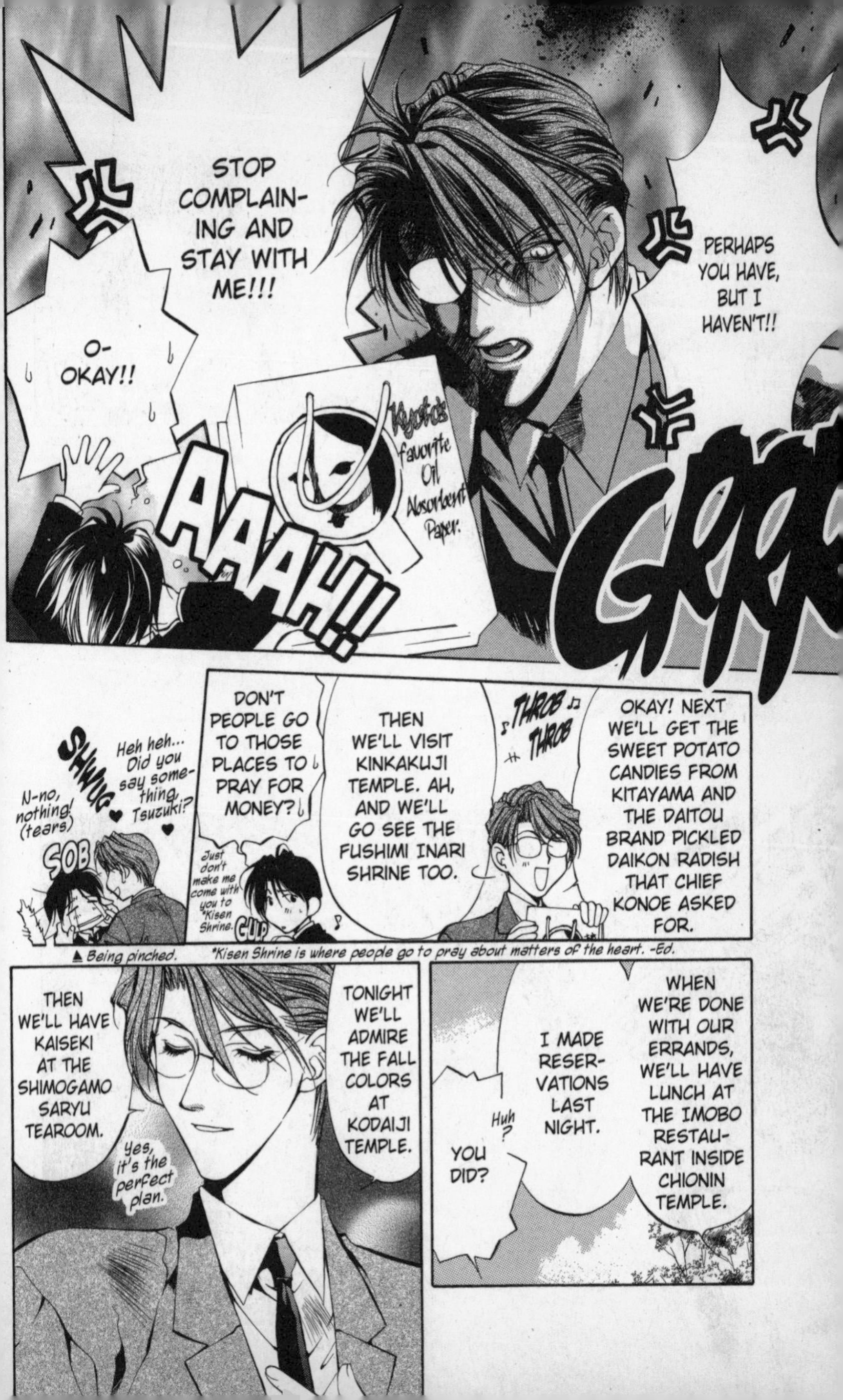
PERHAPS YOU HAVE, BUT I HAVEN'T!!
GRRR
Kyoto's favorite Oil Absorbent Paper.
STOP COMPLAIN-ING AND STAY WITH ME!!!
AAAH!!!
O-OKAY!!
OKAY! NEXT WE'LL GET THE SWEET POTATO CANDIES FROM KITAYAMA AND THE DAITOU BRAND PICKLED DAIKON RADISH THAT CHIEF KONOE ASKED FOR.
THROB THROB
THEN WE'LL VISIT KINKAKUJI TEMPLE. AH, AND WE'LL GO SEE THE FUSHIMI INARI SHRINE TOO.
DON'T PEOPLE GO TO THOSE PLACES TO PRAY FOR MONEY?
Just don't make me come with you to *Kisen Shrine.
GULP
Heh heh... Did you say some-thing, Tsuzuki?
SHWUG
N-no, nothing! (tears)
SOB
▲ Being pinched.
*Kisen Shrine is where people go to pray about matters of the heart. -Ed.
WHEN WE'RE DONE WITH OUR ERRANDS, WE'LL HAVE LUNCH AT THE IMOBO RESTAU-RANT INSIDE CHIONIN TEMPLE.
I MADE RESER-VATIONS LAST NIGHT.
Huh?
YOU DID?
TONIGHT WE'LL ADMIRE THE FALL COLORS AT KODAIJI TEMPLE.
THEN WE'LL HAVE KAISEKI AT THE SHIMOGAMO SARYU TEAROOM.
Yes, it's the perfect plan.

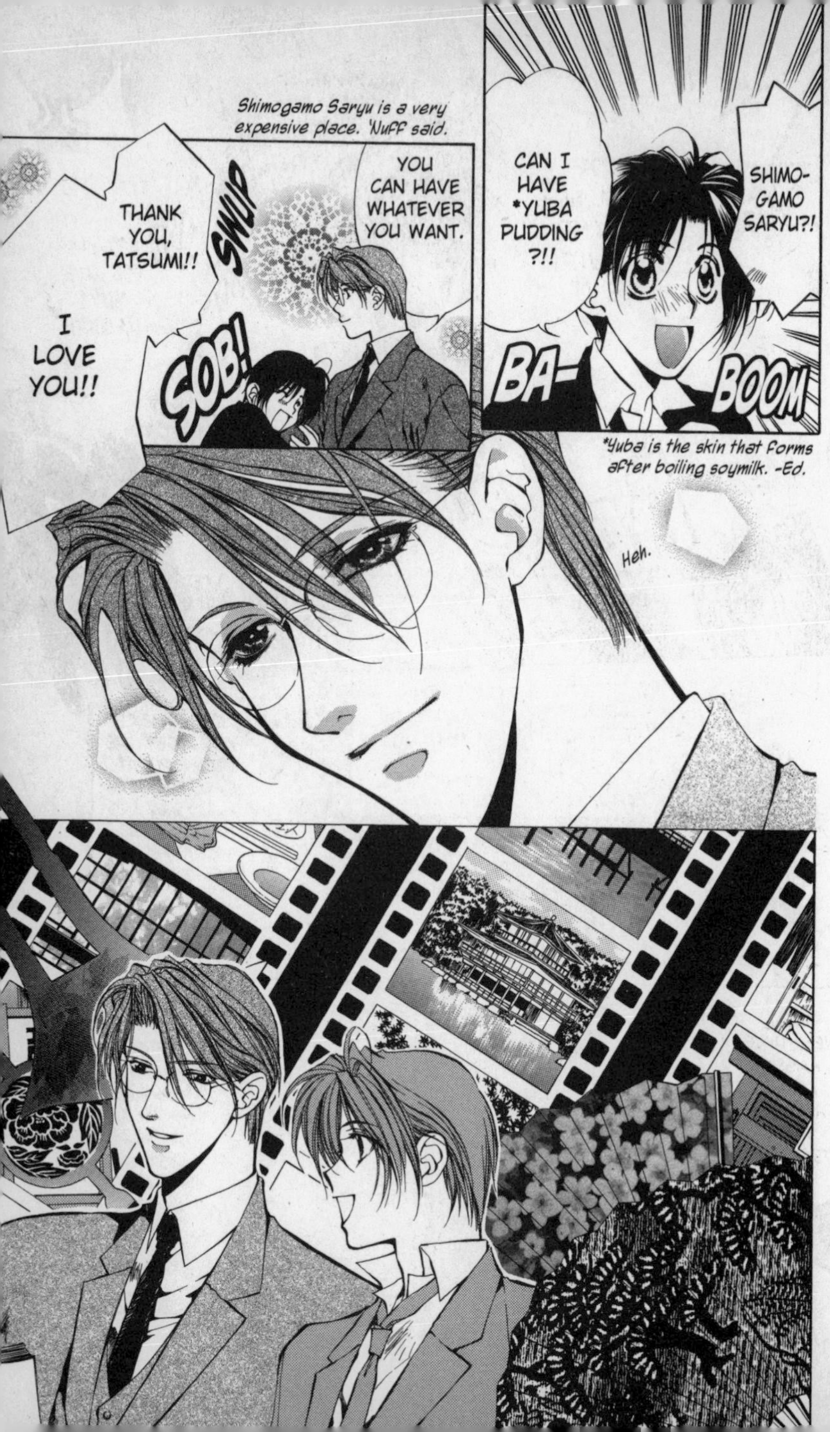
SHIMO-GAMO SARYU?!
CAN I HAVE *YUBA PUDDING ?!!
BA-
BOOM
*Yuba is the skin that forms after boiling soymilk. -Ed.
Shimogamo Saryu is a very expensive place. 'Nuff said.
YOU CAN HAVE WHATEVER YOU WANT.
SWUP
THANK YOU, TATSUMI!!
SOB!
I LOVE YOU!!
Heh.

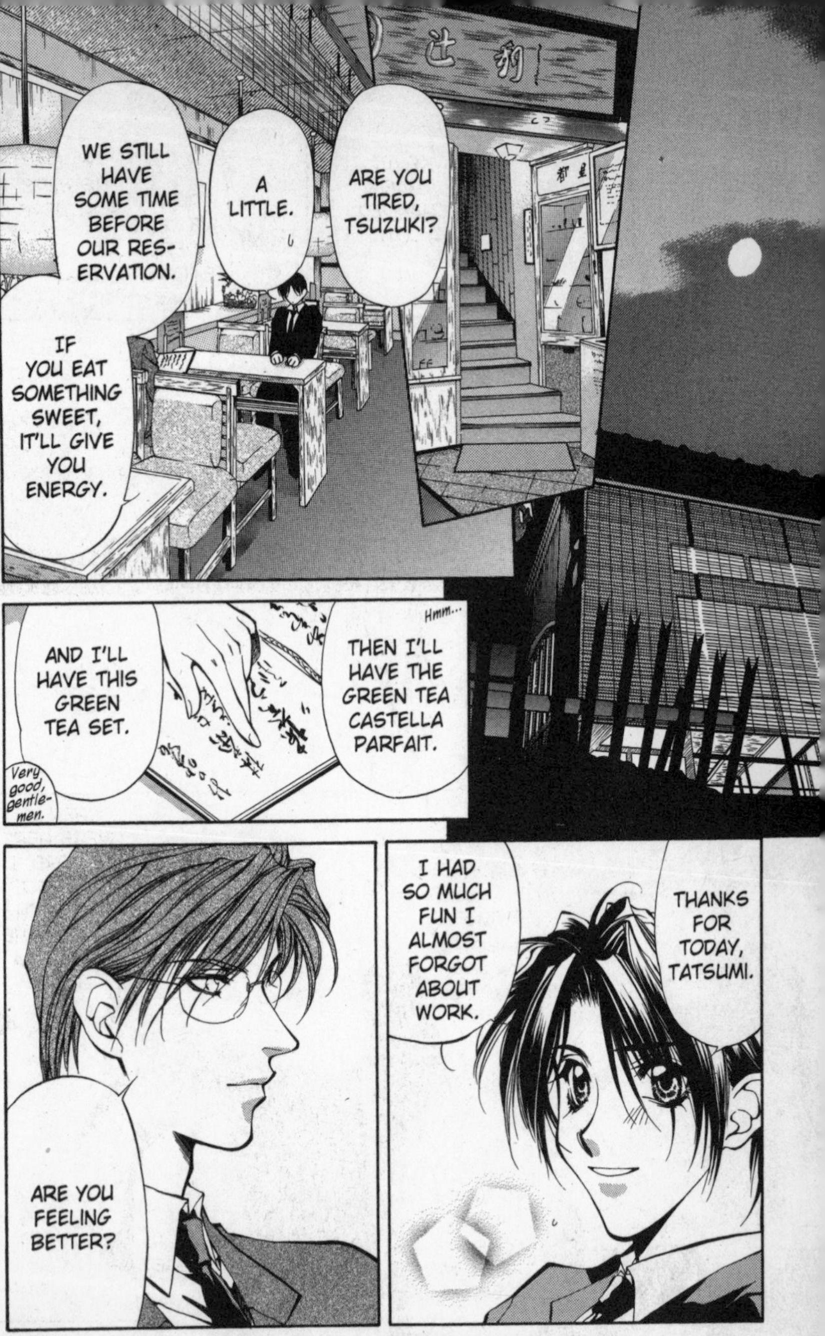
ARE YOU TIRED, TSUZUKI?
A LITTLE.
WE STILL HAVE SOME TIME BEFORE OUR RES-ERVATION.
IF YOU EAT SOMETHING SWEET, IT'LL GIVE YOU ENERGY.
Hmm...
THEN I'LL HAVE THE GREEN TEA CASTELLA PARFAIT.
AND I'LL HAVE THIS GREEN TEA SET.
Very good, gentle-men.
THANKS FOR TODAY, TATSUMI.
I HAD SO MUCH FUN I ALMOST FORGOT ABOUT WORK.
ARE YOU FEELING BETTER?

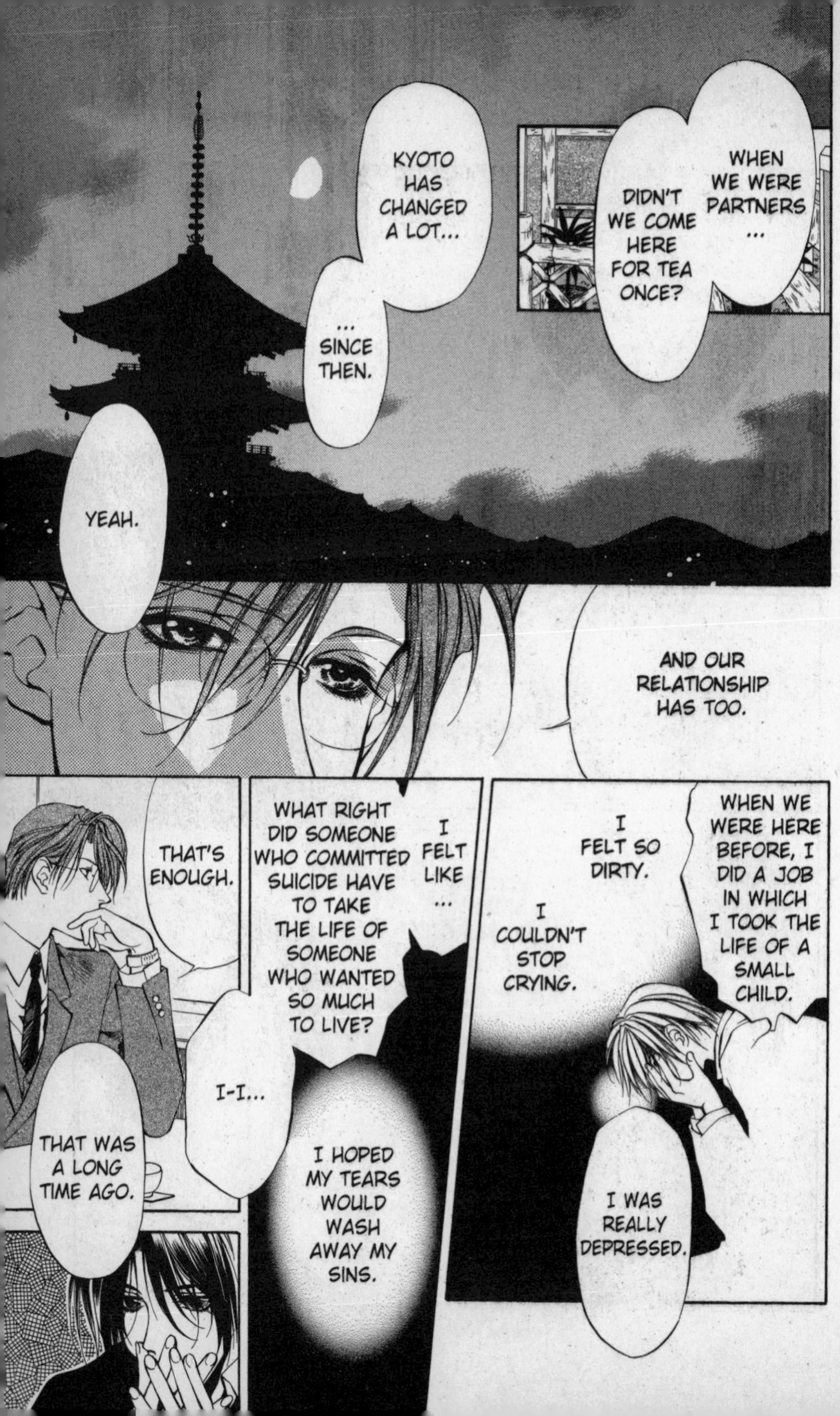
WHEN WE WERE PARTNERS...
DIDN'T WE COME HERE FOR TEA ONCE?
KYOTO HAS CHANGED A LOT...
...SINCE THEN.
YEAH.
AND OUR RELATIONSHIP HAS TOO.
WHEN WE WERE HERE BEFORE, I DID A JOB IN WHICH I TOOK THE LIFE OF A SMALL CHILD.
I FELT SO DIRTY.
I COULDN'T STOP CRYING.
I WAS REALLY DEPRESSED.
I FELT LIKE...
WHAT RIGHT DID SOMEONE WHO COMMITTED SUICIDE HAVE TO TAKE THE LIFE OF SOMEONE WHO WANTED SO MUCH TO LIVE?
I HOPED MY TEARS WOULD WASH AWAY MY SINS.
THAT'S ENOUGH.
I-I...
THAT WAS A LONG TIME AGO.

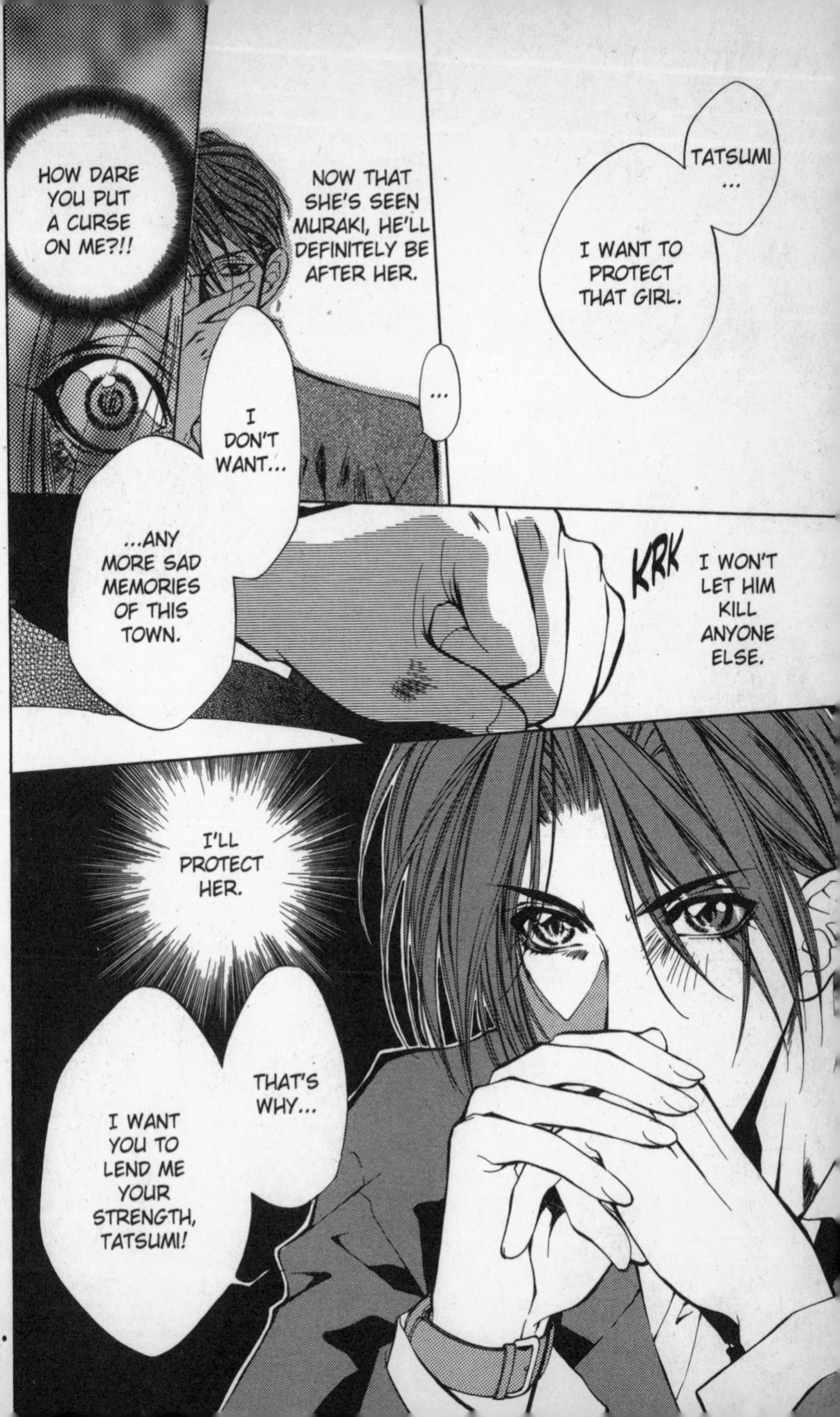
TATSUMI ...
I WANT TO PROTECT THAT GIRL.
NOW THAT SHE'S SEEN MURAKI, HE'LL DEFINITELY BE AFTER HER.
...
HOW DARE YOU PUT A CURSE ON ME?!!
I DON'T WANT...
KRK
I WON'T LET HIM KILL ANYONE ELSE.
...ANY MORE SAD MEMORIES OF THIS TOWN.
I'LL PROTECT HER.
THAT'S WHY...
I WANT YOU TO LEND ME YOUR STRENGTH, TATSUMI!

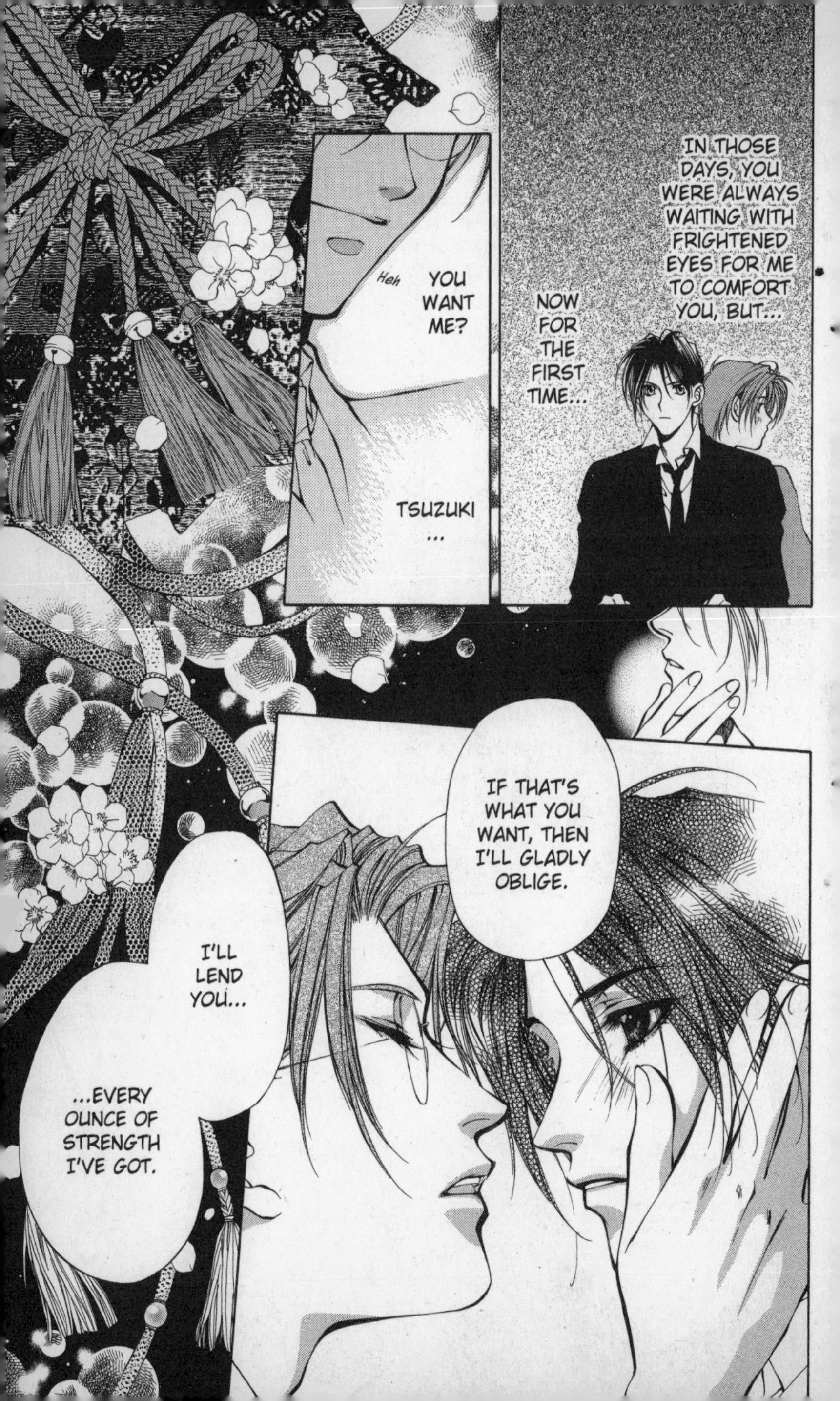

IN THOSE DAYS, YOU WERE ALWAYS WAITING WITH FRIGHTENED EYES FOR ME TO COMFORT YOU, BUT...
NOW FOR THE FIRST TIME...
YOU WANT ME?
Heh
TSUZUKI...
IF THAT'S WHAT YOU WANT, THEN I'LL GLADLY OBLIGE.
I'LL LEND YOU...
...EVERY OUNCE OF STRENGTH I'VE GOT.

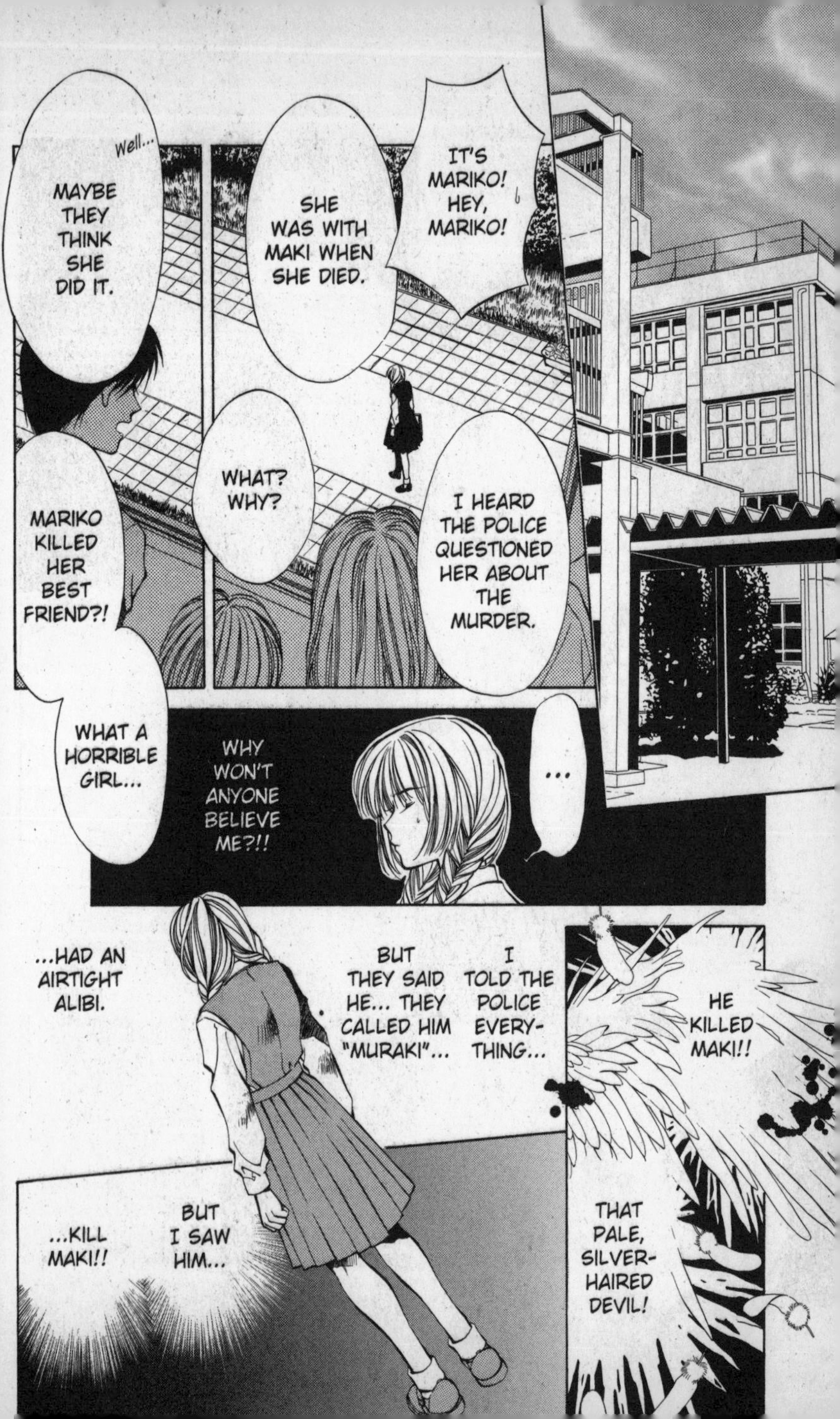
IT'S MARIKO! HEY, MARIKO!
SHE WAS WITH MAKI WHEN SHE DIED.
I HEARD THE POLICE QUESTIONED HER ABOUT THE MURDER.
WHAT? WHY?
Well...
MAYBE THEY THINK SHE DID IT.
MARIKO KILLED HER BEST FRIEND?!
WHAT A HORRIBLE GIRL...
...
WHY WON'T ANYONE BELIEVE ME?!!
HE KILLED MAKI!!
THAT PALE, SILVER-HAIRED DEVIL!
I TOLD THE POLICE EVERY-THING...
BUT THEY SAID HE... THEY CALLED HIM "MURAKI"...
...HAD AN AIRTIGHT ALIBI.
BUT I SAW HIM...
...KILL MAKI!!

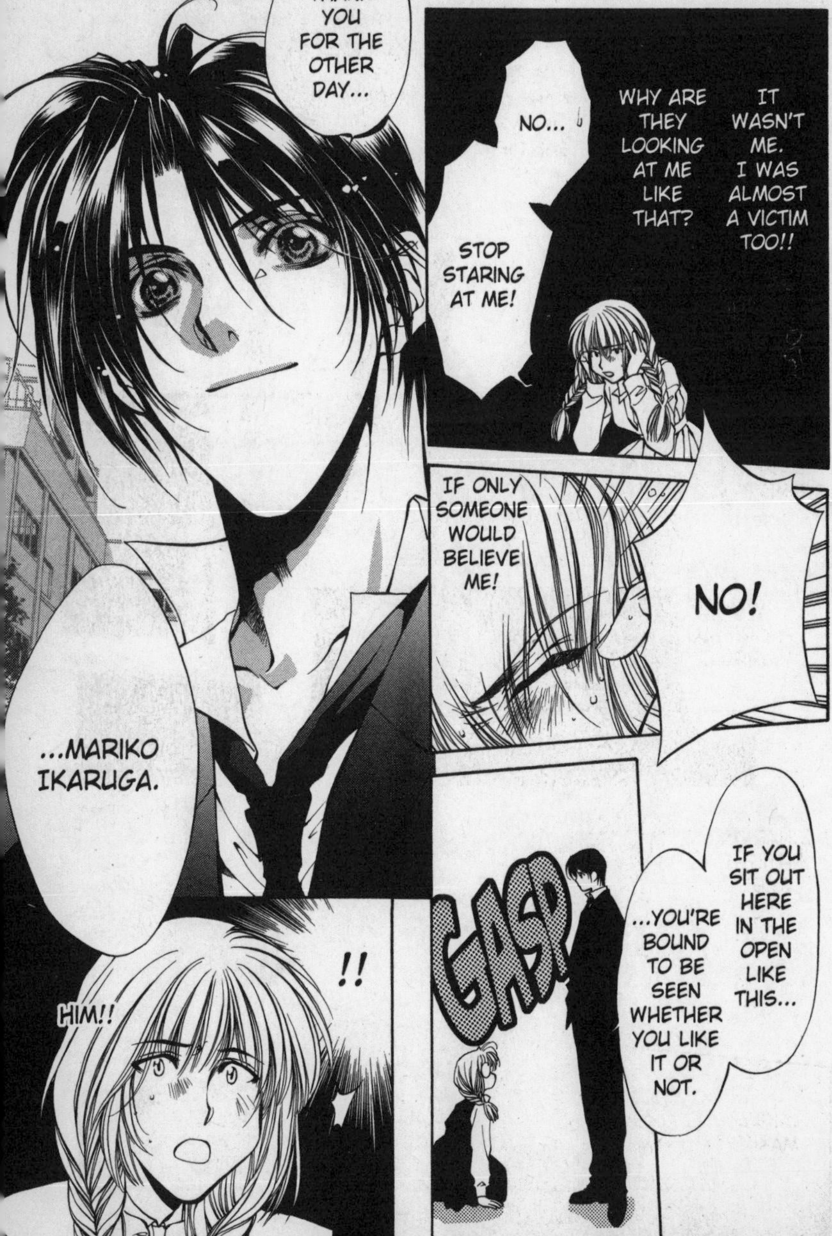
IT WASN'T ME. I WAS ALMOST A VICTIM TOO!!
WHY ARE THEY LOOKING AT ME LIKE THAT?
NO...
STOP STARING AT ME!
NO!
IF ONLY SOMEONE WOULD BELIEVE ME!
IF YOU SIT OUT HERE IN THE OPEN LIKE THIS...
...YOU'RE BOUND TO BE SEEN WHETHER YOU LIKE IT OR NOT.
GASP
THANK YOU FOR THE OTHER DAY...
...MARIKO IKARUGA.
!!
HIM!!

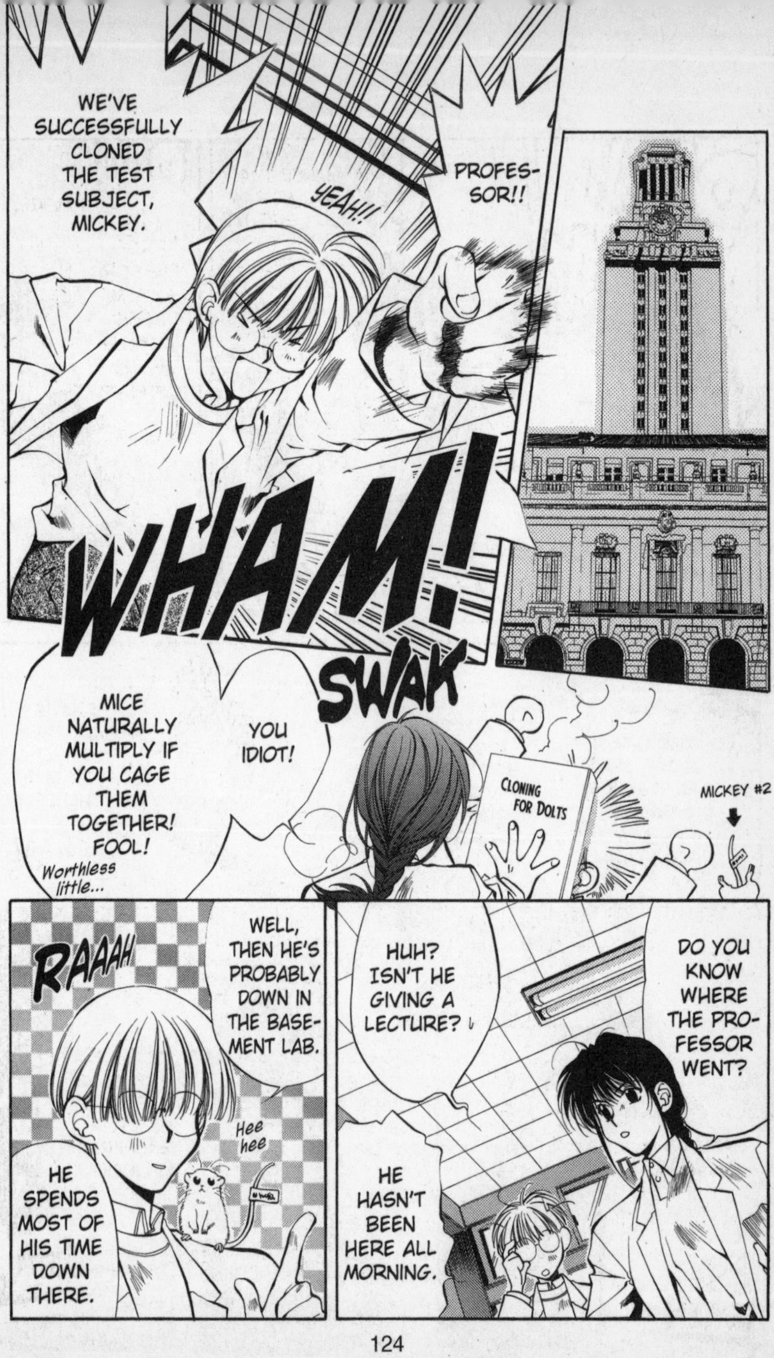
PROFES-SOR!!
YEAH!!
WE'VE SUCCESSFULLY CLONED THE TEST SUBJECT, MICKEY.
WHAM!
SWAK
YOU IDIOT!
MICE NATURALLY MULTIPLY IF YOU CAGE THEM TOGETHER! FOOL!
Worthless little...
CLONING FOR DOLTS
MICKEY #2
DO YOU KNOW WHERE THE PRO-FESSOR WENT?
HUH? ISN'T HE GIVING A LECTURE?
HE HASN'T BEEN HERE ALL MORNING.
WELL, THEN HE'S PROBABLY DOWN IN THE BASE-MENT LAB.
RAAAH
Hee hee
HE SPENDS MOST OF HIS TIME DOWN THERE.

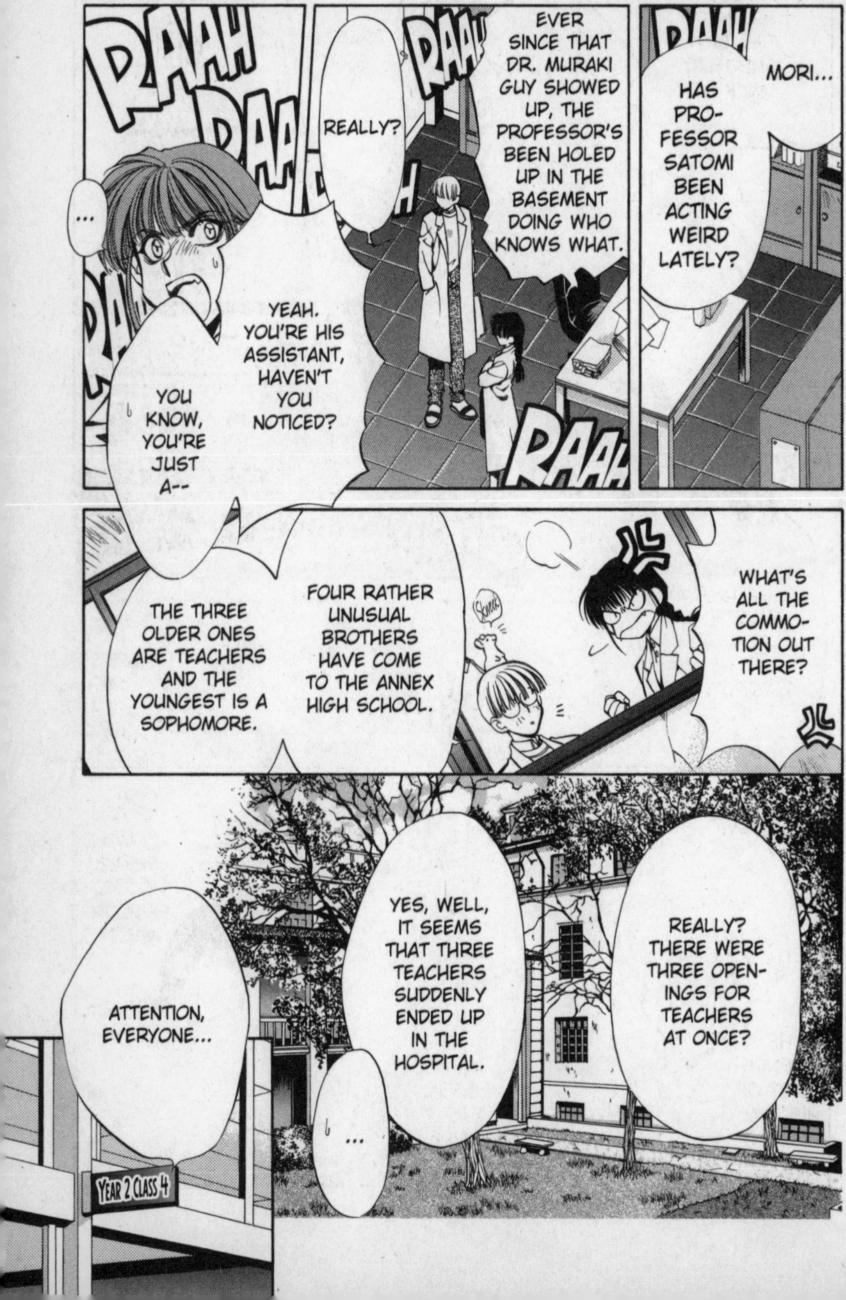
MORI...
HAS PROFESSOR SATOMI BEEN ACTING WEIRD LATELY?
RAAH
EVER SINCE THAT DR. MURAKI GUY SHOWED UP, THE PROFESSOR'S BEEN HOLED UP IN THE BASEMENT DOING WHO KNOWS WHAT.
RAAH
REALLY?
YEAH. YOU'RE HIS ASSISTANT, HAVEN'T YOU NOTICED?
RAAH
RAAH
RAAH
...
YOU KNOW, YOU'RE JUST A--
WHAT'S ALL THE COMMOTION OUT THERE?
FOUR RATHER UNUSUAL BROTHERS HAVE COME TO THE ANNEX HIGH SCHOOL.
THE THREE OLDER ONES ARE TEACHERS AND THE YOUNGEST IS A SOPHOMORE.
REALLY? THERE WERE THREE OPENINGS FOR TEACHERS AT ONCE?
YES, WELL, IT SEEMS THAT THREE TEACHERS SUDDENLY ENDED UP IN THE HOSPITAL.
...
ATTENTION, EVERYONE...
YEAR 2 CLASS 4

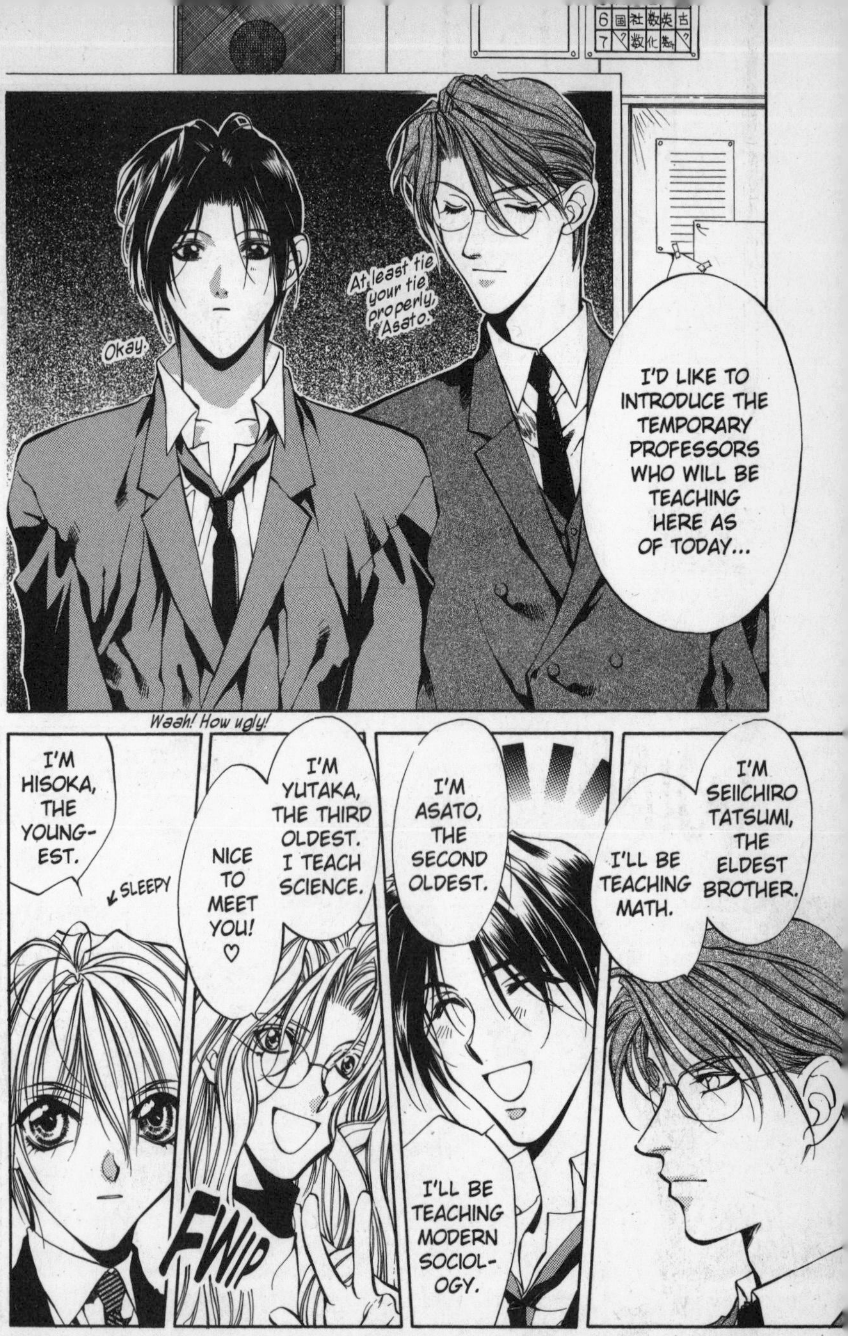
I'D LIKE TO INTRODUCE THE TEMPORARY PROFESSORS WHO WILL BE TEACHING HERE AS OF TODAY...
At least tie your tie properly, Asato.
Okay.
Waah! How ugly!
I'M SEIICHIRO TATSUMI, THE ELDEST BROTHER.
I'LL BE TEACHING MATH.
I'M ASATO, THE SECOND OLDEST.
I'LL BE TEACHING MODERN SOCIOLOGY.
I'M YUTAKA, THE THIRD OLDEST. I TEACH SCIENCE.
NICE TO MEET YOU! ♡
FWIP
I'M HISOKA, THE YOUNGEST.
SLEEPY

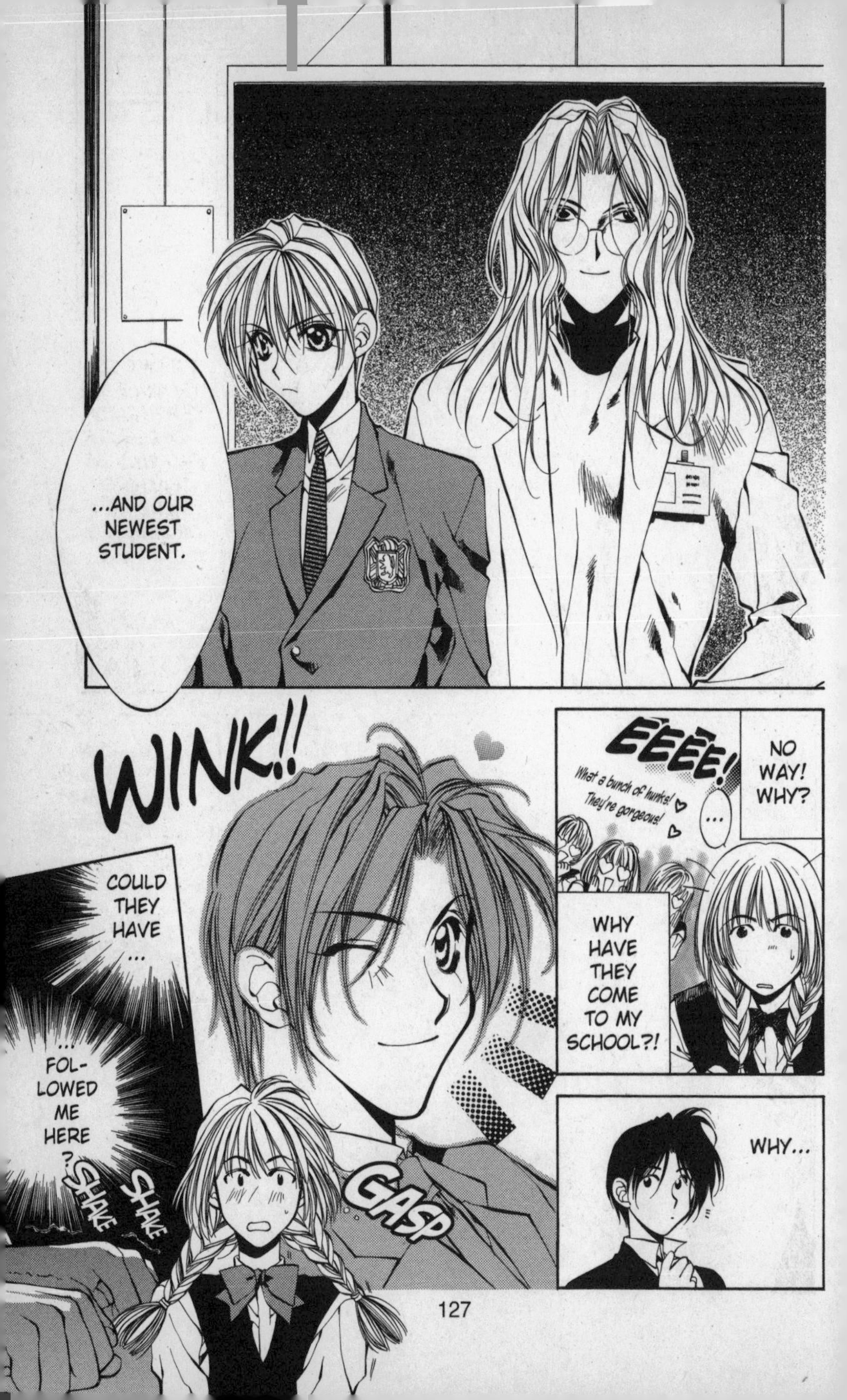
...AND OUR NEWEST STUDENT.
NO WAY! WHY?
EEEE!
What a bunch of hunks! They're gorgeous!
...
WHY HAVE THEY COME TO MY SCHOOL?!
WHY...
WINK!!
COULD THEY HAVE ...
... FOL-LOWED ME HERE?
SHAKE SHAKE
GASP

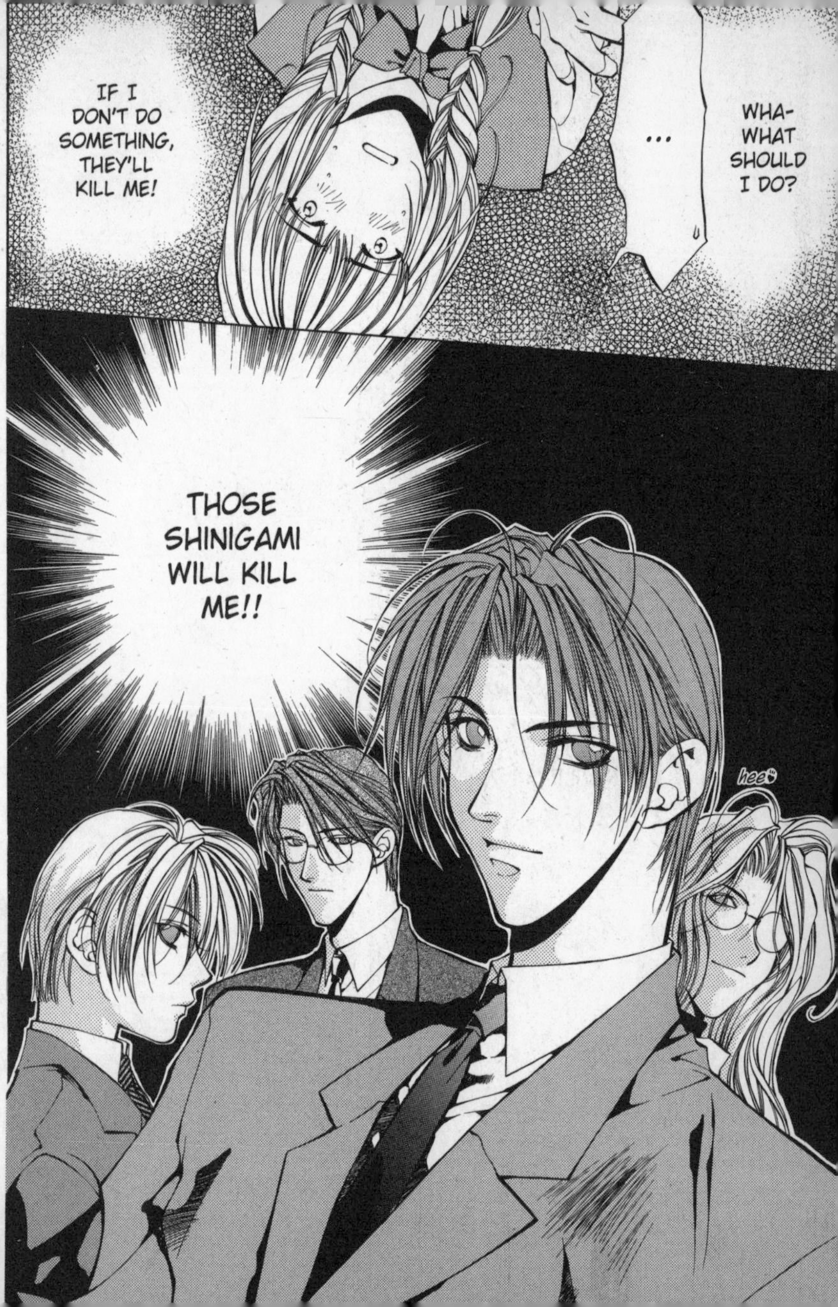
WHA- WHAT SHOULD I DO?
...
IF I DON'T DO SOMETHING, THEY'LL KILL ME!
hee
THOSE SHINIGAMI WILL KILL ME!!

CHAPTER 22

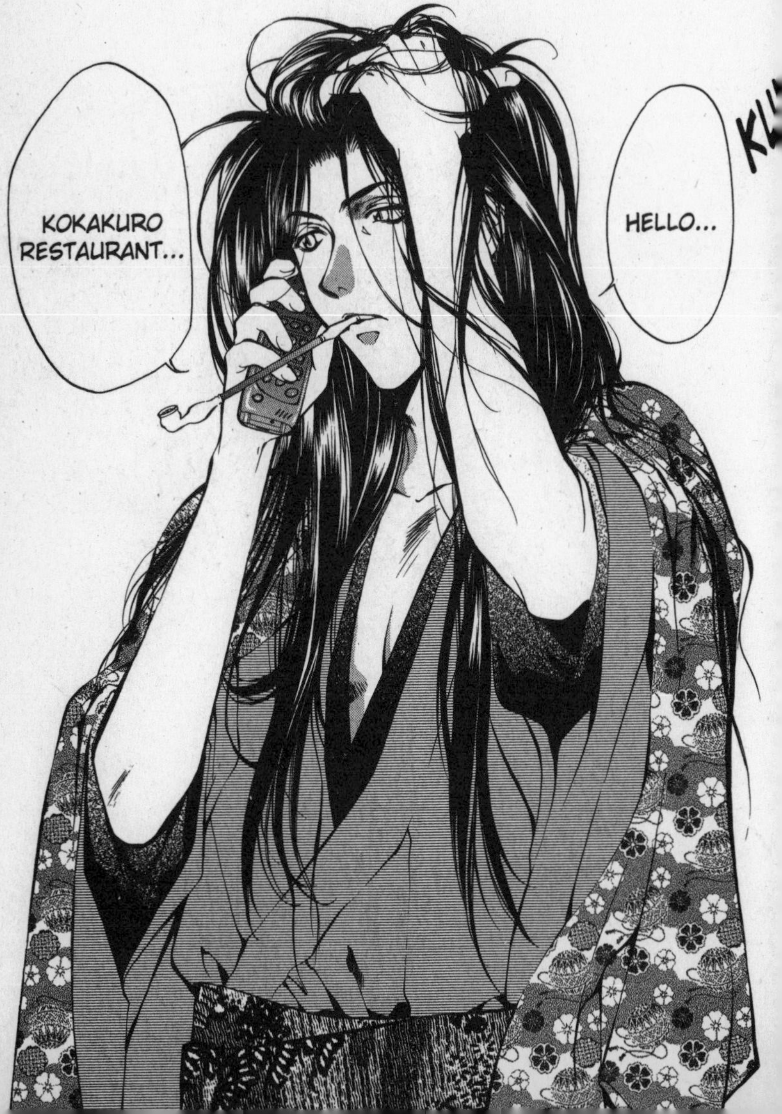
HELLO...
KOKAKURO RESTAURANT...

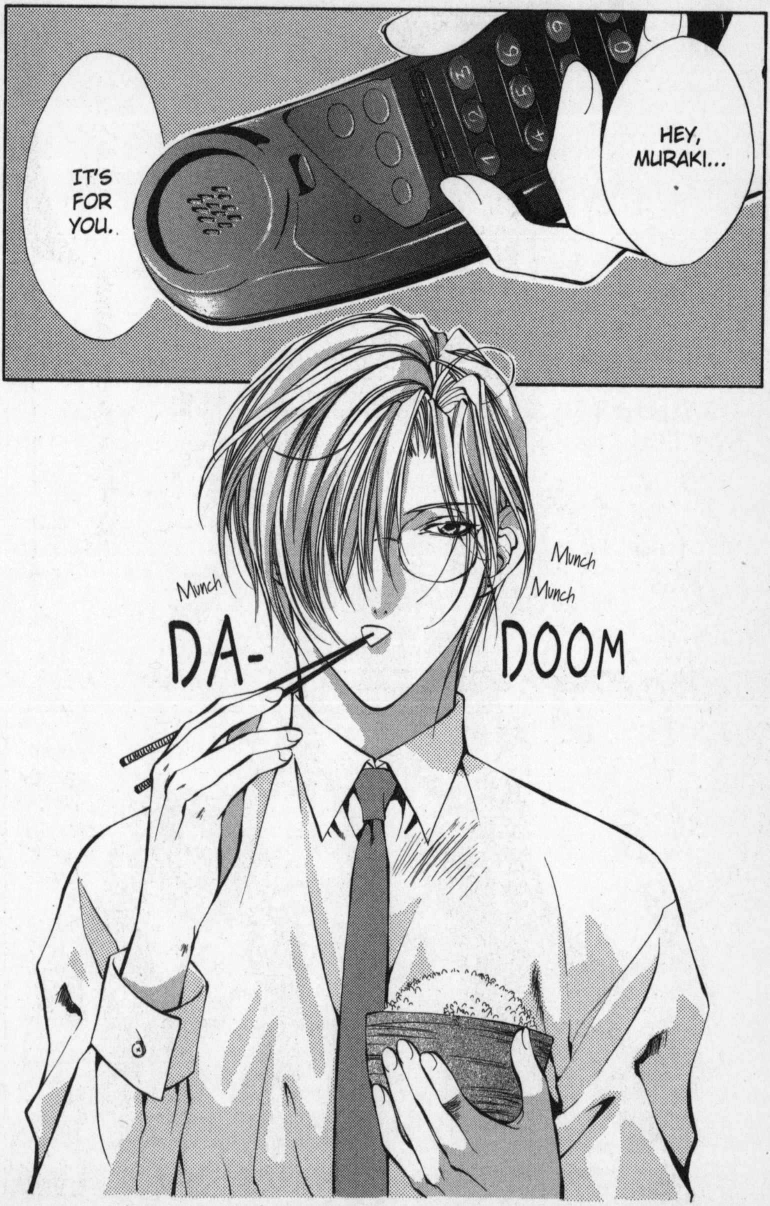
HEY, MURAKI...
IT'S FOR YOU.
Munch
Munch
Munch
DA-DOOM

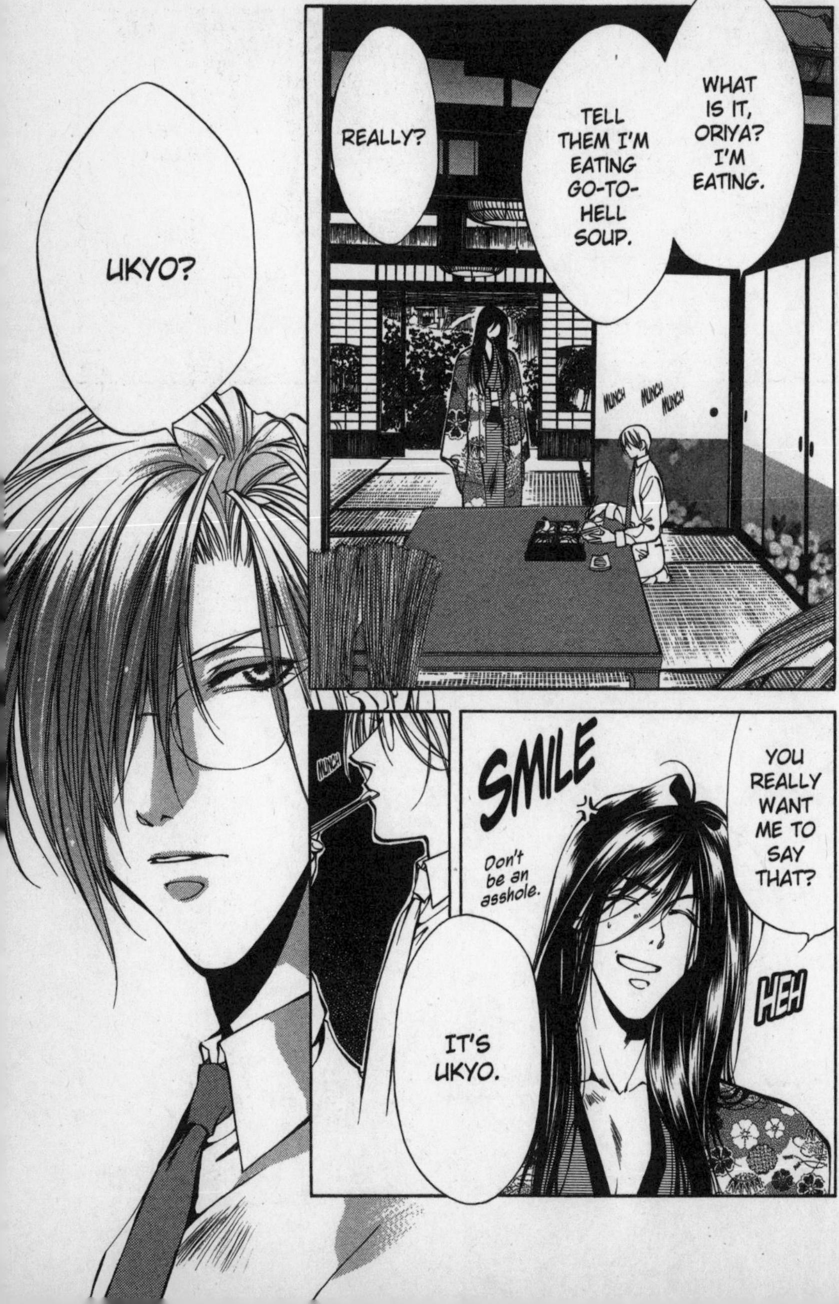
WHAT IS IT, ORIYA? I'M EATING.
TELL THEM I'M EATING GO-TO-HELL SOUP.
REALLY?
MUNCH MUNCH MUNCH
YOU REALLY WANT ME TO SAY THAT?
SMILE
Don't be an asshole.
HEH
IT'S UKYO.
MUNCH
UKYO?

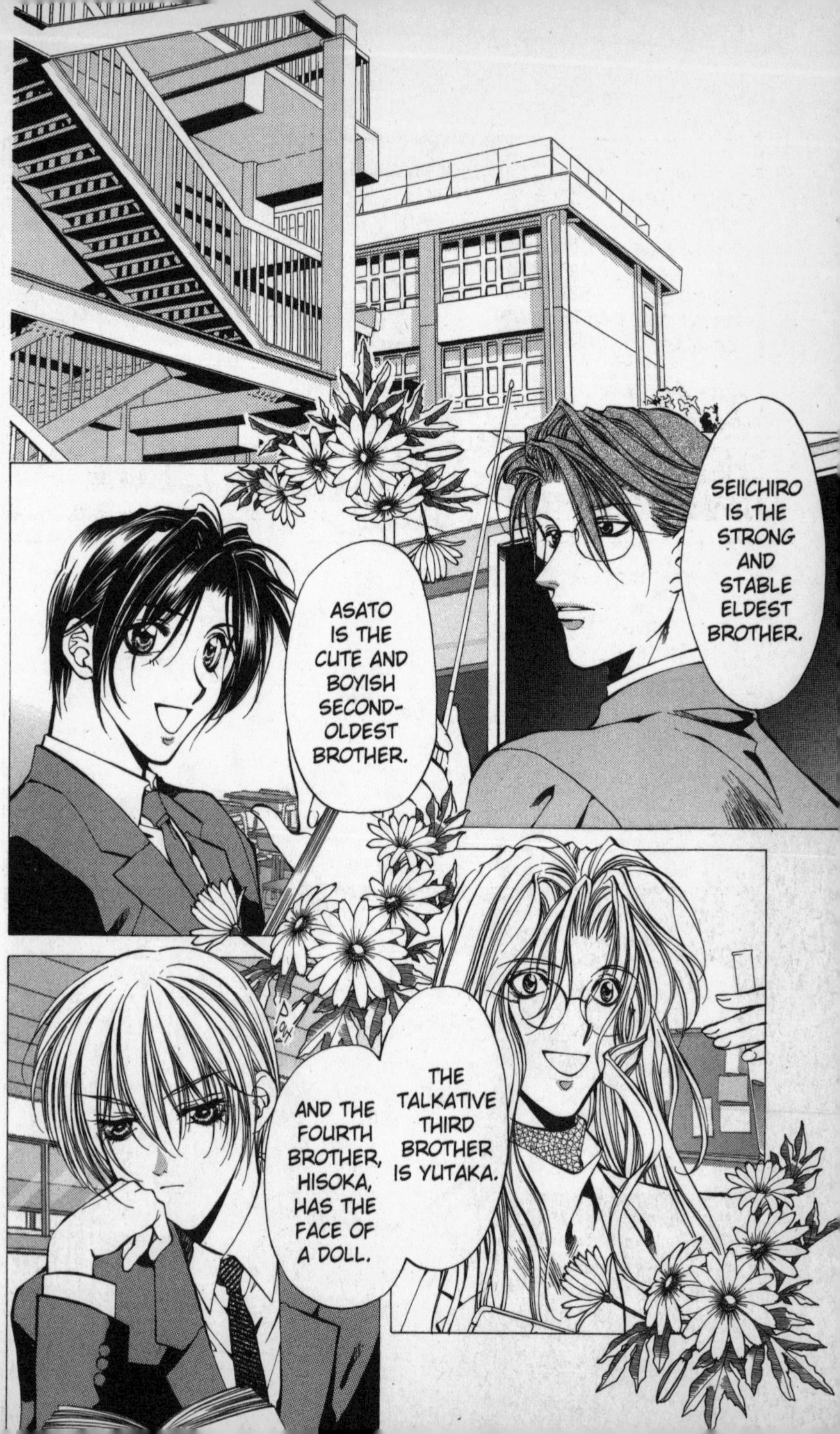
SEIICHIRO IS THE STRONG AND STABLE ELDEST BROTHER.
ASATO IS THE CUTE AND BOYISH SECOND-OLDEST BROTHER.
THE TALKATIVE THIRD BROTHER IS YUTAKA.
AND THE FOURTH BROTHER, HISOKA, HAS THE FACE OF A DOLL.

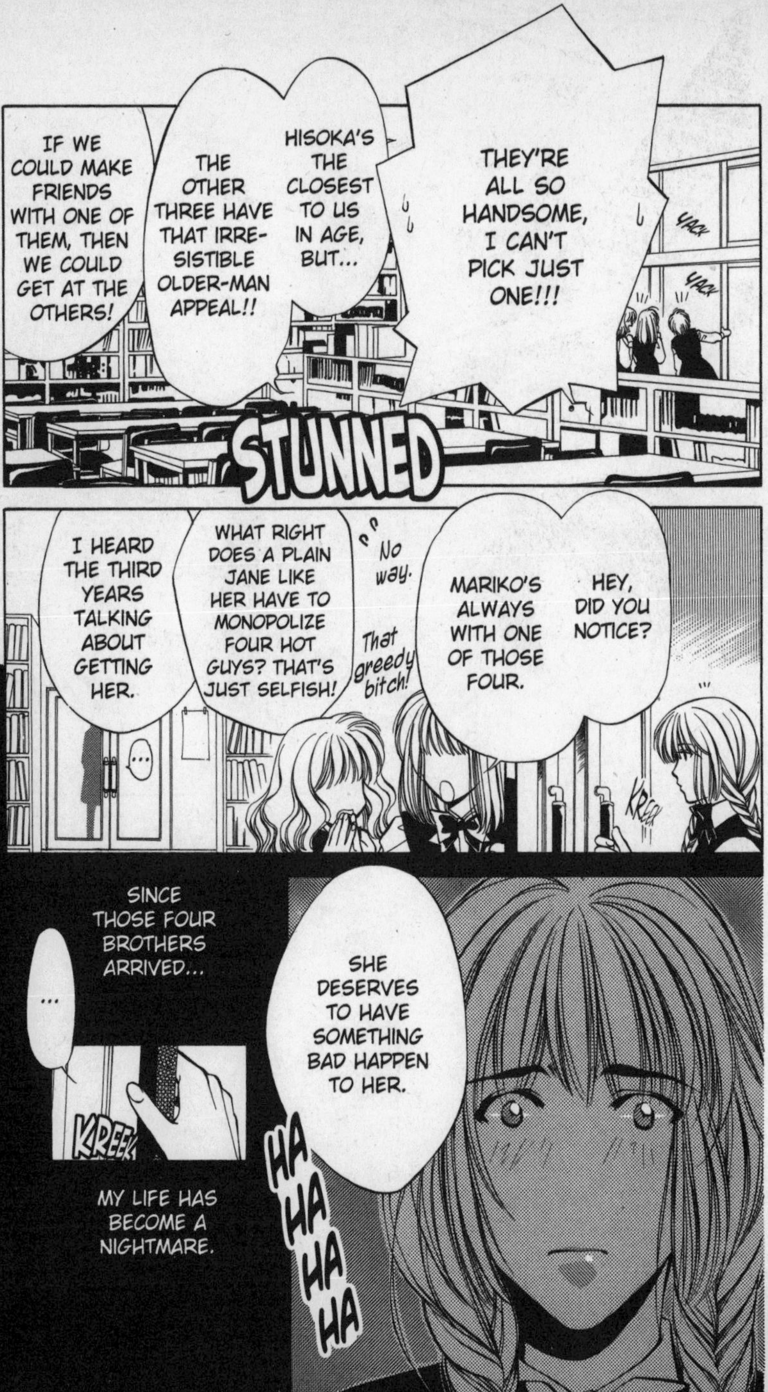
THEY'RE ALL SO HANDSOME, I CAN'T PICK JUST ONE!!!
YACK
YACK
HISOKA'S THE CLOSEST TO US IN AGE, BUT...
THE OTHER THREE HAVE THAT IRRE-SISTIBLE OLDER-MAN APPEAL!!
IF WE COULD MAKE FRIENDS WITH ONE OF THEM, THEN WE COULD GET AT THE OTHERS!
STUNNED
HEY, DID YOU NOTICE?
MARIKO'S ALWAYS WITH ONE OF THOSE FOUR.
No way.
That greedy bitch!
WHAT RIGHT DOES A PLAIN JANE LIKE HER HAVE TO MONOPOLIZE FOUR HOT GUYS? THAT'S JUST SELFISH!
I HEARD THE THIRD YEARS TALKING ABOUT GETTING HER.
KREEK
...
SHE DESERVES TO HAVE SOMETHING BAD HAPPEN TO HER.
HA HA HA HA HA HA
SINCE THOSE FOUR BROTHERS ARRIVED...
...
KREEK
MY LIFE HAS BECOME A NIGHTMARE.

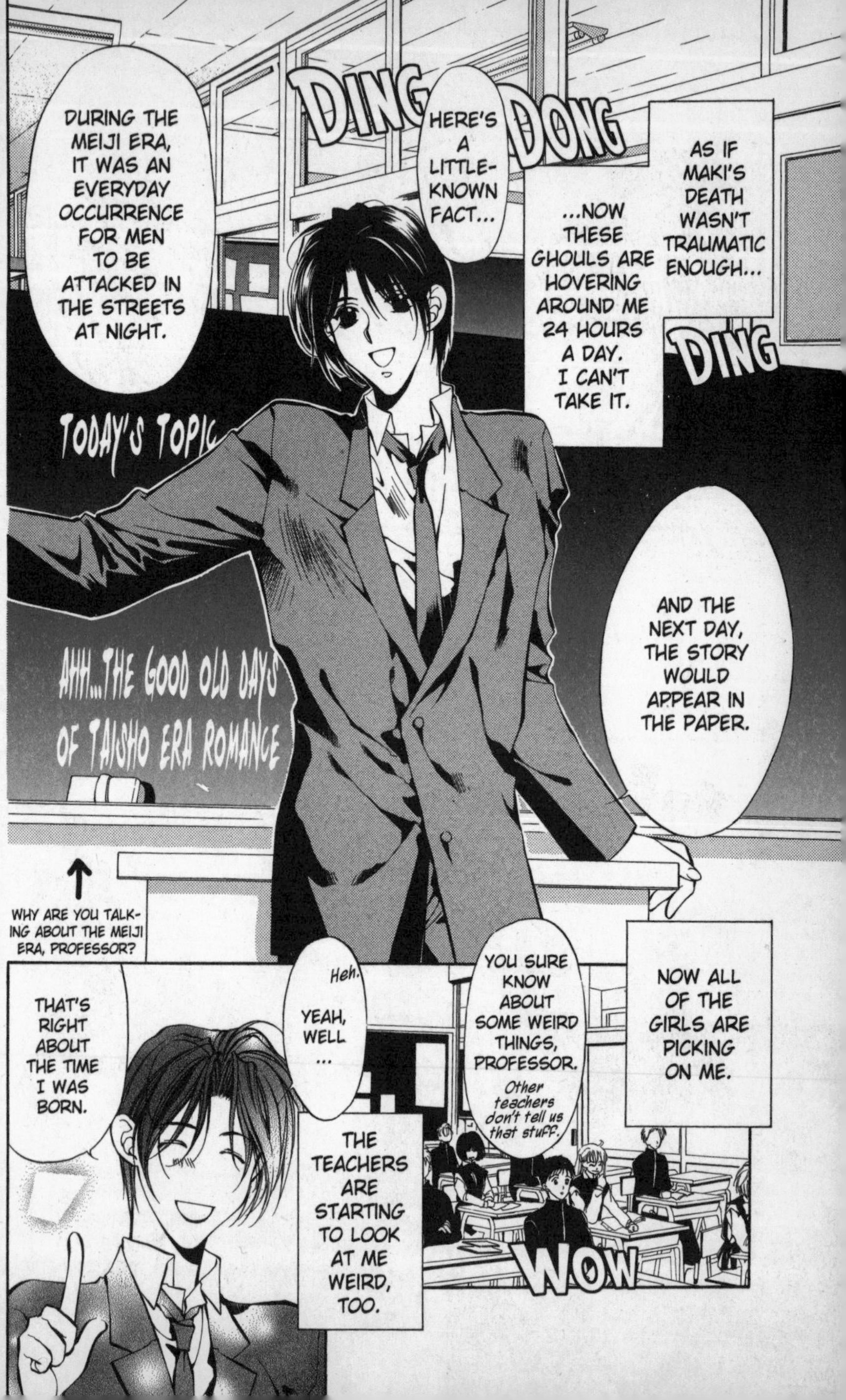
AS IF MAKI'S DEATH WASN'T TRAUMATIC ENOUGH...
...NOW THESE GHOULS ARE HOVERING AROUND ME 24 HOURS A DAY. I CAN'T TAKE IT.
DING DONG DING
HERE'S A LITTLE-KNOWN FACT...
DURING THE MEIJI ERA, IT WAS AN EVERYDAY OCCURRENCE FOR MEN TO BE ATTACKED IN THE STREETS AT NIGHT.
AND THE NEXT DAY, THE STORY WOULD APPEAR IN THE PAPER.
TODAY'S TOPIC
AHH...THE GOOD OLD DAYS OF TAISHO ERA ROMANCE
WHY ARE YOU TALKING ABOUT THE MEIJI ERA, PROFESSOR?
NOW ALL OF THE GIRLS ARE PICKING ON ME.
YOU SURE KNOW ABOUT SOME WEIRD THINGS, PROFESSOR.
Other teachers don't tell us that stuff.
Heh.
YEAH, WELL ...
THE TEACHERS ARE STARTING TO LOOK AT ME WEIRD, TOO.
THAT'S RIGHT ABOUT THE TIME I WAS BORN.
WOW

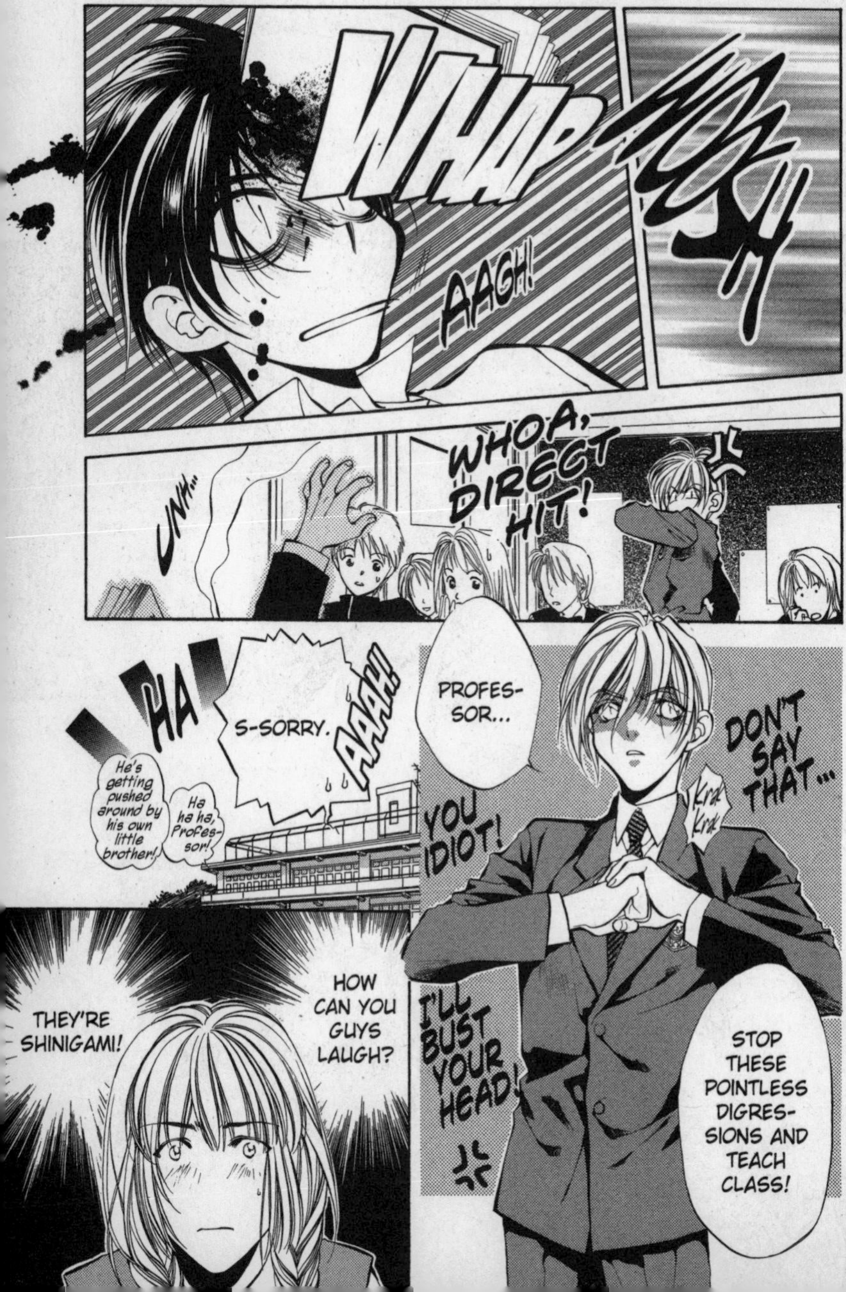
WHOOSH
WHAP
AAGH!
WHOA, DIRECT HIT!
UNH...
PROFES-SOR...
DON'T SAY THAT...
Krak Krak
YOU IDIOT!
I'LL BUST YOUR HEAD!
STOP THESE POINTLESS DIGRES-SIONS AND TEACH CLASS!
AAAH!
S-SORRY.
HA
He's getting pushed around by his own little brother!
Ha ha ha, Profes-sor!
HOW CAN YOU GUYS LAUGH?
THEY'RE SHINIGAMI!

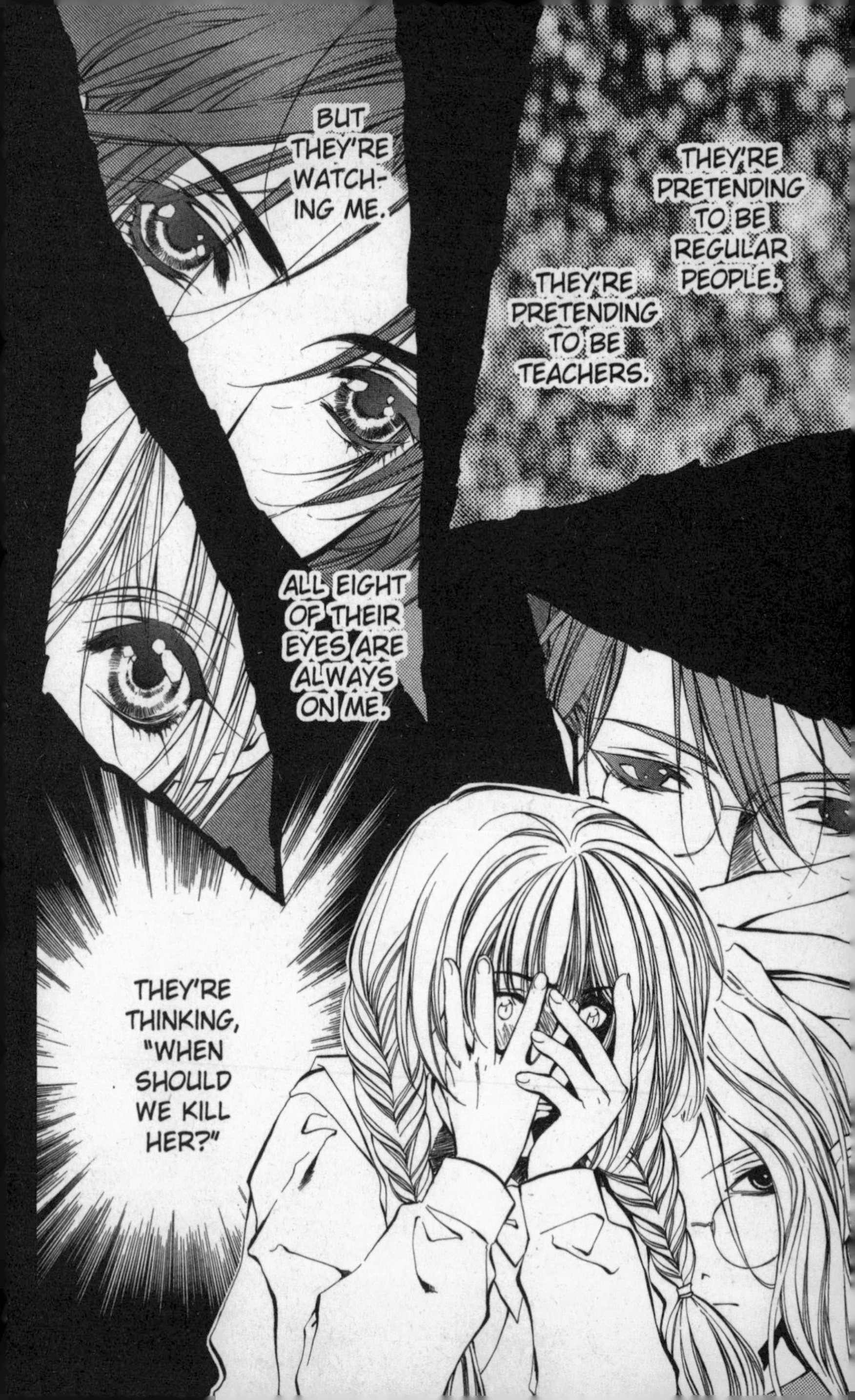
THEY'RE PRETENDING TO BE REGULAR PEOPLE.
THEY'RE PRETENDING TO BE TEACHERS.
BUT THEY'RE WATCH-ING ME.
ALL EIGHT OF THEIR EYES ARE ALWAYS ON ME.
THEY'RE THINKING, "WHEN SHOULD WE KILL HER?"

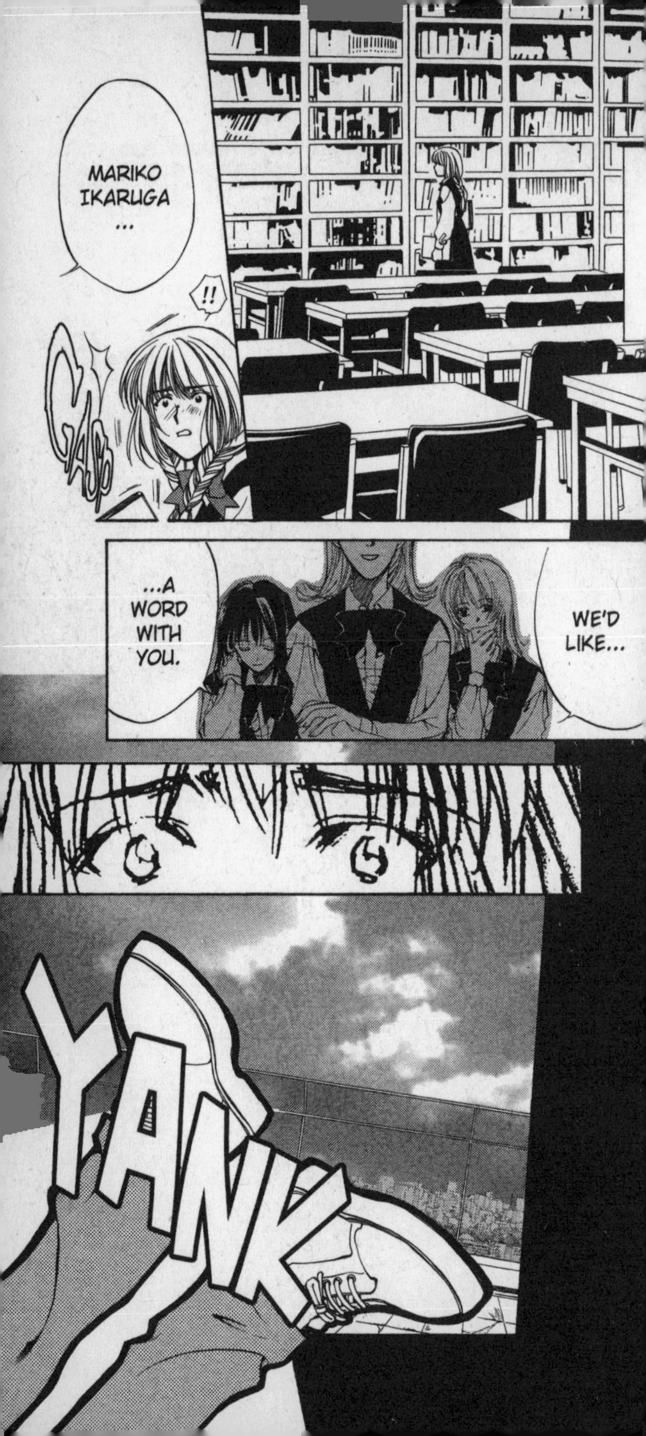
MARIKO IKARUGA ...
!!
GASP
WE'D LIKE...
...A WORD WITH YOU.
YANK

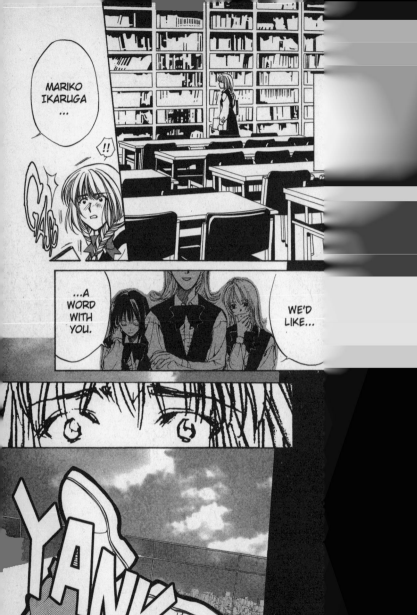

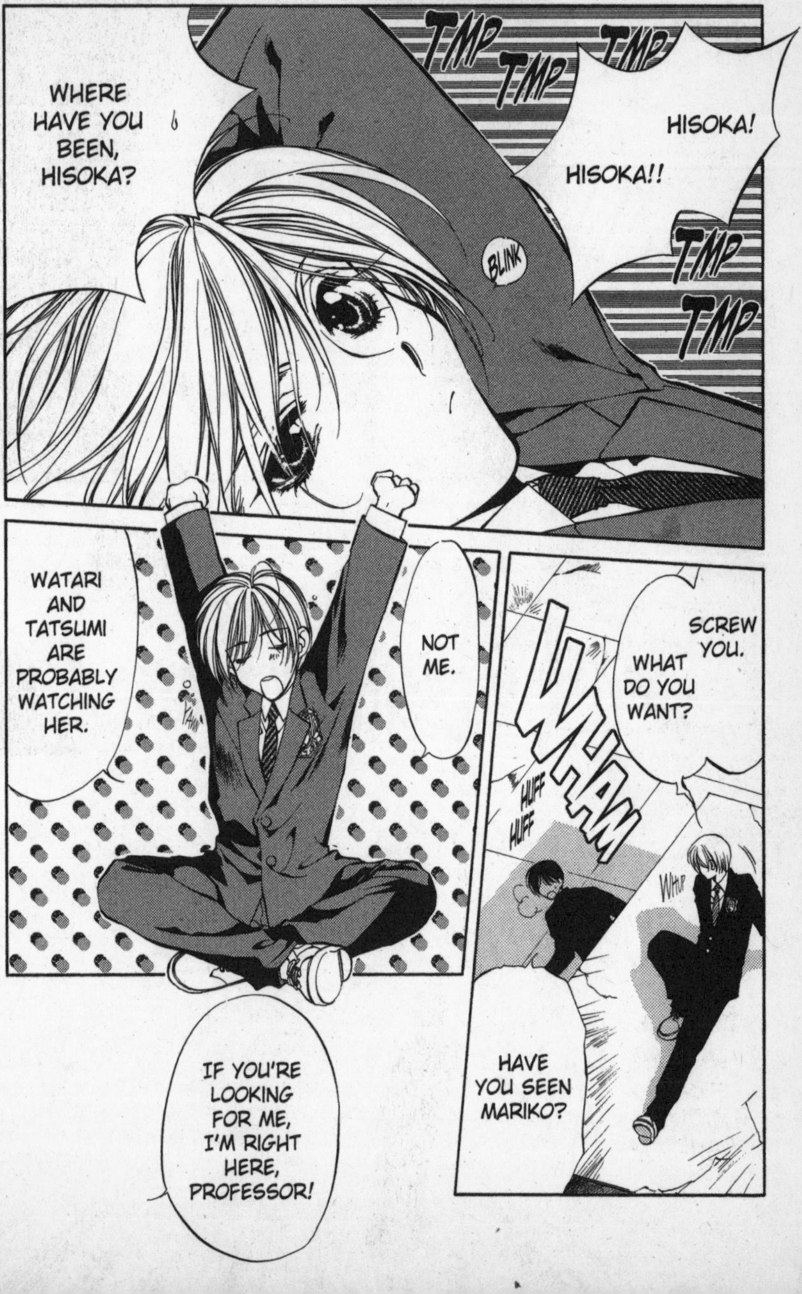
TMP TMP TMP
HISOKA!
HISOKA!!
TMP TMP
BLINK
WHERE HAVE YOU BEEN, HISOKA?
SCREW YOU. WHAT DO YOU WANT?
WHAM
HUFF HUFF
WHUP
HAVE YOU SEEN MARIKO?
NOT ME.
YAWN
WATARI AND TATSUMI ARE PROBABLY WATCHING HER.
IF YOU'RE LOOKING FOR ME, I'M RIGHT HERE, PROFESSOR!

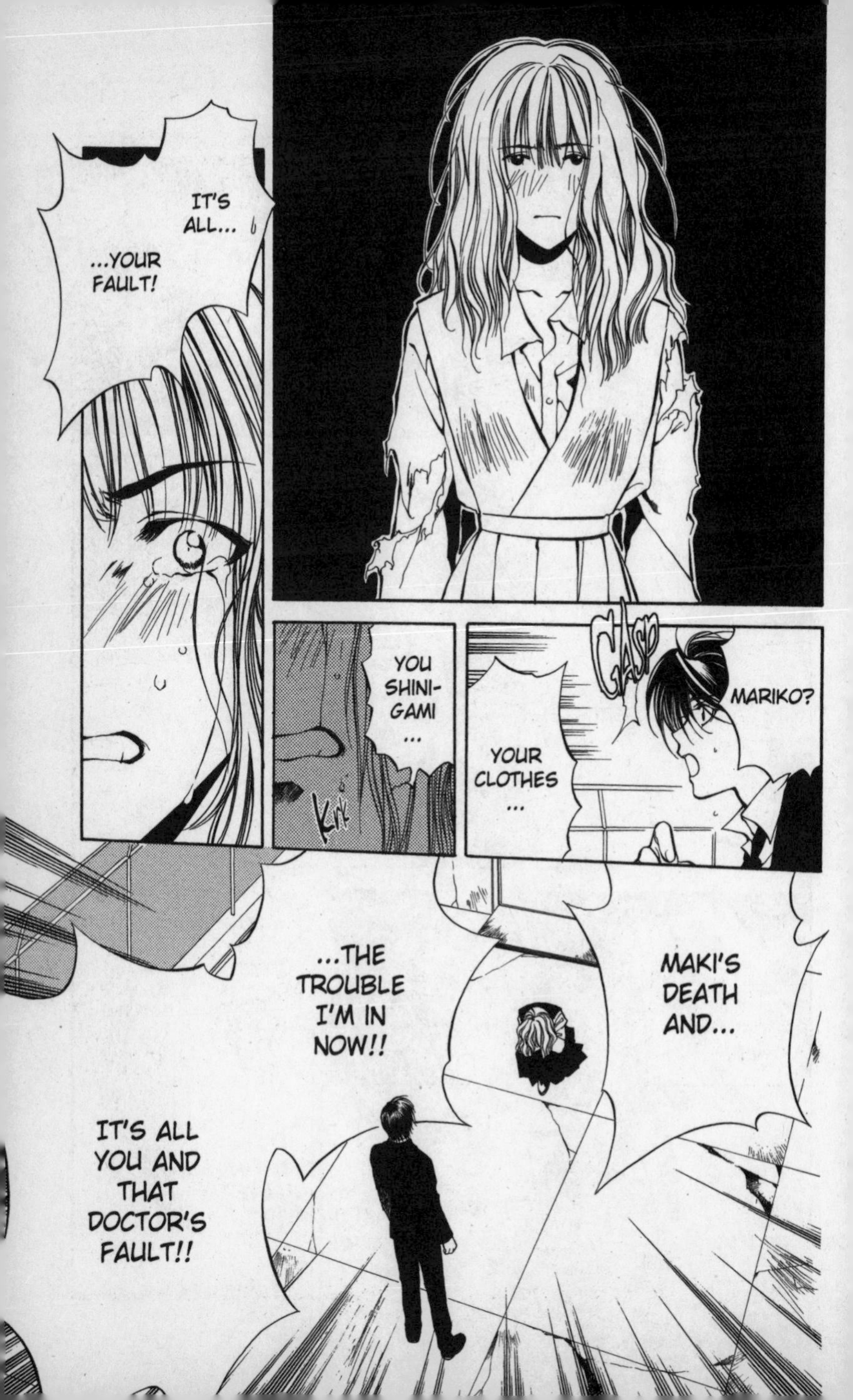
MARIKO?
GASP
YOUR CLOTHES...
YOU SHINI-GAMI...
KRK
IT'S ALL...
...YOUR FAULT!
MAKI'S DEATH AND...
...THE TROUBLE I'M IN NOW!!
IT'S ALL YOU AND THAT DOCTOR'S FAULT!!

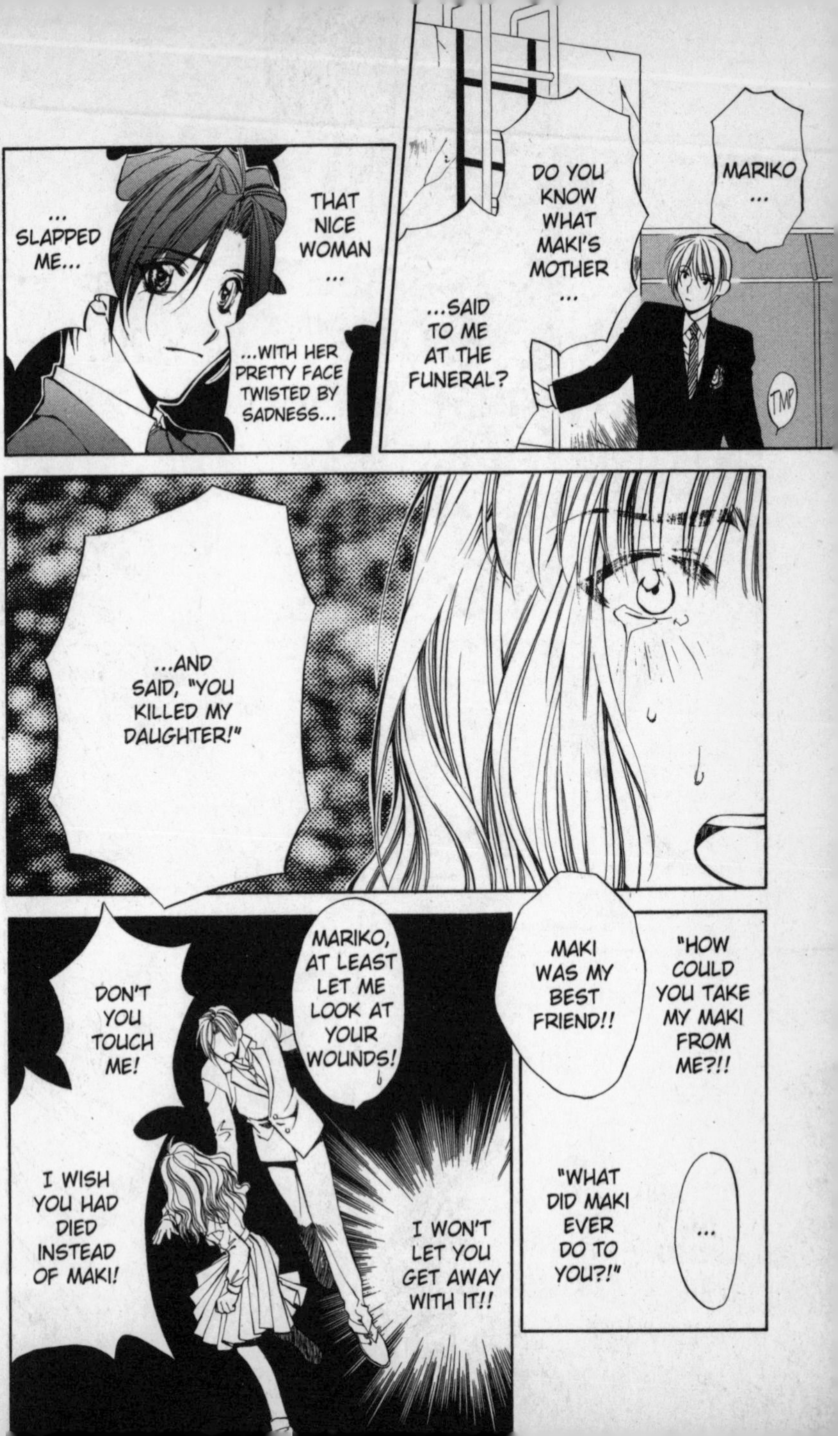
MARIKO ...
DO YOU KNOW WHAT MAKI'S MOTHER ...
...SAID TO ME AT THE FUNERAL?
TMP
THAT NICE WOMAN ...
...WITH HER PRETTY FACE TWISTED BY SADNESS...
... SLAPPED ME...
...AND SAID, "YOU KILLED MY DAUGHTER!"
"HOW COULD YOU TAKE MY MAKI FROM ME?!!
MAKI WAS MY BEST FRIEND!!
"WHAT DID MAKI EVER DO TO YOU?!"
...
MARIKO, AT LEAST LET ME LOOK AT YOUR WOUNDS!
DON'T YOU TOUCH ME!
I WON'T LET YOU GET AWAY WITH IT!!
I WISH YOU HAD DIED INSTEAD OF MAKI!

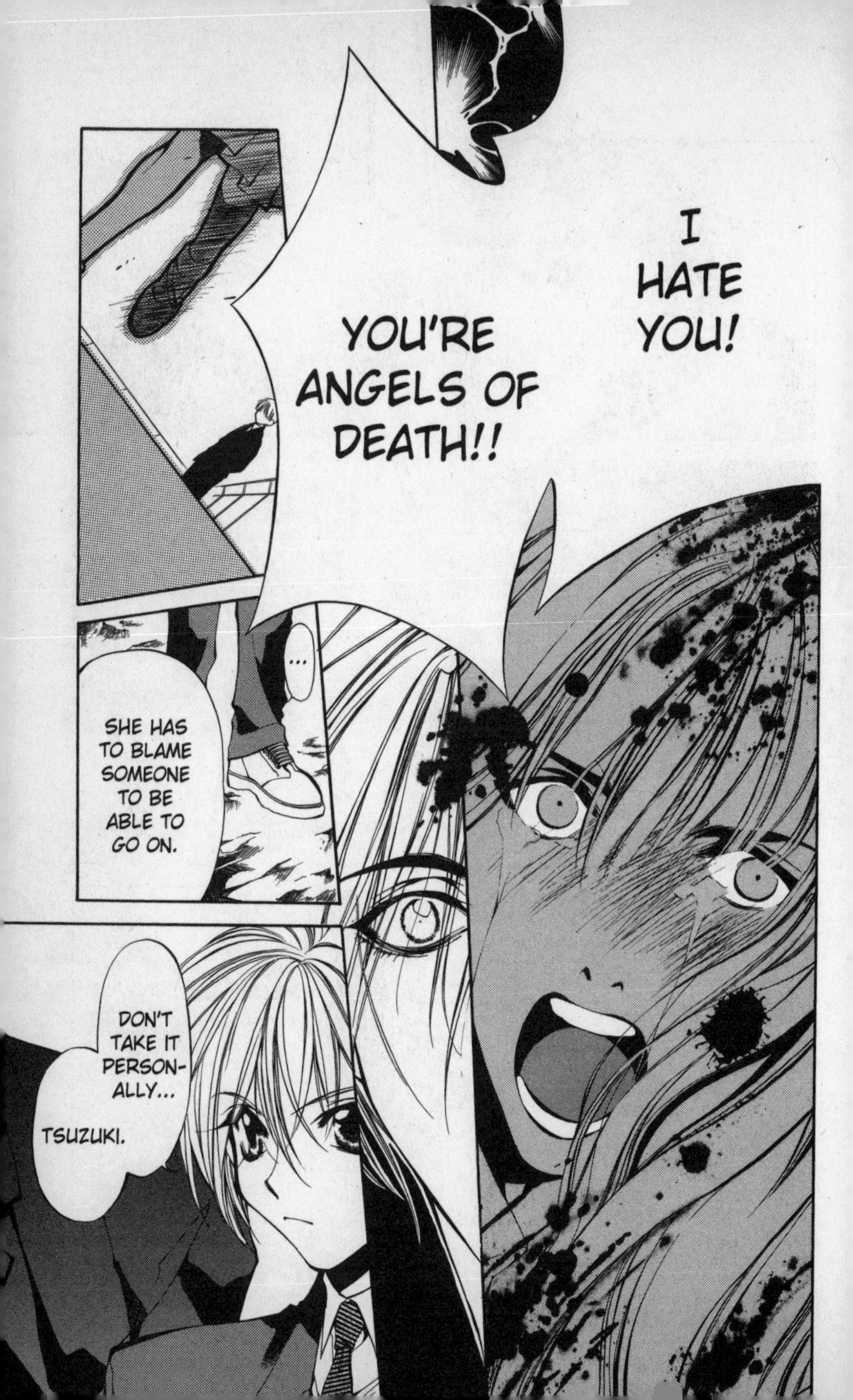
I HATE YOU!
YOU'RE ANGELS OF DEATH!!
...
SHE HAS TO BLAME SOMEONE TO BE ABLE TO GO ON.
DON'T TAKE IT PERSON-ALLY...
TSUZUKI.

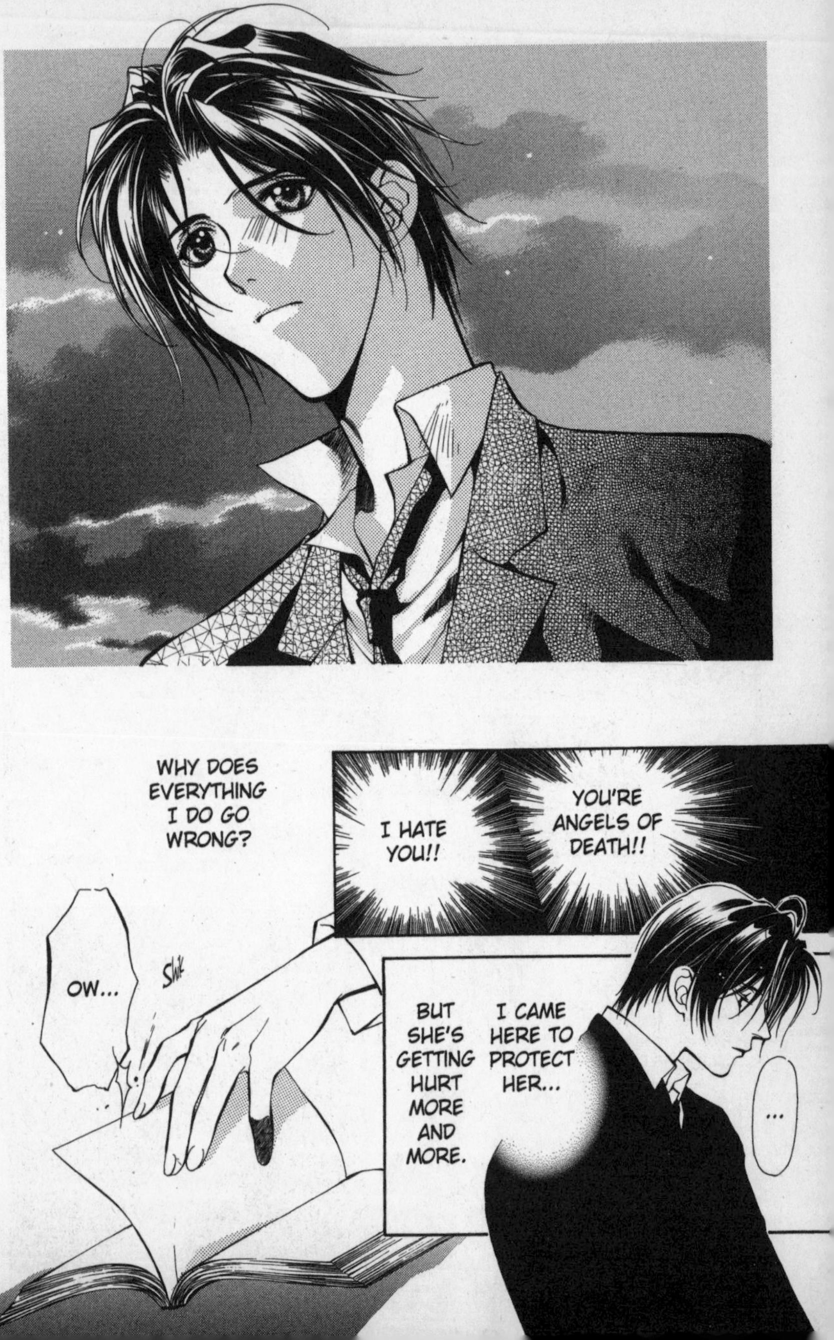
YOU'RE ANGELS OF DEATH!!
I HATE YOU!!
WHY DOES EVERYTHING I DO GO WRONG?
...
I CAME HERE TO PROTECT HER...
BUT SHE'S GETTING HURT MORE AND MORE.
Shik
OW...

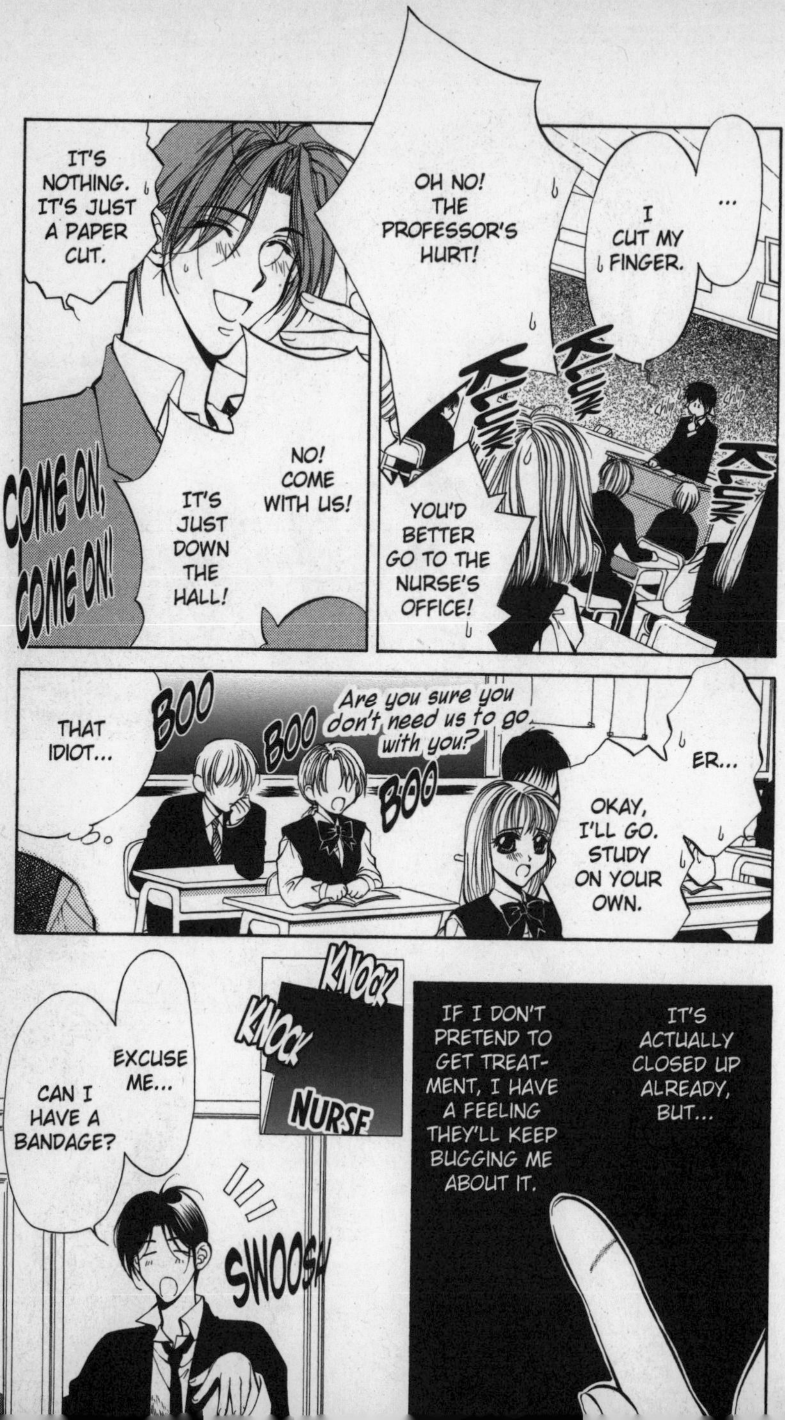
...
I CUT MY FINGER.
OH NO! THE PROFESSOR'S HURT!
KLUNK
KLUNK
KLUNK
KLUNK
YOU'D BETTER GO TO THE NURSE'S OFFICE!
IT'S NOTHING. IT'S JUST A PAPER CUT.
NO! COME WITH US!
IT'S JUST DOWN THE HALL!
COME ON, COME ON!
ER...
OKAY, I'LL GO. STUDY ON YOUR OWN.
Are you sure you don't need us to go with you?
BOO
BOO
BOO
THAT IDIOT...
IT'S ACTUALLY CLOSED UP ALREADY, BUT...
IF I DON'T PRETEND TO GET TREAT-MENT, I HAVE A FEELING THEY'LL KEEP BUGGING ME ABOUT IT.
KNOCK
KNOCK
NURSE
EXCUSE ME...
CAN I HAVE A BANDAGE?
SWOOSH

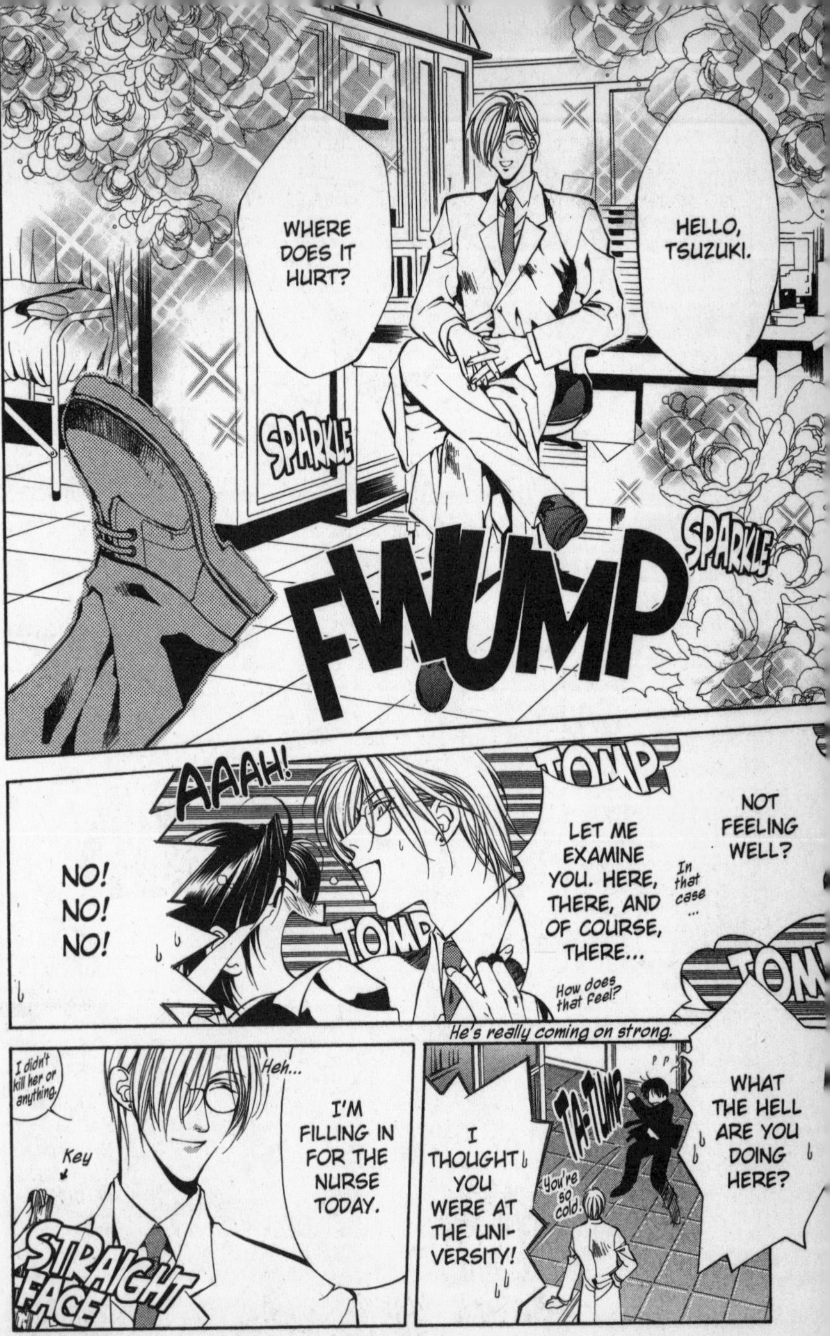
HELLO, TSUZUKI.
WHERE DOES IT HURT?
SPARKLE
SPARKLE
FWUMP
TOMP
NOT FEELING WELL?
In that case ...
LET ME EXAMINE YOU. HERE, THERE, AND OF COURSE, THERE...
How does that feel?
TOM
TOMP
AAAH!
NO! NO! NO!
He's really coming on strong.
WHAT THE HELL ARE YOU DOING HERE?
TA-TUMP
You're so cold.
I THOUGHT YOU WERE AT THE UNI-VERSITY!
I'M FILLING IN FOR THE NURSE TODAY.
Heh...
I didn't kill her or anything.
Key
STRAIGHT FACE

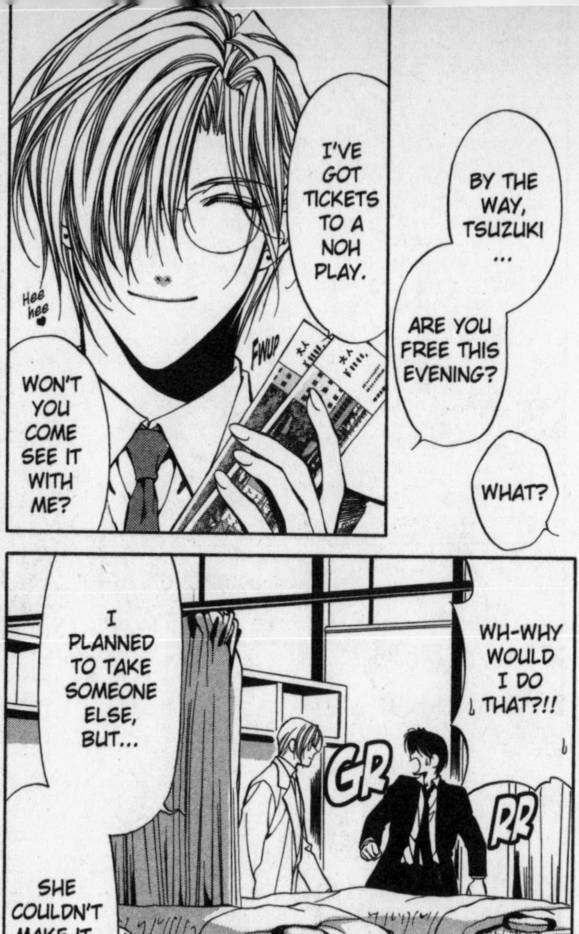
BY THE WAY, TSUZUKI ...
ARE YOU FREE THIS EVENING?
WHAT?
I'VE GOT TICKETS TO A NOH PLAY.
Hee hee
FWUP
WON'T YOU COME SEE IT WITH ME?
WH-WHY WOULD I DO THAT?!!
GR
RR
I PLANNED TO TAKE SOMEONE ELSE, BUT...
SHE COULDN'T MAKE IT.
Heh ...
HOW NAUGHTY OF UKYO TO TURN ME DOWN.
Heh heh ...
SPARKLE
And we hardly ever see each other.
IN HIS OWN WORLD.
A GIRL?
Good. At least he has some normal relation-ships.
SPARKLE SPARKLE

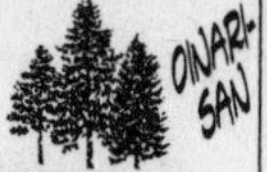

OINARI-SAN

(GUARDIAN STATUES THAT PROTECT A SHRINE.)

When I think of Kyoto, blood comes to mind. (Sorry, Kyoto!) Well, it is the historic capital. There are so many sights to see, you can never have enough film. My assistant and I went out to take pictures without considering how much it would cost to develop them. Flash! Flash! Flash! I had a hard time organizing all those pictures when I got home. My favorites are of the Fushimi Inari shrine. As I walked through the long rows of red *torii, I snapped a few photos. I used two rolls of film just on Fushimi Inari alone.

IDIOT.

And I didn't even use them in this story. But it really is a beautiful place. Both shrines and temples seem to have a kind of force field that creates a sanctuary for the psyche. Even though Japan is heavily influenced by foreign cultures, special places like that can still be found.

It's part of the Japanese spirit.

*Torii are gateways, often made of wood, found at the entrances of Shinto shrines. Ed.

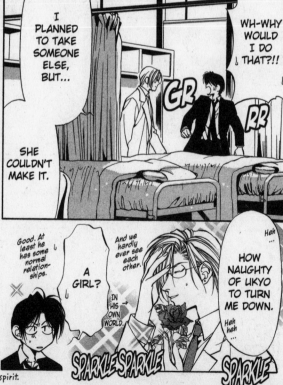

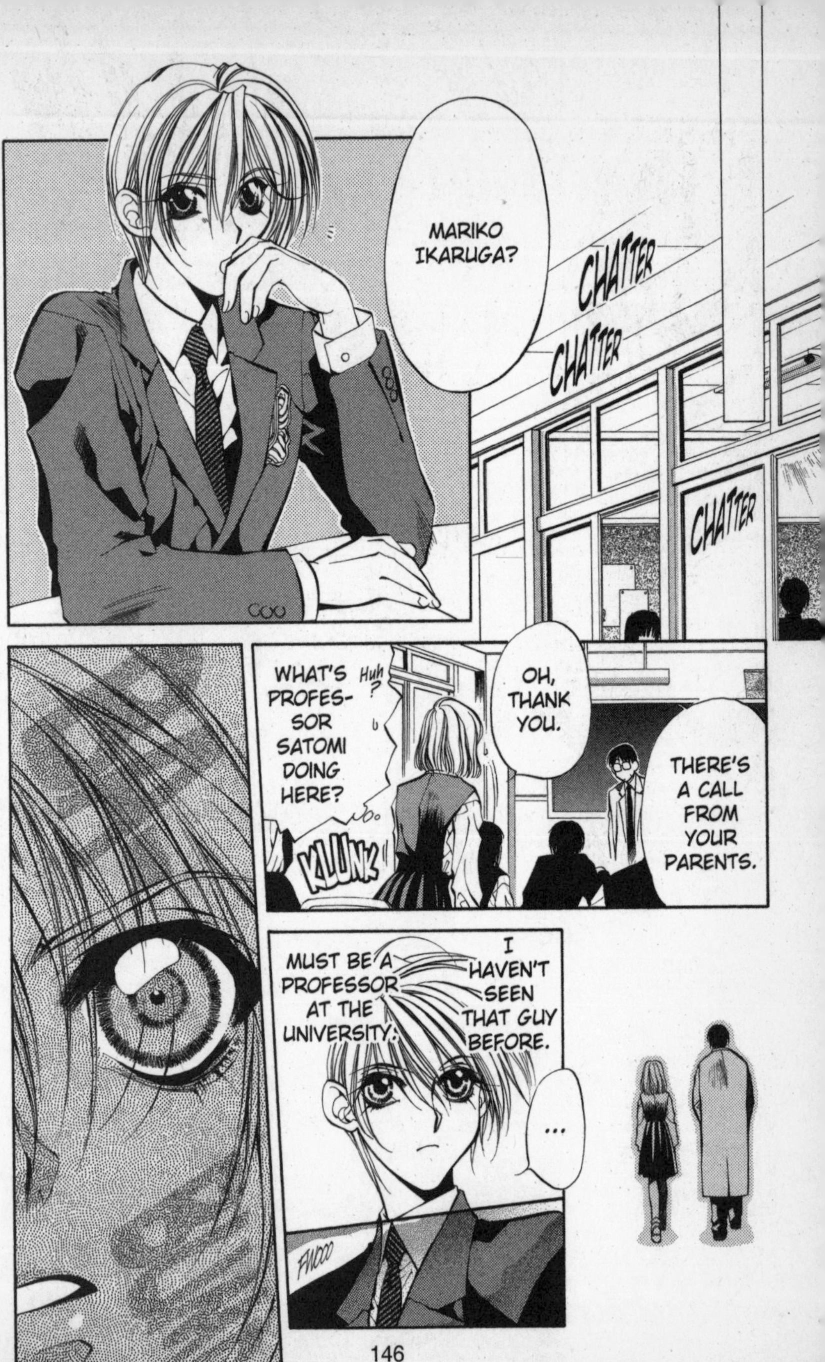
MARIKO IKARUGA?
CHATTER
CHATTER
CHATTER
THERE'S A CALL FROM YOUR PARENTS.
OH, THANK YOU.
Huh?
WHAT'S PROFES-SOR SATOMI DOING HERE?
KLUNK
I HAVEN'T SEEN THAT GUY BEFORE.
MUST BE A PROFESSOR AT THE UNIVERSITY.
...
FWOOO

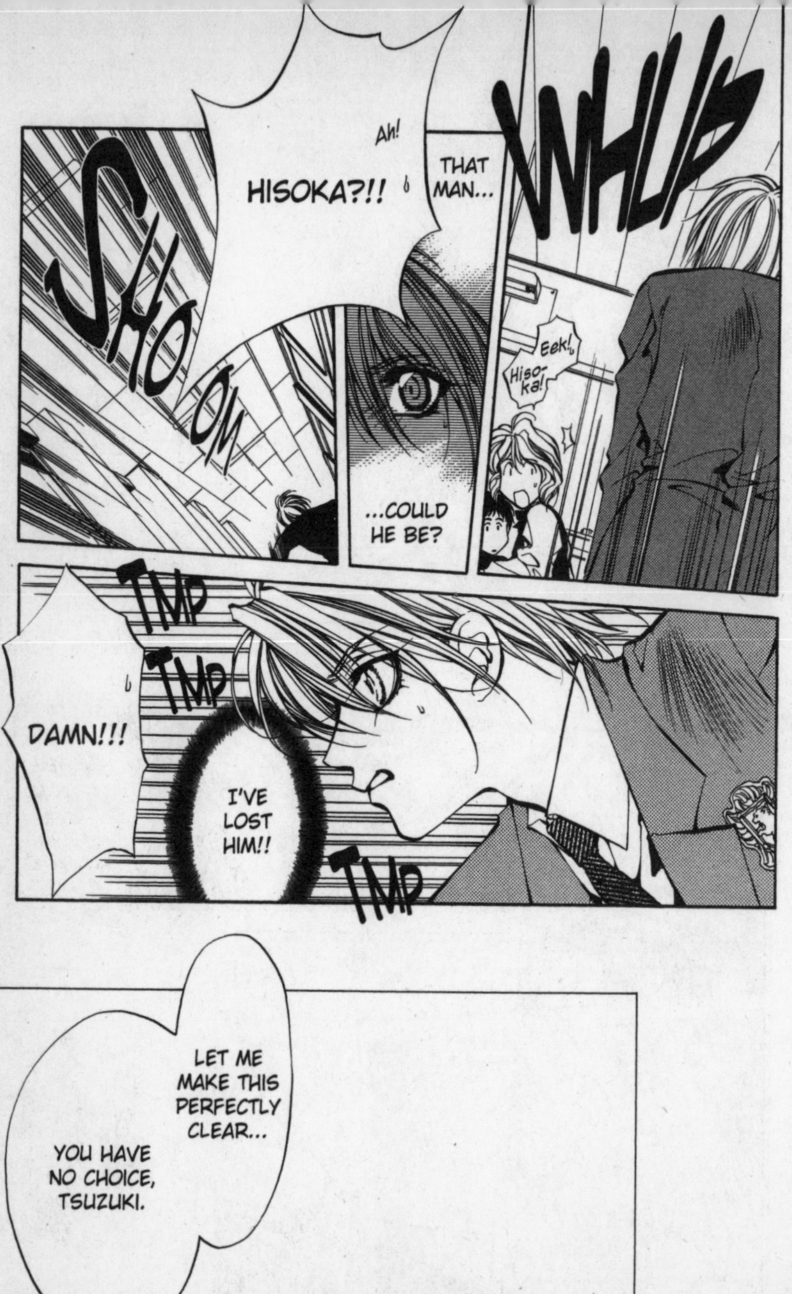
WHUD
Eek! Hiso-ka!
Ah!
HISOKA?!!
THAT MAN...
...COULD HE BE?
SHOOM
TMP TMP
DAMN!!!
I'VE LOST HIM!!
TMP
LET ME MAKE THIS PERFECTLY CLEAR...
YOU HAVE NO CHOICE, TSUZUKI.

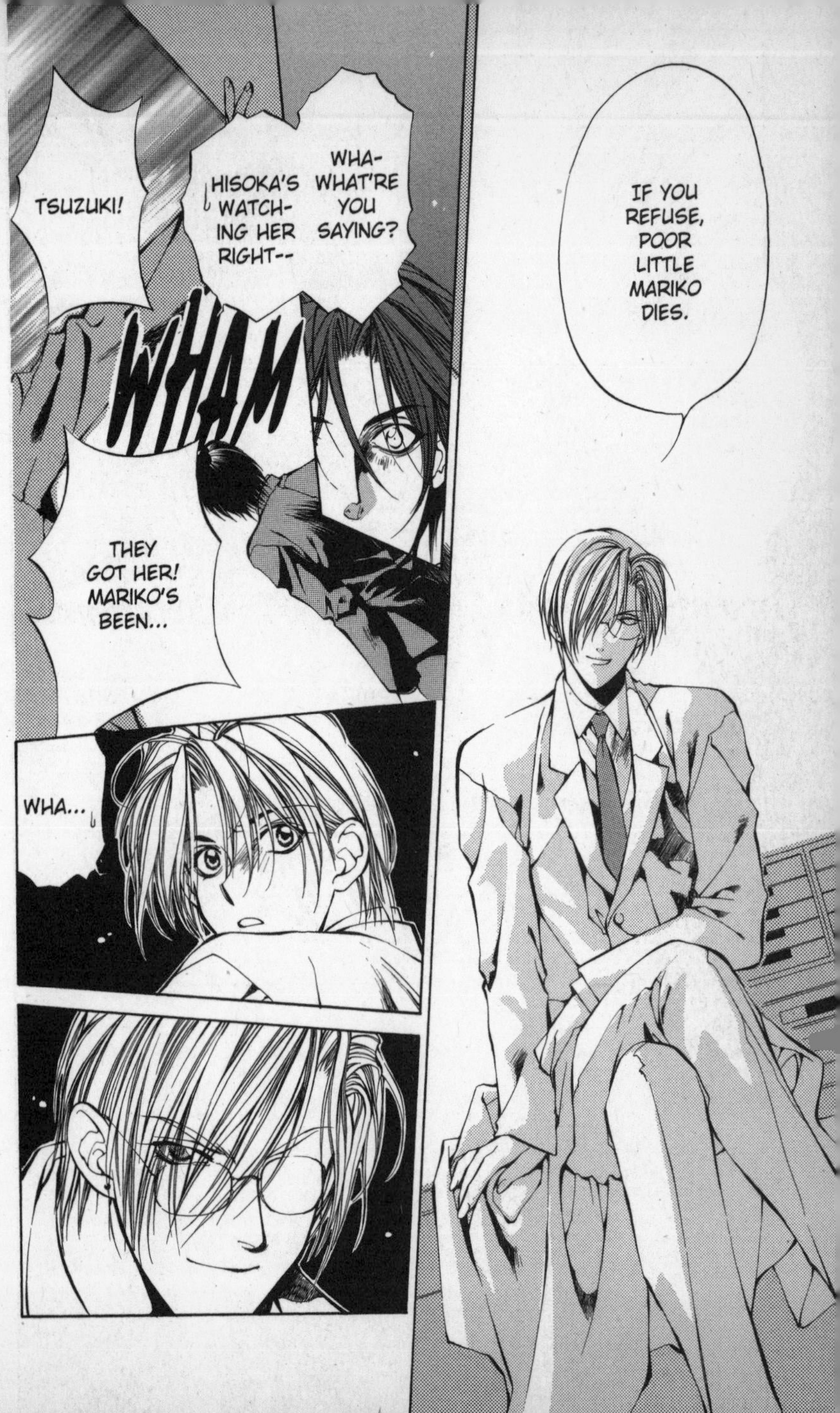
IF YOU REFUSE, POOR LITTLE MARIKO DIES.
WHA- WHAT'RE YOU SAYING?
HISOKA'S WATCHING HER RIGHT--
TSUZUKI!
WHAM
THEY GOT HER! MARIKO'S BEEN...
WHA...

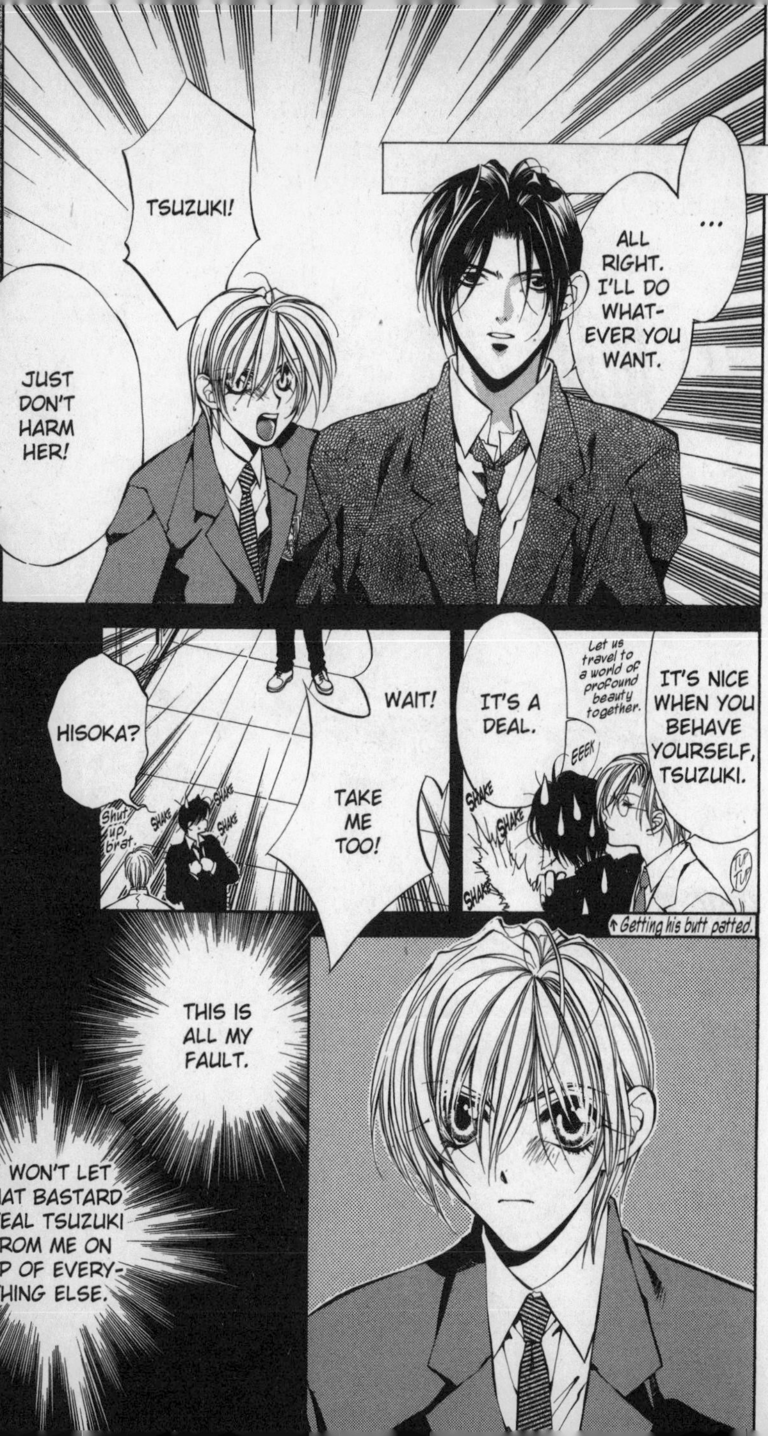
...
ALL RIGHT. I'LL DO WHAT-EVER YOU WANT.
TSUZUKI!
JUST DON'T HARM HER!
IT'S NICE WHEN YOU BEHAVE YOURSELF, TSUZUKI.
Let us travel to a world of profound beauty together.
IT'S A DEAL.
EEEK
SHAKE
SHAKE
SHAKE
TUP TUP
↑ Getting his butt patted.
WAIT!
TAKE ME TOO!
HISOKA?
Shut up, brat.
SHAKE
SHAKE
THIS IS ALL MY FAULT.
I WON'T LET THAT BASTARD STEAL TSUZUKI FROM ME ON TOP OF EVERY-THING ELSE.

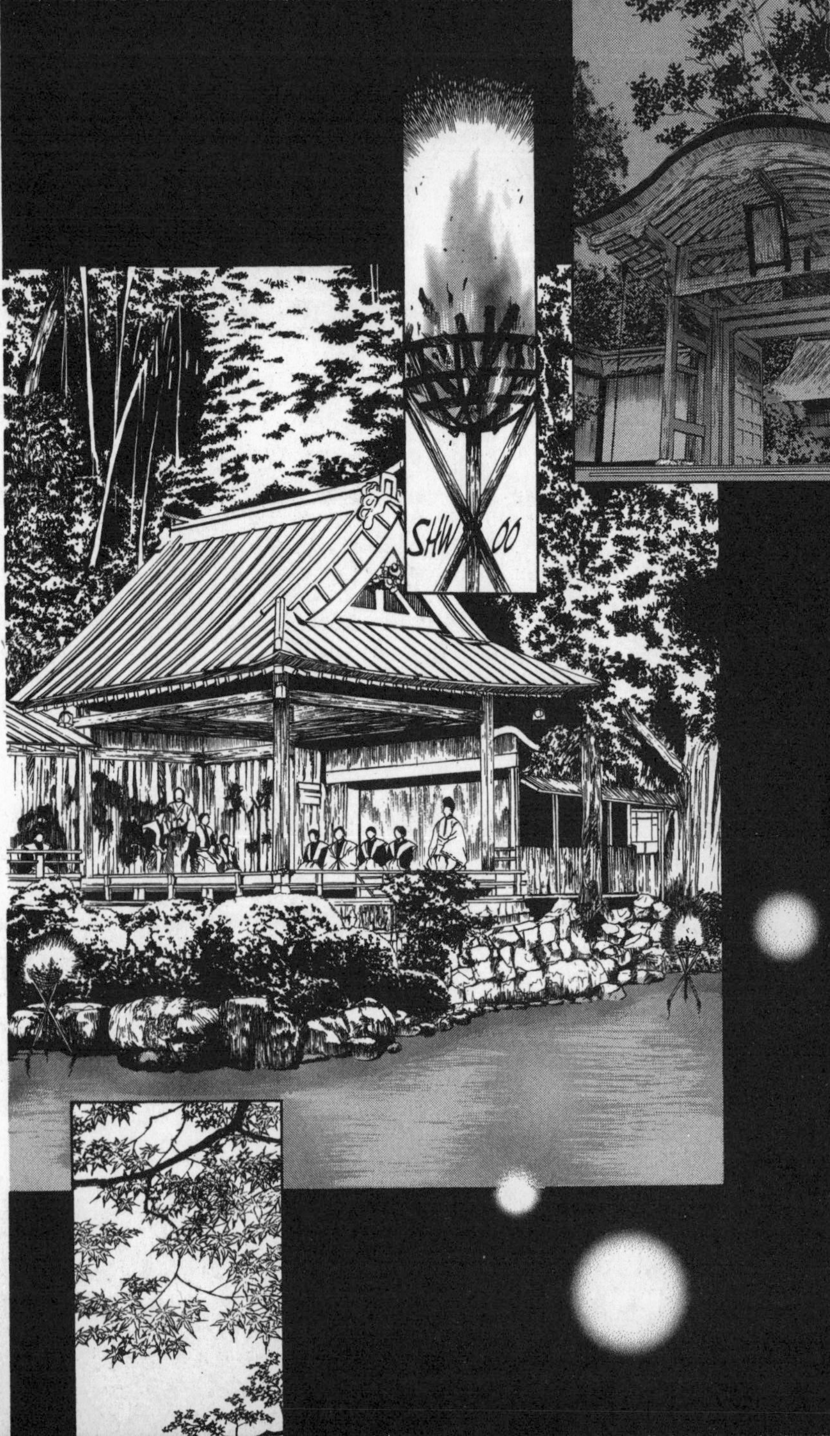
SHWOO

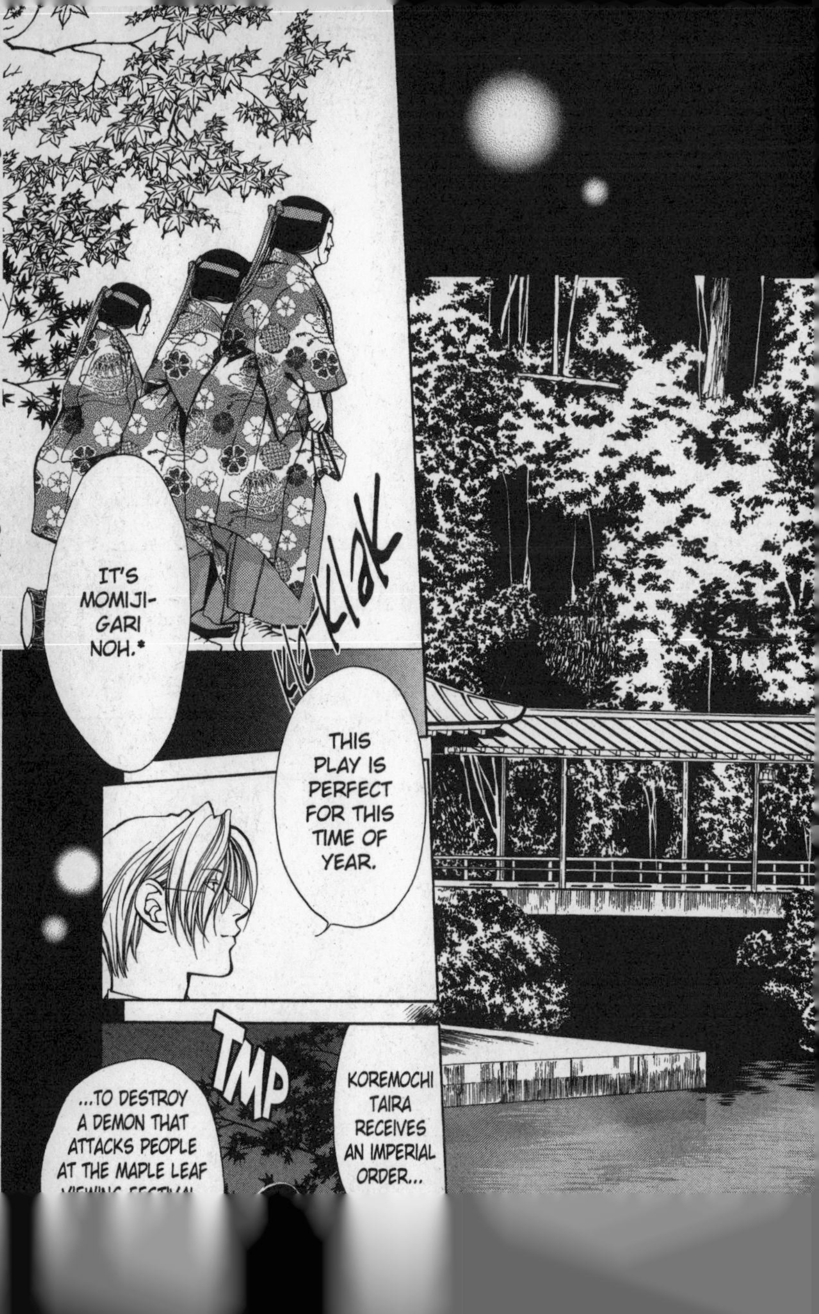
IT'S MOMIJI-GARI NOH.*
KLA-KLAK
THIS PLAY IS PERFECT FOR THIS TIME OF YEAR.
KOREMOCHI TAIRA RECEIVES AN IMPERIAL ORDER...
TMP
...TO DESTROY A DEMON THAT ATTACKS PEOPLE AT THE MAPLE LEAF

*A Famous Noh play. Momiji-gari means "to watch maple leaves change color." -Ed.

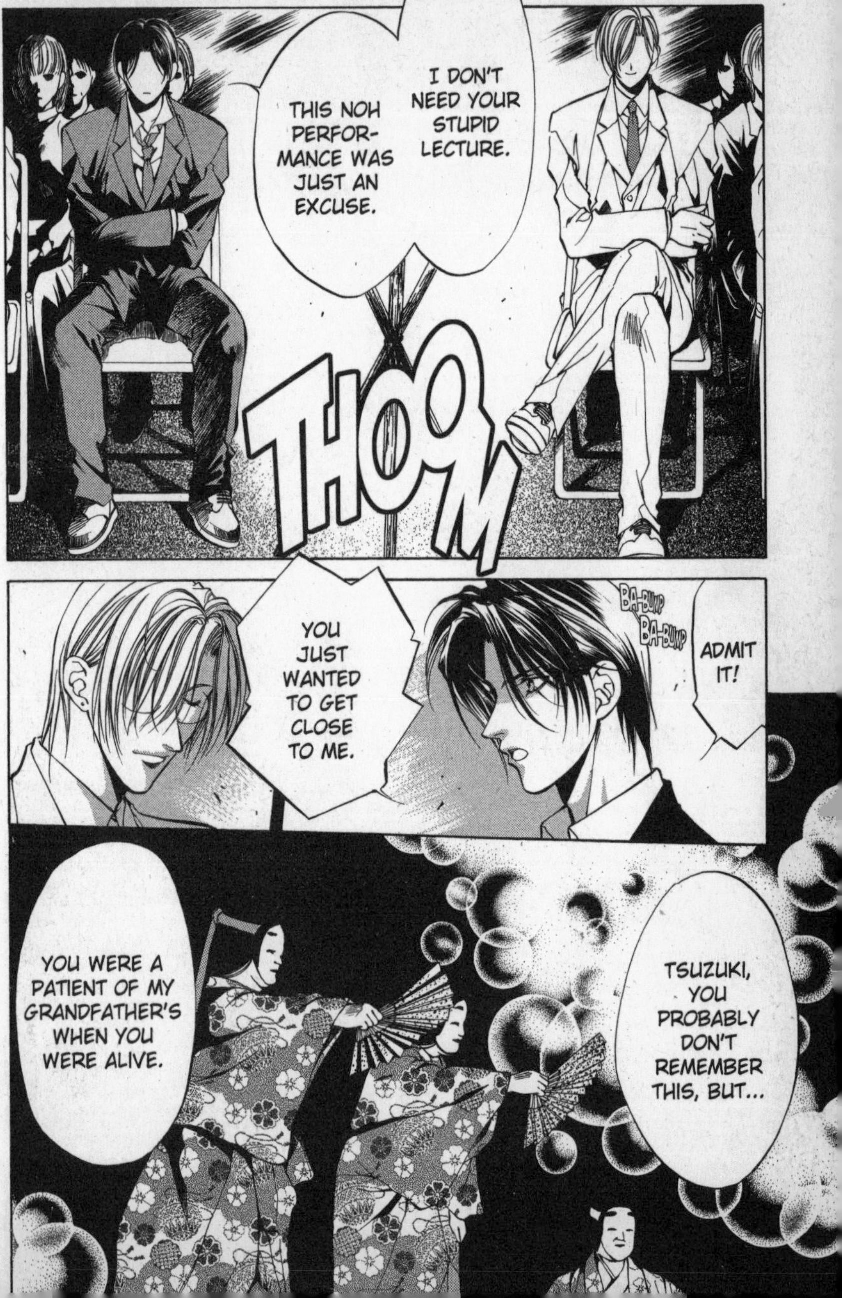
I DON'T NEED YOUR STUPID LECTURE.
THIS NOH PERFORMANCE WAS JUST AN EXCUSE.
THOOM
BA-BUMP BA-BUMP
ADMIT IT!
YOU JUST WANTED TO GET CLOSE TO ME.
TSUZUKI, YOU PROBABLY DON'T REMEMBER THIS, BUT...
YOU WERE A PATIENT OF MY GRANDFATHER'S WHEN YOU WERE ALIVE.

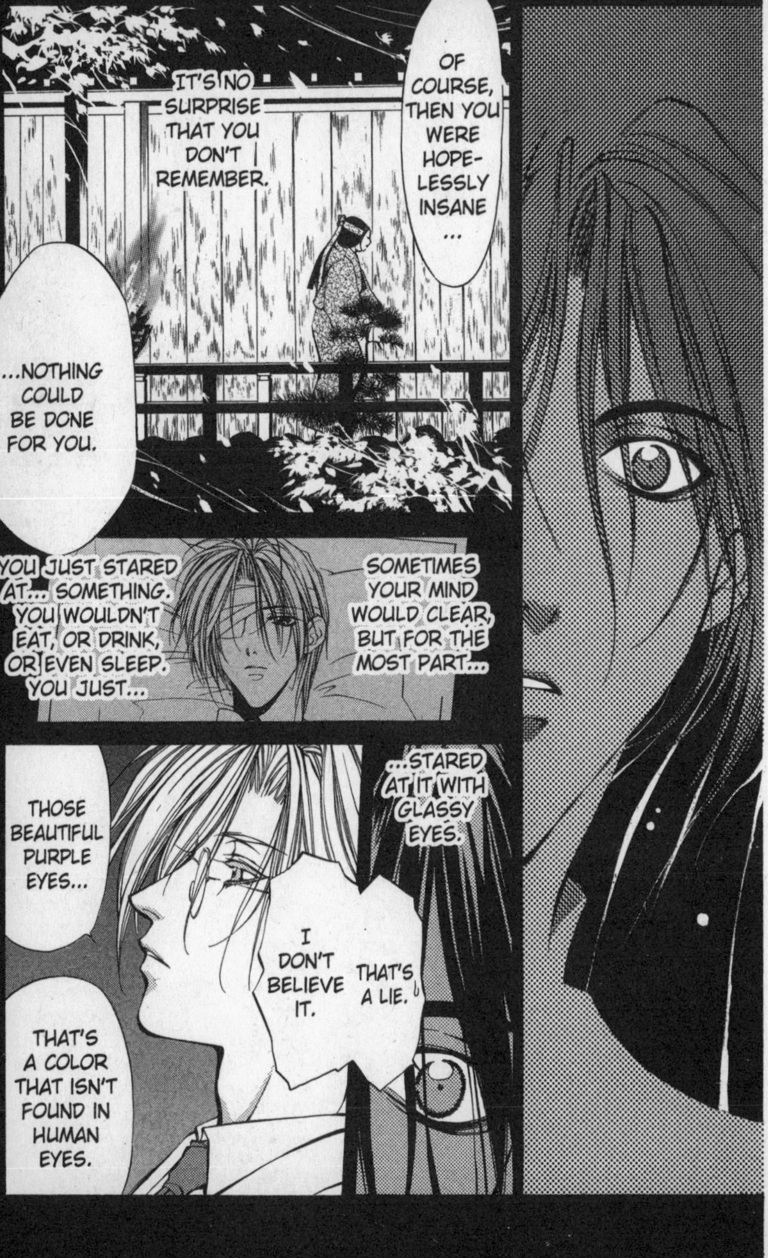
OF COURSE, THEN YOU WERE HOPELESSLY INSANE...
IT'S NO SURPRISE THAT YOU DON'T REMEMBER.
...NOTHING COULD BE DONE FOR YOU.
SOMETIMES YOUR MIND WOULD CLEAR, BUT FOR THE MOST PART...
YOU JUST STARED AT... SOMETHING. YOU WOULDN'T EAT, OR DRINK, OR EVEN SLEEP. YOU JUST...
...STARED AT IT WITH GLASSY EYES.
THOSE BEAUTIFUL PURPLE EYES...
THAT'S A LIE.
I DON'T BELIEVE IT.
THAT'S A COLOR THAT ISN'T FOUND IN HUMAN EYES.

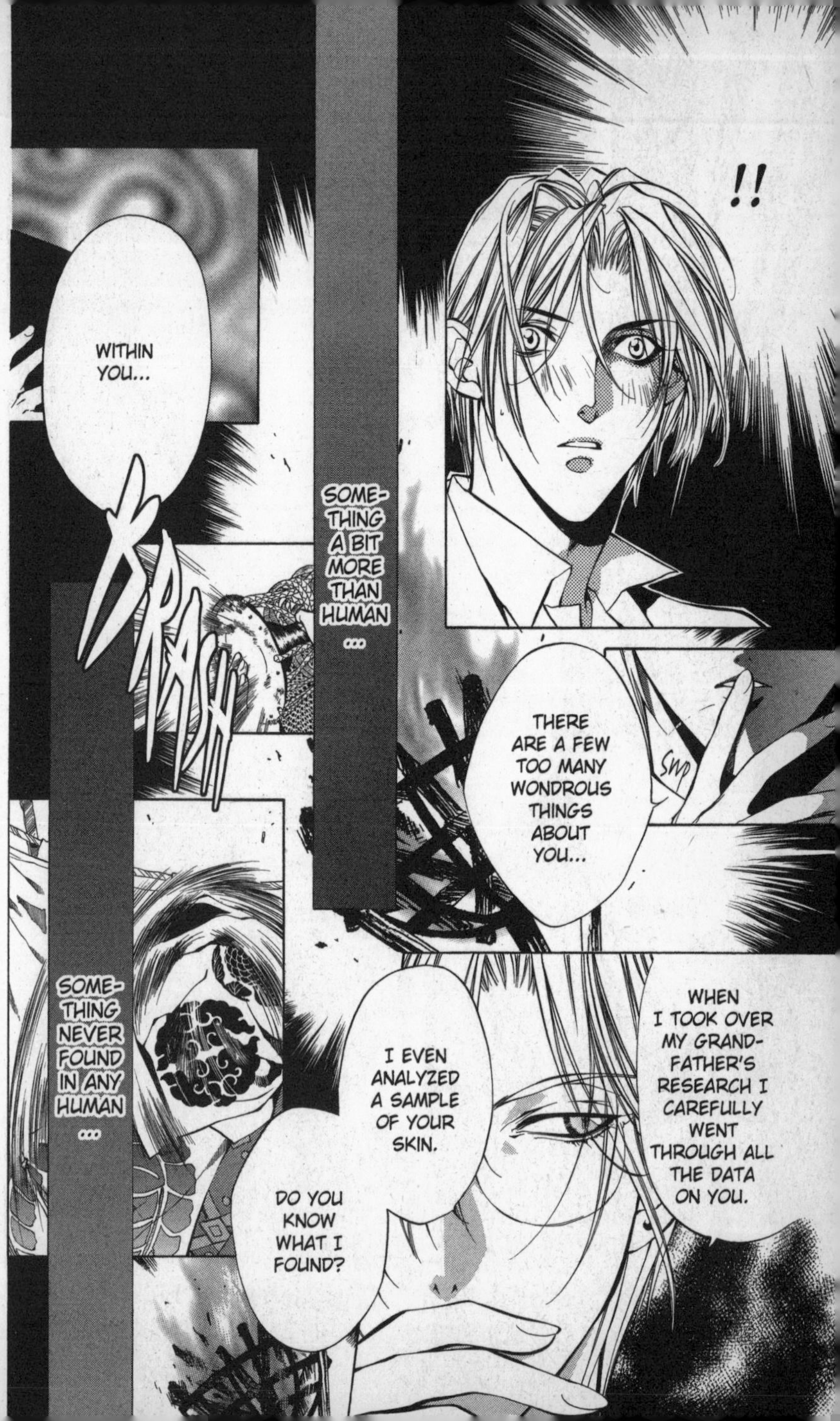
!!
THERE ARE A FEW TOO MANY WONDROUS THINGS ABOUT YOU...
SNP
WHEN I TOOK OVER MY GRAND-FATHER'S RESEARCH I CAREFULLY WENT THROUGH ALL THE DATA ON YOU.
I EVEN ANALYZED A SAMPLE OF YOUR SKIN.
DO YOU KNOW WHAT I FOUND?
SOME-THING A BIT MORE THAN HUMAN...
WITHIN YOU...
KRASH
SOME-THING NEVER FOUND IN ANY HUMAN...

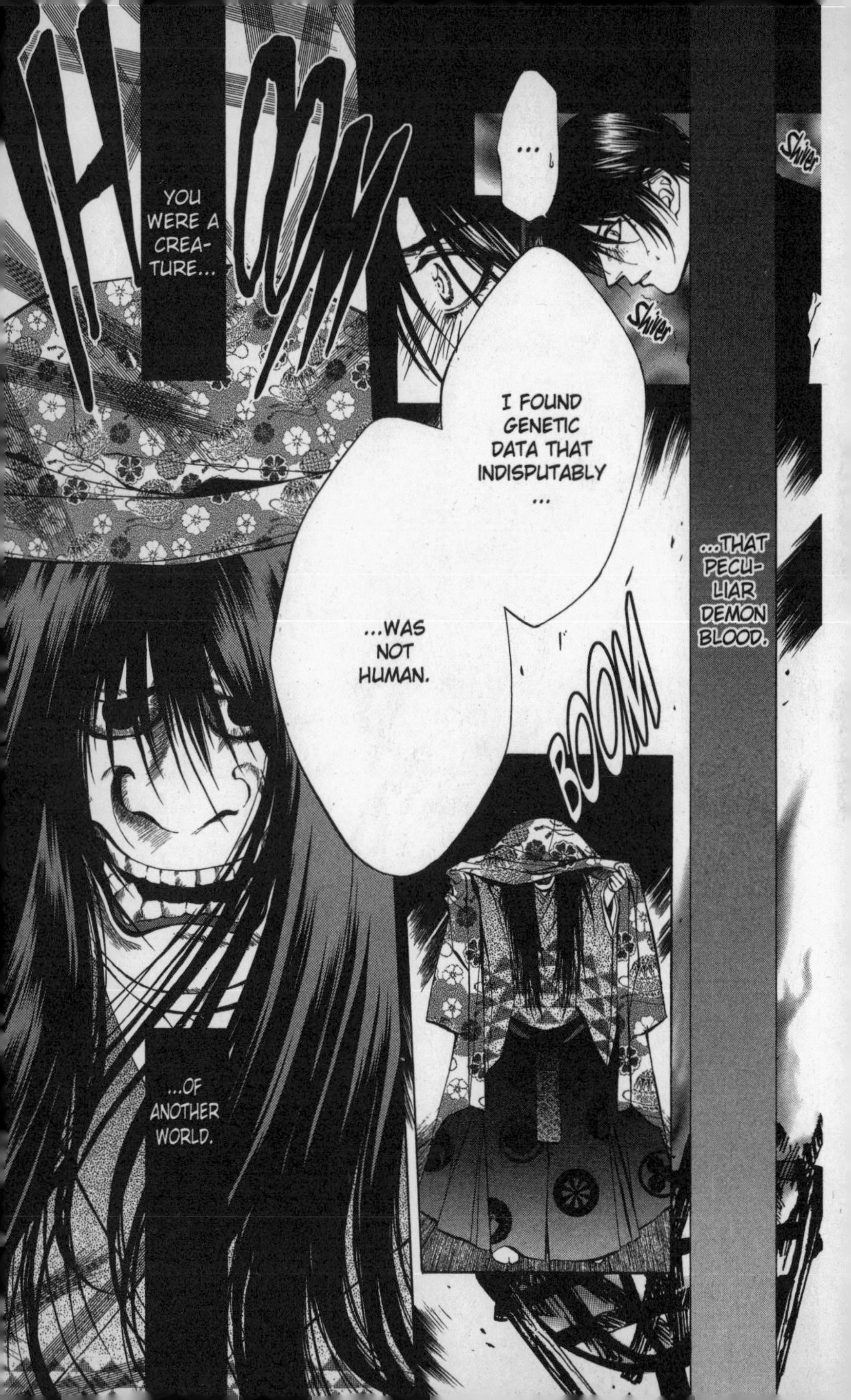
...
Shiver
Shiver
I FOUND GENETIC DATA THAT INDISPUTABLY ...
...WAS NOT HUMAN.
...THAT PECULIAR DEMON BLOOD.
BOOM
YOU WERE A CREATURE...
...OF ANOTHER WORLD.

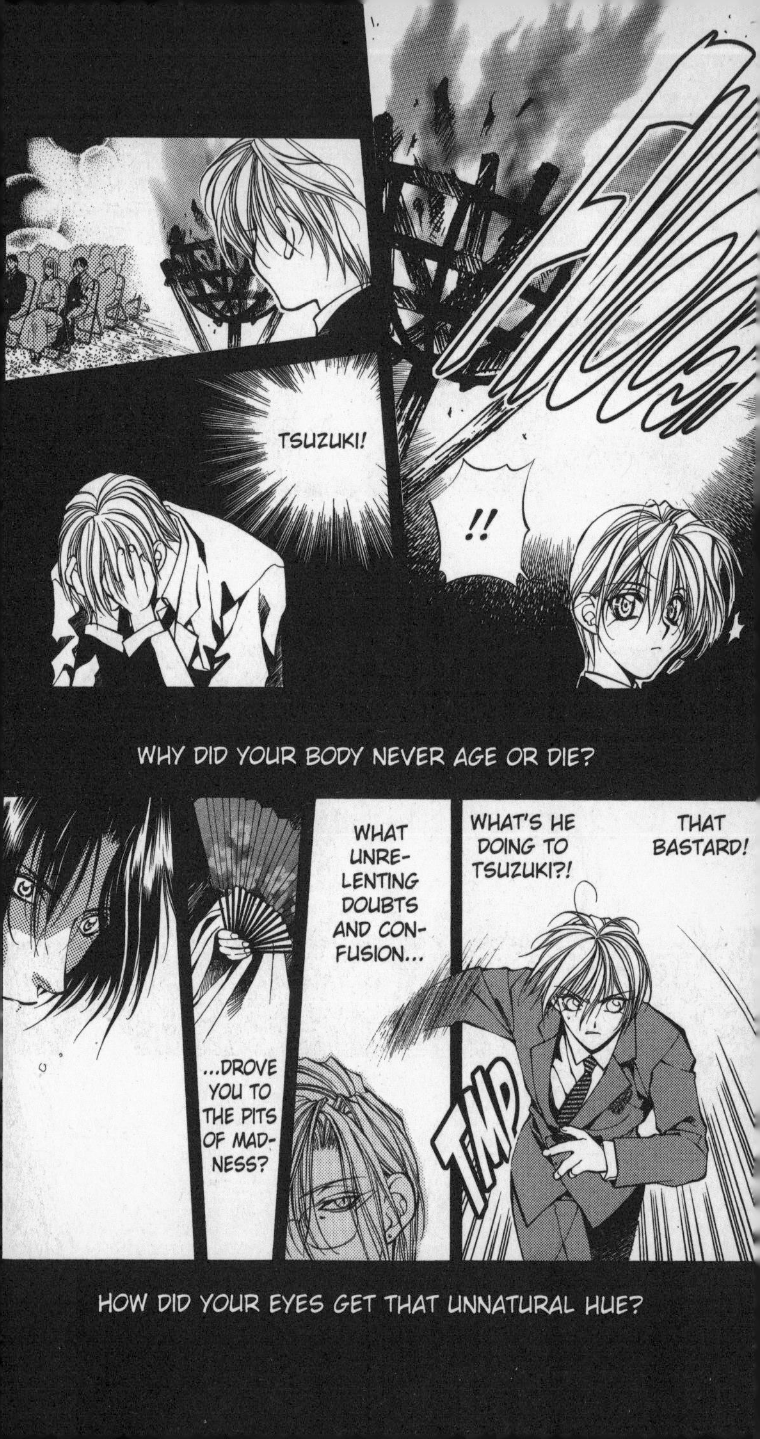
!!
TSUZUKI!
WHY DID YOUR BODY NEVER AGE OR DIE?
THAT BASTARD!
WHAT'S HE DOING TO TSUZUKI?!
TMP
WHAT UNRE-LENTING DOUBTS AND CON-FUSION...
...DROVE YOU TO THE PITS OF MAD-NESS?
HOW DID YOUR EYES GET THAT UNNATURAL HUE?

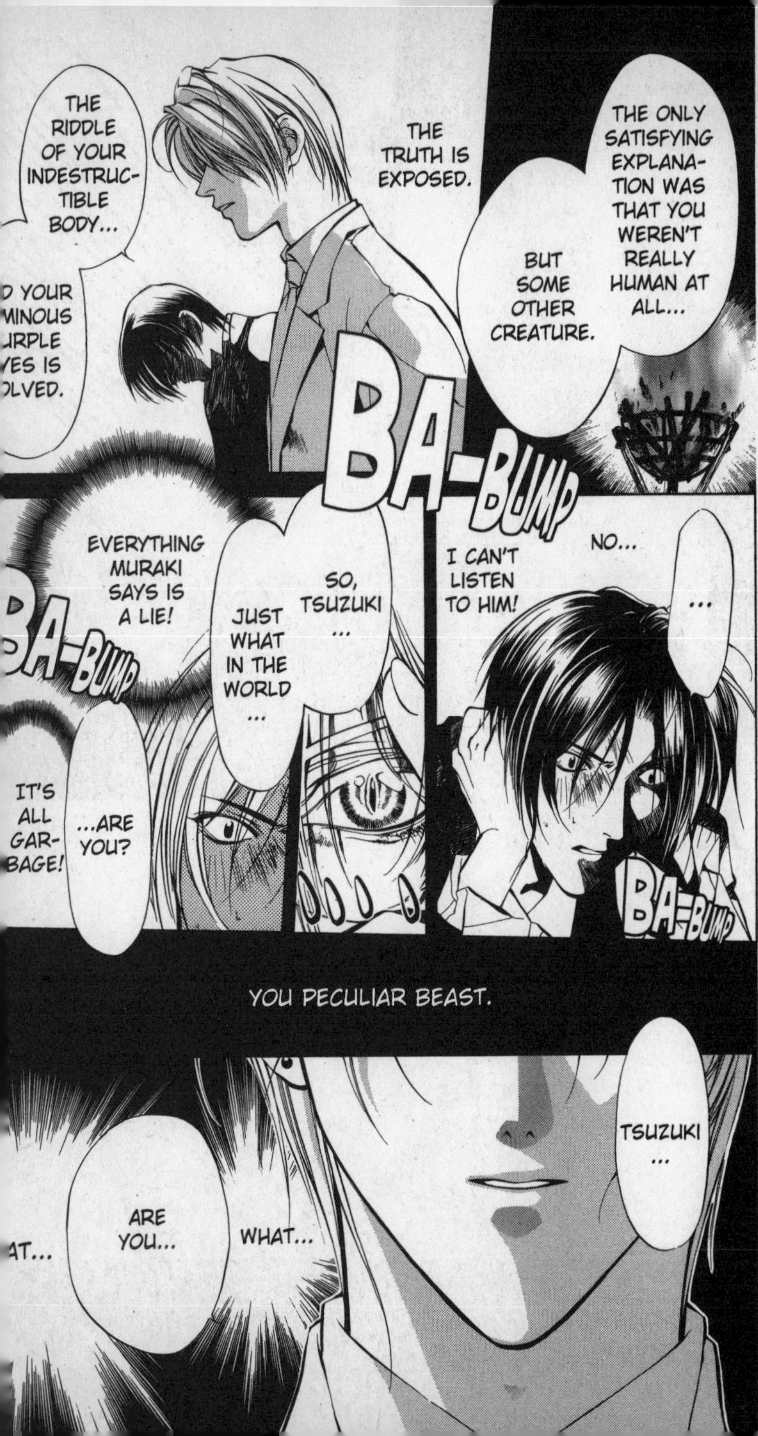
THE ONLY SATISFYING EXPLANATION WAS THAT YOU WEREN'T REALLY HUMAN AT ALL...
BUT SOME OTHER CREATURE.
THE TRUTH IS EXPOSED.
THE RIDDLE OF YOUR INDESTRUCTIBLE BODY...
D YOUR MINOUS URPLE YES IS OLVED.
BA-BUMP
...
NO...
I CAN'T LISTEN TO HIM!
BA-BUMP
SO, TSUZUKI ...
JUST WHAT IN THE WORLD ...
EVERYTHING MURAKI SAYS IS A LIE!
BA-BUMP
...ARE YOU?
IT'S ALL GARBAGE!
YOU PECULIAR BEAST.
TSUZUKI ...
WHAT...
ARE YOU...
AT...

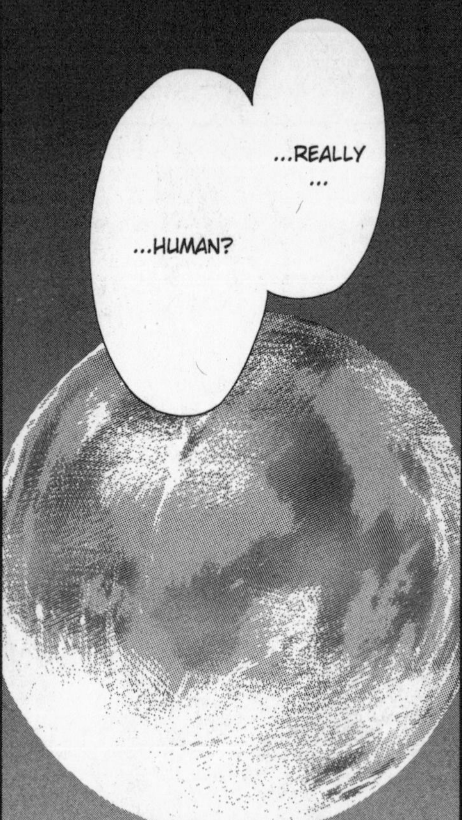
...REALLY ...
...HUMAN?

WHAT IN THE WORLD AM I?

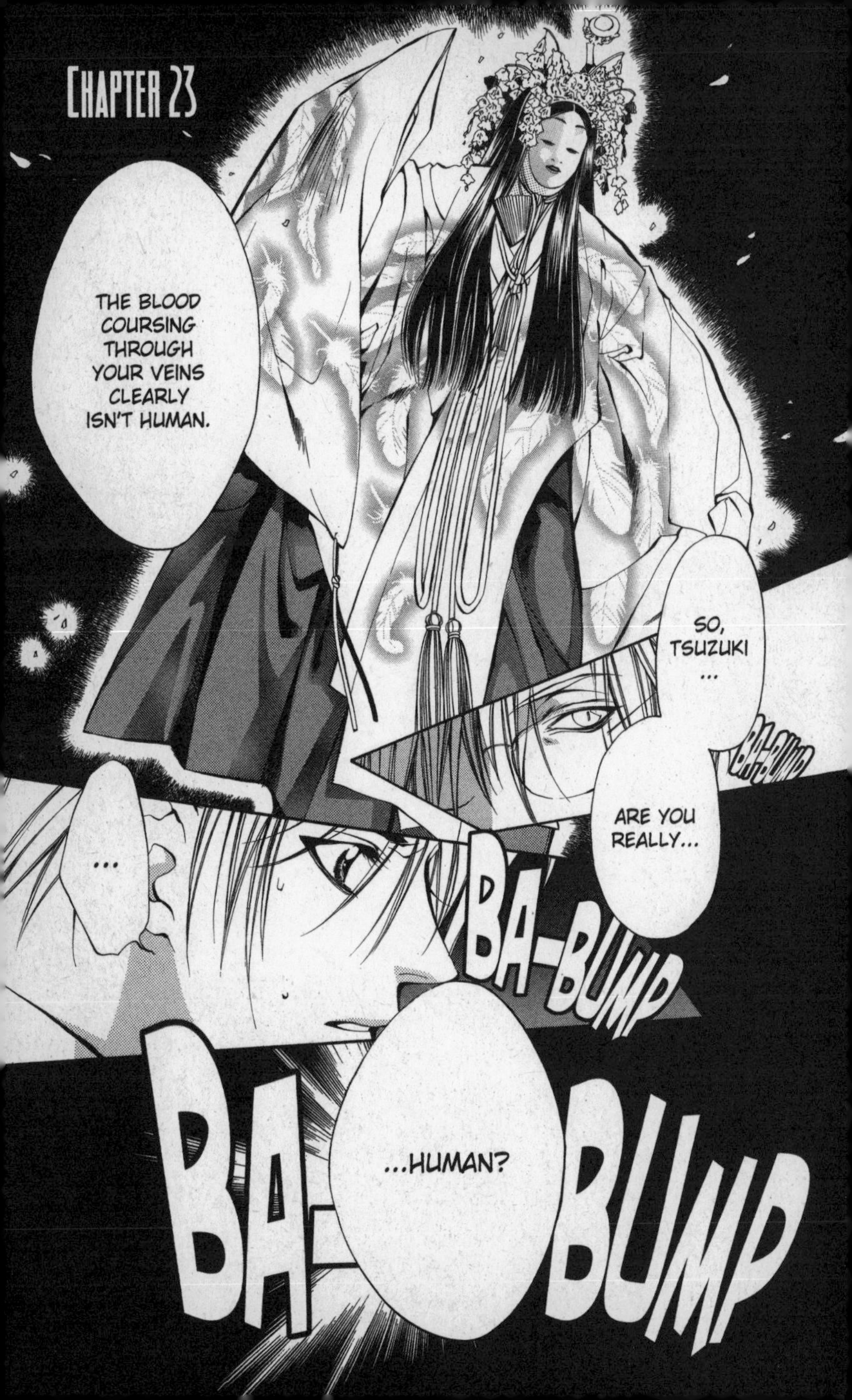
CHAPTER 23
THE BLOOD COURSING THROUGH YOUR VEINS CLEARLY ISN'T HUMAN.
SO, TSUZUKI ...
BA-BUMP
ARE YOU REALLY...
...
BA-BUMP
...HUMAN?
BA-BUMP

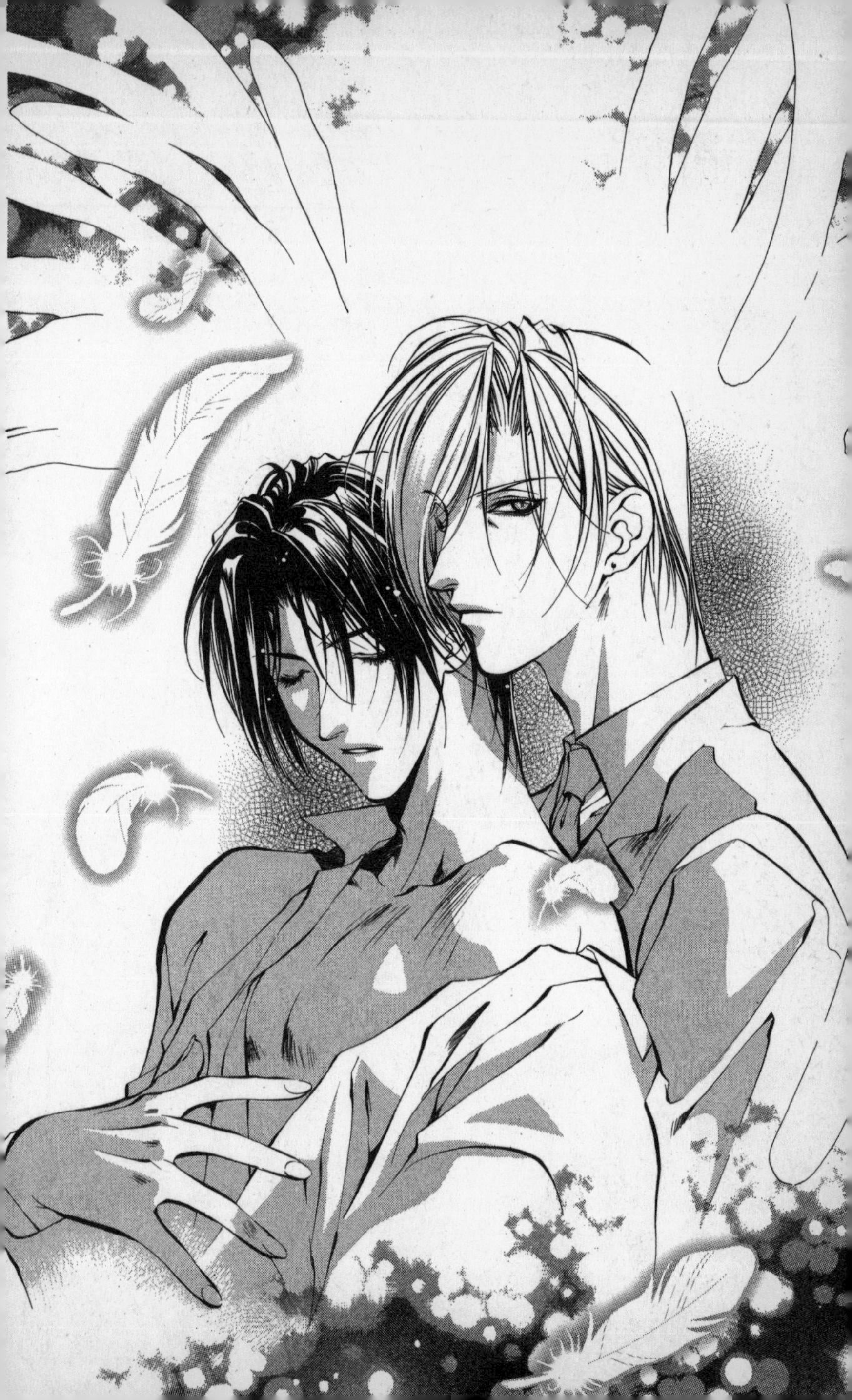

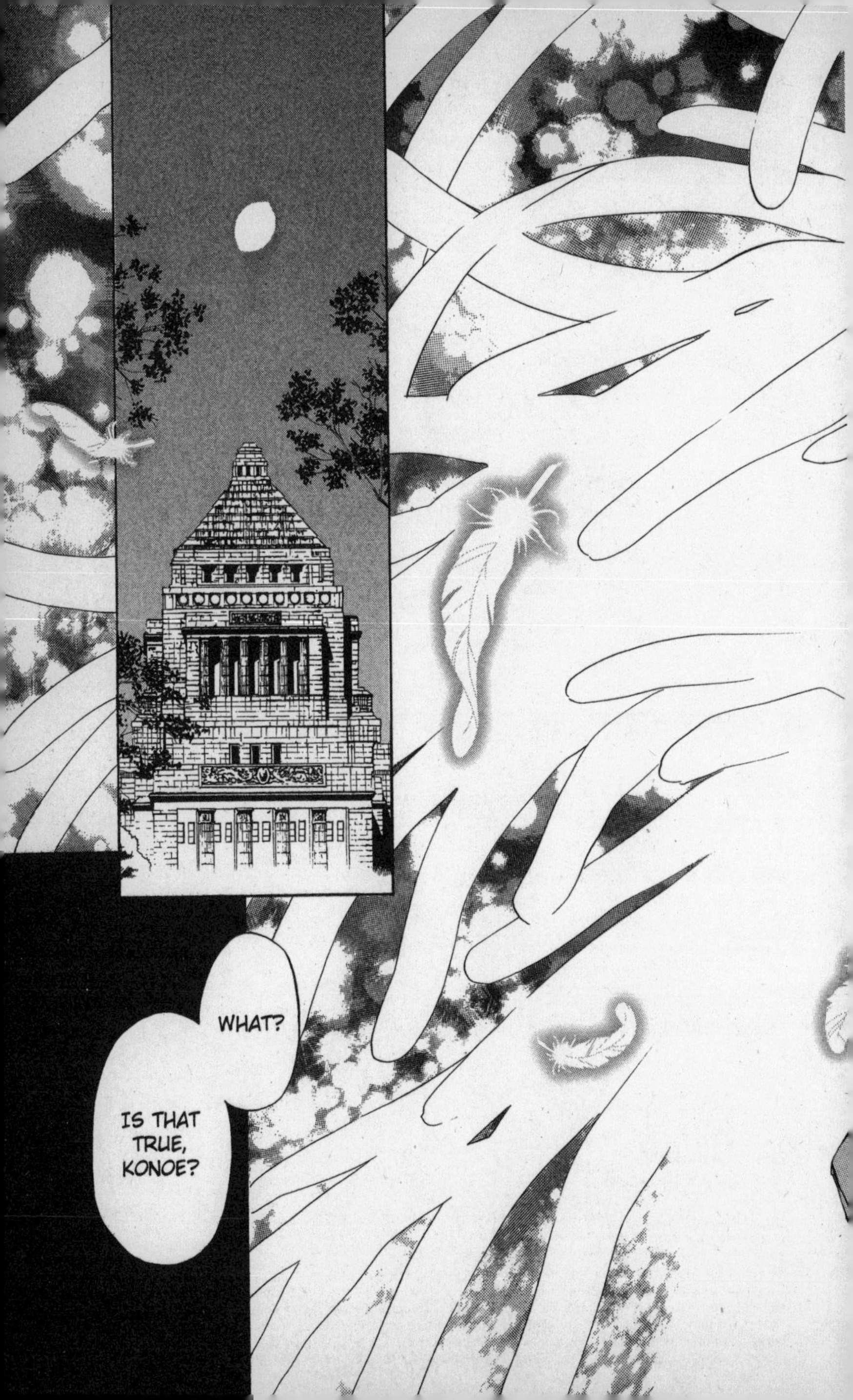
WHAT?
IS THAT TRUE, KONOE?

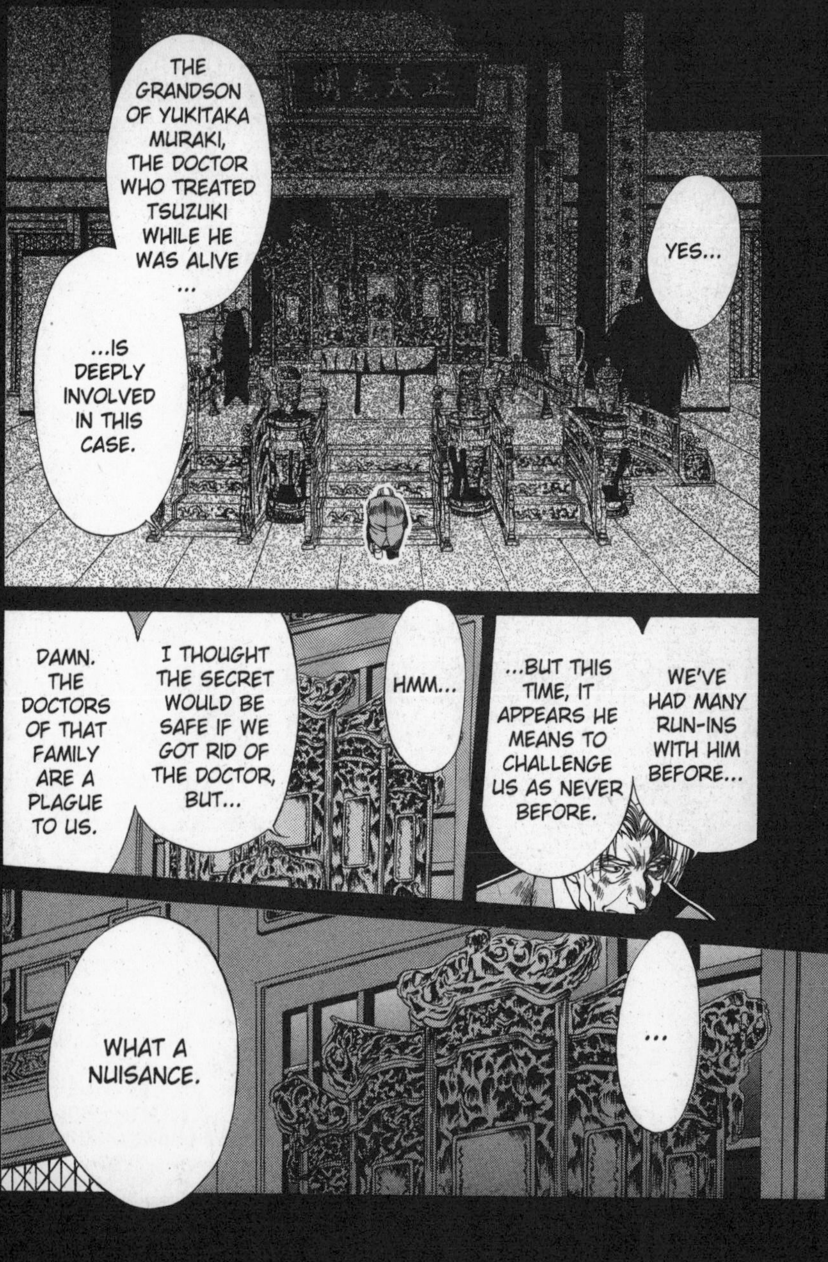
THE GRANDSON OF YUKITAKA MURAKI, THE DOCTOR WHO TREATED TSUZUKI WHILE HE WAS ALIVE ...
...IS DEEPLY INVOLVED IN THIS CASE.
YES...
WE'VE HAD MANY RUN-INS WITH HIM BEFORE...
...BUT THIS TIME, IT APPEARS HE MEANS TO CHALLENGE US AS NEVER BEFORE.
HMM...
I THOUGHT THE SECRET WOULD BE SAFE IF WE GOT RID OF THE DOCTOR, BUT...
DAMN. THE DOCTORS OF THAT FAMILY ARE A PLAGUE TO US.
...
WHAT A NUISANCE.

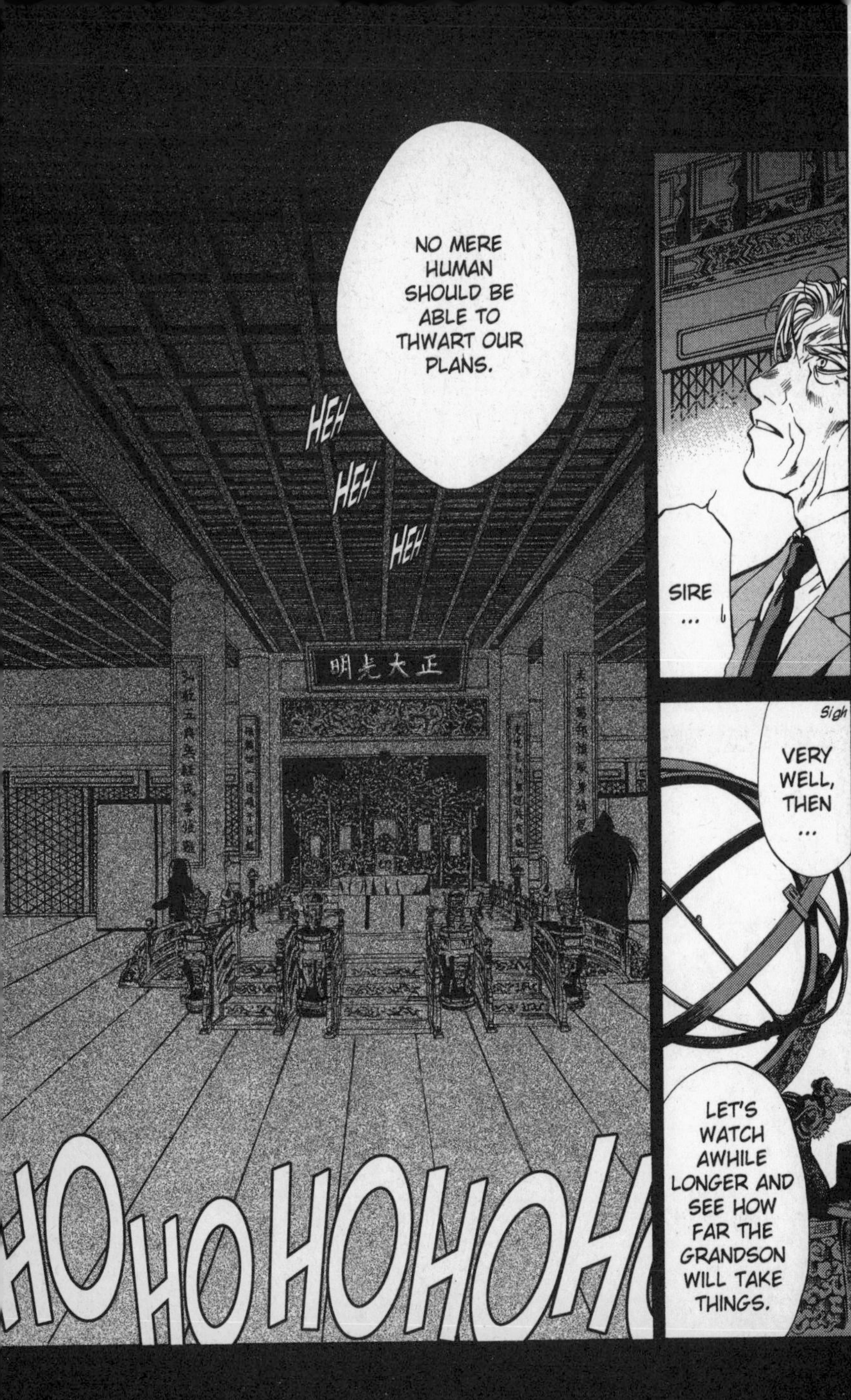
SIRE ...
Sigh
VERY WELL, THEN ...
LET'S WATCH AWHILE LONGER AND SEE HOW FAR THE GRANDSON WILL TAKE THINGS.
NO MERE HUMAN SHOULD BE ABLE TO THWART OUR PLANS.
HEH HEH HEH
正大光明
HO HO HO HOHOHO

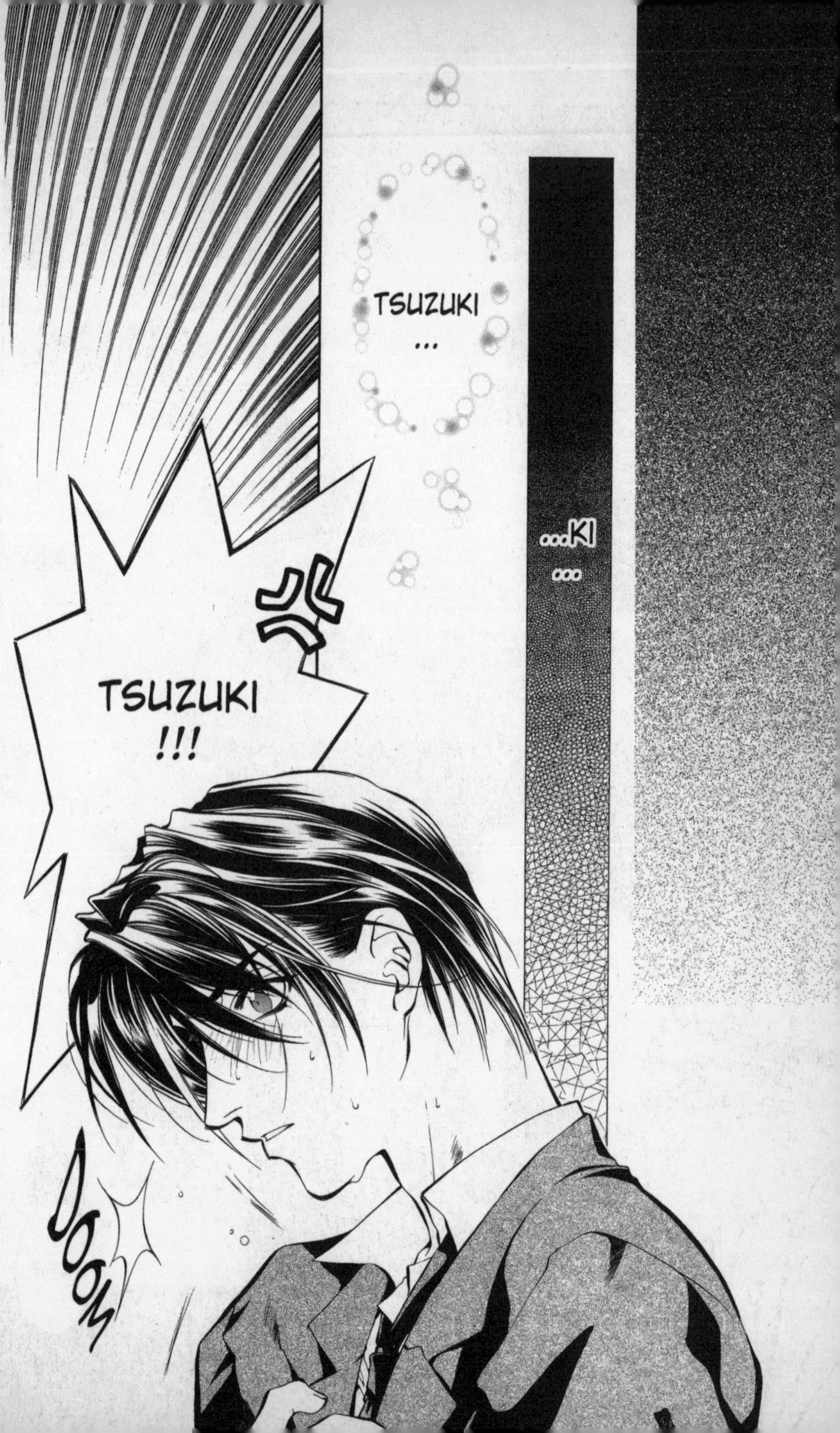
...KI
...
TSUZUKI
...
TSUZUKI
!!!
DOOM

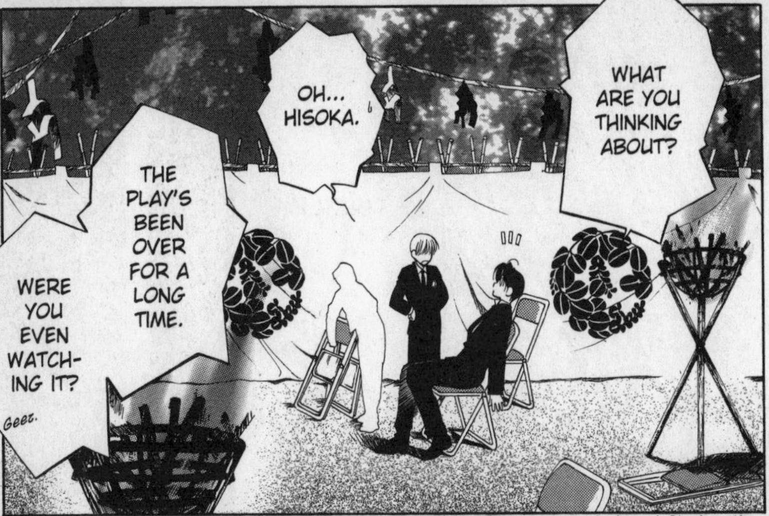
WHAT ARE YOU THINKING ABOUT?
OH... HISOKA.
THE PLAY'S BEEN OVER FOR A LONG TIME.
WERE YOU EVEN WATCHING IT?
Geez.
▲The Doctor seems to have left abruptly.

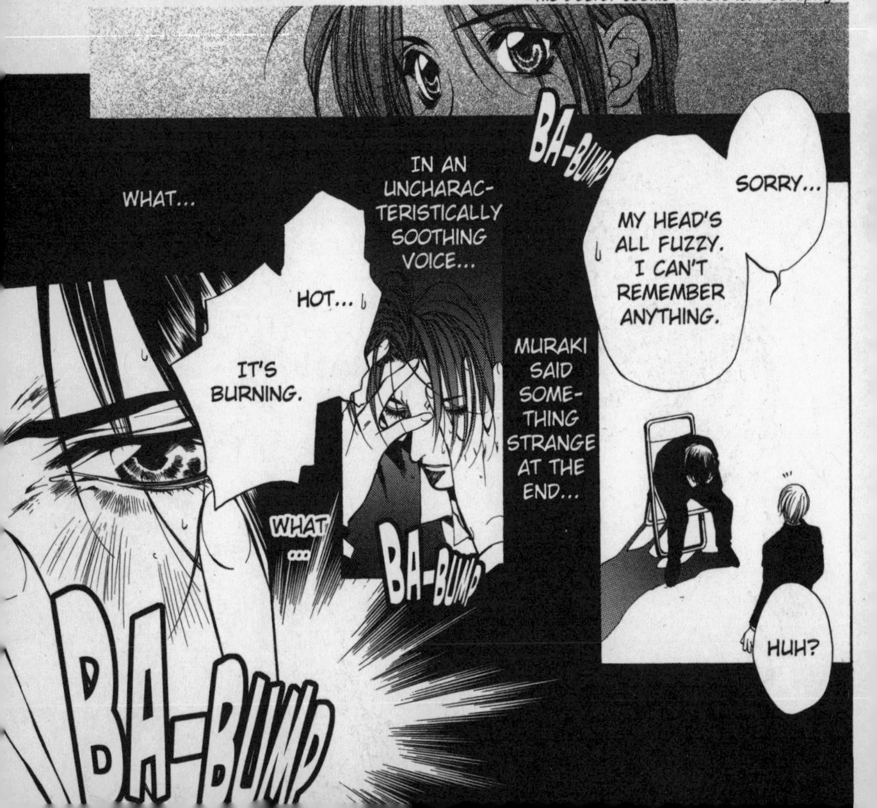
BA-BUMP
SORRY...
MY HEAD'S ALL FUZZY. I CAN'T REMEMBER ANYTHING.
HUH?
MURAKI SAID SOMETHING STRANGE AT THE END...
IN AN UNCHARACTERISTICALLY SOOTHING VOICE...
WHAT...
HOT...
IT'S BURNING.
WHAT...
BA-BUMP
BA-BUMP

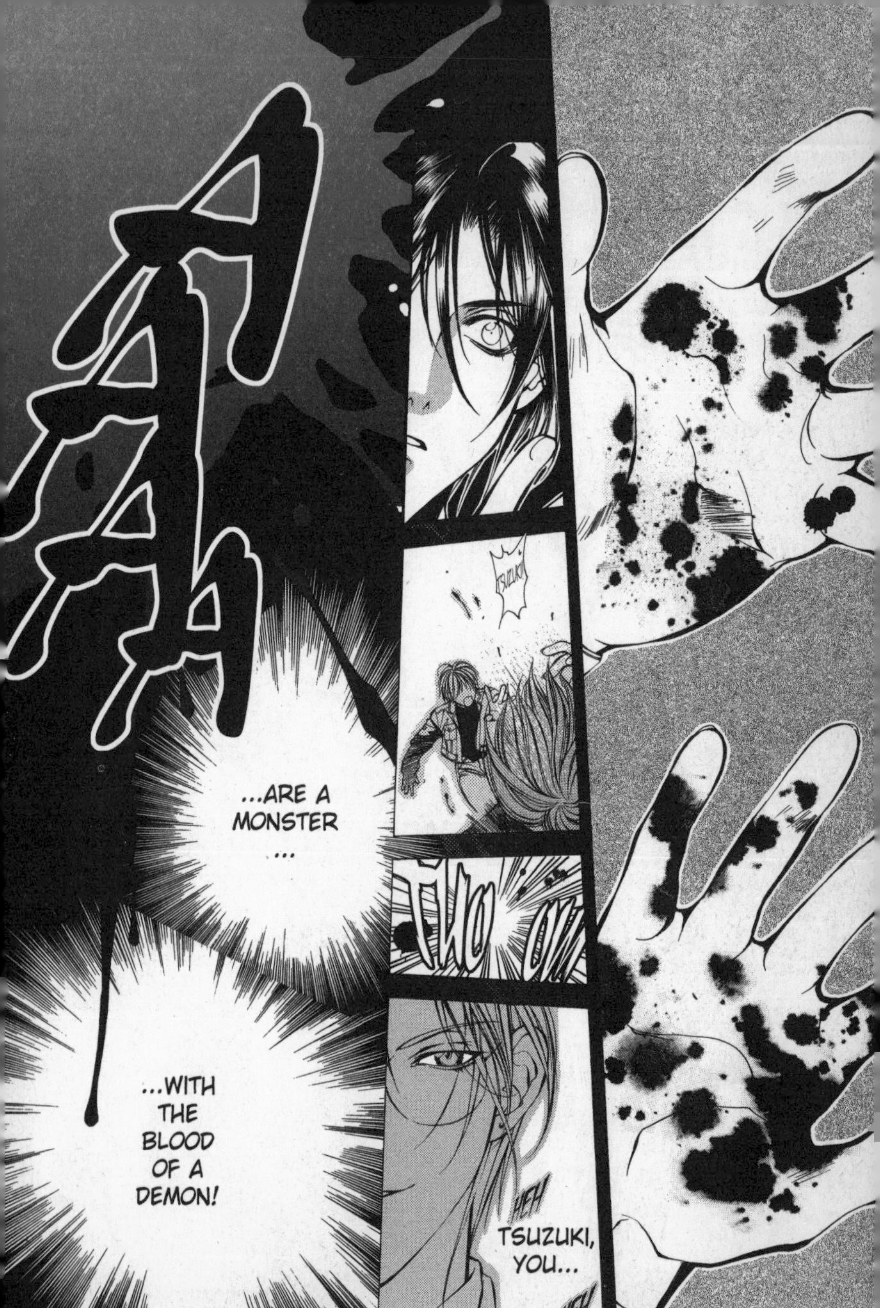
TSUZUKI!
HEH
TSUZUKI, YOU...
HEH
...ARE A MONSTER ...
...WITH THE BLOOD OF A DEMON!

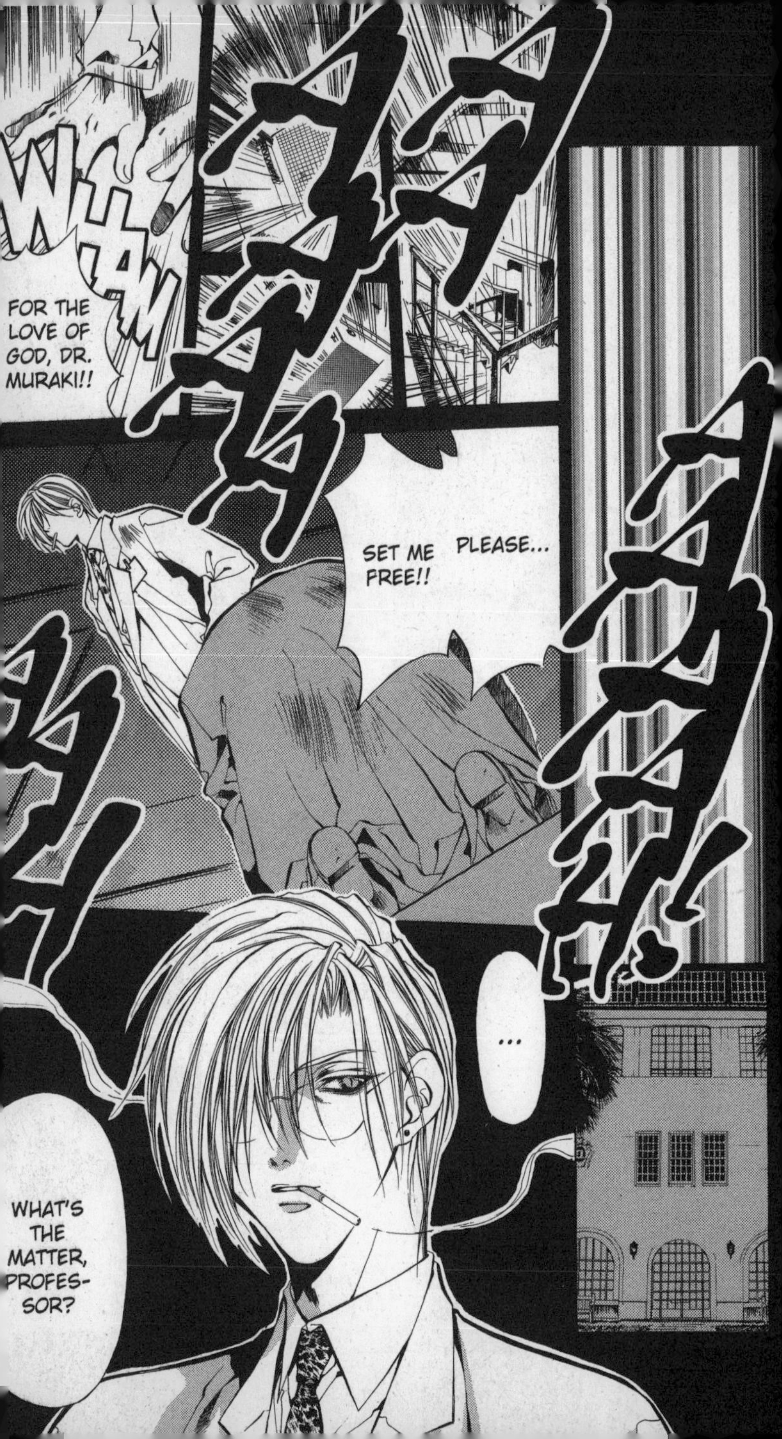
WHAM
FOR THE LOVE OF GOD, DR. MURAKI!!
PLEASE...
SET ME FREE!!
...
WHAT'S THE MATTER, PROFESSOR?

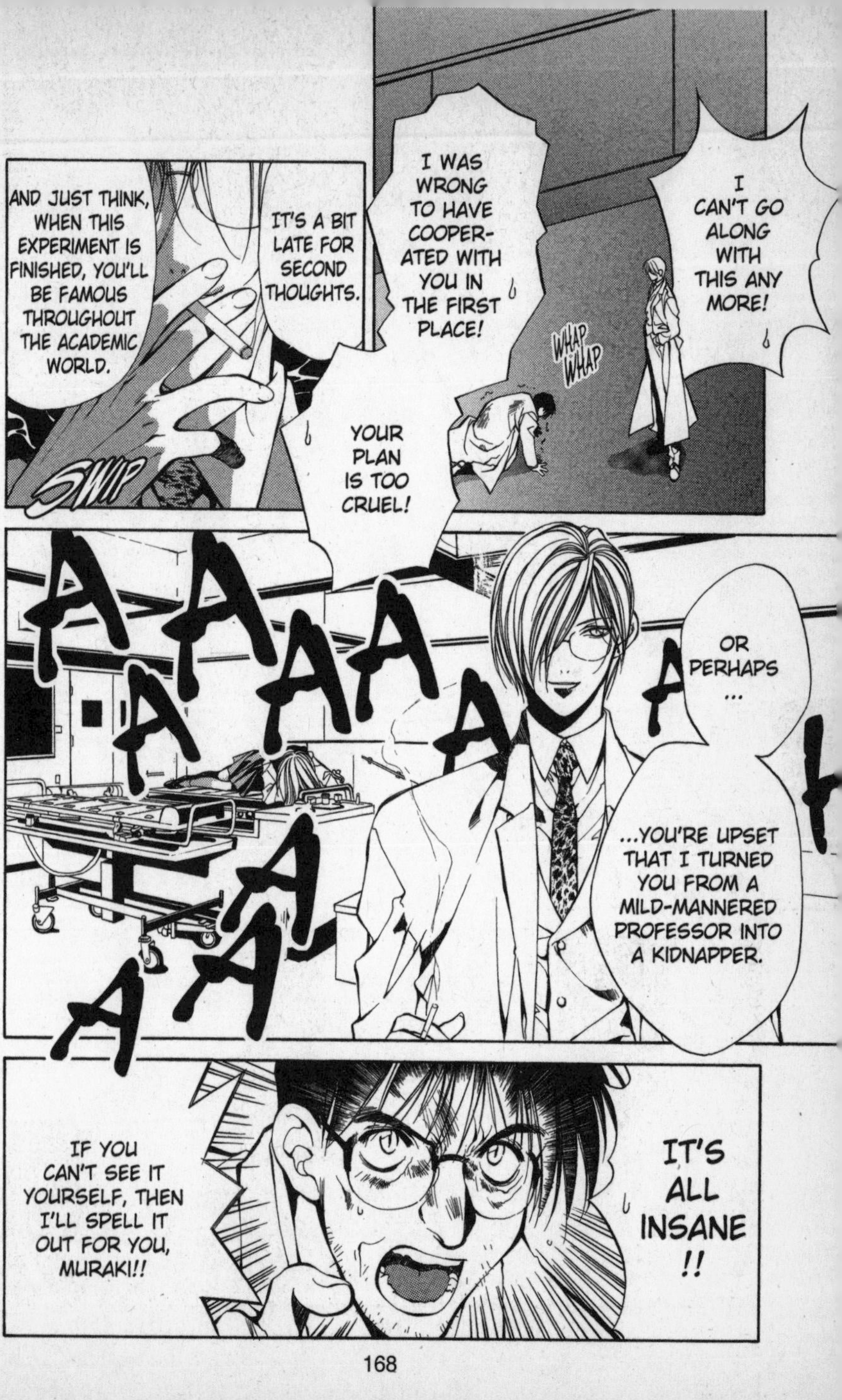
I CAN'T GO ALONG WITH THIS ANY MORE!
WHAP WHAP
I WAS WRONG TO HAVE COOPER-ATED WITH YOU IN THE FIRST PLACE!
YOUR PLAN IS TOO CRUEL!
IT'S A BIT LATE FOR SECOND THOUGHTS.
AND JUST THINK, WHEN THIS EXPERIMENT IS FINISHED, YOU'LL BE FAMOUS THROUGHOUT THE ACADEMIC WORLD.
SWIP
OR PERHAPS ...
...YOU'RE UPSET THAT I TURNED YOU FROM A MILD-MANNERED PROFESSOR INTO A KIDNAPPER.
AAAAAAAAAAAA
IT'S ALL INSANE !!
IF YOU CAN'T SEE IT YOURSELF, THEN I'LL SPELL IT OUT FOR YOU, MURAKI!!

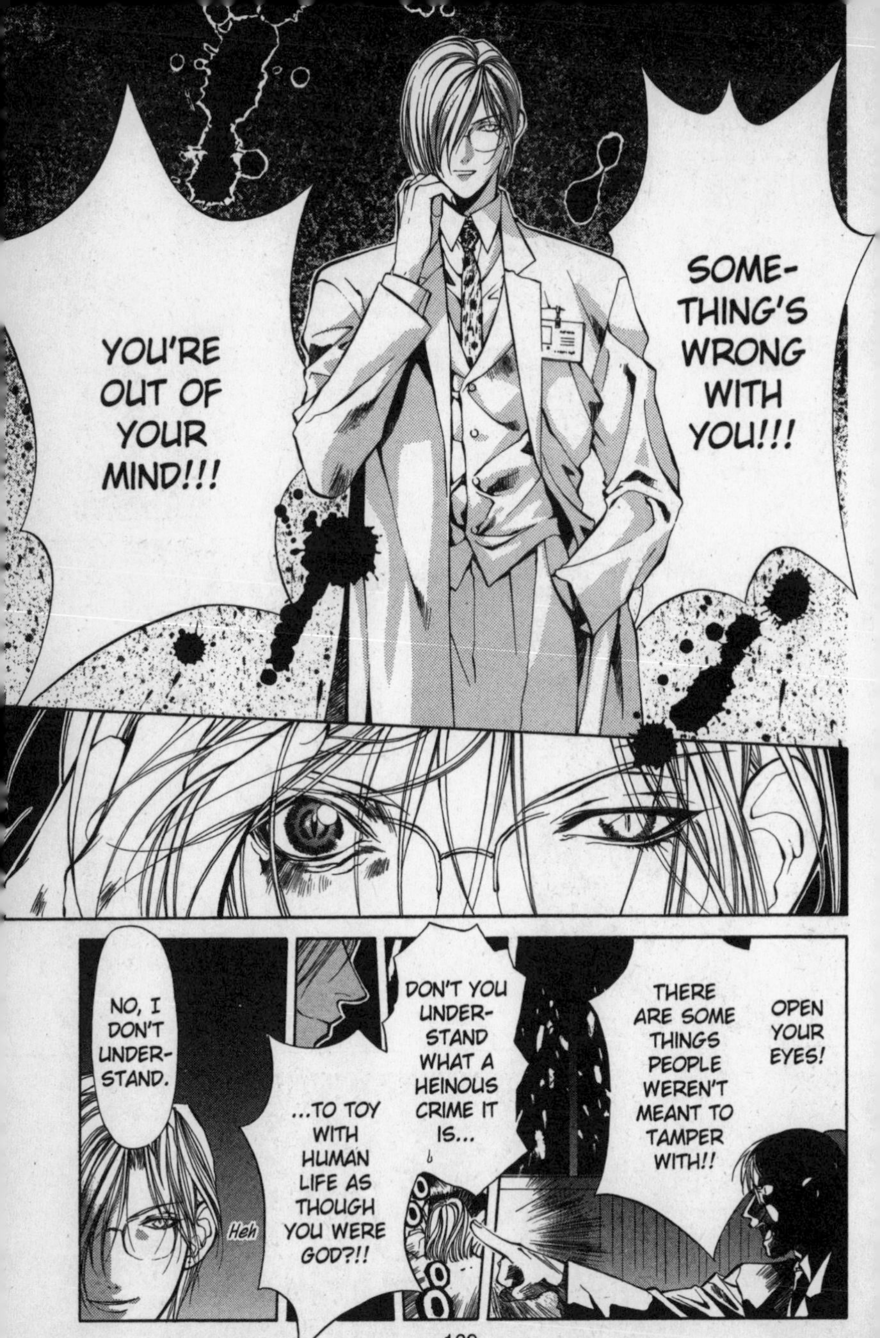
SOME-THING'S WRONG WITH YOU!!!
YOU'RE OUT OF YOUR MIND!!!
OPEN YOUR EYES!
THERE ARE SOME THINGS PEOPLE WEREN'T MEANT TO TAMPER WITH!!
DON'T YOU UNDER-STAND WHAT A HEINOUS CRIME IT IS...
...TO TOY WITH HUMAN LIFE AS THOUGH YOU WERE GOD?!!
NO, I DON'T UNDER-STAND.
Heh

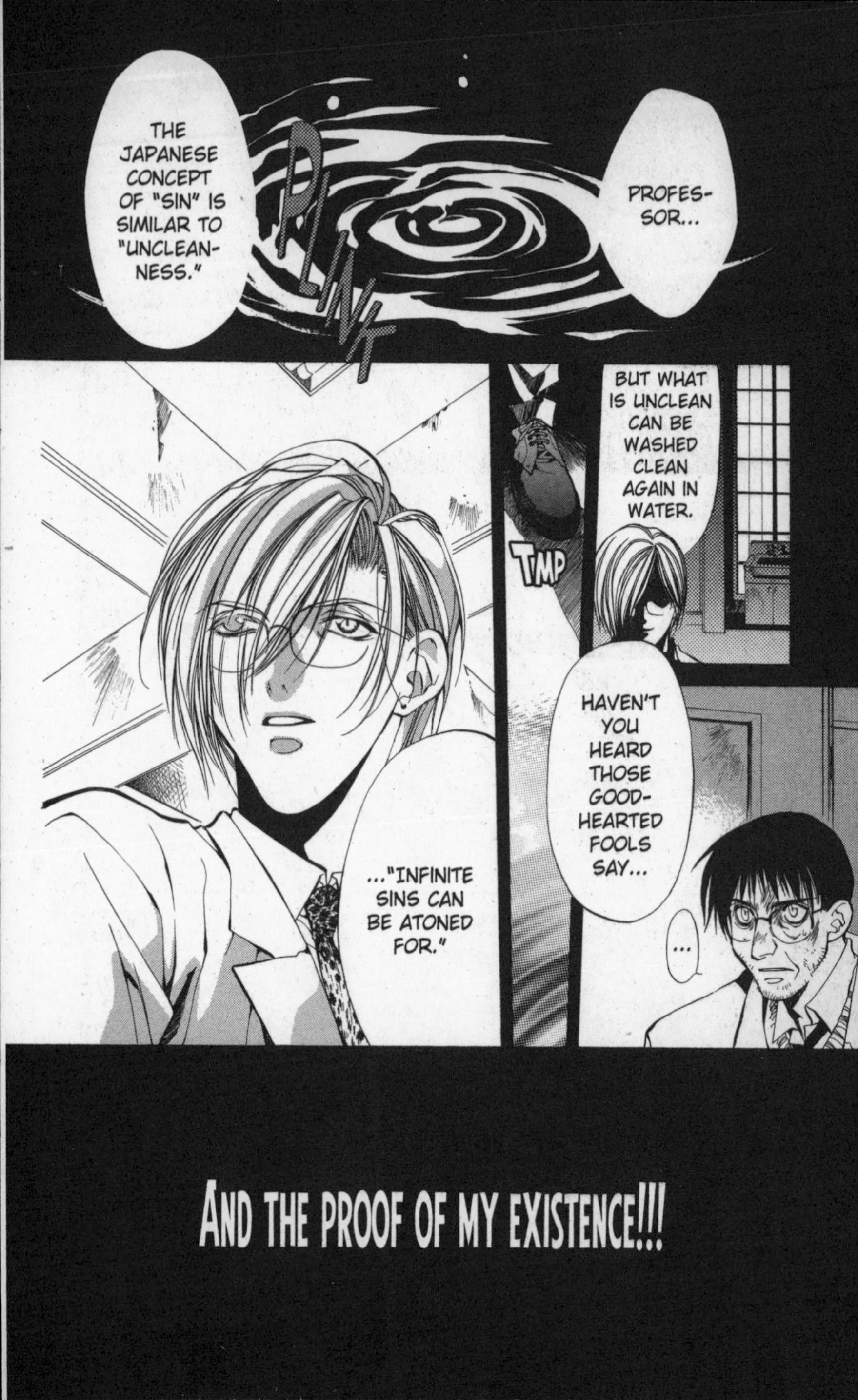
PROFES-SOR...
PLINK
THE JAPANESE CONCEPT OF "SIN" IS SIMILAR TO "UNCLEAN-NESS."
BUT WHAT IS UNCLEAN CAN BE WASHED CLEAN AGAIN IN WATER.
TMP
HAVEN'T YOU HEARD THOSE GOOD-HEARTED FOOLS SAY...
...
..."INFINITE SINS CAN BE ATONED FOR."
AND THE PROOF OF MY EXISTENCE!!!

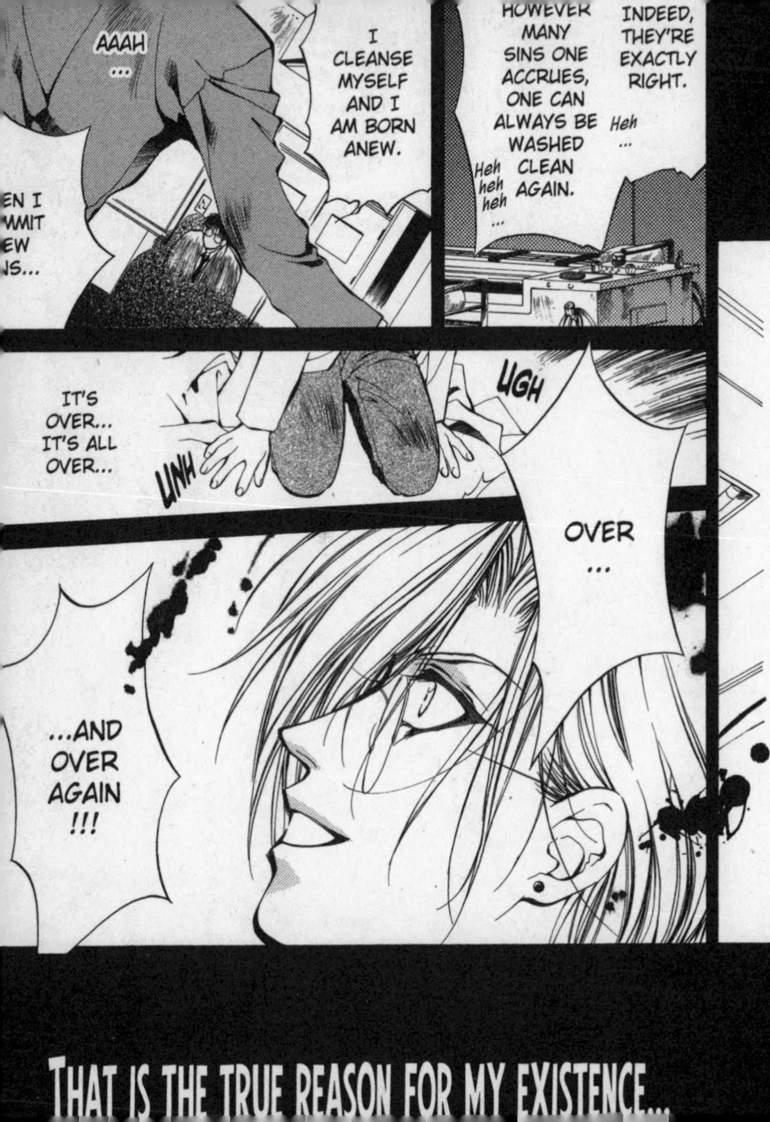
INDEED, THEY'RE EXACTLY RIGHT.
Heh ...
HOWEVER MANY SINS ONE ACCRUES, ONE CAN ALWAYS BE WASHED CLEAN AGAIN.
Heh heh heh ...
I CLEANSE MYSELF AND I AM BORN ANEW.
AAAH ...
EN I MMIT EW NS...
UGH
IT'S OVER... IT'S ALL OVER...
UNH
OVER ...
...AND OVER AGAIN !!!
THAT IS THE TRUE REASON FOR MY EXISTENCE...

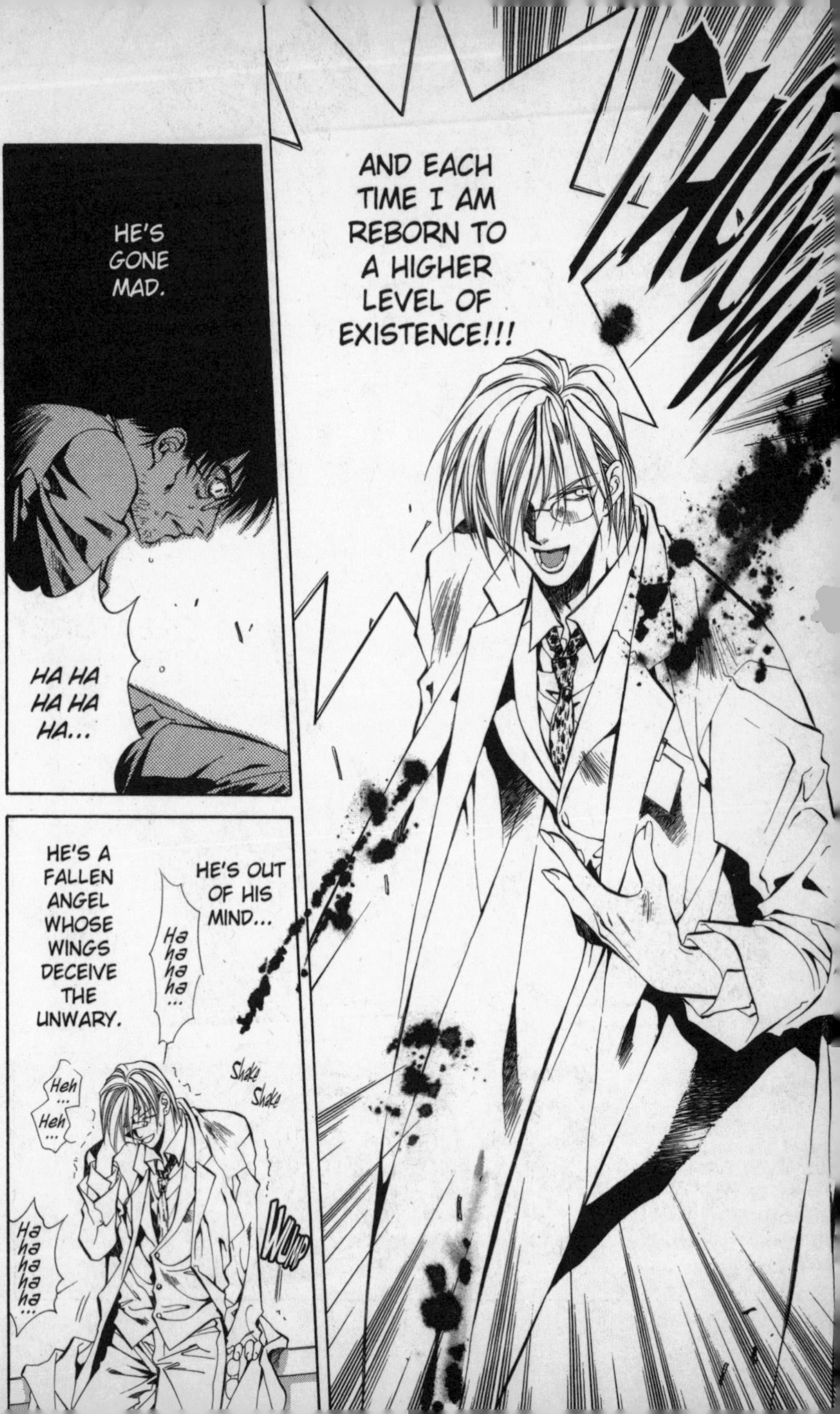
THUM
AND EACH TIME I AM REBORN TO A HIGHER LEVEL OF EXISTENCE!!!
HE'S GONE MAD.
HA HA HA HA HA...
HE'S OUT OF HIS MIND...
HE'S A FALLEN ANGEL WHOSE WINGS DECEIVE THE UNWARY.
Ha ha ha ha ha...
Shake Shake
Heh... Heh...
WUMP
Ha ha ha ha ha ha...

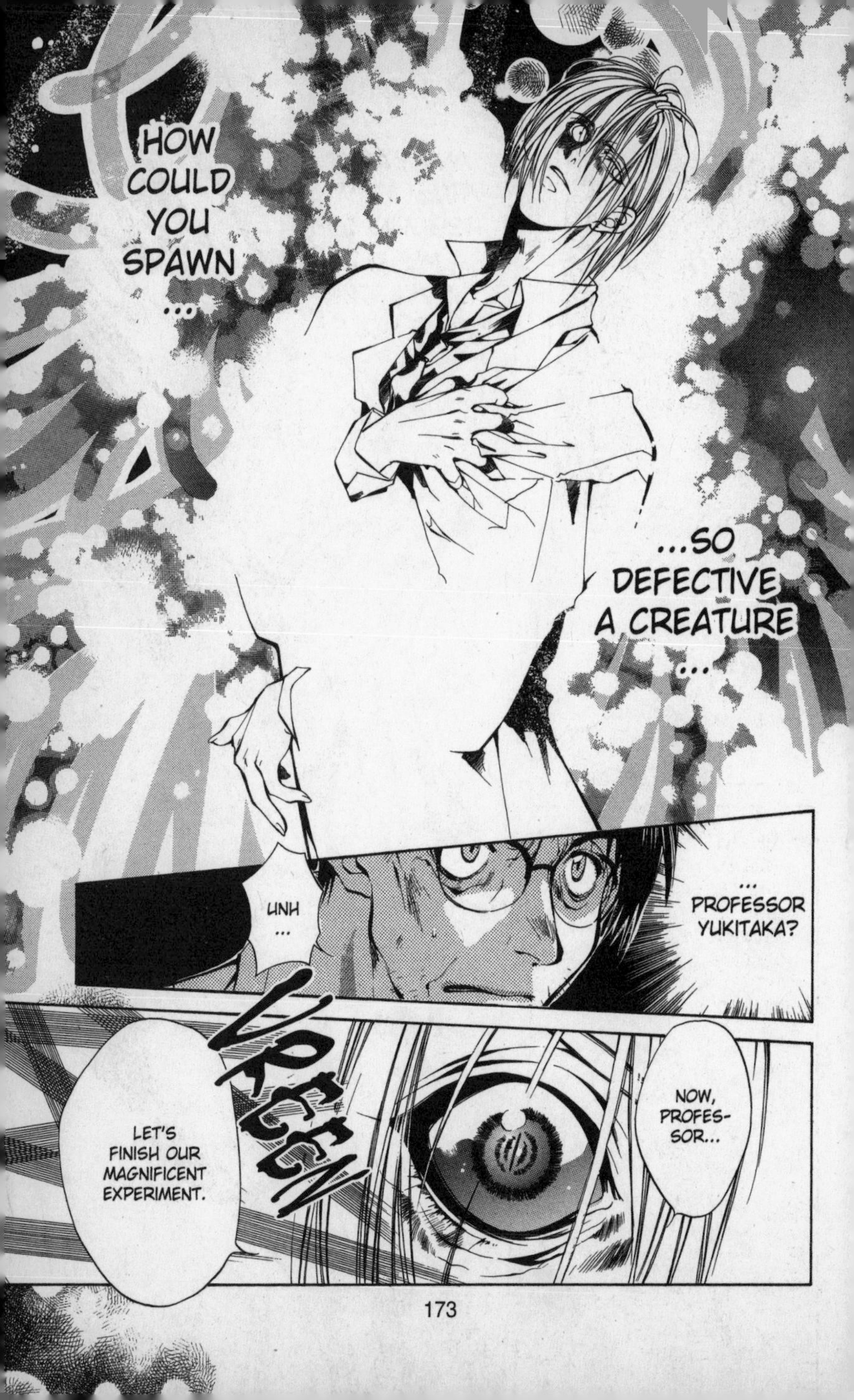
HOW COULD YOU SPAWN ...
...SO DEFECTIVE A CREATURE ...
... PROFESSOR YUKITAKA?
UNH ...
NOW, PROFES-SOR...
VREEN
LET'S FINISH OUR MAGNIFICENT EXPERIMENT.

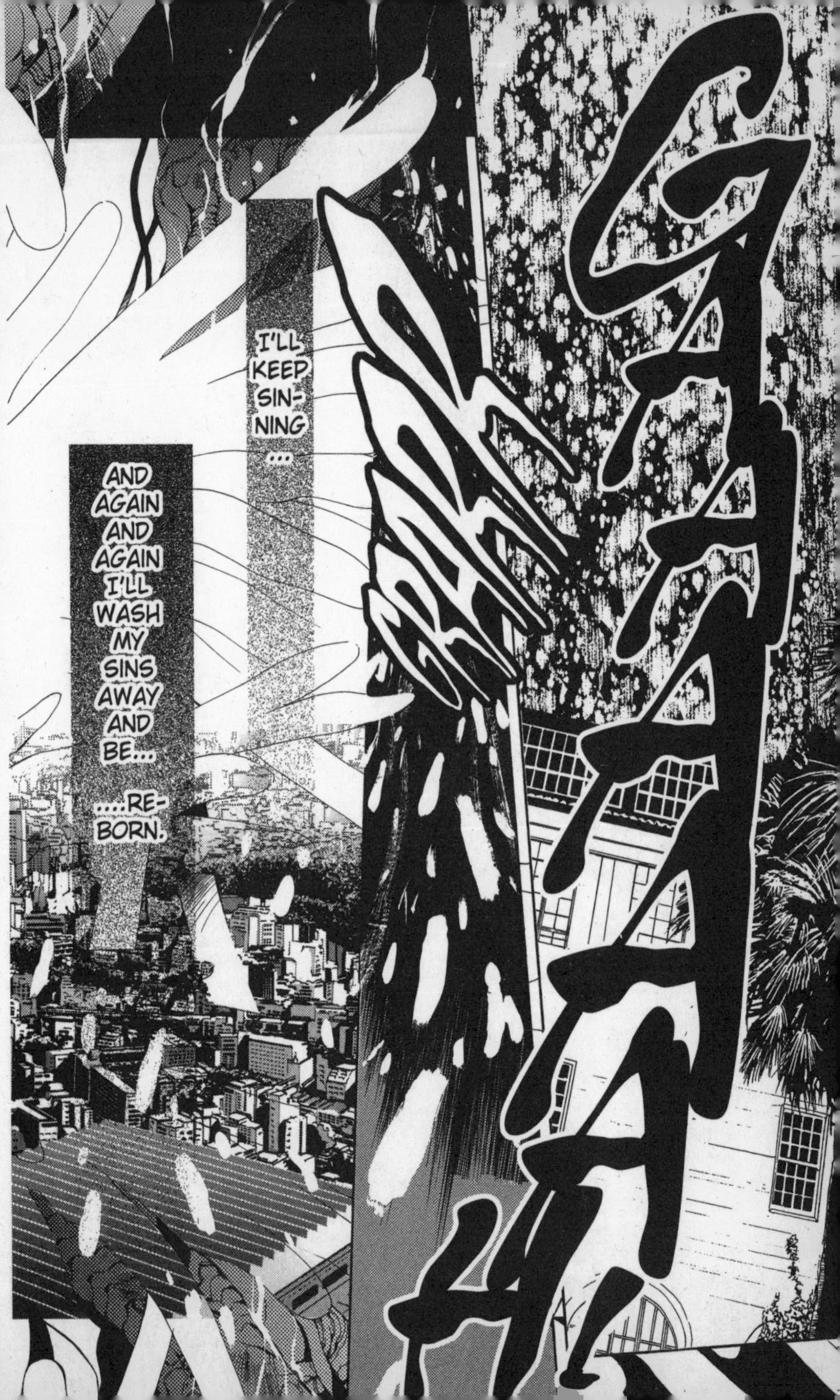
I'LL KEEP SIN-NING...
AND AGAIN AND AGAIN I'LL WASH MY SINS AWAY AND BE...
....RE-BORN.

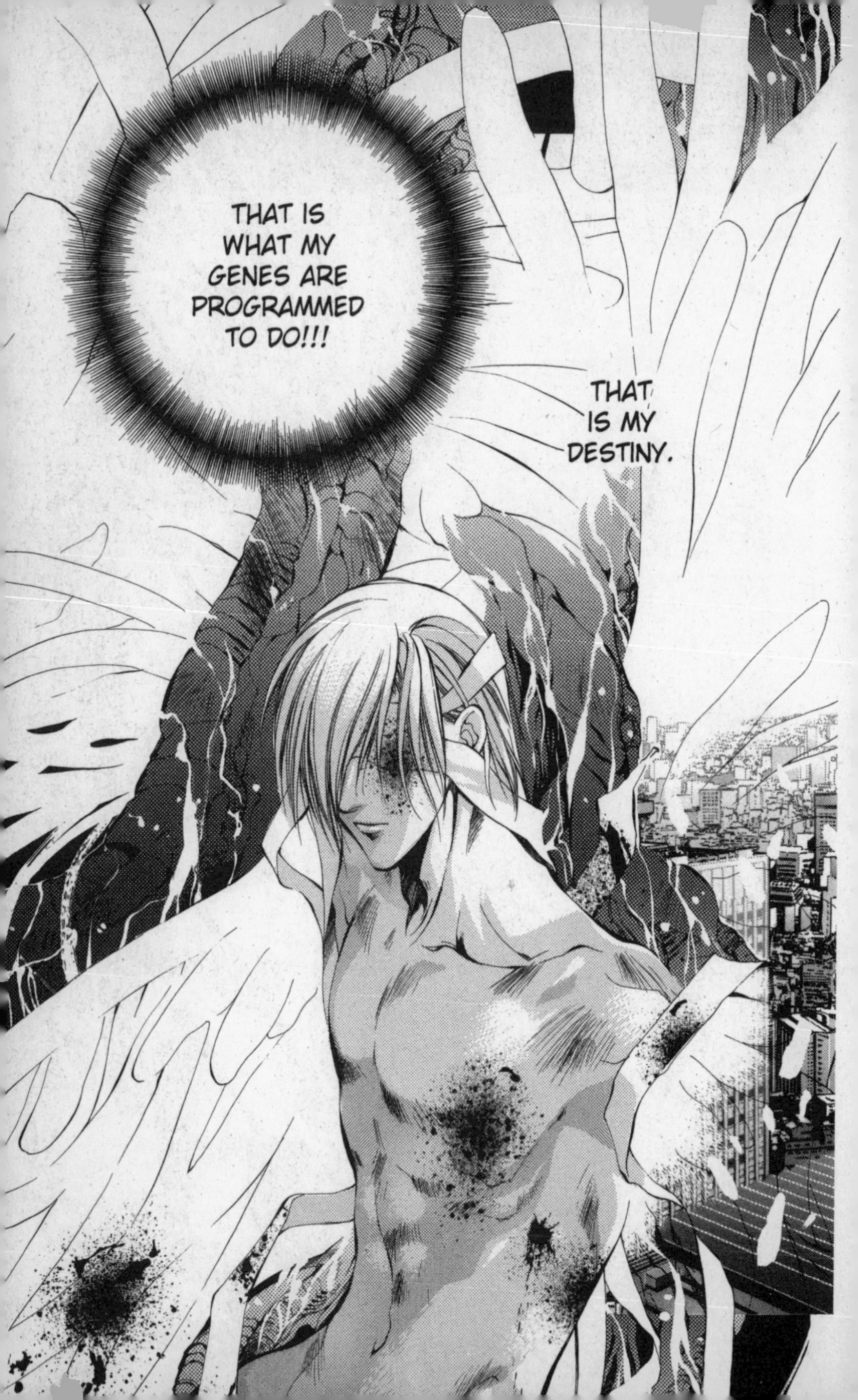
THAT IS WHAT MY GENES ARE PROGRAMMED TO DO!!!
THAT IS MY DESTINY.

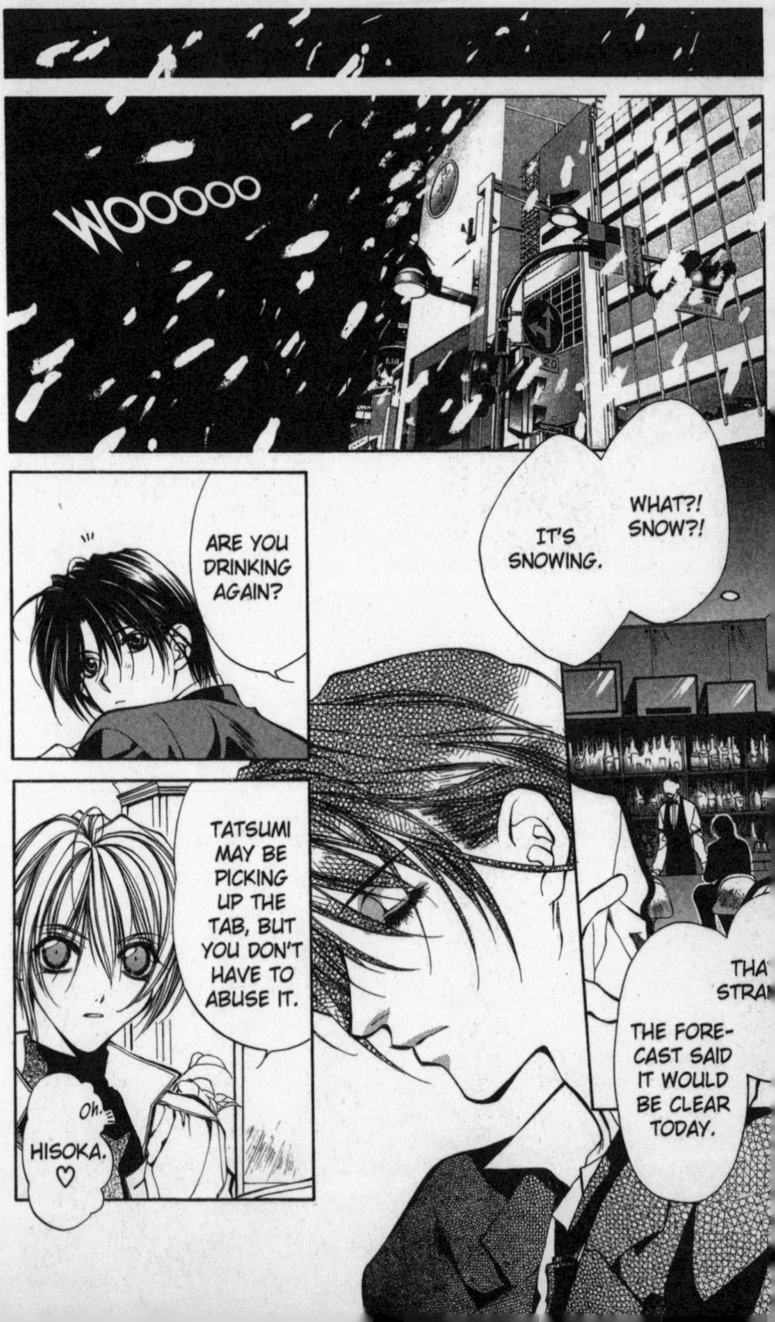

WOOOOO
WHAT?! SNOW?!
IT'S SNOWING.
THE FORE-CAST SAID IT WOULD BE CLEAR TODAY.
ARE YOU DRINKING AGAIN?
TATSUMI MAY BE PICKING UP THE TAB, BUT YOU DON'T HAVE TO ABUSE IT.
Oh. HISOKA. ♡

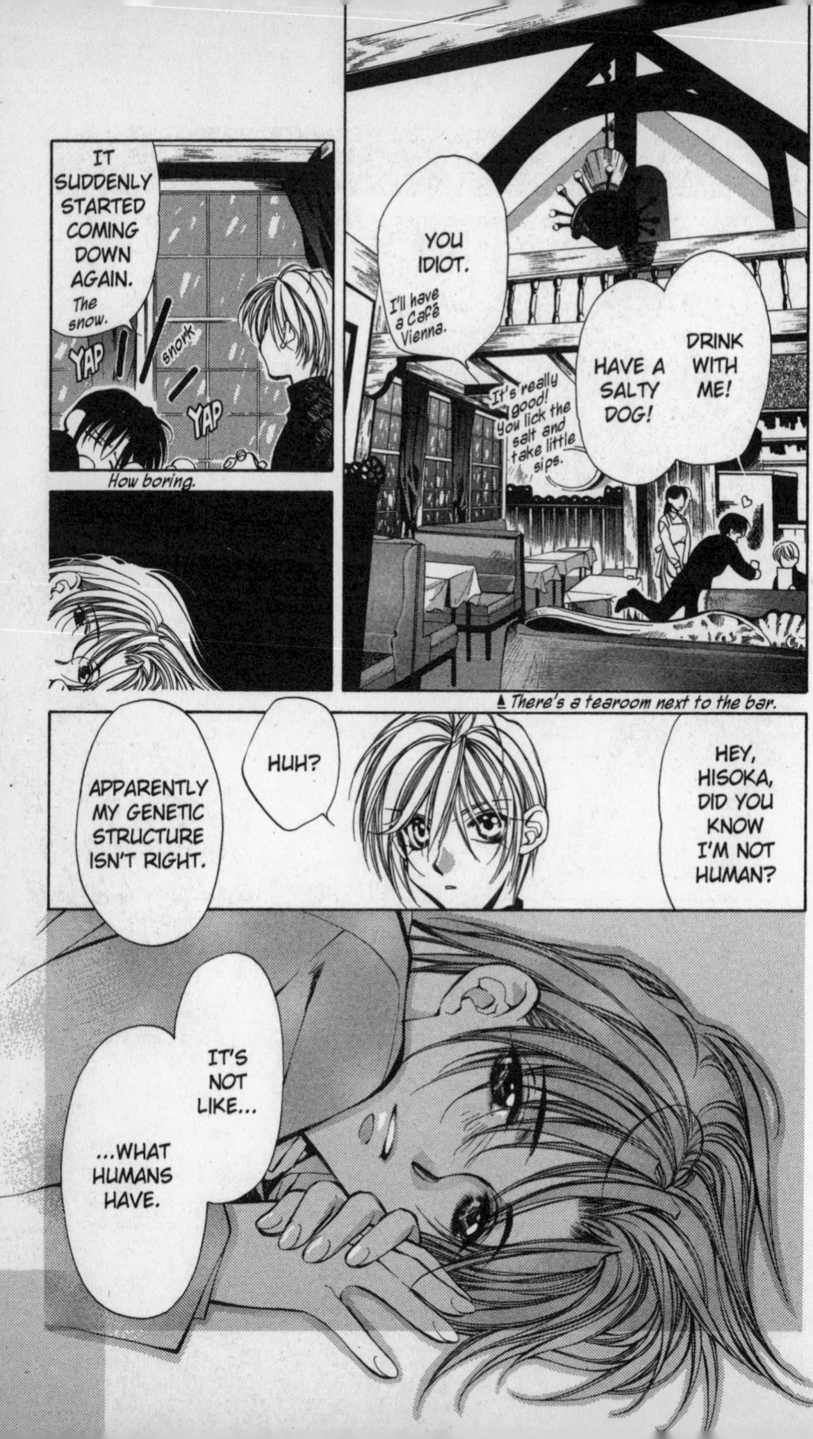
DRINK WITH ME!
HAVE A SALTY DOG!
It's really good! You lick the salt and take little sips.
YOU IDIOT.
I'll have a Café Vienna.
▲There's a tearoom next to the bar.
IT SUDDENLY STARTED COMING DOWN AGAIN.
The snow.
YAP
snork
YAP
How boring.
HEY, HISOKA, DID YOU KNOW I'M NOT HUMAN?
HUH?
APPARENTLY MY GENETIC STRUCTURE ISN'T RIGHT.
IT'S NOT LIKE...
...WHAT HUMANS HAVE.

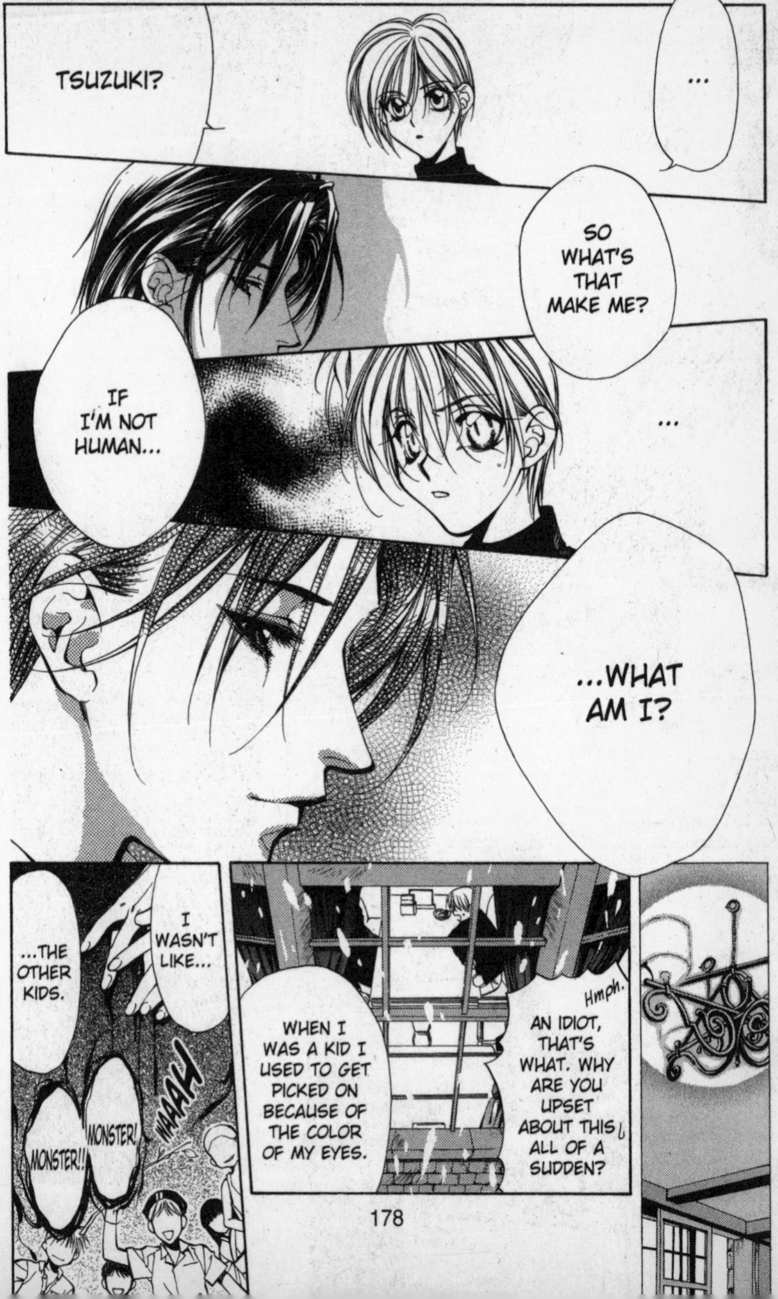
...
TSUZUKI?
SO WHAT'S THAT MAKE ME?
IF I'M NOT HUMAN...
...
...WHAT AM I?
Hmph.
AN IDIOT, THAT'S WHAT. WHY ARE YOU UPSET ABOUT THIS ALL OF A SUDDEN?
WHEN I WAS A KID I USED TO GET PICKED ON BECAUSE OF THE COLOR OF MY EYES.
I WASN'T LIKE...
...THE OTHER KIDS.
WAAAH
MONSTER!
MONSTER!!

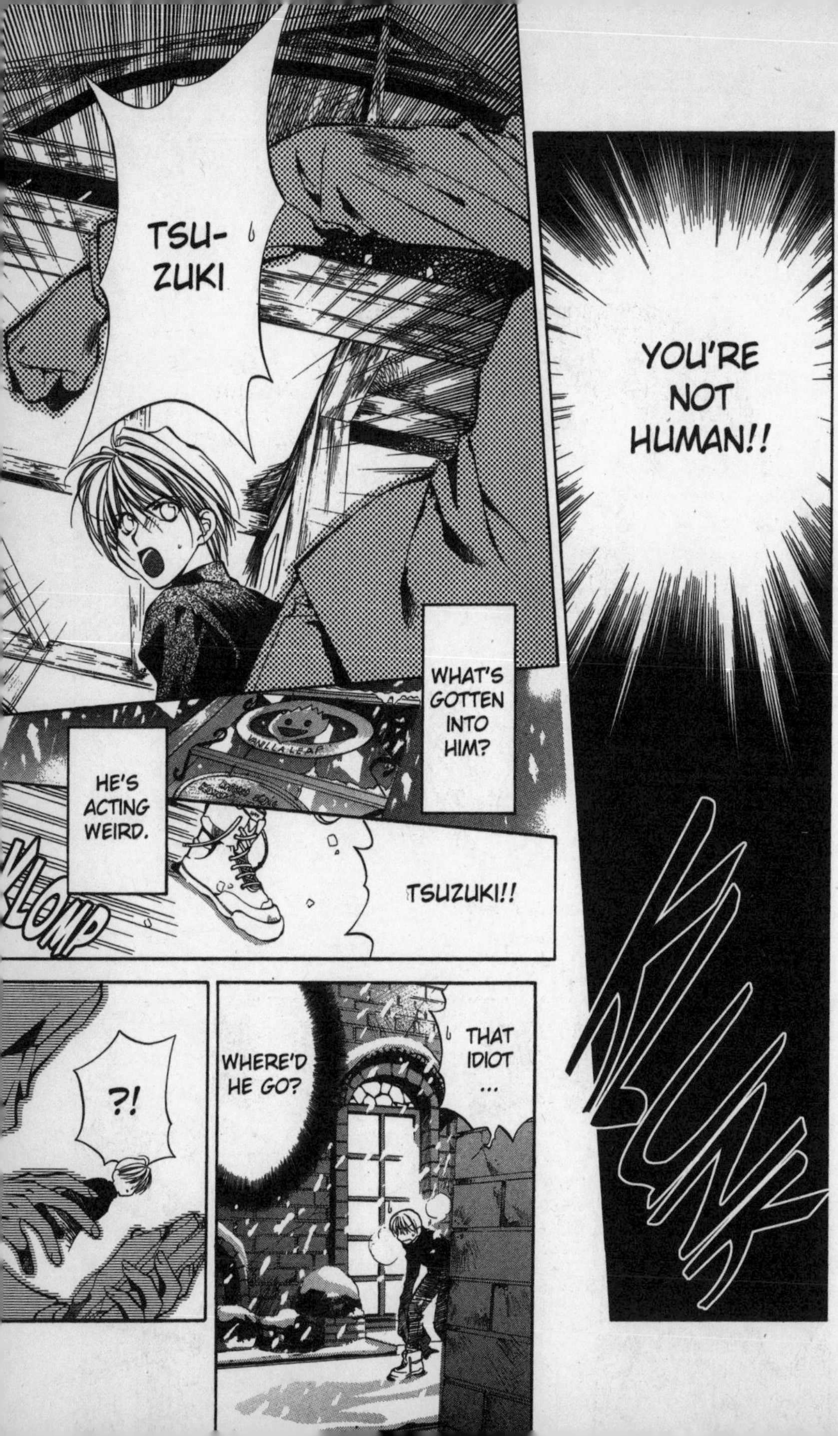
YOU'RE NOT HUMAN!!
TSU-ZUKI
WHAT'S GOTTEN INTO HIM?
HE'S ACTING WEIRD.
TSUZUKI!!
THAT IDIOT ...
WHERE'D HE GO?
?!

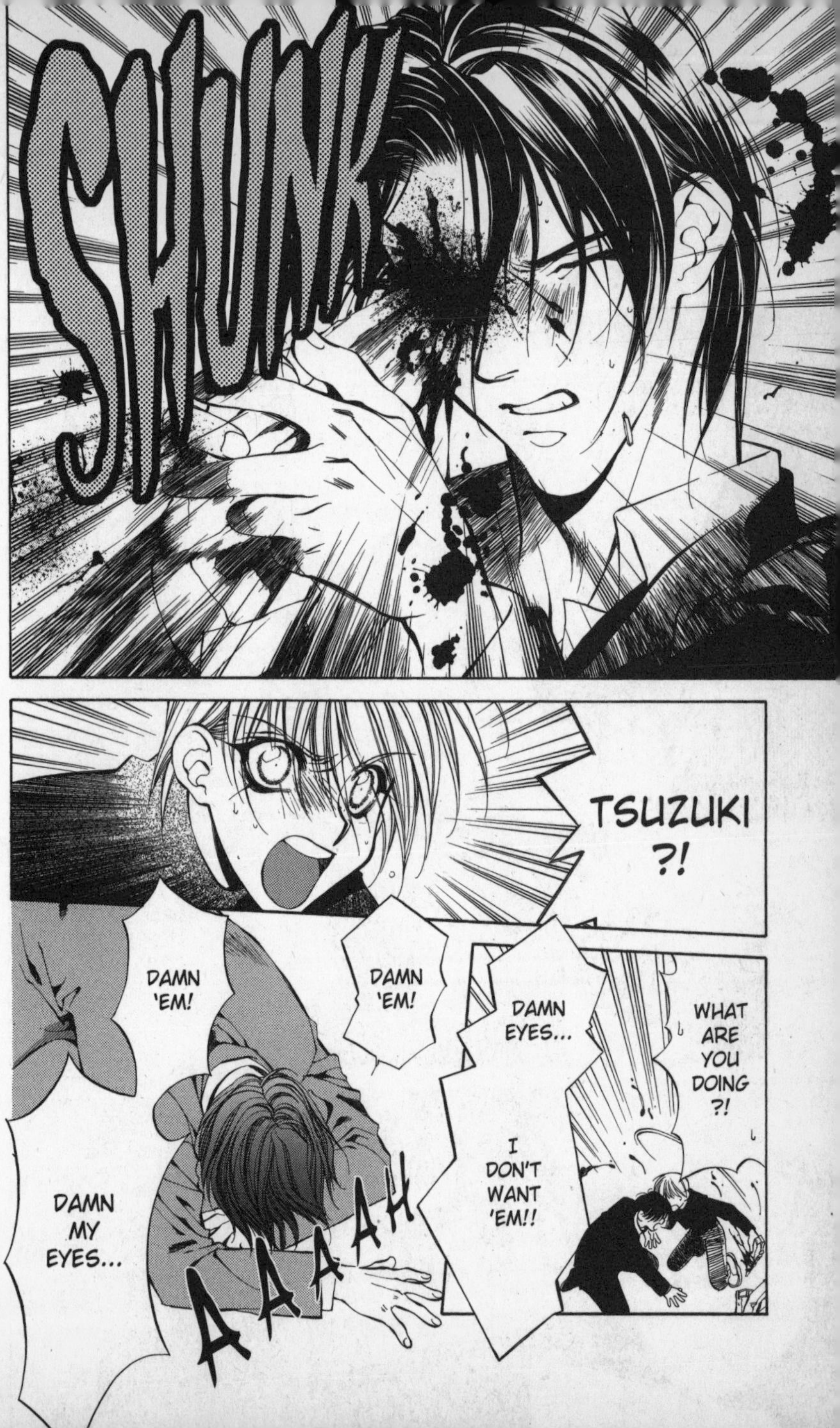
SHUNK!
TSUZUKI ?!
WHAT ARE YOU DOING ?!
DAMN EYES...
I DON'T WANT 'EM!!
DAMN 'EM!
DAMN 'EM!
DAMN MY EYES...
AAAAAH

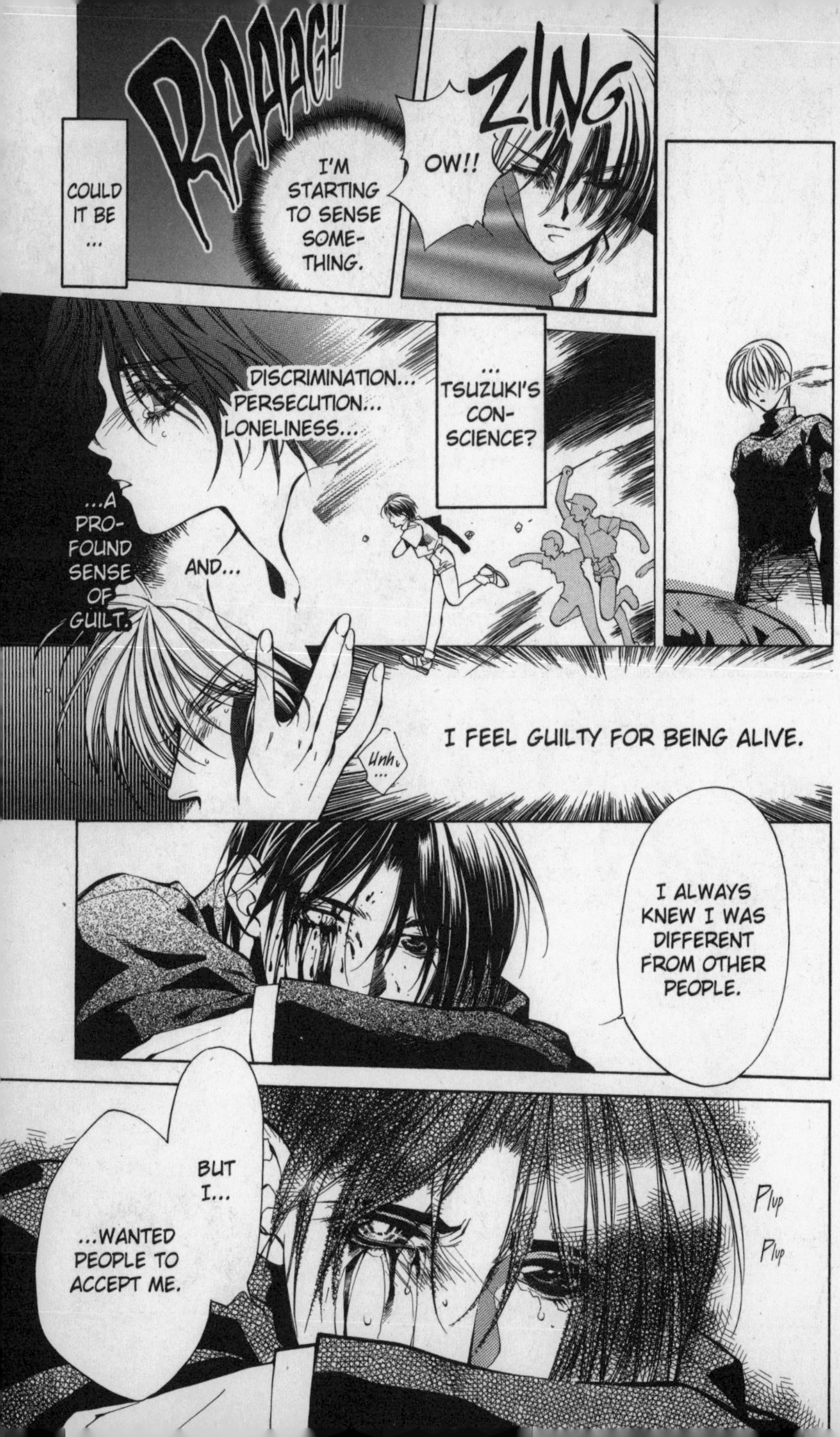
ZING
OW!!
RAAAGH
I'M STARTING TO SENSE SOME-THING.
COULD IT BE ...
... TSUZUKI'S CON-SCIENCE?
DISCRIMINATION... PERSECUTION... LONELINESS...
AND...
...A PRO-FOUND SENSE OF GUILT.
I FEEL GUILTY FOR BEING ALIVE.
Unh, ...
I ALWAYS KNEW I WAS DIFFERENT FROM OTHER PEOPLE.
Plup
Plup
BUT I...
...WANTED PEOPLE TO ACCEPT ME.

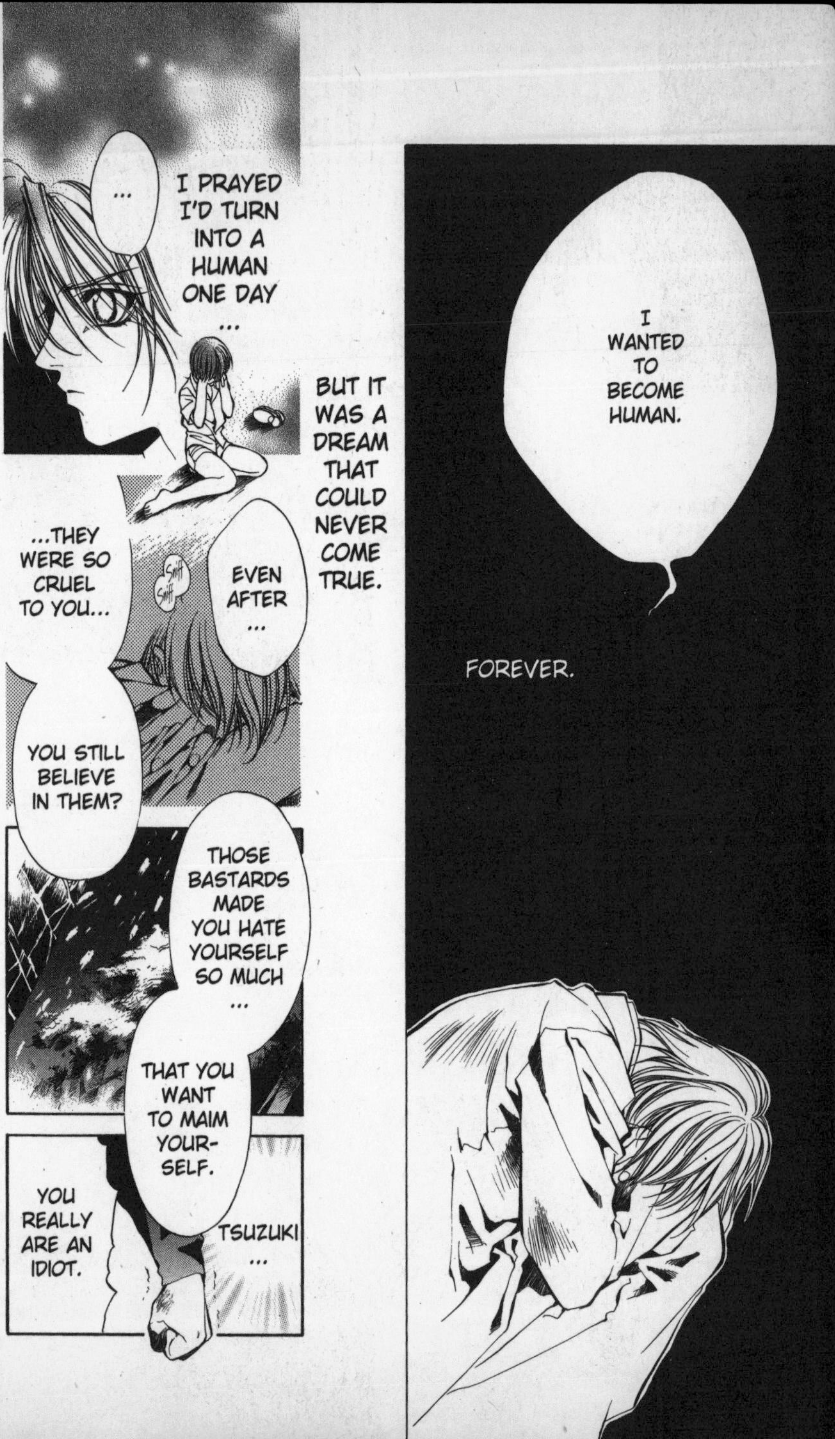
I WANTED TO BECOME HUMAN.
FOREVER.
I PRAYED I'D TURN INTO A HUMAN ONE DAY ...
...
BUT IT WAS A DREAM THAT COULD NEVER COME TRUE.
EVEN AFTER ...
SNIFF SNIFF
...THEY WERE SO CRUEL TO YOU...
YOU STILL BELIEVE IN THEM?
THOSE BASTARDS MADE YOU HATE YOURSELF SO MUCH ...
THAT YOU WANT TO MAIM YOURSELF.
TSUZUKI ...
YOU REALLY ARE AN IDIOT.

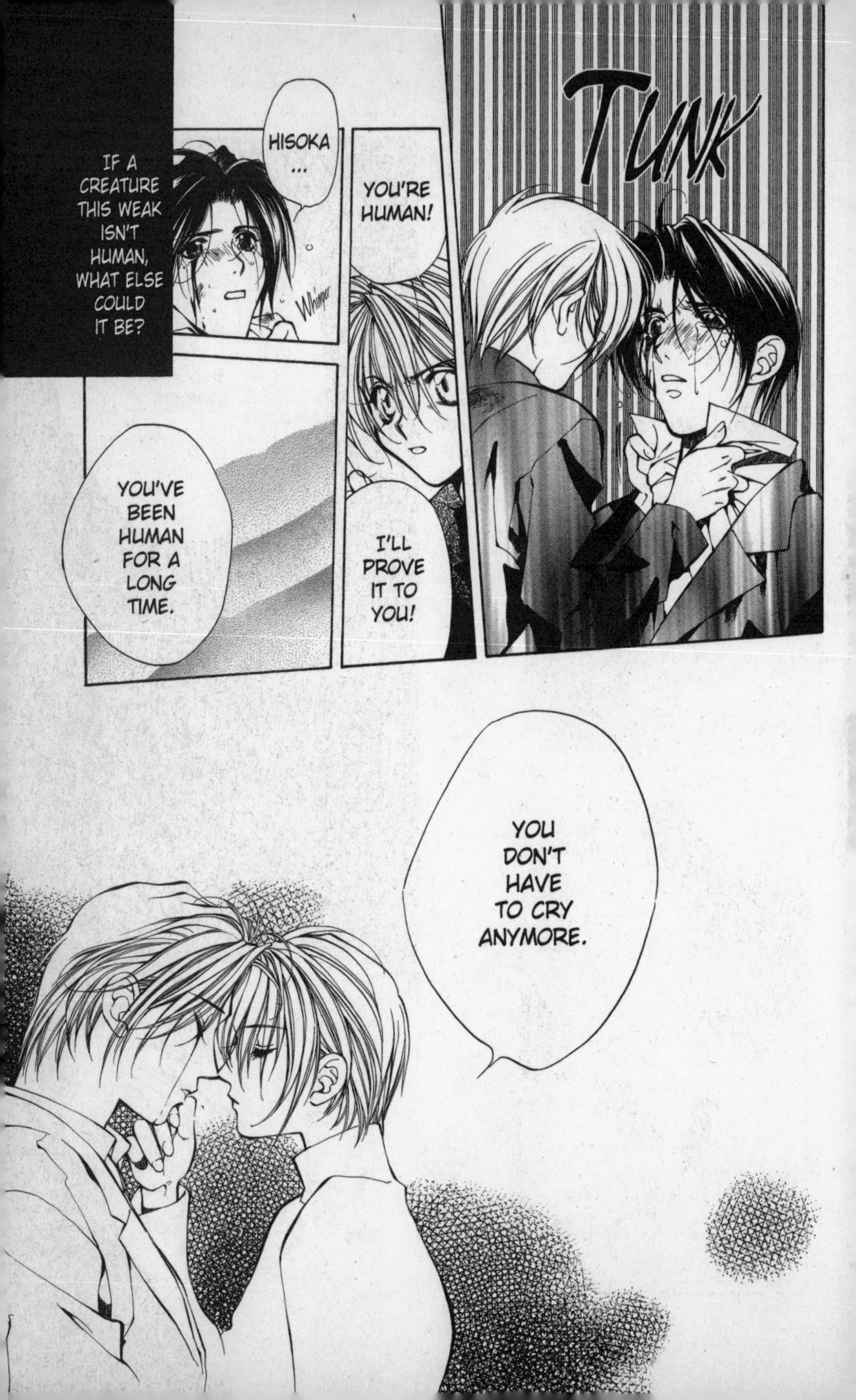
TUNK
YOU'RE HUMAN!
I'LL PROVE IT TO YOU!
IF A CREATURE THIS WEAK ISN'T HUMAN, WHAT ELSE COULD IT BE?
HISOKA...
Whimper
YOU'VE BEEN HUMAN FOR A LONG TIME.
YOU DON'T HAVE TO CRY ANYMORE.

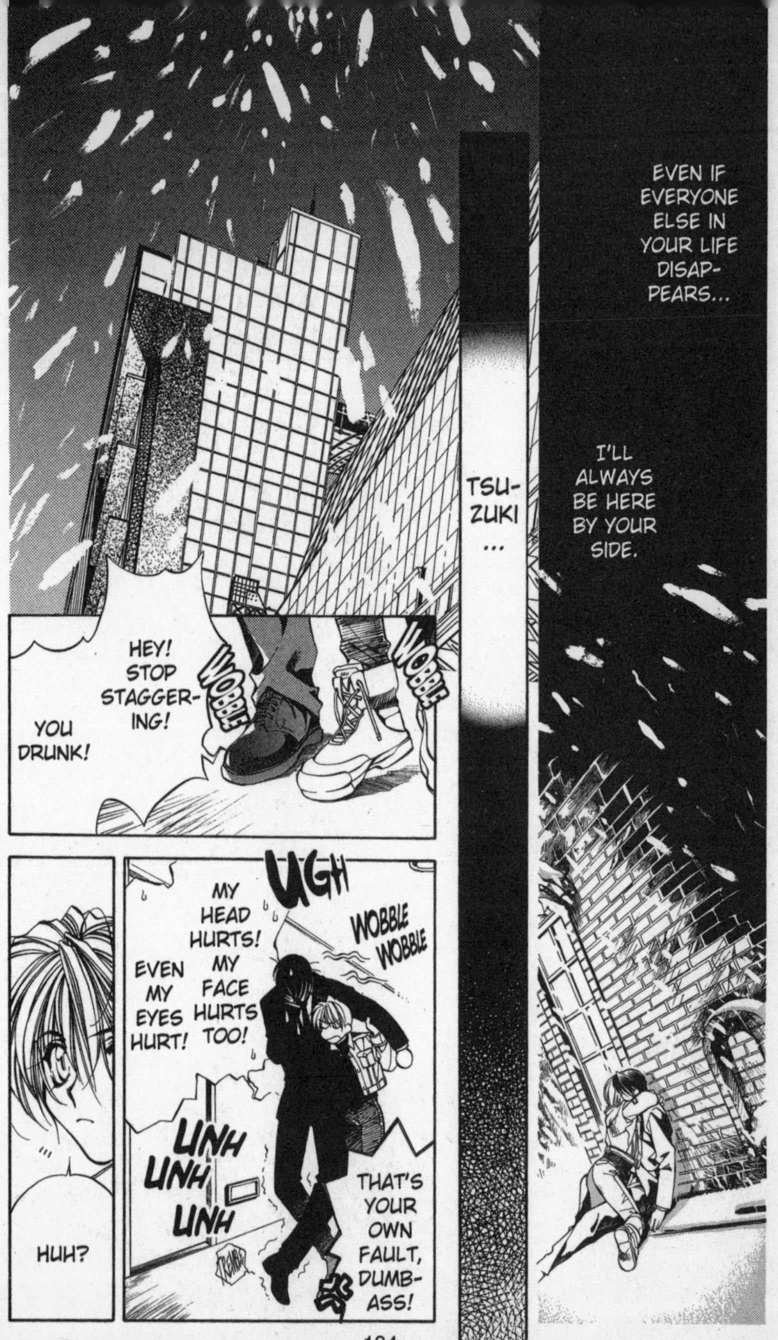
EVEN IF EVERYONE ELSE IN YOUR LIFE DISAPPEARS...
I'LL ALWAYS BE HERE BY YOUR SIDE.
TSUZUKI ...
WOBBLE
WOBBLE
HEY! STOP STAGGERING!
YOU DRUNK!
UGH
WOBBLE WOBBLE
MY HEAD HURTS! MY FACE HURTS TOO!
EVEN MY EYES HURT!
UNH UNH UNH
THAT'S YOUR OWN FAULT, DUMBASS!
HUH?

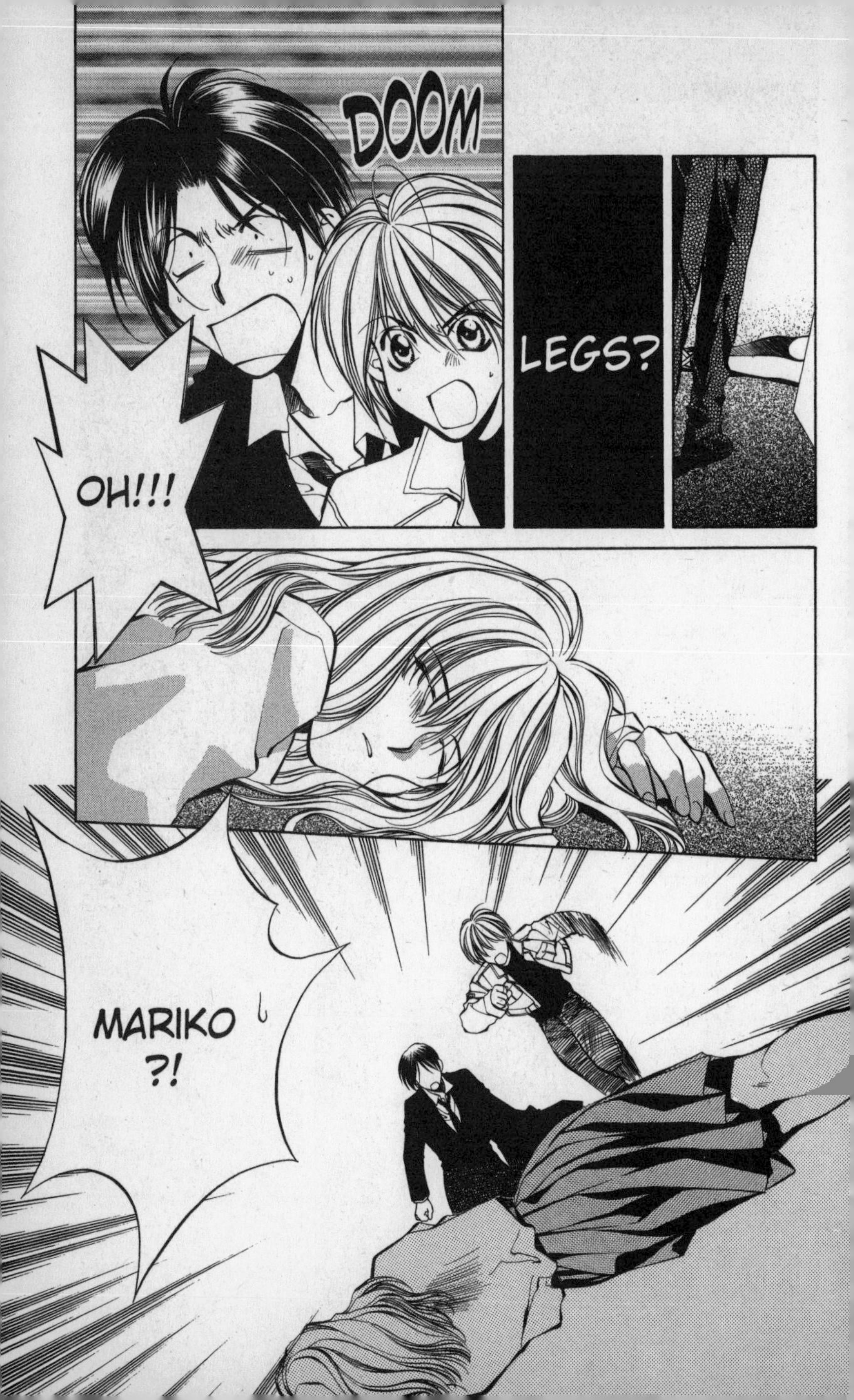
LEGS?
DOOM
OH!!!
MARIKO ?!

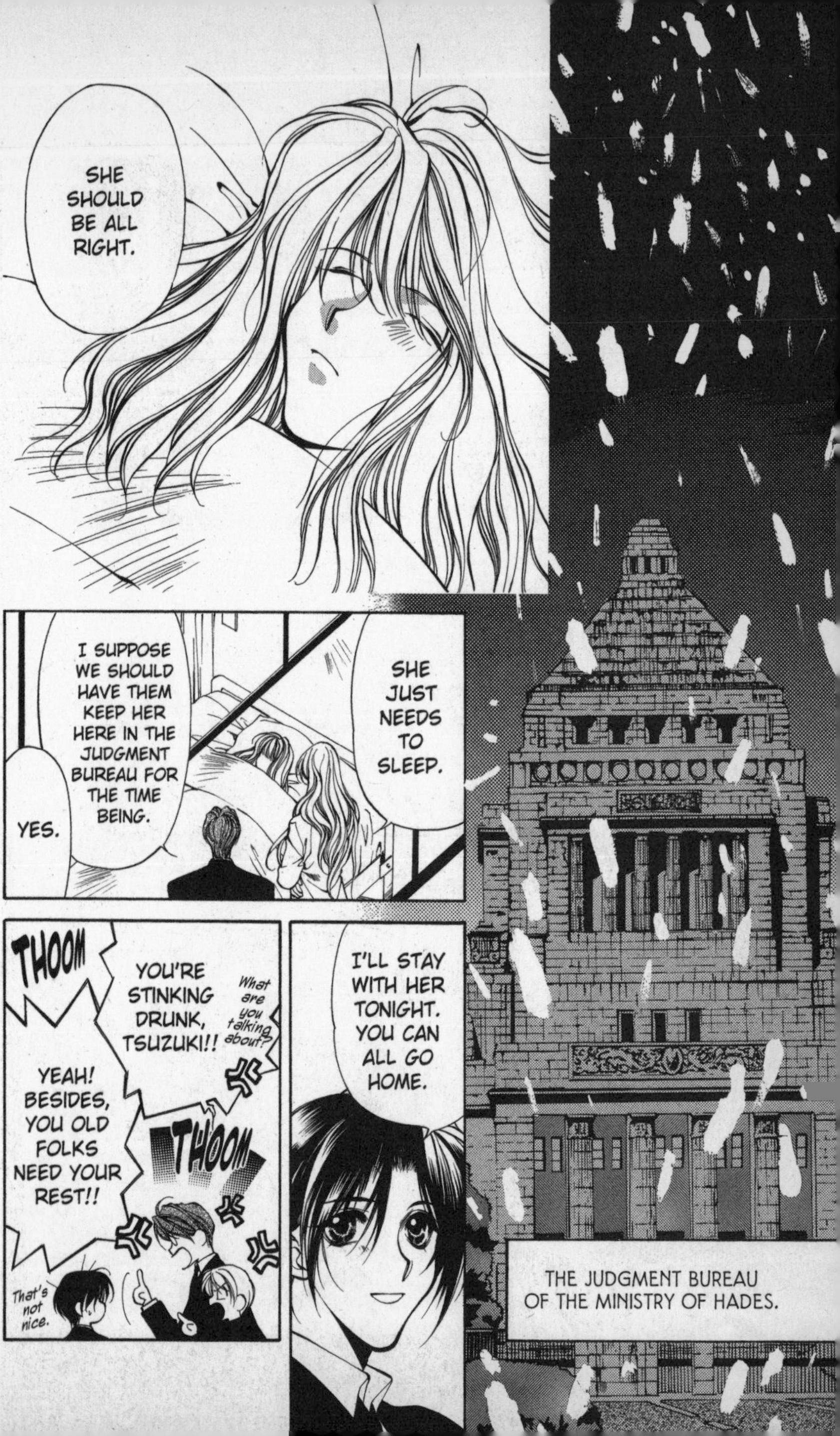
THE JUDGMENT BUREAU OF THE MINISTRY OF HADES.
SHE SHOULD BE ALL RIGHT.
SHE JUST NEEDS TO SLEEP.
I SUPPOSE WE SHOULD HAVE THEM KEEP HER HERE IN THE JUDGMENT BUREAU FOR THE TIME BEING.
YES.
I'LL STAY WITH HER TONIGHT. YOU CAN ALL GO HOME.
THOOM
YOU'RE STINKING DRUNK, TSUZUKI!!
What are you talking about?
YEAH! BESIDES, YOU OLD FOLKS NEED YOUR REST!!
THOOM
That's not nice.

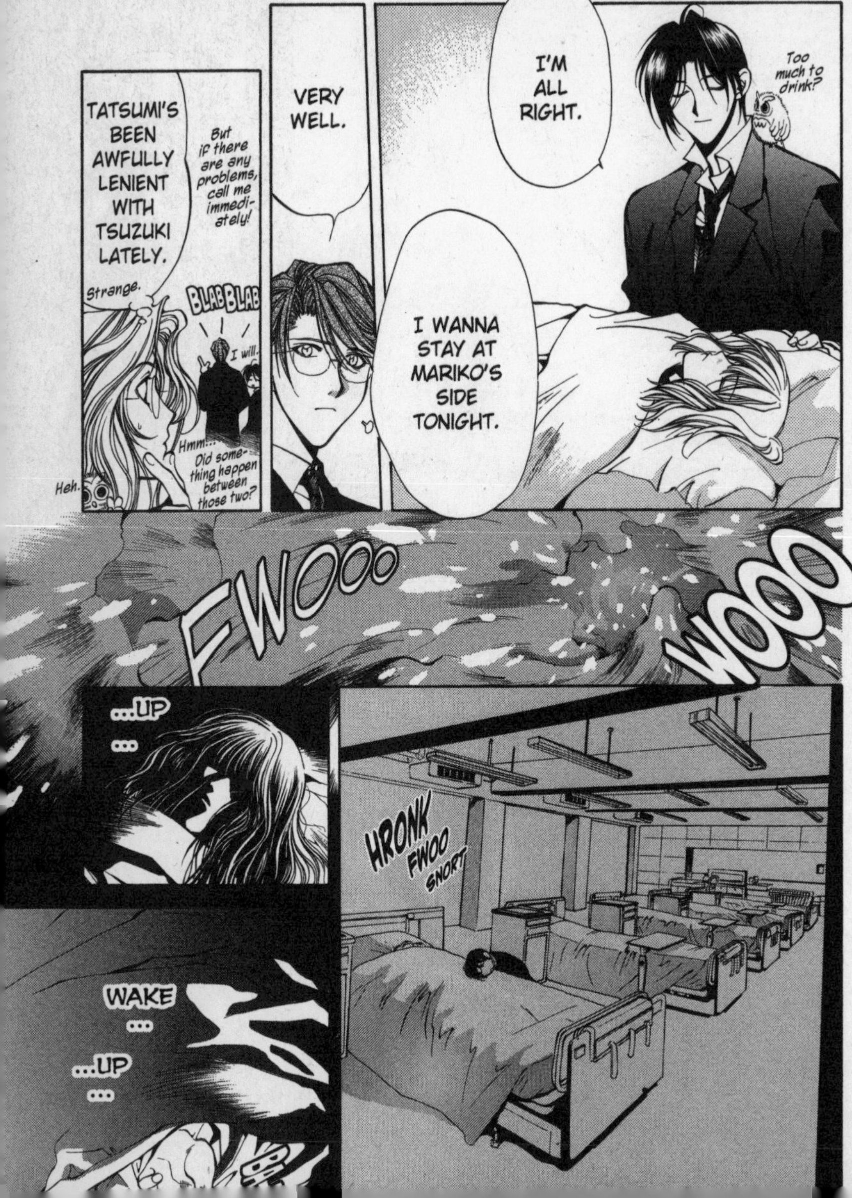
Too much to drink?
I'M ALL RIGHT.
I WANNA STAY AT MARIKO'S SIDE TONIGHT.
VERY WELL.
But if there are any problems, call me immediately!
TATSUMI'S BEEN AWFULLY LENIENT WITH TSUZUKI LATELY.
BLAB BLAB
I will.
Strange.
Hmm... Did something happen between those two?
Heh.
FWOOO
WOOO
HRONK
FWOO
SNORT
...UP
...
WAKE
...
...UP
...

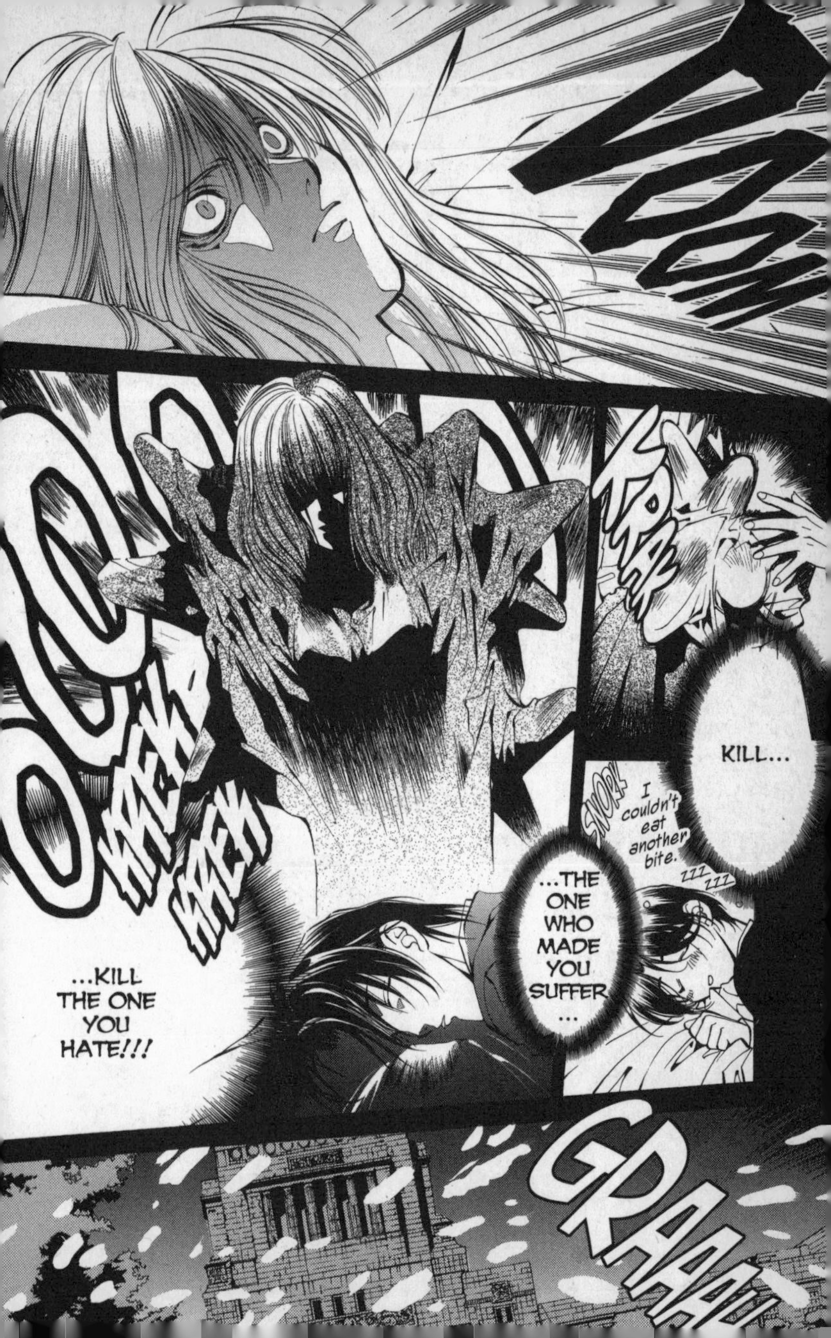
KRAK
KILL...
SNORK
I couldn't eat another bite.
ZZZ ZZZ
...THE ONE WHO MADE YOU SUFFER ...
...KILL THE ONE YOU HATE!!!

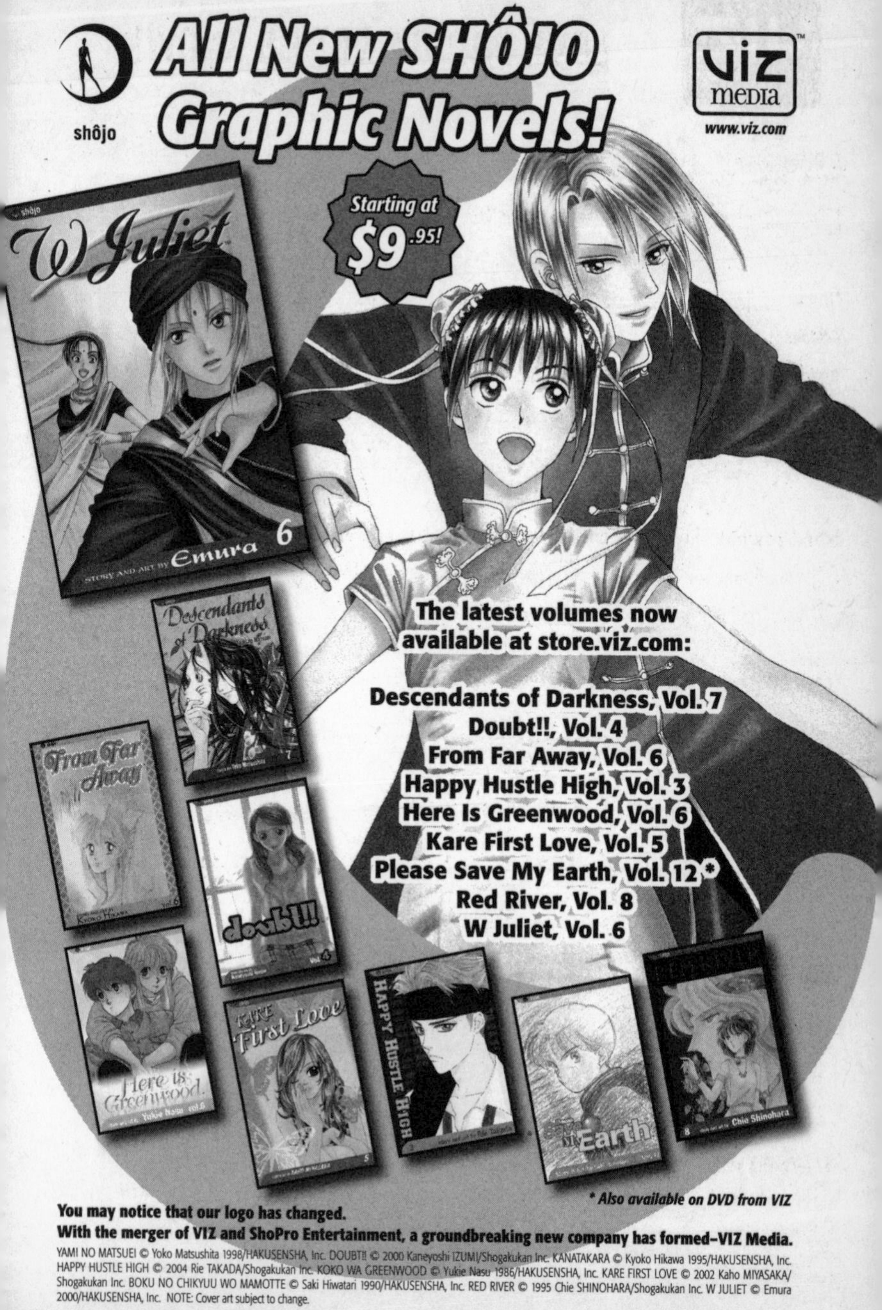
shôjo
All New SHÔJO Graphic Novels!
VIZ media
www.viz.com
Starting at $9.95!
W Juliet
Emura 6
The latest volumes now available at store.viz.com:
Descendants of Darkness, Vol. 7
Doubt!!, Vol. 4
From Far Away, Vol. 6
Happy Hustle High, Vol. 3
Here Is Greenwood, Vol. 6
Kare First Love, Vol. 5
Please Save My Earth, Vol. 12 *
Red River, Vol. 8
W Juliet, Vol. 6
* Also available on DVD from VIZ
You may notice that our logo has changed.
With the merger of VIZ and ShoPro Entertainment, a groundbreaking new company has formed–VIZ Media.
YAMI NO MATSUEI © Yoko Matsushita 1998/HAKUSENSHA, Inc. DOUBT!! © 2000 Kaneyoshi IZUMI/Shogakukan Inc. KANATAKARA © Kyoko Hikawa 1995/HAKUSENSHA, Inc. HAPPY HUSTLE HIGH © 2004 Rie TAKADA/Shogakukan Inc. KOKO WA GREENWOOD © Yukie Nasu 1986/HAKUSENSHA, Inc. KARE FIRST LOVE © 2002 Kaho MIYASAKA/ Shogakukan Inc. BOKU NO CHIKYUU WO MAMOTTE © Saki Hiwatari 1990/HAKUSENSHA, Inc. RED RIVER © 1995 Chie SHINOHARA/Shogakukan Inc. W JULIET © Emura 2000/HAKUSENSHA, Inc. NOTE: Cover art subject to change.

LOVE SHOJO? LET US KNOW!

☐ Please do NOT send me information about VIZ Media products, news and events, special offers, or other information.

☐ Please do NOT send me information from VIZ' trusted business partners.

Name: _____

Address: _____

City: _____ State: _____ Zip: _____

E-mail: _____

☐ Male ☐ Female Date of Birth (mm/dd/yyyy): ___/___/_____ (Under 13? Parental consent required)

What race/ethnicity do you consider yourself? (check all that apply)

☐ White/Caucasian ☐ Black/African American ☐ Hispanic/Latino

☐ Asian/Pacific Islander ☐ Native American/Alaskan Native ☐ Other: _____

What VIZ shojo title(s) did you purchase? (indicate title(s) purchased)

_____

What other shojo titles from other publishers do you own? _____

_____

Reason for purchase: (check all that apply)

☐ Special offer ☐ Favorite title / author / artist / genre

☐ Gift ☐ Recommendation ☐ Collection

☐ Read excerpt in VIZ manga sampler ☐ Other _____

Where did you make your purchase? (please check one)

☐ Comic store ☐ Bookstore ☐ Mass/Grocery Store

☐ Newsstand ☐ Video/Video Game Store

☐ Online (site:_____) ☐ Other _____

How many shojo titles have you purchased in the last year? How many were VIZ shojo titles?
(please check one from each column)

SHOJO MANGA	VIZ SHOJO MANGA
☐ None	☐ None
☐ 1 – 4	☐ 1 – 4
☐ 5 – 10	☐ 5 – 10
☐ 11+	☐ 11+

What do you like most about shojo graphic novels? (check all that apply)

☐ Romance
☐ Drama / conflict
☐ Fantasy
☐ Comedy
☐ Real-life storylines
☐ Relatable characters
☐ Other ______________________

Do you purchase every volume of your favorite shojo series?

☐ Yes! Gotta have 'em as my own
☐ No. Please explain: ______________________

Who are your favorite shojo authors / artists? ______________________

____

What shojo titles would like you translated and sold in English? ______________________

____

THANK YOU! Please send the completed form to:

NJW Research
ATTN: VIZ Media Shojo Survey
42 Catharine Street
Poughkeepsie, NY 12601

r privacy is very important to us. All information provided will be used for internal purposes only and will not be sold otherwise divulged.